Islam in Tribal Societies

ISLAM IN TRIBAL SOCIETIES
From the Atlas to the Indus

Edited by Akbar S. Ahmed
and David M. Hart

Routledge & Kegan Paul
London, Boston, Melbourne and Henley

First published in 1984
by Routledge & Kegan Paul plc
39 Store Street, London WC 1E 7DD,
9 Park Street, Boston, Mass. 02108, USA,
464 St Kilda Road, Melbourne,
Victoria 3004, Australia, and
Broadway House, Newtown Road,
Henley-on-Thames, Oxon RG9 1EN
Printed in Great Britain by
The Thetford Press Ltd, Thetford, Norfolk
© Routledge & Kegan Paul 1984

Library of Congress Cataloging in Publication Data

Islam in tribal societies.
Includes index.
1. Tribes and tribal system--Islamic countries--
Addresses, essays, lectures. 2. Islam--20th century--
Addresses, essays, lectures. I. Ahmed, Akbar S.
II. Hart, David M.
JC49.I76 1983   305.6' 971   83-561

ISBN 0-7100-9320-9

CONTENTS

ACKNOWLEDGMENTS

Chapter 1 - Doctor and saint - by Ernest Gellner, first appeared in Nikki R. Keddie (ed.), 'Scholars, Saints and Sufis: Muslim Religious Institutions since 1500', University of California Press, 1972 (© 1972 Regents of the University of California), and is reprinted by permission of the University of California Press.

Chapter 3 - Segmentary systems and the role of 'five fifths' in tribal Morocco - by David M. Hart, first appeared in 'Revue de l'Occident Musulman et de la Méditerranée', vol. 3, no. 1 (1967), pp. 65-95, and is reprinted by permission.

Chapter 4 - Cultural resistance and religious legitimacy in colonial Algeria - by Fanny Colonna, first appeared in 'Economy and Society', vol. 3, no. 3 (August 1974), pp. 233-52 (© Routledge & Kegan Paul 1974), and is reprinted by permission of Routledge & Kegan Paul.

Chapter 5 - Sufism in Somaliland: a study of tribal Islam - by I.M. Lewis, first appeared in the 'Bulletin of the School of Oriental and African Studies', vol. 17, no. 3 (1955), pp. 581-602, and vol. 18, no. 1 (1956), pp. 145-60, and is reprinted by permission.

INTRODUCTION
Akbar S. Ahmed and David M. Hart

I THE ISLAMIC TRIBE

As this collection is about tribes we could do not better by way
of opening the discussion than highlighting their characteristics.
This is easier said than done. The definition of 'tribe' remains
problematic and a central controversy in anthropology. An
eminent anthropologist has entitled a chapter in his study,
which examines the problem, thus: 'the concept of the "tribe":
a crisis involving merely a concept or the empirical foundations
of anthropology itself?' (Godelier 1977: 70). We wish to avoid
entering academic polemic regarding the definition and concept
of tribe. However, for purposes of the arguments contained in
this volume, we will employ a generalised blanket definition
drawn from characteristics of the tribes mentioned below.
'Tribes', we suggest, are rural groups that have a name and
distinguish between members and non-members, which occupy
a territory, and which within that territory assume either all
responsibility, or at least a significant proportion of the
responsibility, for the maintenance of order. In as far as they
assume such responsibility both internally and externally, they
can be said to possess political and military functions. Under
modern conditions, the state generally tries to monopolise these
functions, and so it is sensible to extend the term 'tribe' even
to groups which have but recently lost the capacity for political
and military action, or rather have been deprived of it, but
which could easily resume it if the central state slackened its
hold. Partly because of the confrontation with larger states,
some kind of tribal genealogical charter assumes almost mythical
importance and is memorised from generation to generation,
making allowances, of course, for 'lost' ancestors.

If there is a problem in defining a tribe it is compounded
when defining an Islamic tribe. What is an Islamic tribe? The
definition, indeed self-apperception of these groups, relates
to the following key questions: How do tribal societies that are
Muslim view themeselves? How do they see themselves in relation to non-tribal but Islamic groups? How are they seen by
non-Islamic societies? What inbuilt structural mechanism helps
to perpetuate traditional Islamic values? What norms and mores
motivate these groups to permit or inhibit change? What is the
relationship between segmentary tribal ideology and Islam? The
papers in this volume attempt to answer some of the key questions in understanding Islamic tribal societies. In doing so the

1

earlier question regarding the Islamic tribe may be resolved.

As has already been intimated, a lively debate is being conducted in the social sciences around certain concepts such as
'tribe', 'segmentary societies' and 'Islam in society'. Contributing to the debate and extending theory are aims of the
collection. This book is thus a contribution to tribal literature
in general and, specifically, to the ethnology and related
problems in the study of Islamic tribal societies.

II ISLAM AND ISLAMIC TRIBAL SOCIETIES

The range of papers in the book deals with societies which are
at once segmentary and Islamic. The concept of segmentary
societies is one that has become a commonplace in anthropological
literature ever since it was originally introduced as diagnostic
of a particular social category by Fortes and Evans-Pritchard
in 'African Political Systems' (1940). Segmentary societies
in a wider sense have certain characteristics. They are:'tribal',
acephalous (in a de facto if not necessarily a de jure sense), tend
towards a relative equality and are segmentary in a narrower sense,
with balance, opposition, fission and fusion, all characteristic of
the segmentary process. The segmentary principle guides relations
between the component and competing segments into which the
society or tribal group in question is divided, at all levels of
segmentation. Hence they also exhibit 'nesting' attributes
(Barnes 1954: 490) and are, ideally, continually segmenting.
These tribal societies are markedly distinguished from the kind
of tribal society which has a segregated warrior class, or
standing armies, hierarchies and a high degree of centralisation.

May the papers contained in this volume be interpreted as
reflecting the traditional segmentary position in the classic
mould of segmentary theory? The first important elaboration
of segmentary theory in the discipline appears, as we know,
with the Nuer study by Evans-Pritchard. The theory became,
and remains, popular particularly in examining Islamic tribal
groups. Studies of the Berbers of the Atlas by Ernest Gellner
and the Somali nomads by I.M. Lewis are highly regarded
examples. The application of the theory to Islamic tribal groups
was made by Evans-Pritchard himself through his study of the
Cyrenaican bedouin (1949). In a sense the segmentary theory
had returned to its natural place of origin, in the segmentary
genealogical charters of Islamic tribal groups, whence it had
originated a century earlier in the writings of Victorian scholar-
travellers, notably W. Robertson Smith. In spite of the criticism that it is not so much a 'new' as a 'Nuer' look at the
bedouin (Dyson-Hudson 1972), Evans-Pritchard's study
remains a good example of diachronic tribal analysis within
the segmentary and Islamic frames.

Recently there has been considerable and mounting criticism
of segmentary theory, particularly in America. The criticism is

led by Clifford and Hildred Geertz and some younger American anthropologists like Dale Eickelman and Lawrence Rosen. The following, in capsule form, are some of the major criticisms against segmentary theory: segments are neither balanced nor is there equality between segments; on the contrary there is disparity in political resources, which is exacerbated with the emergence of lineages claiming seniority, and finally, in times of political crises groups do not combine according to segmentary patterns. In spite of such criticism, however, satisfactory alternative explanations have not been put forward. Reading the papers in this volume it is difficult not to conclude that segmentary theory retains its usefulness in examining Islamic tribal groups. The caveat, however, needs to be added that its usefulness is limited when it is conceptualised as a blueprint for social identity and not for political action.

The primary characteristic of Islamic society may be identified as one providing relationship with the larger world of Islam, making it part of the wider Islamic *umma* or religious community. It is, furthermore, a society that traditionally considers itself Islamic in both a cultural and a religious sense, and is so considered by other groups adjacent to it or otherwise in contact with it, whether these latter groups themselves be either Islamic or not. Thus an Islamic segmentary society, that is, a segmentary society within the context of Islam, is one that exhibits the structure and organisation of societies that are acephalous, egalitarian, etc., but is also one that is Islamic both in its professed religion and in its culture. For Islam, as we know, perhaps more than any other religious system, provides for its practitioners a blueprint of a near-total social order.

Segmentary societies, such as the Nuer, have been traditionally (although they can be no longer) examined in isolation (Evans-Pritchard 1940, 1951, 1956; Fortes and Evans-Pritchard 1940; Middleton and Tait, eds, 1958). The papers in this volume suggest that in terms of theory and methodology in the social sciences the overall religious framework is important, crucially so, in the study of any individual Islamic society. These same papers also suggest that Islamic segmentary societies are not culturally independent but embedded in the wider civilisation of Islam. In great measure they share the religion, concepts and symbols of the entire Muslim world.

Not only does the argument in the preceding paragraph have wide general application, but the very fact that pagan or once-pagan African (Nuer) or even Asian societies (Kafirs, now Nuris, of northeastern Afghanistan) were studied in isolation stands in contrast with the Islamic situation under consideration in these papers. In the tribal Muslim world, a tribe is a tribe not only by virtue of its apposition and opposition to other tribes of the same order, or to some urban centre in whose rural hinterland its territory may vaguely lie, but also to a regional or even a rational political authority (traditionally monarchic and generally dynastic), which has claims over it for purposes of taxes, conscription, or the like. The tribe's resistance to such claims, however, may be another matter, and may reflect its desire, if powerful enough, to work out its own destiny with a minimum of outside interference of any sort whether from other tribes, from towns, or from governments (whether these are or were colonial or national).

As national policies regarding tribes run the gamut from conciliation to coercion so do the tribal responses to them, from complete submission to the state authority and active co-operation with it to outright rebellion and hostility. Nonetheless it should also be noted that when state control, imposed centrally and from above, over a given tribal group, becomes truly effective, the tribe in question begins to lose its marginal character (marginal, that is, to the central power) and its structural self-sufficiency, and to turn gradually into an undifferentiated rural peasantry. The 'detribalisation' or 'sedentarisation' process, it would appear, is yet another aspect of the interaction between tribe and state.

The dual issue, of segmentary-cum-Islamic, leads first to the important questions of whether the segmentary societies here under consideration were pre- or post-Islamic, and how their structures and organisations have been adapted to Islam and/or vice versa. In the first place, it seems reasonable to assume that there were probably segmentary factors present in most of these societies, or in those ancestral to them, in their original pre-Islamic contexts but, as we do not know for certain, the question must unfortunately remain an open one. Apart from a few speculative papers (Aswad 1970; Eickelman 1967; Wolf 1951), there is little anthropological literature on tribes in early Islam. One interesting available yardstick, however, for comparative purposes is that provided by the bedouin tribes of pre-Islamic Arabia (Chelhod 1971; Gabrieli 1953; Jacob 1897; Procksch 1899; and Robertson Smith 1903). Such evidence as there is from the early North African Berbers prior to the Muslim conquests of the Maghrib also seems suggestive (Desanges 1962; Gaid 1972; Gsell 1913-28), although in some of these cases, as among the Tuareg today, the matrilineal principle may, contrary to the patrilineal principle accepted elsewhere, have been invoked (Keenan 1977; Marcy 1941).

In the second place, as Coulson (1964: 17) and others have argued, Muslim inheritance regulations as they exist today represent a 'mitigated agnatic succession', which was decreed by the Prophet of Islam himself in order to give daughters a better stake in the family patrimony than that which they had had in the pre-Islamic *jahiliya* or 'time of ignorance'. Daughters were now allotted a half-share of what sons receive, with two daughters thus equalling one son, whereas previously they had received nothing; and indeed in many Muslim tribal and segmentary societies they still receive nothing in a de facto sense. It is possible that the practice of female infanticide in pre-

Islamic Arabia, which the Prophet tabooed completely, may also
be pertinent here but the question remains just how widespread
it was. The pre-Islamic dispensation may thus be described as
'unmitigated agnatic succession', and the evidence suggests
that agnation and agnatic descent, a fundamental and unilineal
precondition of segmentary organisation, were thus already
present when Islam appeared on the scene. Nonetheless, the
adaptation of these early segmentary societies, as postulated,
to Islam and any structural modifications which they may have
undergone as a result of such adaptation are most important.
The question is of particular relevance, too, in the light of the
complete identification with Islam of the present-day societies
considered here, and in their refusal to be identified in any
way with either pre-Islamic or non-Islamic forms, whether the latter
be represented by Punic, Roman or 'Portuguese' (as known
locally) ruins in North Africa or by Greco-Buddhist statues
and stupas in Afghanistan and Pakistan.

Muslim tribal societies themselves may well show marked
internal differentiation in structure and organisation however
similar the cultural carapace of society. The argument clearly
indicates systems within systems in the Islamic world.

Various examples may be given to support the argument: one
is the traditional oscillation between two contrasting social
forms in the Western High Atlas of Morocco. This oscillation,
already well under way and documented during the second half
of the nineteenth century, took place between egalitarian and
'anarchic' tribal assemblies of small mountains 'cantons',
organised on a compromise basis between segmentary and territorial considerations, on the one hand, and, on the other,
local strongmen, like the famous three 'Big Qaids' (the Glawi
in particular), who sought to widen their power bases and
increase their personal followings at the expense of neighbours
who may have balked at playing their game - and whose
opportunities during protectorate times became virtually unli-
mited (Montagne 1930). Another such example may reside in
the contrast between the ordinary camel-herding bedouin of
a given tribe in, say, Saudi Arabia and the members of that
tribe's dominant shaikhly clan, the clan which has always
traditionally provided the paramount shaikh, or *shaikh ash-
shuyukh*, and which is also almost always considerably better
off materially than the rank and file of the tribe, with an
emphasis on Land Rovers and limousines rather than on camels
(Braeunlich 1933-4; Cole 1975; Montagne 1947).

Finally, an example of internal differentiation in structure
and organisation resides in the contrast among tribal Pukhtuns
in Afghanistan and Pakistan between the *nang* (lit. 'honour')
groups which are egalitarian, acephalous and largely unencapsulated, and the *qalang* (lit. 'taxes and rents') groups, like
the northern khanates of Swat, Dir and Bajaur, which are
hierarchical, ranked and encapsulated into large state systems
(Ahmed, A.S. 1976, 1977, 1980a). Nang and qalang are locally

perceived as the main affective and conative symbols in society
and thus provide a useful opposition in societies with surface
cultural similarities. It is, of course, the nang groups among
the Pukhtuns, the ordinary camel-herding groups among the
bedouin and the democratic Berber assemblies as opposed to
the strongmen and their followings which correspond to the
segmentary, acephalous 'Group B' societies in 'African Political
Systems' (Fortes and Evans-Pritchard 1940). Most of the papers
in this collection discuss what we may refer to as nang-type
groups.

It is important to point out that these tribal societies consider themselves to be 'purely' Islamic, although they are often
illiterate and may even be unorthodox in form. Subjectively
they all regard themselves as 'pure' Muslims. In so doing they
thus live out the circular movements which regenerate urban or
settled Islam, in what amounts to a simplistic version of Ibn
Khaldun's famous three-generations rise and fall theory based
on the tribal concept of ^{c}asabiya, social cohesion or 'group
feeling' (Ibn Khaldun, Rosenthal and Dawood 1967) - characterised as 'agnation in action' (Hart 1962).

As many segmentary tribes often claim putative genealogical
links and descent from the Prophet (the bedouin of Cole or the
Somalis of Lewis in this volume) or his companions (the Pukhtuns
of Ahmed and at least one major Berber tribe of the Moroccan
Rif - Hart 1976), it is important to conceptualise and discuss
what the position and role are of the exclusively religious or
holy lineages. The religious authority or sanction in genealogical tradition in such groups is already inherent, ratified
as it is by agnatic links to the Prophet (through, of course,
his daughter Hazrat Fatima). This authority and sanction vary
from the Berber *igurramen* of the Moroccan Central Atlas (see
Gellner), where such groups actively participate in the election
of chiefs, and the *imrabdhen* of the Moroccan Rif, where they
merely preside at council meetings (Hart 1976), to the limited
authority of the *mians* of Pakistan (Ahmed, A.S. 1980a). However, religious groups do rise to overall political supremacy
for short periods in 'extraordinary times' (Ahmed, A.S. 1976).
An important visible function performed by holy lineages is 'to
anchor the local society in the wider system of Islam' as pointed
out by Ernest Gellner in his paper in this volume. Holy lineages thus provide both an ideological and a social reference
point in and to society.

Islamic tradition, reinforced by the tradition of egalitarianism
among tribes, discourages saintly groups (as distinct from
saintly leaders). Hence using the gloss 'saints' for religious
groups or lineages, as some anthropologists have done (Bailey
1972; Barth 1972), may be misleading (Ahmed, A.S. 1976). In
society, and before God, all are Muslims; perhaps one is better,
more orthodox, more conservative than another but in the eyes
of Allah they remain equal until Judgment Day. Any person,
regardless of birth, if his behaviour approximates to the ideal,

can, and does, assume leadership in Islamic society, especially in times of crisis. A correlation, however, appears to exist for religious leadership: genealogy in stable times and appearance of charismatic leadership in disturbed times (for example, during the colonisation of Islamic nations in the last century, briefly discussed in the next section). This does not follow that there is necessarily a correlation between leadership and holy genealogies in ordinary times.

A major point that follows from the above, and emerges from the studies in this volume, affords a framework for a comprehensive and holistic view of Islamic society: that is, the universality and persistence of Islamic symbolism so important to Muslims and so visibly embedded in society. Although anthropologists have individually differed in their interests, approaches and explanations in the analysis of symbolic forms and functions, they have collectively been concerned with the interdependence between symbolism, power and social relationships. Symbols in the dynamics of Islamic sociopolitical life are valences being not only cognitive but also agitative and conative. The latter provide the motivation to Islamic action on most levels of life in a Muslim society. In that sense they provide a key in the understanding of the perpetuation of Islamic values and their universality in society. Islamic symbols are active, visible and cogent where the state is Islamic, as in Iran or Saudi Arabia (1982) or dormant but recognisable, as in the high price the Holy Qur'an will fetch among Soviet Muslims (again in 1982). These symbols, whether visible or invisible, provide points that affect behaviour and determine interaction with other groups. Social causation is often prompted, related or a result of interaction with Islamic symbols.

First, such key symbols (for instance, the five pillars) are universally recognisable wherever Muslims live. The persistence of these symbols for over 1,300 years of Islamic history prove their strength. These are the defined and known symbols of society. In addition there are other symbols, such as jihad which, though ambiguous, remain emotive and may take various, often martial, forms (for a fresh discussion of jihad with reference to contemporary Islam, see Ahmed, A.S. 1983).

The five pillars of Islam (the profession of faith stating the oneness of God; praying, *salat*, five times daily; fasting during the month of Ramadan; performing hajj, the pilgrimage, at least once; and paying *zakat*, alms) are recognisable social symbols in Islamic societies. In addition there are the traditional rites de passage originating from Arabia; together they provide the key to understanding and identifying Islamic social organisation and behaviour and indeed general social life; and, as some of the papers point out, in cases where pre-Islamic practices survive they have been 'Islamised'.

The primary symbol is the *shahada* or *kalima*, that which proclaims the uniqueness of Allah and the Prophethood of Muhammad. Islam is a monotheistic religion and the central concept of unity (*tawhid*) is fundamental to it. There is no allotheism in Islam. Muslims do not anthropomorphise or, conversely, encourage belief in anthropolatry. Allah is omnipotent, omnipresent, the sole source and owner of power.

Authority, leadership and succession, the central questions in the social and political life of tribal society, are linked with early Islam. 'Certain styles of political legitimation emerged prominently at the very inception of the Muslim community. The consensus of "the" Community, the authority of "the" Book, kinship with "the" Prophet: these were the ideas which were invoked when leadership, authority or succession were in dispute' (Gellner, Foreword to Ahmed, A.S. 1976: ix9.

Islamic memory is characterised by a remarkable reference to tradition and a persistent anamnesis of past historical events. The battles of Uhud and Badr, the tragedy of Karbala, the martyrdom of the Prophet's grandchildren, are part of Muslim folklore as much as part of the actual history of early Islam. It is notable that antonomasiac titles such as the Ayatullah, or in the last century the Akhund or Mahdi, have an association for Muslims that reaches beyond society and into the world of historical consciousness. Some of the material in the papers illustrate that in this regard a remarkable historical continuity has been maintained in Islamic society where and when ideas of leadership and authority have been invoked.

The categories of rulers in Islamic countries and the forms of legitimisation they employ reveal the complexity of the problem of studying the Islamic world. The rulers range from absolute monarchs to absolute visionaries; the complexity is increased as both legitimise their rule by references to the Prophet and his life (*sunna*). However, there are certain discernible structural and organisational similarities in Islamic tribal societies of the nang category such as discussed in this collection. It is one of the purposes of this collection to indicate these similarities in spite of wide cultural and geographical differences and elucidate principles whereby understanding of these societies is assisted.

III ISLAMIC TRIBES AND THE COLONIAL ENCOUNTER

In spite of the wide cultural and political diversity in the Islamic world a common bond, providing a theme, is perceptible of a long and bitter encounter with Western powers during the colonising phase of their history: the British in Africa and Asia, the French (and Spanish) in north and central Africa, the Dutch in Indonesia, the Russians in Central Asia, and the Americans in the Philippines (where the Muslim problem remains as a legacy to agitate the Muslim mind although distant from the Islamic heartlands).

Muslim anthropologists see this encounter and its impact on knowledge, particularly the social sciences, thus:

All these disciplines are rooted in that complex historical encounter between the West and the Third World which commenced about the sixteenth century: when capitalist Europe began to emerge out of feudal Christendom; when the conquistadors who expelled the last of the Arabs from Christian Spain went on to colonise the New World and also to bring about the direct confrontation of 'civilised' Europe with 'savage' and 'barbaric' peoples. (Asad 1973: 103)

In most cases such sociocultural interaction as there was between the two systems operated mechanically, not dialectically:

As recent rulers of vast Muslim populations, the imperalist rulers could attempt to legitimise their own governing position with arguments supplied by the orientalists: that Islamic rule has historically been oppressive rule (colonial rule is by contrast humane), that Islamic political theory recognises the legitimacy of the effective *de facto* ruler (colonial rule is manifestly better than the corruption, inefficiency and disorder of pre-colonial rule), the political domination in Muslim lands is typically external to the essential articulation of Islamic social and religious life (therefore no radical damage has been done to Islam by conquering it as its central political tradition remains unbroken). (Ibid.: 117)

The accusation that anthropology is a tool of imperialism is rooted in the colonial encounter: 'Anthropologists are regarded as reactionaries by the majority of the African intellectuals; and hence statements to the effect that "most social anthropologists held and still hold radical or liberal political views" hardly find much sympathy among African intellectuals' (Ahmed, A.G.M. 1973: 260). Such reactions are partly responsible for suggesting a radical re-examination of traditional Orientalist Islamic studies (Jansen 1979; Said 1978).

However, outside an academic interest in these societies there is a general popular appeal about them which is rooted in romantic Victorian élite attitudes to primitive people which saw British civilisation confronting and edifying 'noble savages'. Some of the most evocative figures of Victorian England, when England dominated the world in thought and might, are linked in the public mind with such Islamic tribal groups: for instance, Churchill fighting the Pukhtuns at the Malakand Pass on the North-West Frontier of India, and Gordon and Kitchener facing the followers of the Mahdi in Sudan. Names such as the Akhund of Swat, the Mahdi of Sudan and the Sanusi of Cyrenaica became widely known (interestingly enough such leaders were supported by nang groups, in the forefront of the colonial struggle, across the Islamic world). Although romantic to the European coloniser it has been argued that the colonial

encounter was seen as bitter and barren by tribesmen themselves (Ahmed, A.S. 1978, 1980b).

There have been, indeed are, historical, theological and
cultural differences that have often acted as barriers to understanding between Islamic and non-Islamic societies. A certain
legacy of the deep-rooted misunderstanding and a sensitivity
to the problem still remain. The generalised non-Muslim view of
the predatory Muslim warrior with scimitar in one hand and
Qu'ran in the other, and the Muslim view of the Westerner -
mainly the Christian European - as perfidious and avaricious,
exploiting and colonising are even now only slowly fading
popular images.

We support and recommend that any ethnocentric study must
be avoided. The typical ethnocentric study may take two
extreme forms, both academically reprehensible, and both
reflecting a cultural if not political aspect of the colonial encounter. One is of the variety in which the Western/colonial
scholar studies and comments on primitive savages. At the
other extreme is the result of the recent growth in 'native'
scholarship. This form has been termed as the 'narcissistic
ethnic study' (see Ahmed's foreword in Afridi 1980). In this
category a member of a traditional society examining his own
group finds much to admire in it, and is so fascinated by the
view as to be almost overwhelmed by its perfection and beauty,
as for instance, a nang Pukhtun describing a nang tribe (ibid.).
The 'narcissistic ethnic study' raises certain interesting theoretical and methodological questions for professional anthropology.

Does this type of study unconsciously gloss over what are
or imagined to be, defects in society? Or does it not see them
altogether? Or because of kin identification and extension of
the local understanding of concepts such as 'honour', does it
consciously throw a curtain over facts it thinks would be
compromising for the group? Can such studies, given the
intimate nature of the author-subject relationship, be objective?
Balanced by this set of questions is the obvious advantage of
insight into and access to society which the 'insider' scholar
enjoys. Nothing is secret or hidden from him. 'Narcissistic
ethnic studies' will increase in the coming decades as the so-
called less developed countries produce more local social scientists. National pride, a discernible anti-Western trend, political
considerations or simple jingoism may combine to encourage the
'narcissistic ethnic study'.

If a certain ambiguity exists in perception by insiders, a
similar set of problems faces outsiders who comment on Muslim
society. Herein, perhaps, lies the challenge of studying society.
The richness and diversity of the subject is brought out
clearly in the work of two outstanding scholars, Clifford Geertz
(1968, 1973, 1979) and Ernest Gellner, (1969, 1972), examining
tribal groups in Morocco. Indeed, the opposed models they build
to explain social structure and organisation, the former

emphasising culture, the latter segmentary structure, point to the methodological fecundity of the discipline.

Making allowances for cultural irreducibility, especially in the context of colonialism, the writing of, or on, European political administrators suggests a rich and authoritative source of ethnographic material for the social sciences. An important step is the study by anthropologists of the administrators themselves in the context of the tribes among which they worked. Such studies could ensure a degree of academic objectivity for the subject, on the one hand, and personal empathy for the administrator on the other. Perhaps such a method may provide a way out for the anthropologist not wishing to fall between the two stools mentioned above. The topic has certain methodological and theoretical ramifications and is explored at greater length elsewhere (Ahmed and Hart, 'Islamic Tribes and European Administrators: Readings in the Colonial Encounter', book under preparation). It is hoped that anthropological method, which often brings together scholar and subject from different countries, will help in maintaining objectivity and perspective. A balance between the two extreme forms of ethnocentric studies is necessary if our discipline is to grow or even maintain its claim to scientific objectivity. The job of the anthropologist is, and must remain, to record and analyse impartially.

IV   THE RE-EMERGENCE OF ISLAM

A brief section on 'the re-emergence of Islam' may be relevant, and also topical, as there appears to be a 'resurgence', 'revival' or perhaps more correctly 're-emergence' of Islam in the world today, which urgently necessitates a closer look at traditional societies in the Islamic framework. There is a ferment in Islamic countries even at the 'grass roots' or village level, termed in the mass media and analysed as 'the "resurgence" or "revival" of Islam'. This ferment has in places taken a volatile shape and a violent direction, often displacing strongly entrenched leaders such as the Shah of Iran. To analyse the mood merely as 'resurgence' or 'revival' is simplistic and misleading. Muslim leaders, tribal and non-tribal, have led a religious organisation which has subsequently converted to or merged into a political organisation. A well-documented example in anthropological studies, that of the Sanusi of Cyrenaica (Evans-Pritchard 1949), was cited earlier. Similarly, the Mahdi's family in Sudan and the Akhund's descendants in Swat converted a religious base into political leadership (Ahmed, A.S. 1976). The interconnection between religion and politics has its source in the history of the Prophet's own family.

The phenomenon of Imam Khomeini which has provided reactions ranging from horror to reverence, and is fascinating the world and, as a consequence, increasing interest in Islamic

studies, is not new in Islam. Its dramatic quality has been
underlined and enhanced by the twentieth-century mass media:
television brings events into the drawing-room on the same day
they are happening in remote villages and deserts. The Ayatullah is a religious leader in a Muslim society such as the Mahdi,
the Akhund and the Sanusi were in the last century; like
those leaders he represents one aspect of Islamic reaction to
colonial or neo-colonial forces. We may therefore view the
Islamic mood not so much as a 'revival' but as an illustration of
the latent strength in society of Islamic symbols, norms and
mores, and their capacity to be mobilised. In the Iranian case
they were mobilised so successfully as to overthrow the most
powerful of kings supported by the entire paraphernalia of a
state apparatus including a modern army and police force. The
'resurgence' is more a 're-emergence' of Islam on the world
stage.

A conscious attempt to re-examine the major methodological
and theoretical assumptions in the study of Islamic societies
must be made in the light of the cumulative development in
knowledge in the post-war decades. The times demand this
re-examination. Images are changing; from a popular prototype
of Islamic society as congenitally valetudinarian, symbolised by
the epithet in the last century for the only Islamic country in
Europe, Turkey: 'the sick man of Europe', to the new, more
virile and aggressive image in the late twentieth century. But
the reasons for the new images they invoke lie elsewhere. Many
Muslim lands are oil-rich and the industrialised West, or indeed
any industrialised nation, is dependent to some degree on oil.

Not only images but Islamic societies are changing too. The
point to be underlined is that Islamic societies are undergoing
change and the attitudes of non-Islamic societies to them are
also, and correspondingly, changing. This change is often
effected with a swiftness that bewilders both actor and spectator. Two things now appear certain in the last quarter of the
twentieth century: Islam as a world force has re-emerged after
three to four centuries and its people and lands will command
attention if only because of their oil and strategic placement
in world geopolitics. It is perhaps significant that the 1980s
began with world attention focused on the crises in Iran and
Afghanistan.

The tribal societies that we are considering in this volume
have been affected to some degree by the colonial encounter
and are being affected by the re-emergence of Islam (it would
seem that some of the forms the latter is assuming are a
consequence of the former). Perhaps the degree of change in
society is kept to a minimum due to the generally inaccessible
nature of the terrain (barren mountains and remote valleys).
This leads to a related point: the sociological or anthropological 'purity' of the Islamic tribes is safeguarded to an extent
and the analyses may thus present a picture more static than
the effects of the two factors discussed above would suggest.

V METHODOLOGY

The papers in this symposium are not involved with, or do not advocate, any theological or ecclesiastical position. They are, rather, anthropological analyses of Islamic segmentary societies, which is to say, societies that are culturally and traditionally part of the Muslim world and that consciously claim to be Islamic, whatever their extent of deviation or aberration from mainstream or orthodox Islam as interpreted by urban scholars, the learned Muslim doctors - or ^c*ulama*.

It has been argued by social scientists, both Muslim and non-Muslim, that the mainstream of British and French social anthropology has tended to minimise, ignore or play down the Islamic factor in such societies thus far studied, owing to an intrinsic hostility towards Islamic societies in general, for various historical reasons. Chief among these are cultural 'hang-ups' resulting from colonialism (Asad 1973; Daniel 1966; Laroui 1974, 1977; Said 1978). In this book we will examine these societies as anthropologists and not as orientalists (whether historians, linguists or whatever). We hope to look at the subject scientifically, with objectivity and impartiality.

Usually such anthologies or symposia in social anthropology represent an intellectual consensus that in itself reflects and presupposes the pre-eminence of a given school or nationality: for example, 'Themes in Economic Anthropology' (Firth 1967), in which six out of nine authors represented are listed as trained in or affiliated with the London School of Economics, or 'Tribes Without Rulers' (Middleton and Tait 1958), wherein five of the seven authors are Oxonians or as in the case of 'African Political Systems', where the contributors are mostly British. Such ties, which are almost tribal in their own way, may lead to a certain cultural and/or academic ethnocentricity in both the presentation and the analysis of data. This volume, to the contrary, reflects in our view a healthy diversity of academic thought (for instance, Marxist, structuralist, holistic, etc. analyses) and of national backgrounds (Algerian, American, British, French, Pakistani and Soviet Russian) that nullify or balance any tendency towards a monolithic trend in this volume. This fact is in itself a guarantee against ethnocentricity, referred to above, and provides an opportunity to examine Islamic tribal societies from several different angles, thus allowing the reader to draw his own conclusions.

We feel that the exercise as presented here is justified even if it had only been reduced simply to collecting and presenting the papers as they were written. The 'common' religious/cultural and 'segmentary'/tribal factors that are so central to the enterprise are precisely those that make it worthwhile. However, it should be noted, and emphasised, that these cultural and structural similarities among the various societies in question do indeed exist in spite of being placed within such widely different ranges of national political framework as monarchies

or former monarchies (Morocco, Saudi Arabia, Iran and Afghanistan), Arab socialist republics (Algeria, Libya, Somalia), the
most powerful Communist state (Soviet Russia), and a semi-
autonomous and largely unencapsulated situation (the Tribal
Areas of Pakistan, on the Pakistan-Afghanistan frontier).

The physical limits of Islamic segmentary societies, which
are well covered in this book, are an extension of the Middle
East itself, in a wide sense, the area of Coon's 'mosaic of
peoples' (1951). The areas covered, as seen from Saudi Arabia
where Islam originated, are the Moroccan Atlantic coast and
Atlas ranges in the west to the Indus River in Pakistan in the
east (hence the title), and from Soviet Turkistan (the Turkmen
SSR) in the north(east) to Baluchistan (Iran and Pakistan) in
the south(east). In between these outlying areas, Algeria,
Libya, Somalia, the Arabian Peninsula, Iran and Afghanistan
are also covered in the book.

However, although the large agricultural peasant societies of
Pakistan south and east of the Indus, of India, of Bangladesh,
and of Malaysia, Indonesia and the Southern Philippines – to say
nothing of those of black Africa south of the Sahara – may be
just as Muslim as any of the societies under consideration in our
symposium, they, nonetheless, fall outside our area not only
geographically but also in large part structurally. Indeed, it
should be noted that the majority of the world's nearly 800
million Muslims live outside the area encompassed in this book,
while the segmentary tribesmen within it represent a small
percentage of the total population.

The physical limits covered by the tribes in this volume coincide in general with prototype images of the tribal Muslim:
nomadic, fierce warriors living in barren zones and by a strict
code of behaviour. The camel and the date-palm have become
popular symbols of these groups (important for the household
economy, the former providing locomotion, milk, hides and the
latter, food and shelter). Indeed, there is some truth in the
prototype images and, for instance, the further we move south
of the Indus the more completely the camel and the date-palm
begin to give way to the water buffalo and standing crops
(paddy, wheat or sugar-cane).

The papers assembled in this symposium are by anthropologists, many of whom have won their spurs studying Islamic
societies. The contributors have conducted field-work among
Islamic tribal societies and have been and/or are still engaged
in their examination of such societies. How they have analysed
these societies is of wide interest, as are the common factors
that emerge from one geographical and political extremity to
the other. Some of the papers have been previously published
and are well known, while others appear here for the first time.
Papers previously published elsewhere are, of course, so
acknowledged in the text.

There follows a brief introduction to the individual contributions (generally from west to east): The role and status of

holy genealogies in tribal Morocco are discussed by Professor Ernest Gellner. Magali Morsy provides a discussion of the arbitration process in the Moroccan political system from pre-Islamic times to the present. David M. Hart and I.M. Lewis discuss particular localised aspects of the structural features of Islamic societies at the two extremes of North Africa, Hart for Morocco in the west and Lewis for Somalia in the east. Both papers have implications for a wider and more general Islamic segmentary framework. The resistance to colonialism and its ramifications for Algerian society are the subject of Fanny Colonna's paper. The importance of alliances and relationship through females in contrast to the traditional wisdom that emphasised agnatic kinship relations is underscored in Donald P. Cole's paper on the Al Murra bedouin of the Saudi Arabian Empty Quarter. Emrys Peters discusses the role of ritual in Islamic tribal societies and raises important questions regarding segmentary theory.

Moving out of the Arabic-speaking world, Professor Basilov describes forms of shamanism, ritual and belief in the supernatural among the Soviet Turkmen; he postulates that many of these forms, now 'Islamised', are pre-Islamic in origin. Richard Tapper describes three tribal societies, unrelated but similar in their environments in their pastoral nomadic systems of production and in being non-Arab Muslim: the Shahsevan of northwestern Iran (Turki-speaking Shi^{c}ites), the Basseri of south-west Iran (Persian-speaking Shi^{c}ites) and the Durrani of north-central Afghanistan (Pashtu-speaking Sunni). Louis Dupree relates folklore and tribal war among Afghan tribes. Religiosity, values and economic change among a nomadic group in Afghanistan are discussed by Bahram Tavakolian. Crossing into the Indo-Pakistan subcontinent, Stephen L. Pastner argues how 'feuding in the realm of the spirit becomes a surrogate for secular competition, with the saint emerging as a hero whose exploits provide his followers with a vicarious sense of self-esteem' in Baluchistan. Religious symbolism in Pukhtun society and its homologous relationship with the wider Islamic world and with Islamic tradition are discussed by Akbar S. Ahmed.

The regularity with which our informants, from Morocco to Pakistan, present us with segmentary models of their societies is notable. It also provides overwhelming evidence for the fact that even if such models are pre-Islamic, Islam appropriated them, incorporated them and made them its own (see, for instance, Lewis and Basilov). Whether in fact these models are applicable in given individual cases or not is another matter; there is, for example, a growing tendency among anthropologists to look for 'deep structures' and hence to disregard much of what their informants tell them. Certainly any traditional material that comes to light should be used as a cross-check on what one's informants say: our own inclination is to take the more charitable and 'traditional' view that unless they are clearly and demonstrably wrong, they should be given the

benefit of the doubt. However, this raises questions of anthropological methodology that are not germane to the issue here,
which is that the identity of segmentary tribal societies appears
to be co-extensive with the whole Muslim Middle East.

We have decided to let the papers speak for themselves and
not to force them into any theoretical or conceptual mould. This
has allowed the contributors a flexibility in selecting their
approach and choice of subject. As will be seen below, some
have selected religious themes (lineages, orders or symbolism)
others, social ones (structure and organisation) to describe
and analyse their tribal groups. A certain 'local' disunity is
thus maintained which balances the overall theoretical and
methodological unity of the volume. The cultural diversity of
the societies is apparent, and so are certain similarities. For
example, most (though not all) Islamic tribal societies (a) are
characterised by low populations; (b) are located in low production areas; (c) remain highly conscious of their genealogical
charter and of the privileged position that it ascribes to them;
(d) do not encourage the formation of townships (though this
is becoming less and less the case); and (e) are acutely aware
of their Islamic identity both in a theological and sociological
sense.

With respect to at least two of the above points, it is worth
noting, for example, Caro Baroja's observation (made in contrasting the rural Ghmara villagers of north-western Morocco
with the bedouin tribesmen of the western Sahara) to the effect
that population density stands in inverse ratio to the density
of the lineage system and the genealogy (Caro Baroja 1957: 146).
However, this, as well as the other points just enumerated,
should be regarded only as guidelines, and by no means as
absolute truths. It should also be borne in mind that the *qabila-*
concept, the Muslim concept of 'tribe', is in reality a very
elastic one: not only is its meaning in Morocco different from
what it may connote in Saudi Arabia, but also there may well be
significant variation in this meaning, as culturally and structurally perceived by the people themselves, from one part of
Morocco (or wherever) to another.

In the end, as to the crucial question of segmentary tribes
and their Islamic identity, what are the common denominators
of this identity, beyond the obvious one of active participation
in a wider national and international socio-religious system as
perceived by Islamic scholars (for instance, in Hodgson's
'The Venture of Islam', 3 vols, 1974)? Our suggestion is that in
most Islamic tribal societies the notions of both the orthodox
Shari'a and of the less orthodox Sufism, and of what these
concepts imply in the local context, are probably equally
important, despite the fact that greater lip service is generally
paid to the former. In his own view, that is in the way the
native Muslim perceives the world, he is orthodox, and there is
certainly no question about his conservatism. As for participation in the wider sociocultural and religious system, we need

only mention the five pillars of Islam, highlighting in particular the stringent observance by adults of the Ramadan fast, and also noting that the hajj to Makkah (Mecca), a tremendous physical hardship for the majority of Muslims even as recently as thirty or forty years ago, has today become the world's biggest peacetime exercise in logistics, on the part of the Saudi Arabian government (Amin 1978).

Finally, it is our pleasant duty to thank the participants for their enthusiastic response in contributing to this volume. We extend our hope that the collection will further the knowledge and understanding of Islamic societies in general and of segmentary tribal societies in particular. Furthermore, it is hoped this knowledge will practically benefit tribal societies especially in situations of rapid change; we believe anthropology can contribute effectively to solving modern tribal problems (Ahmed, A.S. 1980c). Needless to say, the views expressed in this introduction do not necessarily reflect those of our colleagues.

BIBLIOGRAPHY

Afridi, O.K. (1980), 'Mahsud Monograph', foreword by
   A.S. Ahmed, Tribal Research Cell, NWFP, Peshawar.
Ahmed, A.G.M. (1973), Some Remarks from the Third World
   on Anthropology and Colonialism: The Sudan, in 'Anth-
   ropology and the Colonial Encounter', ed. by Talal Asad,
   Ithaca Press, London.
Ahmed, A.S. (1976), 'Millennium and Charisma Among Pathans:
   A Critical Essay in Social Anthropology', Routledge & Kegan
   Paul, London.
Ahmed, A.S. (1977), 'Social and Economic Change in the Tribal
   Areas', Oxford University Press, Karachi.
Ahmed, A.S. (1978), The Colonial Encounter on the NWFP:
   Myth and Mystification, 'Journal of the Anthropological
   Society of Oxford', vol. IX, no. 3, Oxford.
Ahmed, A.S. (1980a), 'Pukhtun Economy and Society: Tradi-
   tional Structure and Economic Development in a Tribal
   Society', Routledge & Kegan Paul, London.
Ahmed, A.S. (1980b), Tribes and States in Central and South
   Asia, 'Asian Affairs', June, vol. XI, part II.
Ahmed, A.S. (1980c), How to aid Afghan Refugees, in 'Royal
   Anthropological Institute News', no. 39, August.
Ahmed, A.S. (1983), 'Religion and Politics in Muslim Society:
   Order and Conflict in Pakistan', Cambridge University Press.
Ahmed, A.S., and D.M. Hart (eds), 'Islamic Tribes and
   European Administrators: Readings in the Colonial Encounter'
   (book under preparation).
Amin, M.A. (1978), 'Pilgrimage to Mecca', Macdonald & Jane's,
   London.
Asad, T. (ed.) (1973), 'Anthropology and the Colonial

Encounter', Ithaca Press, London.

Aswad, B.C. (1970), Social and Ecological Aspects in the Formation of Islam, in 'Peoples and Cultures of the Middle East', ed. by L.E. Sweet, vol. I, Natural History Press.

Bailey, F.G. (1972), Conceptual Systems in the Study of Politics, in 'Rural Politics and Social Change in the Middle East', ed. by R. Antoun and I. Harik, Indiana University Press.

Barnes, J.A. (1954), 'Politics in a Changing Society: A Political History of the Fort Jameson Ngoni', University of Manchester Press, Manchester, for Institute of Social Research, University of Zambia, 2nd edn, 1967.

Barth, F. (1972), 'Political Leadership among Swat Pathans', Athlone Press, London.

Braeunlich, E. (1933-4), Beitraege zur Gesellschaftsordnung der arabischen Beduinenstaemme, in 'Islamica', vol. VI, nos. 1-2, pp. 68-111, 182-229, Leipzig.

Burke, E. III (1979), Islamic History as World History: Marshall Hodgson, 'The Venture of Islam', in 'International Journal of Middle Eastern Studies', vol. 10, no. 2, pp. 241-64.

Caro Baroja, J. (1957), 'Estudios Mogrebies', Instituto de Estudios Africanos, Madrid.

Chelhod, J. (1971), 'Le Droit dans la Société Bédouine: Recherches Ethnologiques sur le 'Orf ou Droit Coutumier des Bédouins', Marcel Rivière, Paris.

Cole, D.P. (1975), 'Nomads of the Nomads: The Al Murrah Bedouin of the Empty Quarter', Aldine, Chicago.

Coon, C.S. (1951), 'Caravan: The Story of the Middle East', Holt, New York, 3rd edn, Holt, Rinehart & Winston, New York, 1962.

Coulson, N.J. (1964), 'A History of Islamic Law', Islamic Surveys no. 2, Edinburgh University Press, Edinburgh.

Daniel, N. (1966), 'Islam, Europe and Empire', Edinburgh University Press, Edinburgh.

Desanges, J. (1962), 'Catalogue des Tribus Africaines de l'Antiquité Classique à l'Ouest du Nil', Section d'Histoire 4, Faculté des Lettres et Sciences Humaines, University de Dakar, Dakar.

Dyson-Hudson, N. (1972), The Study of Nomads, in 'Perspectives on Nomadism', ed. by William Irons and Neville Dyson-Hudson, E.J. Brill, Leiden, pp. 2-29.

Eickelman, D.F. (1967), Musaylima: An Approach to the Social Anthropology of Seventh Century Arabia, 'Journal of the Economic and Social History of the Orient', no. 10.

Evans-Pritchard, E.E. (1940), 'The Nuer: A Description of the Modes of Livelihood and Political Institutions of a Nilotic People', Clarendon Press, Oxford.

Evans-Pritchard, E.E. (1949), 'The Sanusi of Cyrenaica', Clarendon Press, Oxford, 2nd edn, 1954.

Evans-Pritchard, E.E. (1951), 'Kinship and Marriage among

the Nuer', Clarendon Press, Oxford.
Evans-Pritchard, E.E. (1956), 'Nuer Religion', Clarendon Press, Oxford.
Firth, R. (ed.) (1967), 'Themes in Economic Anthropology', Association of Social Anthropologists (ASA) Monograph no. 6, Tavistock, London, 3rd edn, 1970.
Fortes, M., and E.E. Evans-Pritchard (eds) (1940), 'African Political Systems', Oxford University Press for International African Institute, London, New York, Toronto.
Gabrieli, F. (ed) (1953), 'L'Antica Società Beduina', Studi Semitici 2, Istituto di Studi Orientali, University of Rome.
Gaid, M. (1972), 'Aguellids et Romains en Berbérie', Société Nationale d'Edition et de Diffusion (SNED), Algiers.
Geertz, C. (1968), 'Islam Observed: Religious Development in Morocco and Indonesia', Yale University Press.
Geertz, C. (1973), 'The Interpretation of Cultures', Basic Books, New York.
Geertz, C., H. Geertz and L. Rosen (1979), 'Meaning and Order in Moroccan Society: Three Essays in Cultural Analysis', Cambridge University Press.
Gellner, E. (1969), 'Saints of the Atlas', Weidenfeld & Nicolson, London, and Chicago, University of Chicago Press.
Gellner, E. (1972), Doctor and Saint, in 'Scholars, Saints and Sufis: Muslim Religious Institutions in the Middle East Since 1500', ed. by N.R. Keddie, University of California Press, Berkeley, Los Angeles, London, pp. 307-26.
Gellner, E. (1976), Foreword in Ahmed, A.S. (1976) above.
Godelier, M. (1977), 'Perspectives in Marxist Anthropology', Cambridge University Press.
Gsell, S. (1913-28), 'Histoire Ancienne de l'Afrique du Nord', 8 vols, Hachette, Paris (especially vol. 5, 1927).
Hart, D.M. (1962), The Social Structure of the Rgibat Bedouins of the Western Sahara, 'Middle East Journal', vol. XVI, no. 4, pp. 515-27.
Hart, D.M. (1976), 'The Aith Waryaghar of the Moroccan Rif: An Ethnography and History', Viking Fund Publications in Anthropology no. 55, University of Arizona Press, Tucson.
Hodgson, M.G.S. (1974), 'The Venture of Islam: Conscience and History in a World Civilization' (vol. I: 'The Classical Age of Islam'; vol. II: 'The Expansion of Islam in the Middle Periods'; vol. III: 'The Gunpowder Empires and Modern Times'), University of Chicago Press.
Ibn Khaldun (1967), 'The Muqaddimah: An Introduction to History', trans. by Franz Rosenthal and ed. by N.J. Dawood, Princeton University Press (Bollington Series).
Jacob, G. (1897), 'Altarabisches Beduinenleben', Mayer & Mueller, Berlin.
Jansen, G.H. (1979), 'Militant Islam', Pan Books, London.
Keenan, J. (1977), 'The Tuareg: People of Ahaggar', Allen Lane, London.
Laroui, A. (1974), 'La Crise des Intellectuels Arabes: Tradi-

tionalisme ou Historicisme?', François Maspéro, Paris.
Laroui, A. (1977), 'Les Origines Sociales et Culturelles du
  Nationalisme Marocain 1830-1912', François Maspéro, Paris.
Marcy, G. (1941), Les Vestiges de la Parenté Maternelle en
  Droit Coutumier Berbère et le Régime des Successions
  Touarègues, 'Revue Africaine', vol. LXXXV, nos 3-4,
  Algiers, pp. 187-211.
Middleton, J., and D. Tait (eds) (1958), 'Tribes Without
  Rulers: Studies in African Segmentary Systems', Routledge
  & Kegan Paul, London.
Montagne, R. (1930), 'Les Barbères et le Makhzen dans le Sud
  du Maroc: Essai sur la Transformation Politique des Berbères
  Sédentaires (Gruuse Chlouh)', Félix Alcan, Paris.
Montagne, R. (1947), 'La Civilisation du Desert: Nomades
  d'Orient et d'Afrique', Hachette, Paris.
Procksch, O. (1899) 'Ueber die Blutrache bei den vorislamischen
  Arabern und Muhammads Stellung zu ihr', Teubner, Leipzig.
Robertson Smith, W. (1903), 'Kinship and Marriage in Early
  Arabia', ed. by Stanley A. Cook, A. & C. Black, London,
  2nd edn, ed. by E.L. Peters, Beacon Press, Boston,
  n.d. (c. 1966).
Said, E.W. (1978), 'Orientalism', Routledge & Kegan Paul,
  London.
Wolf, E.R. (1951), The Social Organization of Mecca and the
  Origins of Islam, 'South Western Journal of Anthropology',
  vol. 7, no. 4.

1   DOCTOR AND SAINT*

Ernest Gellner

Accounts of societies in terms of the beliefs and values of their members often assume that each member has one set of beliefs about the world, and one set of values. This seems to me a major mistake. Any professional sports team invariably has more than one reserve in addition to the set normally presented to the public, ever ready to replace the first lot, either one by one or, if necessary, as a whole. The same is generally true about our cosmological picture or about our moral values. There is, of course, an interesting difference. When the cosmological picture or the moral values claim unique and exclusive validity, the overt possession and display of rival alternatives would be shameful, heretical, and scandalous. Apart from anything else, it would undermine confidence in that unique cosmological picture or set of moral values. One of the points of having the picture and the values is, of course, to reassure both oneself and others, and to proclaim that certain ideas and certain attitudes are simply not negotiable. A person who made it plain that his confidence in his own supposedly unnegotiable basic positions is less than total, and that he is keeping an alternative ready and available, would thereby undermine the credibility of his own stance and encourage intransigence in others. This would never do.

Thus the alternatives are decently hidden away. There is nothing unusual about this, and there are many parallels in social and political fields. For instance, a government recognizes the legal and legitimate authorities in a neighboring country, and it would be a hostile and provocative act to recognize at the same time some 'government in exile,' heading a revolutionary movement which hopes to dislodge the present rulers of the neighboring state. But, of course, it would be most unwise to have no relationships at all with that revolutionary movement: after all, they might win. So, while the department of state charged with diplomacy entertains cordial and exclusive relationships with the official government, the covert intelligence services are at liberty to maintain just as significant relationships with the revolutionaries.

The importance of the ulama is that they are the openly displayed, official first eleven of Islam. They are the norm-givers

*The material used in this paper is presented in greater detail in 'Saints of the Atlas' (London and Chicago, 1969).

of the community of the faithful; they are the repositories and arbiters of legitimacy. So much for theory. There is one well-known manner in which reality diverges from theory: the verdict of the ulama regarding legitimacy, like the flight of that much overrated bird the Owl of Minerva, takes place only after the event, and hence in effect ratifies the actual power situation, rather than sitting in judgment on it. From the viewpoint of understanding the general social structure of Islam this particular limitation does not matter too much, perhaps: it does mean that in general the ulama cannot do very much about determining the identity of the ruler, but are constrained to ratify whichever ruler prevails by force of arms. This is indeed so. But while they cannot determine the specific identity of the ruler, and must bow to superior strength, whether they like it or not, it does not preclude them from being extremely influential on the general kind of society over which the ruler presides. A group of men may be powerless with respect to filling individual roles in a society and yet extremely influential with respect to what kind of system of roles there is to be filled. This, I suspect, is indeed the role of the ulama in Islamic society: not very powerful in deciding between one ruler or dynasty and another, they were most influential in determining the general nature of the society.

But there is another limitation on their influence of quite a different kind: the limitation not on their choice of personnel, but on their influence on the general social structure. This limitation is notoriously well attested by the fact that such large segments of Muslim populations look not only, and not so much, toward the ulama for spiritual guidance, as they do toward other types of religiously significant groups, whom there is a tendency to lump together under the heading of Sufism.

It should be said that this kind of indiscriminate lumping together of what is in effect residual category is probably a mistake. Under the general category of Sufism, people tend, for instance, to group together genuin mystics, and tribal holy men whose connection with mysticism is minimal. Both may be classified by the same kind of terminology, not only by scholars but also by the local populations, but this does not mean that the two phenomena are homogeneous and deserve to be classed together, either from the viewpoint of social significance or from that of religious phenomenology. Roughly speaking: urban Sufi mysticism is an alternative to the legalistic, restrained, arid (as it seems to its critics) Islam of the ulama. Rural and tribal 'Sufism' is a substitute for it. In the one case, an alternative is sought for the Islam of the ulama because it does not fully satisfy. In the other case, a substitute for it is required because, though its endorsement is desired, it is, in its proper and urban form, locally unavailable, or is unusable in the tribal context.

There are within Islam three major types of legitimation: the Book (including its extension by tradition), the consensus of the community, and the line of succession.

The Book is a repository of the divine word, publicly available, not incarnated in any one person, group, institution, or policy, and hence capable of sitting in judgment on any one of them. This transethnic and transsocial quality of the Book is, of course, of the utmost importance in understanding the political life both of Muslim societies and of the expansion of Islam. Even if the sociologists were right in supposing that the divine is merely the social in camouflage, it is a fact of the greatest importance that the camouflage (if such it be) is so rigorously maintained, and hence emphatically ensures the nonidentification of the divine with any one concrete human or social representative of it.

Another important form of legitimation, in Islam and elsewhere, is, of course, the consensus of the community. In Islam, this approach has complemented rather than opposed the Book. Islamic societies have never been what might be called 'pure' democratic societies; they have not maintained that the only sort of legitimacy is the consent of the community. That consent was invoked only for the supplementing of divine truth by interpretation where interpretation was required, rather than as an independent and equally powerful source. In practice, the Book required scholars to read it and consensus to interpret it, and hence, concretely speaking, the authority of the ulama as religious scholars, and that of the community as interpreters of the Words, were in harmony.

But there is a third type of legitimation within Islam, that of succession. Succession can be either physical or spiritual, and sometimes one genealogical line may employ both physical and spiritual links. The physical links, of course, arise from the fact that there is no requirement of celibacy on religious leaders. The spiritual links are made possible by mystical doctrine: mystical illumination can be passed on from teacher to disciple in a legitimacy-preserving way, analogous to the manner in which paternity maintains legitimacy of authority from father to son.

This third principle of legitimation is, of course, not always in harmony with the other two. In Shi^{c}i Islam, it becomes, of course, the main principle bringing with it the possibility of overruling the other two. But even within Sunni Islam, which does not have the same stress on locating religious legitimacy in a lineage, succession can become extremely important, and particularly so in social conditions that display a particularly strong requirement that the Word should become Flesh. There are such milieus. The most obvious examples are, of course, tribal societies, cut off from the Book by the fact that their members are illiterate (and, one should add, that they do not possess the means for sustaining or protecting a class of literate scholars), and in some measure cut off from the wider Islamic consensus by a relationship of hostility (and yet of economic interdependence) with those urban centers which are somehow the visible incarnation and center of gravity of the Muslim civilization. In such tribal milieus, there is a shift of stress in legitimation from the Book or the abstract consensus, toward the lineage. The stress is, of course, exemplified in practice rather than expressed in any kind of theory.

This, then, is the general setting: the significance of the tribal holy lineages is that they satisfy a need for the incarnation of the Word in a milieu that through lack of literacy and of towns cannot use the ulama. Thus the lineages of holy men are an alternative to the ulama, an alternative that at the same time, within the wider spiritual economy of Islam, is parasitical on them. It provides an alternative and in effect serves and represents values other than those of the ulama, and yet at the same time indirectly endorses the values and views of the ulama. Tribal society has its values and attitudes, and these are served and symbolized by the tribal holy men. The tribesmen do not wish to be any different from what they are. But they are, in the eyes of their more learned urban folk, sinful and/or heretical. They know that this is how they are seen, and they do not really repudiate the judgment. They accept it, and yet wish to persist in their attitudes. At the same time, they do not in any way desire to opt out of the wider community of Islam. Their attitude really is that of Saint Augustine: Lord, make me pure, but not yet. They recognize standards of purity in terms of which their own tribal society fails, yet at the same time wish to remain as they are, indefinitely. They are quite aware of the conflict and contradiction, yet at the same time the contradiction is not articulated clearly or stressed. It is there, yet is clouded in decent obscurity.

The significance of the tribal holy men lies in the manner in which they help to perpetuate this situation.

The Berbers of the central high Atlas are an outstandingly fine example of the manner in which the Word must become Flesh when incarnated in a tribal society. In addition to factors frequently found elsewhere in Islam, there are here some additional ones, which perhaps once operated throughout the Maghreb, but which in any case are most clearly preserved here. These local factors are a most remarkable case of tribal separation of powers, inspired not by either modern or any political theory, but tied in beautifully with the requirements of religious representation.

The political and social system of these tribes is segmentary, which is to say, each tribe divides and subdivides again and so forth until family units are reached. At each level of size, all segments are equal and there is no division of labor between them, either of an economic or of a political nature. Neither within segments nor between them are there any specialized political institutions or groups. Thus, from the viewpoint of the tribe as a whole, the tribe possesses a treelike structure, dividing and subdividing in the manner of the branches of a tree - though there is no central and preeminent trunk, all branches being equal. From the viewpoint of any one individual or family, this means that he or it are at the center of a number of concentric circles - the intravillage clan, the village, the group of villages forming a local clan, the larger clan, the tribe, and so forth. None of these superimposed groupings, from the individual's viewpoint, ever cuts across another and thus ideally they give no rise to conflicting obligations. Conflict at a lower level in no way precludes cohesion and cooperation at a higher level: in other words, two clans may be hostile to each other .yet cooperate jointly as members of the tribe against another tribe. Everything is symmetrical and egalitarian: although, of course, some men and some groups manage temporarily to be richer or more influential than others, this gives no rise either to a permanent, or a symbolically ratified, stratification. Only complete outsiders to the tribe can be located, socially speaking, above or below: negroid or Jewish artisans and holy men are the only significant exceptions, in the traditional system, to the pervasive symmetry and equality.

The general features of such segmentary societies, with their diffusion of power and the maintenance of order by the opposition of groups to one another at all levels, are well known. The only remarkable thing about the Berbers of the central high Atlas is the degree of perfection to which they have brought the system. They approximate more closely an ideal type of segmentary society than do most other societies of this kind, including those most frequently cited when the principles of segmentation are expounded.

A crucial feature of the society, which conveys its general nature, is chieftaincy. Chieftaincy among these tribes is elective and annual. Moreover, the manner of election is remarkable: it observes the principles of which I call 'rotation and complementarity.' These work as follows: suppose a tribe to be subdivided into three clans, A, B, and C. Any given year it will be the turn of one clan only to supply the chief. But the clan that supplies the chief does not elect him. Suppose Clan A supplies the chief: then it is the turn of the men of clans B and C to be the electors. In other words, any given year, a clan can supply either candidates or voters, but not both.

This system of rotation and complementarity operates at a number of levels of segmentation at once, so that the political system as a whole could be compared to a number of rotating wheels-within-wheels. The system is somewhat modified at the top and at the bottom ends of the scale, in terms of size. At the top, the wheel may turn only if there is need of it: in concrete terms, a topmost chief may be elected only if there is need of him, if there is some issue of concern to the topmost unit. There will be no filling of chieftaincy posts for the sake of continuity alone. At the very bottom, rotation and complementarity may not be observed. If it is a matter of choosing heads of tiny segments, say, of the three subclans within a village, the total population of which is in the neighborhood of two or three hundred people, then the chief of these minuscule subsegments will be chosen from the segment as a whole and not from a restricted area of candidacy, so to speak. At that level, the number of people available with suitable talents may be so small that such restriction would prove too cumbersome. But for the village of about two or three hundred inhabitants, rotation and implementing will be observed.

The relationship of lower level chiefs to higher level chiefs is obscure and eludes the categories of neat political or administrative theory. The lower level chiefs are at once elective heads of their units, and representatives within their units of the higher level chiefs.

A particularly bewildering feature of the system is what I call leap-frogging in the hierarchy. It works as follows. Suppose there are four levels of size of segmentary units. It may happen that top chiefs of units at the level of size 1 will have their agents and representatives chiefs at level 3, whereas chiefs at level 2 will act through representatives at level 4. In other words, there will be two hierarchies which, as it were, pass through each other without affecting each other, articulated as they are in two different media. In an ordinary, centralized, nonsegmentary society, where the maintenance of order is the concern of some specialized agencies in the society, this would be madness. It would be inconceivable for the government, or for the courts, or for the police to be concerned with conflicts and violence only selectively, according to the level of size at which they occur, with one police force concerned with conflicts at one set of levels and another police force concerned with conflicts at another set, the two sets being related to each other like alternate layers in a cake. In a segmentary society, where violence and aggression is a tort and not a crime, and where conflicts of units of different size are kept apart and do not implicate one another, this kind of arrangement makes perfectly good sense.

The political system of the lay tribes of the central Atlas does not concern us directly, but only for its implications for the holy lineages. What are the relevant features of this political system? Its most obvious features are weak chieftaincy and lack of continuity. All chiefs are lame ducks. As soon as elected they are within a year of the termination of their office (even if, rather exceptionally, their tenure may be prolonged). Moreover, they depend on the votes of the members of the rival clans, in a society built upon the rivalry of clans. They have no agents or sanctions, other than minor chieftains elected in a manner similar to their own: they have no secretariat and no police force. The only backing they have are the moral pressures of public opinion and the normal mechanisms of segmented societies – the anger of the offended subgroup in the case of an offense against it.

All these factors militate against the emergence of permanent and tyrannical chieftains and privileged political lineages, and indeed, their political system did enable the Berbers of the central High Atlas to escape the kind of ephemeral but harsh tyranny which characterized, for instance, the western High Atlas in this century.

But if the merit of the system is to provide checks and balances against tyranny and political ambition, its corresponding weakness is, as indicated, a lack of continuity and of order-maintaining agency. Yet these tribes do need a measure of order. They are not made up of small, inward-turned communities. They are ecologically most diversified and complementary. The natural environment is highly diversified, with extremes of climate and season between the Sahara edge and the high pastures of the Atlas mountains, whose highest point rises above 4,000 meters. The shepherds and their flocks can survive thanks only to a complex pattern of transhumance, involving movement over large distances and the drawing up of complex pasture rights, synchronized use, and deferment of use, of the better pastures, and the drawing of boundaries in time (seasonally) as well as in space. Many tribes must trade if they are to survive, being grossly deficient in their production of staple cereals, and all of them trade if they are to procure salt, and what might be called the essential luxuries of sugar and tea, and, in the olden days, firearms and ammunition. At the same time, order is not maintained, in the traditional situation, by the central government: on the contrary, the tribes ensure that central government does not interfere in their affairs. In brief, we have a situation of great ecological and economic interdependence, combined with only very weak and, in themselves, inadequate political institutions for the maintenance of the order required by economic life and for purposes of communication. How is this paradox resolved?

This is, of course, the point at which the holy lineages enter the argument.

It might be best first of all to describe them briefly. The holy men (*igurramen*, in the local Berber dialect) live in settlements generally centered on the shrine of the founding saintly ancestor. They possess a genealogy linking them to this ancestor. In the central High Atlas, the genealogy generally stretches back beyond the founding ancestor and leading, finally, to the Prophet through his daughter and his son-in-law, Our Lord Ali.

The settlements around the shrine may be quite large and have up to something like three hundred inhabitants. In some cases, virtually all the members of the settlement may be descendants of the founding saint (in the sense of believing themselves to be such and having the claim generally recognized). Nevertheless, even in these cases in which this genealogical qualification is widely diffused, by no means all of them will actually perform the function ascribed to igurramen.

This function will only be performed by a small number among them, and in a limiting case, by only one of them. The others may be described as laicized or latent saints. Presumably their ancestors once were effective saints, but the offspring were pushed out into a lay condition by demographic pressure and by the crucial fact that it is of the very nature of this kind of sanctity, that it is concentrated in a small number of people. Excessive diffusion is incompatible with its very nature.

What is the role of the effective saints? They provide the continuity and the stable framework that the political system of the lay tribes so conspicuously lacks. For instance: the lay chiefs are elective. But elections are procedures that require some kind of institutional background, and this society, needless to say, has no civil service or secretariat or anything of the kind that could look after these matters. So the elections take place at the settlement and near the shrine of the hereditary holy men, which is, of course, also a sanctuary within which one must not feud. Thus the saints provide the physical locale and the moral guarantee that make it possible for rival clans to assemble and carry out their elections. They also provide the means of moral persuasion and the mediation that help ensure that the elections, in the end, arrive at a unanimous conclusion.

Or again: the saints provide the cornerstone for the legal system (or perhaps one should say, arbitration system) of the lay tribes. The legal decision procedure is trial by collective oath, with the number of cojurors dependent on the gravity of the offense. A theft might require two cojurors; a rape, four; a murder of a woman, twenty; a murder of a man, forty. The rule is that issues requiring less than ten cojurors are settled on the spot, among the lay tribes, but issues requiring ten or more cojurors are taken up to the shrine of the founding saint of the holy lineage, and settled with the moral assistance of the saints who are the progeny of the enshrined founder.

The saints and their settlements are thus arbitrators between tribes, and between their clans, and they are physically located on important boundaries. This indicates a further important function performed by them: their physical location at important boundaries indicates and guarantees those boundaries. Their moral authority also helps to guarantee the complex seasonal arrangements connected with transhumancy between the high mountain pastures and the desert edge. Their location on the frontier also greatly assists trade. Tribesmen visiting markets in neighboring tribes can pass through the settlement of the saints, deposit their arms there, and be accompanied on their way to the market by a saint from the settlement or a representative of an important saint. This holy fellow traveler then provides simultaneously a guarantee of their safety from their hosts and a guarantee of their good conduct toward their hosts.

The political life of the saints is quite different from that of the lay tribes. There is a neat contrast in almost every respect. Lay chiefs are chosen by the people: saints are chosen only by God. Lay chiefs are, in principle, annual: saints are permanent, and in principle permanent over generations. Lay tribesmen are addicted to feuding and litigation: saints are obligatorily pacific and must not litigate. (In the tribal mind, litigation and violence are very close to each other. The collective oath is the continuation of the feud by other means.)

The basic contradiction in the life of the saints arises from the fact that there must not be too many of them: their role and influence hinges on the one-many relationship between them and the tribes, for one saint must arbitrate among many tribes or tribal segments. At the same time, saints proliferate, and yet they have no rule of succession to decide the inheritance of saintly role. The rule of inheritance among the saints is the same as among the lay tribes, and is symmetrical as between brothers. There is only a very slight predisposition in favor of primogeniture, a predisposition that is certainly not decisive.

How then is the succession decided? In the local mind, it is only God who decides. It would be presumptuous indeed for men to decide where grace, *baraka*, is to flow. God makes his choice manifest through the possession by the elect of the crucial attributes of pacifism, uncalculating generosity and hospitality, and prosperity.

In reality it is, of course, a kind of unconscious choice by the tribesmen which decides the succession. By using this rather than that son, by using this rather than that rival saintly lineage, the tribesmen in effect choose and elect the given son or lineage as the 'real' saint. But the fact that the voice of God is really the voice of the people is not made manifest and explicit. The voice of the people manifests itself through making feasible the possession or attribution of characteristics which are then seen as signs of divine election. A man who is used by the tribesmen as a saint and revered as such can afford to be pacific, to turn the other cheek, with impunity. A man who is not respected as a saint would, if he behaved in this kind of way, only attract aggression. A man who is revered by the tribesmen as a saint will receive plentiful donations and can afford to act with what appears to be uncalculating generosity, and yet also retain that other attribute of election, namely, prosperity. A man, on the other hand, who did not receive adequate donations from the tribes but who behaved as if he were in effect a saint would impoverish himself and thereby make most manifest his lack of divine grace.

Thus the choice of the tribesmen externalizes itself and comes to appear as a divine choice. The mediating factor is, of course, the stress of the specifically saintly virtues of pacifism and of uncalculating generosity. The possession of these virtues is the test: one can acquire them only with the cooperation of the lay tribesmen. Pacifism and a consider-the-lilies attitude among the saints cannot be explained as some kind of diffusion

or survival of values derived from the Sermon on the Mount.
They are much too inherently and visibly a necessary
corollary of the local social structure, of the role performed by
saints within it and the manner of attributing sanctity within
it. They are in no way generalized beyond the role that requires
them.

Thus both the conceptualization and the rhythm of political
life are quite different among the saints from those that are
found among lay tribes. The political life of the saints is a
game of very slow musical chairs, played out over generations
not by the removal of chairs but by the addition to the number
of contestants. Success and failure in it are in principle for
keeps and are seen as the consequences of supernatural, divine
favor. By contrast, election to chieftaincy among the lay tribes
is in the hands of men, not of God, and is for a limited period
only. There is a belief among nonanthropologists that tribesmen
generally see their tribal arrangements as supernaturally sanctioned. Berbers of the central High Atlas do not: they know
their own tribal arrangements to be secular and based on the
will of men, and they have the conceptual equipment that
enables them to be clear about it. This equipment is, of course,
derived not from secularist philosophers, but simply from the
fact that within their own society, they need to distinguish
between the divine factor in political life, represented by the
saints, and the secular factor, complementing it and represented
by themselves. What the saints decide is, in local belief, a
reflection of divine will: but what the tribal assembly decides,
though deserving of respect as perpetuation of ancestral custom, springs from a human source and can on occasion be
consciously and deliberately changed by consent.

There is, however, one further function performed by the
saints, over and above the invaluable role they visibly fulfill in
the local sociopolitical structure. This additional role is to
anchor the local society in the wider system of Islam. The
saints are not merely saints: they are also, in local belief, the
descendants of the Prophet. The tribesmen know that in the
eyes of inhabitants of the urban centers of literate Islam, they
are held to be at worst heretical and sinful, and at best sadly
ignorant of religion. They know that only Muslims may own
land, and that a tribe convicted of not being Muslim would
provide a most enviable justification for all its neighbors to
dispossess it. Admittedly, the city dwellers would not have the
means to deprive a mountain or desert tribe of its land, but
they could encourage other tribes to combine in a joint act of
aggression against it. So every tribe needs, and in any case
wishes, to display its Muslim status. They can hardly do this
through Qur'anic scholarship. They are illiterate. But they
can do it by showing due reverence to those supposed descendants of the Prophet who are so conveniently settled among
them, helping to guarantee tribal frontiers and in other ways

assisting the tribes to manage their affairs.

This, then, is one further function of the holy lineages. Though the holy lineages are often assimilated to Sufism, their real life and function has little to do with mysticism and the diffusion of mystical ideas. (On the contrary, some supposedly Sufi practices may in fact derive from tribal customs, tribal styles of dancing, and so forth.)

The political system in which permanent and pacific saints divide the political role with elective, secular, and feud-addicted tribal chieftains is elegant and, structurally, sufficient unto itself. But it is not conceptually sufficient unto itself. Conceptually, it is other-directed and looks toward the wider world of Islam. Spiritually speaking, the holy lineages are lords of the marches. They represent the religion of the central tradition of the wider society for the tribesmen, and guarantee the tribesmen's incorporation in it. As described, they also help the tribesmen to avoid being saddled with physical, military lords of the marches, by giving continuity and stability to a system otherwise possessing only minimal political leadership.

How is this local other-directedness concretely manifested?

The manifestations vary in kind. They are found both among the lay tribes and the holy lineages. Take, as a simple example, some legends circulating both about and among one of the most backward, savage, and religiously ignorant among the Atlas tribes, the Ait CAbdi of the Ait Sukhman. When I say that this tribe is particularly backward, savage, and ignorant of religion, I refer to a stereotype held of it not just by outsiders to the region, urban folk and such, but by other tribes within the region itself, and, most significantly, by the tribe itself. Though all mountain tribes without distinction may seem to be licentious, violent, heterodox savages to the bourgeoisie of Fez, once you get in among the tribes you find, as so often, that further subtle distinctions and nuances can be made by anyone with local knowledge. All tribesmen may seem savages from Fez, but for the connoisseur, some are much more so than others, even, or especially, in their own estimation.

The Ait CAbdi are at the end of the road, literally and figuratively speaking. Or rather, literally speaking they are a good way beyond the end of the road, for no road at all makes its way to their desolate and stony plateau. Even nowadays, you can get there only on foot or on the back of a mule, and the plateau is held to be almost inaccessible in winter. Figuratively speaking, they are at the end of the road, for almost anyone can look down on them as savages, and as far as I know there is no one more savage on whom they can look down, though there are some who are perhaps their equals in this respect.

The interesting thing is that the Ait CAbdi themselves share this view. There is one legend that circulates among and about them which is particularly suggestive. This legend is something utterly familiar to every child among the Ait CAbdi, as Father

Christmas is to a child in Western society.

The legend runs as follows: a false teacher of Islam, in fact a Jew, appeared among the Ait ^CAbdi, and was received by them and recognized as a true religious teacher. He made a good living among them as a *fqih*, that is to say, scribe and Qur'anic teacher. He was in fact quite devoid of the religious knowledge he was supposed to teach, but he did not allow this to dismay him: instead of reciting the Qur'an, he simply rattled off various well-known local place names, ending this recitation with the words – I show you your land, O heads of asses – 'ighfawen n-ighyal.' Despite this blatant effrontery, it took the Ait ^CAbdi quite some time to unmask him – and the rest of the legend does not concern us.

Note the point of the story: it illustrates, of course, the perfidy, cunning, and effrontery of the infidel-foreigner, but it also illustrates, indeed highlights, the stupidity, gullibility, and total religious ignorance of the Ait ^CAbdi themselves. Yet they themselves tell the story!

This is not the only legend in which the Ait ^CAbdi display a kind of joking relationship to their own image and history. Another story, as popular and familiar among them and their neighbors as is the story of the scurrilous religious teacher, concerns a man, u-Himmish, and his wife, Tuda Lahsin, whose intransigence and pugnacity triggered a murderous chain reaction of feud and killing, all started by a trivial quarrel on a pasture. It is actually forbidden among the Ait ^CAbdi to tell this story, on the assumption that its recounting will bring bad luck and perhaps a repetition of such episodes, yet at the same time the story is utterly familiar to all of them. The moral of the situation is – we know we ought not to be so quarrelsome and feud-addicted, and we know at the same time perfectly well that this is just how we are.

Another legend – this one told about rather than among them – explains why it is that they find themselves on their particularly bare and stony plateau: the reason is that they fought so ferociously against their rightful Sultan, Mulay al-Hasan (referring to the nineteenth-century monarch of this name, and not to the present king). It is a curious explanation, insofar as they were by no means the only tribe, or even the most important one, which joined in resisting the attempts of that ruler to penetrate the mountains. But, as so often in these legends, the explanation is, so to speak, differential: what counts as an explanation in one case would not count as such in another. Explanations are not universalized.

What concerns us of course is that the legend underscores once again the recognition of a value – submission to the central state – which is in fact not practiced by the very tribes who repeat the story (or rather, was not practiced till the modern world forced them to practice it, and of course the legend antedates the centralization imposed under modern conditions).

So much by way of illustration of the kind of self-ironizing attitude, the joking relationship with one's own image, as manifested in legends circulating among the lay tribes. The situation becomes even clearer and more conspicuous among the holy lineages.

Here nature has arranged a nice experimental situation. All other factors being held constant, one factor alone is varied, as if for our benefit. This independent variable is: the proximity to the plain and hence to the urban centers from which scripturalist, puritanical, and reformist Islam emanates.

In the central High Atlas, there are a number of centers of sanctity, of holy settlements that act as sanctuaries, centers of arbitration, and pilgrimage, for the surrounding tribes. In many ways, these centers are very similar to one another (though of course they differ in size, influence, and one or two other associated features). On their own account, of course, they ought indeed to resemble one another, insofar as they all have the same ancestor: within quite a wide area of the mountainous terrain where the Middle Atlas fuses with the High Atlas, most holy men, and virtually all holy men of influence, are descended from one founding saint, Sidi Said Ahansal. They are, or believe themselves to be, of one flesh and blood, though this of course does not preclude bitter rivalry among them.

But as stated, they are geographically separated, living as generally they do on important frontiers between lay tribes. Some of them are in the very heart of the mountains while others are not far from the edge of the plain. For purposes of comparison, we shall take the dramatic contrast between the founding and central lodge, Zawiya Ahansal, and another lodge, somewhat to the north and much closer to the plain, named Tamga.

The holy men of both lodges agree on one important point of faith and morals - namely that dancing (*ahaidus*) is immoral and un-Islamic. This point is widely accepted in Morocco and has received much support and endorsement from the Muslim Reform movement. At the same time, of course, this form of dancing is a well-established and extremely popular part of the folklore of the Berber tribes. The issue of the dance has all the potent emotive coloring that the theater had for seventeenth-century puritans. What urban Muslims and those under their influence find particularly shocking is that in the course of this kind of tribal dance, men and women mingle and it can even happen that they dance shoulder to shoulder! This reaction was shared by the great leftist leader Mehdi Ben Barka, later kidnapped and presumably murdered, who was a great champion of the equality of women. For instance, he rejected with scorn the argument that Muslim polygamy was acceptable because it was merely a legalized version of the informal polygamy current among Europeans, with their habit of having mistresses. As he put it, polygamy, whether legalized or informal, was wrong.

In consequence of his nationalist activity, Mehdi Ben Barka had at one time been imprisoned by the French and placed for safe custody among one of the central High Atlas tribes, the Ait Hadiddu. In the course of his imprisonment in the mountain fastness, he had opportunity to witness this form of dancing. Yet even he, left-wing modernist, was shocked, as he later told me, by these dances and the possibility of women, even married women, being involved!

This perhaps illustrates the deep feeling that is involved in this rejection of tribal dancing. Anyway, to return to our saintly lineages: the two centers, both the founding lodge and Tamga, agreed that dancing is highly improper. Some time probably before the turn of the century, the two saintly settlements held a joint meeting to discuss such theological and no doubt other outstanding issues, and in the course of it decided that henceforth, as good Muslims and descendants of the Prophet, they would refrain from dancing. As a matter of fact, Tamga and its group of lodges have kept to this self-denying ordinance to this day, at least to the extent of imposing and enforcing fines on any of their own number who are caught dancing. The meeting at which this was agreed, and the subsequent events can be roughly dated; they occurred when a man named Ahmad u Ahmad was leader in the main lodge, and his 'reign' overlapped with the passage of Father de Foucauld through the area of Ahansal influence - though he was unable to visit the lodges in question. Father de Foucauld's passage through the area took place in 1883 and 1884.

As stated, the saints of Tamga and their group stuck to the agreed principles. Not so the saints of the main or founding lodge. Soon after the agreement, a male infant was born in one of the leading families. The overjoyed family and their kinsmen simply could not restrain themselves, and in no time, as anyone who is familiar with the habits of the main lodge would indeed expect, they were off, dancing like nobody's business.

This blatant transgression of holy law and violation of solemn agreement did not, of course, pass unnoticed. Such a combination of religious transgression and violation of solemn agreement was too much for the men of Tamga, and they took up arms against their lax, irreligious, and self-indulgent cousins. The conflict and feud are said to have lasted seven years (a suspect figure, which with some other evidence suggests that the whole episode is now on the borderline of history and legend). In the end, the conflict was brought to a close by the intervention and arbitration of the surrounding lay, feud-addicted tribes. The irony of this part of the story of course in no way escapes the attention of either the lay tribes or the saints. The ferocious, savage, feud-addicted lay tribes had to exercise strong moral pressure and arbitration to bring to an end murderous violence between holy, obligatorily and essentially pacific saints.

One should add that another feature of the situation is quite obvious to all the locals: they are not at all taken in by the

theological occasion of the conflict between the two saintly
centers. 'Everyone knows' that, however emotively septic the
issue of dancing may be, the real underlying cause of the conflict was a rivalry between the two lodges for influence - a
rivalry that normally is kept within the bounds imposed by the
obligation of pacifism on saints, but which on this occasion
transcended those bounds.

The whole story is highly instructive from a number of view-
points. It illustrates our general argument in the following way:
everyone concerned endorses and formally accepts the values
that are believed to be those of urban, central Islam, exemplified above all by Fez. In particular, those values prohibit
dancing. There is no disagreement at the level of theoretical
endorsement.

But some are under greater pressure to conform to these
values than others. The Tamga group of lodges is close to the
edge of the plain, and some of its client tribes are right on the
edge of the plain. In other words, they have to satisfy a tribal
clientele who are also close to urban centers of religious prop-
aganda, and they have to compete for the favors of this clientele
with other religious leaders, some of them actually urban, who
can exemplify values and ideals closer to the scriptural and
puritanical ideals of the ulama. To meet this competition and
answer its arguments, the holy men of Tamga and its groups
have no choice but to try to emulate those standards.

The main lodge is in quite a different position. It is much
older established than Tamga and thus, not being on the make,
does not have to extend itself to establish its own holiness.
More important, it is located right in the depth of the mountains,
within half a day's march of the main Sahara-Atlantic watershed.
The tribes that form its clientele are likewise overwhelmingly
drawn from the heart of the mountains, and from the area
between the mountains and the Sahara. Though these saints
also need to compete for their followership with other saints,
they do not need to compete with any urban-based religious
centers. In other words, the urban puritanical ideals are far
away and have no local anchorage or sanction. No wonder that
there was so little countervailing power available in the hearts
of the men of the main lodge, to help them to resist the temptation of the dance!

In the purely tribal context, exemplified by the main lodge,
the 'central' values are endorsed but not practiced. The local
tribesmen require the holy lineages, the incarnation of Islam,
mainly for purposes such as arbitration, mediation, social continuity, facilitation of trade, and so forth, and are not at all
interested in purity. On the contrary, they are interested in
a kind of cover for impurity. If they can have their own, very
own, local saints, who like themselves dance but at the same
time, being descendants of the Prophet, can claim to be as
close to the source of Islam as the learned men of the city, so
much the better. That way, one can legitimate one's Muslim

status and persist in the ancient practices, and no very serious
tension need be felt by anyone.

Things become a bit different as one comes closer to the plain,
or when for one reason or another the urban world exercises
stronger pressures. The hereditary holy men of Tamga still
perform the same functions as do their cousins of the main
lodge, but they have to do so in a context that in part is open
to the influence from the plain.

Thus the same ideals are proclaimed throughout, but the way
in which a compromise is reached with the exigencies of tribal
life differs according to circumstance.

Or take another illustration. In the area of Ahansal influence
there is one legend that is particularly popular and which with
some variation in detail is often recounted. I shall call it the
Kingmaker story.

Its hero is Sidi Mhammad n'ut Baba, an ancestor of the effectively saintly sublineage within the main lodge. If this legend
is true, he would have had to have been alive toward the end
of the seventeenth century. The story begins during the reign
of the Sultan Mulay Rashid. This sultan apparently sent a
messenger to the saint, to inquire how he managed to acquire
so much holiness. The saint impressed the messenger by
additional displays of saintly powers, such as making a mule
give birth to a young mule. In return he asked the monarch
to liberate some tribesmen from among his client tribes, whom
the monarch had imprisoned. The monarch refused, and the
incensed saint decided to punish the monarch by magical means.
He hammered a magical *tagust* into the ground. A tagust is a
metal peg used for attaching animals, and as it is hammered
into the ground it is extremely phallic in appearance and function. The word is in fact also used to mean 'penis.' But I shall
not dwell on the obvious and suggestive Freudian aspects of
the story.

As a result of hammering the tagust into the ground the
monarchy came upon a troubled period and in the end Mulay
Rashid died. This was not the worst: his death was followed by
one of those anarchic interregna which are not infrequent in
Moroccan history.

The next sultan-to-be, Mulay Isma^cil, failing to overcome
these difficulties, came to the saint for advice. He stayed at
the main lodge for a few days, presenting his case. The saint,
evidently convinced by the strength of this pretender's claims,
in the end gave him advice. The details of this advice and
Mulay Isma^cil's adventures in carrying it out do not concern
us, but they involved his finding the magical tagust, pulling
it out of the ground as prearranged by the saint, and finding
himself at that moment back in Fez, acclaimed by the populace
as King!

Given the Freudian undertones of the liberated tagust, the
legend is a fine specimen of a 'Waste Land' story, in which the

peace and prosperity of the kingdom depends on the virility of
the monarch. But this is not the aspect I wish to dwell on.

The aspect that is interesting from the viewpoint of our
theme is a certain ideological naïveté of the story. The manifest
purpose and moral of the story is obvious: it is meant to
heighten the prestige of the local holy lineage by turning it
and its ancestor, contrary to all historical probability, into a
kingmaker and arbitrator of the political fortunes in the distant
capital of Fez. (The legend is unhistorical to the extent that the
striking feature of this particular holy lineage is its stability
and continuity in its mountain homeland, and its abstention,
in the main, from interference in or impact on politics at the
urban centers of the country. The two things may well be connected.)

This is the only too obvious purpose of anyone telling the
story: the story wears its heart on its sleeve, and it would be
almost impossible to retell the story without empathizing its
moral. Yet unwittingly, in its simplemindedness, the story also
endorses the ultimate legitimacy of that central monarchy, which
had no effective power locally and which the local tribesmen
defied, and from whose power they had collectively seceded.
The local tribesmen paid no taxes to Fez and received no
officials from it: if the peripatetic court and army attempted
to enter their territory, they fought to stop it. In order to
raise the prestige of their own little local holy men and their
link with Islam, they retell the story showing how influential
and crucial those holy men are. Yet in telling the story, they
unwittingly recognize the ultimate authority of the center.
The story does not even hint that its hero, the saint, should
have himself become a sultan: it only hints that by magical
means it was he who enabled the sultan to rule effectively.

These various legends and situations illustrate, though of
course they do not by themselves prove, the main contention
of this argument: Islam embraces various types of social structure, and while the ulama are its ultimate and most important
expression, its constitutional court so to speak, yet many of
those social structures, notably tribal ones, cannot accommodate or use these learned scribes, and need other anchorages
for religion. A typical specimen of these anchorages are the
holy lineages, so highly developed among the Berbers, but by
no means unparalleled elsewhere. These holy lineages are tied
by links of terminology and even organization to mystical urban
clubs, but despite the similarity of terminology, and sometimes
organizational relations, the two phenomena are quite distinct
in nature and function. Thus very little is explained by any
simple reference to the diffusion of Sufi ideas. It is important
to understand just what the saints do and what they mean in
their context. In the case of the holy lineages of the recesses
of the mountains, their acquaintance with or interest in Sufi
ideas is negligible. What they do and what they mean can only

be understood by reference to the tribes whom they serve.

But while these lineages are very unlike urban ulama, and sadly deficient when the standards proclaimed or even practiced by urban ulama are applied to them, they should not be seen as unambiguously hostile to them. Their role is inherently ambiguous. They must serve tribal, non-urban ends, but they must also link the tribes with a wider and urban-oriented ideal of Islam. They serve both local tribal needs and universal Islamic identification. They hamper the diffusion of good and proper Islam, in a way, by giving the tribesmen an excuse for pretending that they are already good Muslims, that they already possess the institutional framework of faith: and yet at the same time, they keep the door open for the propagation of 'purer' Islam by endorsing it in the course of those very practices in which they deviate from it.

2 ARBITRATION AS A POLITICAL INSTITUTION: AN INTERPRETATION OF THE STATUS OF MONARCHY IN MOROCCO

Magali Morsy

The paradox of Morocco is that it is both the result of trends dominating the history of the Mediterranean and a permanent, original national reality reasserting itself through changing circumstances. The paradox is not merely factual, but also characterizes the observer's standpoint by referring to two distinct discourses. When faced with societies which do not correspond to recognized patterns of state formation, observers tend either to see them as the result of forces exerting pressure or domination from outside on what are posed as subsidiary and historically irrelevant nations. This is illustrated by such chapter headings as 'Roman Africa', 'the Arab Invasion', 'the Colonial Scramble', or, more recently, 'Centre and Periphery'. At the same time the actual definition of such societies is left to anthropologists originally committed to purely local observation, with no reference to multidimensional impact, either in synchronistic or diachronic terms. In this paper, I put forward a number of hypotheses with a view to bridging the gap between two disconnected types of analysis in order to achieve a more comprehensive historical interpretation of the working of such societies. I am here more particularly concerned with the nature of political power in a segmentary tribal system such as that of Morocco.

Some preliminary comments are necessary to clarify this viewpoint. The first is that domination through the accretion of power is a complex phenomenon. It can be seen in economic terms, or in the social or political fields, or from a cultural angle. I am here more interested in the latter since the problem of modern states and nations in North Africa can be seen as the result of a particular use of a cultural idiom, namely Islam, in the context of a segmentary tribal society. That both before and after the advent of Islam Morocco was a tribal polity recognized as a state by outside observers is, moreover, apparent from historical evidence over the centuries. Herodotus or the earlier Arab historians consistently described Morocco in terms of an extended and cohesive tribal pattern, as did Ibn Khaldun or others who have left us accounts of the powerful empires of the Al-Murabitun and the Al-Muwahhidun.

A second preliminary comment referes to the basic premises of this paper. My starting point is that defined by Clastres in his symposium 'La Société contre l'état'.(1) Clastres convincingly demonstrates that the political organization of tribal society is based on mechanisms to obviate the accretion of

power and to neutralize the expression of domination through
political institutions. The non-existence of the latter or their
lack of organization may retard state formation, and the examples to which Clastres refers, namely the Indian tribes of
South America, generally illustrate this. It can also make such
societies weak, especially under pressure from other nations
which have evolved power-wielding institutions. But one may
also argue that tribal societies, including those referred to by
Clastres, show a high degree of resilience which makes them
survive and reassert themselves, even in the context of a
dominant capitalist economy. That is not, however, the point
of this paper which is intended to stress that segmentary tribal
society can also lead to state formation, Morocco being a major
case in point. I am thus going beyond Clastres's own conclusions since I consider the type of political institution derived
from the segmentary system and its role in the national history
of Morocco. That this is also a dialectic movement in which the
efforts of individuals or groups to achieve a power-stand are
countered in order to achieve the counterpoise on which the
segmentary order is based, will also be shown.

A further introductory comment is necessary to explain and
justify my contribution to this collective work in the field of
anthropology. Most historians' accounts of Morocco tend to be
based less on inner forces than on those which European
observers consider relevant, precisely because they are characterized by power which is accrued and exerted, thus privileg-
ing foreign influences, particularly modern ones. This prevalent
type of historical writing has recourse to documentary evidence
as the tool of dominant ideology. When dealing with the long-
term history of Morocco which goes back beyond French and
other foreign records, the historian is at a standstill unless
he can make use of other concepts and other methods of analysis. In this paper I am suggesting that anthropology can help
bridge certain gaps both with respect to time and to levels of
social organization.

One might perhaps also suggest that if certain fundamental
traits of the historical structure of tribal society cannot easily
be accounted for, it is also because tribal society itself refuses
to provide its own descriptive idiom. The refusal to implement
power-wielding structures may also explain why tribal societies
refuse overt self-definition as is apparent, for example, in the
absence of collective names. Thus at the highest level, ethnic
groups - Berbers in general, or Kabyles in Algeria - have no
general name for themselves except through recourse to a
foreign language. It is further significant that where such a
name exists, as is the case with 'Imazighen' or 'Free Men' used
in several regions including the Sahara, this is often the result of class stratification. In a similar way, Berber societies
that have specific, widely used terms to designate smaller segments of tribes are very vague at higher levels. The word for
'tribe', *taqbilt*, is itself a fairly recent borrowing from Arabic.

Moreover, extensive political alliances bear no particular name in Berber and are referred to merely through the technical devices by which they are brought into existence. This highlights the importance of the complex cultural process of which religion is part, since it is the idiom through which group-consciousness is construed.

Let us see how this functions in practice, in a general long-term view of the political process, before seeing how the advent of Islam has altered the traditional equilibrium of tribal society.

I THE TRIBAL PATTERN

An overall picture of Berber society underscores one all-pervading fact: the limited scope for private undertakings or personal influence, or rather the absence of institutionalized means to uphold and channel the power of a particular person or group. Authority is vested almost entirely in the community and expresses itself through public meetings, the aim of which is apparent general agreement. This does not in any way mean that Berber society is egalitarian. As a patriarchal society exploiting female and servile labour, where land tenure establishes degrees of wealth and influence, where status is hereditary, inequality is the rule. What the tribe obviates is the institutionalized means of implementing power, control remaining within the segmentary order of society.

A power-exerting stance is potentially present in all social structures, even in tribal ones geared to making it inoperative. Thus, most Berber tribes have a figurehead, an *amghar*. But it is also characteristic that not only does he have no means of coercion beyond general acceptance of his rulings, but he is in no position to build up his power because he is elected on an annual basis. Moreover, the office passes from one tribal segment to another, tribes being generally for this purpose divided into five units.(2) Even more evidently, periods of strife necessitate cohesion, rapid decisions and forceful action. This is made possible through the election of a war chief (usually distinct from the civil *amghar*). The war chief may be ousted in the course of fighting. If not, his tenure of office ends when a truce or peace are negotiated, nor does he himself take part in such negotiations. This is nonetheless a potentially power-accruing position.

War involves a disruption of tribal life and can lead to important changes in groups and land-tenure. Moreover, if protracted, as is often the case, local struggles can provide a more lasting basis to a war chief's influence. It is not surprising, therefore, that accounts of Moroccan tribes very often highlight the power wielded by warlords who may even develop into a military aristocracy. We must, however, bear in mind that such instances to which historical documents refer are very often the direct result of foreign pressure which is the most

favourable condition for a disruption of the tribal order, both
in terms of the rise to power of military men and the incapacity
of the tribe to maintain them under control. To give but one
example of this inherent tendency, the Roman conquest of North
Africa brought to the fore a national leader, Jugurtha, King of
Numidia, in the second century B.C. Sallust's account of the
latter, however, points out that:

1 Jugurtha was chosen as leader in a context marked by
  Roman imperialism;
2 he was chosen from a dominant lineage;
3 the decision was made essentially because of his military
  experience (acquired fighting in Spain);
4 and, more important still, it was imposed on Berber society
  by a now powerful military group. As Sallust has it: 'the
  Numidians were divided into two factions. The majority
  pronounced itself in favour of Adherbal whereas the principal members of the army were in favour of Jugurtha.
  Jugurtha gathered as many soldiers as he could, and by
  military and peaceful means became the master of several
  cities ... and in this way became the lord of Numidia'.(3)

Thus Jugurtha's case may be seen as the ultimate development
of the power-accruing stand which the tribal system is constantly
at pains to check.

The appearance of such a power group leads to domination and
exploitation of tribal society. To develop his own privileged
position, Jugurtha was committed to facing up to the Romans,
both in terms of diplomacy and military action. This led to a
system of local oppression with the army drawing from the
land the means by which it upheld its dominant position. Hence
the situation the Romans found when they ultimately conquered
the land: the peasants were hard at work and, everywhere,
in each town, in each village, Jugurtha's bailiffs were present
at the head of huge stores of wheat and other goods. That the
development of a feudal system is possible is shown up by
many other Moroccan examples up into the twentieth century.
That, in actual fact, such situations were generally short-lived
is not a proof, as European-oriented historians would have it,
of Berber 'anarchy',(4) but rather of the capacity of the
Moroccan nation to bring such power-based situations under
control. But this in turn poses another question: what is the
structure within tribal society which is capable of asserting
itself, even in the face of such challenges? By what means are
individual tendencies to self-aggrandizement neutralized?

A basic principle of segmentary societies is the presence of
moieties or paired segments both as an overall pattern (a plane
or two-dimensional level), and as a defining principle applied
to ever-widening social entities (a three-dimensional perspective as one passes from brothers to agnatic lineages to whole
tribes). It is perhaps worth pointing out that whatever the

contribution of Evans-Pritchard and modern anthropology to
the definition of the concept of segmentation, the notion is
also actively present in the tribe's view of itself, as one can
see from the metaphorical use Berbers make of parts of the
body to define levels of segmentation. Arabs who are also of
tribal origin and who, with Islam, introduced the dominant
culture in Maghribi society, go further in making this explicit.
We can find in Al-Nuwayri a semantic definition of the tribe
which would probably be accepted by most anthropologists.
'It is named *qabila* because its components are placed face to
face and in equal numbers'.(5) The verbal root Q-B-L means
'to be or stand exactly opposite someone or something', 'to be
face to face with'.

The pairing of segments, generally conveyed in the largely
symbolic idiom of filiation, presupposes an underlying con-
nective structure. This implies not only social control of levels
of interaction but also a process of linkage between levels which
is never automatic but is part of the decision-making process.
Segmentation is not a mechanistic process but instead the
structural means through which levels of involvement are
decided on and brought into play or not, according to the
appreciation of a given situation. This implies:

1 that it has a conscientious function, and
2 that this responsibility makes reference to an overall pattern as well as to particular segments.

We can thus consider segmentary societies as having the
political will to make of the linkage system within the tribe the
locus of interaction. It is further characterized by the use of
a non-disruptive idiom of confrontation - namely language and
discussion - which safeguards the segments. This locus of
interaction is commonly referred to as arbitration.

In view of its transtribal structure and its definition as being
outside the dynamics of segmentation, arbitration very early on
forged a social category to implement its function. The arbiters
as a specialized group are posed as non-tribal. Hence, in
Morocco and elsewhere, the custom is widespread of asking a
passing stranger to arbitrate a discussion or conflict. In a
general way, however, tribes have permanent arbiters. Various
devices make it possible either to attach an actual stranger to
the tribe, or to have recourse to someone within the tribe
whilst posing him as a stranger. Different practical means are
used to associate the arbiter to the tribe and its destiny without
considering him as directly committed to tribal involvements.
A common practice consists in connecting the stranger to the
community by marriage ties. Hence it is that an arbiter usually
has several wives, even in a predominantly monogamous context.
These wives are usually from different important lineages. This
is a pre-Islamic custom, as can be seen from Sallust's comment
on a similar practice with respect to lay chiefs.(6) The function

of arbiter can also be held by members of the tribe who for
particular reasons can be considered as outsiders. Thus old
men often act in this capacity. The Berber *agurram*, the Arab
shaykh – both terms mean an 'old man' before meaning a wise,
respected or important person – are chosen because they are
supposed, by virtue of age, to be 'wise' both in the sense of
not being swayed by present passions, and of having an age-
old experience of tribal lore. More rarely – but the case may
have been more frequent at an earlier period when male-
domination was not as absolute – women could play a similar
role. An example in point is, of course, the Algerian Kahina.
In the Western Sahara since the seventeenth century, the
tributary, vanquished Berber lineages have specialized in
arbitration for the dominant lay Hassani tribes.

Tribal custom, moreover, evolved regulations with a view
to emphasizing the arbiter's non-tribal involvement. He is
installed in a non-warring capacity and the prevalent view is
that he should not be allowed to carry weapons of any sort or
take part in fighting. Even his material involvement in society
is generally curtailed since such land as he does have is
generally worked by tribesmen. Regular gifts and a part of the
harvest are his 'income' in exchange for which he is expected
to be at the disposal of tribesmen to help them solve their
problems.

This, in turn, highlights the way in which the function of
arbitration is exercised, namely through negotiation and discussion. It is therefore a specialized task entailing specific
knowledge, both of tribal lore and particular techniques (language and the convincing use of arguments) which are not the
stock-in-trade of the ordinary tribesman. Language, however,
has a mysterious power of its own. It acts upon people in the
same ill-defined way as the forces in nature. It is awe-inspiring
and potentially dangerous. Thus society tends to create a
special category of people who are entrusted with the use of
language for collective purposes. They are not part of the
tribe and yet they voice the language of the tribe. Arbiters
thus not only preside over public debates but mediate between
the group and its ecological environment. This, from an early
stage, involved shamanistic attributes, a saintly status, and
esoteric techniques.

The relationship to the sacred also has political implications.
The wisdom that arbiters' attitudes and comments are seen as
embodying, refer to the general good of the community and
constitute a trans-segmentary view. The common good which
involves establishing positive relations with supernatural
forces which pervade nature, no less than the appropriate
advice to the tribe, means prosperity. Peace and plenty testify
to the success of the arbiter. A plentiful harvest resulting
from adequate rainfall is thus associated with the approval and
benediction of those transcendental forces that rule over men's
destinies. Through the mediator, tribal society opens up to

transcendence which, in historical terms, can also be seen as a view of the future.

But the present is also determined by the past. Peace and harmony in society are not only something that is constantly to be worked out, they also result from respect for the laws of society, the following of precedent and, in the last resort, submission to the mysteriously binding presence of ancestors. The arbiter who is specialized in the knowledge of tribal lore and custom, is also a connecting link with the past. Moreover his 'sacred' character renders him more apt for the dangerous contact with the deceased. Herodotus notes that ancient Berbers already used to make their oaths binding by reference to the deceased, or appealed to them to inform the present.

> This is their way of taking oaths and of soothsaying. They place their hands on the tombs of those among them who, in their lifetime, had the reputation of having been just and honourable men and they swear by them. For sooth-saying, they go to the tombs of their ancestors and pray there, and then sleep. If, during their sleep, they have some dream, they decide from that what course of action they will take.

Since Herodotus' time, Berber society has gone a long way towards giving the arbiter the monopoly of the relationship between past and present, between the tribe and the super-natural. These connections have been deflected into the field of arbitration and, at the same time, excluded from the private or lay level of society. In some cases one may even point to an actual taboo. This is particularly apparent in the relation of the tribe to its past and to the more occult forces connected in other parts of the world with the cult of ancestors. It seems to me striking and significant that the more elaborate forms of burial which predominated in ancient Libya (notably tumuli and the use of niches in cliffs) disappeared at a later historical period prior to Islam. Even the typical Muslim graveyards with their concentration of low tombs marked at head and foot by stone blocks, are in no way a typical scene of Berberland where, often, no allotted burial ground is apparent. Significantly, too, references to the tribal ancestor are purely cultural (legends or traditions) and limited in scope. His burial place is generally unknown and, in any case, is not the object of any particular cult. But, parallel to this, one sees just as consistently the presence of a 'sacred tomb', generally near the dwelling-place of the lineage of arbitrators. This tomb is held to be that of the ancestor of the hereditary family of arbiters who thus benefit from his effluent spirit or *baraka*. The tomb of the ancestor of the saintly lineage has in effect replaced that of the lay tribal ancestor.

One can thus formulate a hypothesis concerning the historical development of the Berbers and see in the institution of arbitration the basis for the tribe's collective expression of itself, an institution that has growingly monopolized the collective expression of the tribe and its destiny in space and time. The ever more elaborate view which society has of itself is paralleled in the ever more elaborate functioning of the institution of arbitration. This leads not only to specialization of personnel in the exercise of this function by means of certain hereditary lineages, but to polarization of the collective political, religious, and cultural dimensions of history in terms of these lineages. Their special knowledge, but also their special links with supernatural forces, give them a shamanistic status in Berber society, already apparent in an early historical period. How this status is affected by the advent of Islam is the next problem posed by the cultural and social evolution of the region.

II   TRIBAL ARBITERS AND ISLAM

That the advent of Islam in the seventh and eighth centuries A.D. constitutes probably the most important event in the modern history of North Africa will readily be admitted, and yet how this occurred and what its implications were for Berber society, is far less clear. What is nonetheless obvious is that Islam represents a change of attitude but one that was, on the whole, willingly and rapidly accepted. As far as the arbiters were concerned, we can also see that they were, so to speak, in the front line. The new religion was most immediately and most directly a challenge to them and to their position. How and why they so rapidly converted their idiom and stand are tantalizing questions. The answer to such questions is obviously in the first place the result of evolution within tribal society at large. We can sometimes prove, but more often simply infer, that the relationship of men to environment in a semi-agricultural, semi-pastoral society had produced and developed an important network of trade. This, in its turn, influenced the constitution of large tribal working patterns on a vast regional basis. These tribal and intertribal relations involve growing self-consciousness and a sense of the overall pattern as distinct from conflicting tribal solidarities. I have suggested that the fundamental and typical choice made by Berber societies was the use of the institution of arbitration to elaborate on this sense of the trans-tribal, as also to define the relation of the tribe to the outside world. Islam is itself a transcendent ideology, originally part of a tribal society. It came to Morocco with an already elaborate structure, a formulated world-view, and the idiom through which individuals and groups could be integrated into the new pattern. In other words, Islam offered arbiters the definition, the discourse, and the technical means of concretizing their abstract niche in the tribal pattern.

Islam reformulated the world-view which arbiters collectively

upheld to counterbalance the disruptive tendencies of the
segmentary tribal systems. Islam brought with it:

1 A given, objectively defined reference. This was no longer
dependent on tribal lore, or connected with the cult of legendary ancestors, but was an actual, explicit model, independent
of the tribe, but evolved from a tribal structure. This new
model was concretized in the example of the Prophet and his
companions. Their behaviour was the human and social counter-
part of the divine pattern and as such could also be projected
into the future, no longer through dreams or divination, but
as a God-given order based on religious equality, social harmony, and the promise of general prosperity. It further
extended into eternity through divine judgment implying sanctions and rewards. The present was thus no longer an uncertainty, hedged in by obscure and unaccountable forces, but
commanded by the common obligation to bring the present into
line both with past and future through a now clear definition
of the path of righteousness. Religion, namely the Qur'an and
the Prophet's example, afforded the concrete means for a
tribal society to appreciate the historical and transcendent
significance of any given course of action.

2 A justification. The arbiters saw their status confirmed both
by the Qur'an and by the Prophet's example. Was not the
Prophet himself an arbiter - *hakam* - who in that capacity was
welcomed to Yathrib? His early social action thus consisted in
mediating between various groups. The Qur'an itself uses the
verb *hakama* to qualify the settlement of disputes and conflicts,
as distinct from the verb *qâda* applied to divine rulings. The
practice of arbitration was further reasserted by the early
Muslim communities who, in the new spirit of peace preached by
Islam, recommended that conflicts be submitted to arbiters and
further advocated that the latter should, if possible, be
chosen from among the Prophet's own tribe of Quraysh. These
early religious advisers were faced with precisely the task
with which arbiters were familiar, namely relating general
moral principles such as are given in the Qu'ran to *sunna*, or
accepted practice. Later, of course, all this was standardized,
brought down to an established, rigid set of precepts with, in
parallel, the ever-growing influence of legally trained religious
judges. But, at the start, the intellectual stimulus of Islam was
well in accord with the arbiters' own concerns.

3 A challenge. Whatever the objective importance and value
of such a doctrine for the class of arbiters who could find there
the justification of their role as negotiators, it is obvious that
it also entailed a major challenge. The new doctrine came in
a different language, namely Arabic, and involved a new tool:
the written word. Moreover, in the wake of the conquering
army came an appointed personnel already specialized in the
new cultural field. How the challenge was met, how arbiters
individually and collectively reacted is perhaps hypothetical
since we do not actually have documents or case studies for

this early period. But one can nonetheless point to a number
of uncontroverted facts.

The first and most obvious is that Berber arbiters met this
challenge vigorously and accepted all the efforts reconversion
entailed for them. That they did so is proved by the fact that
they were able to hold their own and were nowhere put aside
or replaced (as for example the African witch doctor was), even
if they did have to make concessions by opening up their ranks
to Arab scholars. The predominant system remained and such
incoming elements as there were, were integrated into the
arbiter class, whilst local men acquired the necessary knowledge
to operate efficiently in the new religious and cultural context.
When one considers the difficulties involved for these up-to-
now Berber-speaking and generally illiterate negotiators to
learn Arabic, to learn to read and write and recite the Qur'an,
when one further considers the hardships endured in foreign
centres of study including, from early times, the holy places,
and the social humiliations involved, one is impressed by the
strong collective urge to become proficient. Thus arbiters soon
made of Arabic their common professional language, and the
knowledge of law and other related sciences became the new
basis for tribal negotiations. Further, they became the recognized teachers in all the rural areas. Whatever individual
ignorances may have been, whatever uncertainty may sometimes, wittingly or not, have prevailed in arbiter rulings, it
is striking that they remained undisputed masters on the tribal
scene because they gave themselves the means – both intellectual and technical – to make their position secure by monopolizing the cultural field.

Why did rural negotiators go out of their way to acquire
knowledge related to Islam? Why did they go to such lengths
to become proficient? The answers may be found in the changes
which the reformulated superstructure made in their own
position. Arbiters had up to then been fundamentally dependent
on tribal consent, not only for such authority as they had, but
for the validity of their rulings since these were derived from
tribal practice. As 'strangers' they were merely the mirror in
which the tribe saw itself reflected. Islam was the possibility
given arbiters to become an accepted status group wielding
effective power.

The 'stranger' now has his own personality, directly derived
from Islam. Thus he is held to be a 'pilgrim' come from the East,
often from the Prophet's own tribe, or perhaps from the Western
Sahara in accordance with the general expectation of a Mahdi.
Gradually he will come to be identified as a *sharif* or descendant
of the Prophet. In the case of many local arbiters this preten-
sion was sometimes difficult to uphold, however much a tribe
wished to believe in the 'aristocratic' origins of its own local
patented mediators, but as generations passed it was increasingly easy to accredit a sharifian ancestor. It should, however,
be pointed out that this was a long drawn-out process lasting

well into the eighteenth century and, further, that the switch-
over generally took place en masse during periods of upheaval.
Why such periods of social unrest should lead to renewed
emphasis on descent from the Prophet's family, notably in the
Idrisid line, is a point of historical interest but one that is
beyond the scope of this paper. The ancestor was associated
with a sacred tomb which expressed group-consciousness.
The blessing a tribe could hope for was thus mediated through
the family of the Prophet down to his contemporary descendants.
Islamic culture further made it possible to give an autonomous
religious definition of arbiter lineages as saintly families whose
history was no mere reflection of tribal life and migration but
had its own life cycle, bringing to the fore reputed members
of the lineage whose wanderings became the subject of legends,
and were conceived in terms of a personal quest for sanctity
and knowledge. The stages of this Muslim 'Pilgrim's Progress'
were protracted stays in learned places of study, and, of
course, in Makkah (Mecca) and Medina. The local saint thus becomes
himself part of a cultural universe where we often find him
rivalling with other members of the holy fraternity, however
many miles or years separated them in actual life. Thus arbiters
became a distinct and impressive group in their own right,
characterized and defined by a milieu to which the ordinary
tribesmen did not have access.

The new position of arbiters is visible in the Moroccan landscape where their presence is signified not only by the squat
whitewashed and green-tiled cupolas over shrines, but also by
often extensive buildings: the tower that marks the local mosque,
a house for passing guests, a school, the homes of the sharifian
lineage, and other places of study or negotiation. They express
the new authority (and affluence) the rural religious class
acquired through Islam, and also the new fields of activity it
developed to establish its control over society. Let us consider
the more significant aspects of this rise to power of arbiter
lineages.

1 The monopoly of Islamic culture. This change of emphasis
from public places connected with tribal discussion and arbitration to private buildings connected with religion and learning,
is also an illustration of the means through which the change
of status was effected. One must here re-emphasize, not only
the fact that arbiters were associated with the new knowledge
brought by Islam, but also that they maintained control over
this sector throughout rural Morocco. It is in and around the
zawiya-s - the generally accepted meaning of the term in
Morocco is the set of buildings housing a saintly lineage - that
seats of learning appeared and monopolized the field of education, both the general schooling given to laymen and the more
specialized training of local learned men. Traditional rural
negotiators were able to resist the competition of the Arab
town-based universities as they developed. In fact, as a closer

examination of such a compendium as Lévi-Provençal's 'Les
Historiens des Chorfa' shows, they were able, over the centuries, in spite of social opposition from urban elites, largely to
invest these traditional centres of higher education, or at least
to use their diplomas - *ijaza* - to further their own local influence, whilst at the same time resisting encroachments by members of the urban elite on tribal territory.

Recent studies,(7) and more particularly Mukhtar al-Susi's
account of Southern Morocco,(8) have amply demonstrated the
varied types of education which could be obtained locally, and
the very high standards of many of the rural *zawiya*-s. Their
collection of manuscripts was often extensive. Thus the seventeenth-century establishment of Tamgrut had the reputation of
being one of the most famous libraries in Morocco, and many
other examples come to mind. These reading rooms had copies
of representative works of Arab culture, and even maintained
alive specific fields of study when they had declined in the
better known universities: astrology and medicine, for example.
The literary production of local scholars was considerable.
Moreover, they did not limit themselves to classical subjects,
but also often directly related their acquired culture to their
own tribal environment. Some of their writings were connected
with the local Berber background and even, in a few exceptional
cases, efforts were made to express local legends or tribal
history in written Arabic, or even to write them down in Berber,
using Arabic script. More notably still, these centres of learning concentrated on problems of tribal law, thus bridging the
gap between the established rules of Berber society and the
binding prescriptions of the Shari^{c}a. We may conclude that the
growing authority of saintly families was the result of intense
and fruitful activity in the cultural field, this having more
immediate social consequences in Muslim lands than elsewhere.
But what is probably more significant, both historically and
structurally, is the use this was put to, namely the manipulation
of given situations to create effective power holdings.

2 Control by notaries of tribal society. By their monopoly of
teaching (i.e. of written Arabic) and of knowledge (i.e. the
rules by which society is to be governed), arbiters who up to
Islamic times had merely supervised the working of tribal
society, were now vested with power since they could approve
or condemn a decision by virtue of a commandment of which the
ordinary tribesman would be ignorant. But their active scholarly
centres went further and undertook to exert an effective control on public proceedings. They produced a class of scribes
and notaries to bring this into effect. Although little research
has as yet been done in this field, one cannot but be struck
by the development in Berber areas, probably at a fairly late
period - around the sixteenth century - of written documents.
These correspond to contracts between parties or individuals,
and it should be recalled that this is, in fact, a Qur'anic prescription, but one which was in marked contrast to tribal

practice with its public discussions and oral agreements by co-jurors and collective oath. The authority thus passes from the community itself to a scribe whose name figures on the document and usually shows him to have some connection with the local zawiya. He is responsible for summarizing the proceedings of a meeting, noting the names of the participants or delegates, and specifying the agreement reached. It was also probably at about the same time that the traditional regulations concerning such collective institutions as granary-fortresses which up to then had been purely oral, were written down in the form of elaborate codes of customary law. A further example is that of title deeds for lands which are commonplace in Berber households. They are written on scrolls and often kept in the hollow stems of reeds. The dates vary, but the earliest also seem to go back to the seventeenth century. All these documents are in Arabic.

This new reliance on the written text may be explained in terms of the development of the literate religious class which had, by then, evolved a specialized legal idiom. It may further be supposed that by the sixteenth century, this had become the standard form for such agreements on a large scale and over a wide zone, extending from the Atlas to the Sahara. Recent research by Mezzine(9) has shown that all these documents are in more or less the same conventional style, made up of a set of stereotyped Arabic phrases and a number of Berber terms recast in an Arabic mould. This generally accepted legal idiom, in conjunction with the presence in the tribes of scribes capable of reading and writing this artificial language and adapting it to particular needs, makes the written text a common, and soon a necessary, condition of tribal agreement. Needless to say, it gave the religious leaders an effective control on rural society through their erstwhile pupils or attached set of secretaries.

3 Arbiters and trade. No less important for tribes and for the growing power of arbiters was the protection the latter afforded markets and commercial activities in general. Thus we find them guaranteeing the Moroccan network of weekly markets. The suq is held on neutral ground, either on tribal boundaries or in precincts posed as non-tribal. Zawiyas are often located on the edge of the market, although whether the religious establishment preceded the suq or the other way round is a moot point. Moreover, holy lineages afforded protection to travellers and particularly to traders who were escorted through tribal territory by a member of the arbiter's household.

Islam was a religion which developed in a trading centre and the Prophet himself had been connected with the caravan trade. Further, the ethics and practice of trade play an important role in the Islamic world-view. This was brought to bear on the position of arbiters as the pattern of commercial exchanges developed. Holy lineages came increasingly to be seen not only in terms of a privileged connection with a given population but

in terms of an interconnected pattern of relays illustrating the
structure of intertribal exchanges. Thus trade routes and
zawiyas are closely interwoven as a study of zawiya localization
would show. Trade also contributed to the cohesion of the
arbiter network and to its inner hierarchization which is
largely built up out of the commercial pattern.

The important zawiyas and influential lineages are increasingly in the modern period those connected with extended trade
and more particularly that which passed through the Sahara
bringing precious goods, including *tibr* or gold-dust and
slaves from the *bilad al-Sudan* to the towns and international
ports of Morocco. The two most recent of Morocco's dynasties,
that of the Sa^{c}dis and that of the ^{c}Alawis, marked the rise to
national importance of Sharifian families traditionally connected
with trans-Saharan trade since the former came from an oasis
of the Dra^c valley and the latter from Tafilat.

Thus by the seventeenth century, which was a period of
upheaval and tribal redeployment, arbitration had proved itself
the institution through which a nation-wide control of tribal
relations could be implemented, and through which transtribal
relations of a commercial, administrative, or cultural nature
were channelled. This leads us to consider the nature of state
power in Morocco and its connection with tribal arbiters.

III   THE INSTITUTION OF ARBITRATION AND THE MONARCHY

I have so far put forward two main hypotheses: (1) that arbitration is the fundamental political institution of tribal Morocco;
(2) that Islam was the means through which tribal negotiators
achieved effective social power. A third and ultimate question
comes to mind: what is the relation of arbitration to state
formation? I put forward here a further hypothesis, namely
that in Morocco the state is largely derived from and dependent
on the institution of arbitration.

The first point which even a cursory glance at the past shows
up is that a supra-tribal authority, operating at what one might
call a 'national' level, is an integral part of Moroccan history.
Even in the pre-Islamic period this is attested both by the
Romans and the early Arab conquerors. However, research in
this field has been extremely limited so that it is difficult to
appreciate the part of the present-day system which survives
from an earlier period whilst we tend to be more aware of those
elements which we can connect with social changes brought
about under the influence of Islam.

Whilst it is obviously beyond the scope of this paper to sketch
out the history of the development of the state through the
Islamic period, it may perhaps be useful to point to the continuity and originality of the Moroccan system by reference to
its earliest expression, the Idrisid dynasty, and to its most

recent one, the present ^CAlawi dynasty. It is indeed significant that at the height of Muslim impact when, in the eighth century, the Middle Eastern Empire of the ^CAbbasids was increasingly characterized by a centralized state, Morocco should have opposed this extension and asserted its own national institution represented by the Idrisids. Moreover, an examination of the role of this first independent Muslim dynasty of Morocco(10) shows that it is in fact a projection at national level of a head of the arbiter institution.

Even if the early Arab historians, our informants for this distant period, tend to focus on the personalities of Idris I and Idris II, we can nonetheless see in the traits they mention those very characteristics which define the Islamic arbitrator of tribal Morocco. They tell us that Idris I was a sharif who came to Morocco in 788. He is said to have come on his own, i.e. as a stranger, accompanied only by his freed slave Rashid. And it is as an arbiter that he was invited into the ^CAwraba tribe (near present-day Fes) and was married to a local tribeswoman, Kinza, probably from a dominant lay lineage. That in fact the tribes of the region were in the process of political unification is proved not only by their choice of a prestigious sharif as negotiator and figurehead, but more concretely by the fact that soon after his arrival, the Moroccan nation appeared sufficiently powerful and cohesive a political entity to pose a local threat to ^CAbbasid supremacy. Harun al-Rashid sent an emissary to Morocco and the latter is said to have poisoned Idris I in 792. Not only does the 'empire' stake a claim on the international scene, but the state institution evolved was maintained by the tribes, even in the absence of an immediate successor. Idris's posthumous son, Idris II, was officially recognized in 803, and reigned until his death in 828-9.

It is worth paying some attention to the policy pursued by Idris II in terms of state formation because, as we shall see, it illustrates a characteristic building up of the head arbiter's powers, both with respect to the network of arbitration and with respect to tribes. The definition of head of state which Idris II was to put into application was derived from Islam, not merely as is the case with arbiters as legitimate *hakam*-s, but as effective leaders (*khalifa* and *imam*) of the community of believers (the *umma*). Further, he took over from the classical Muslim state those formal expressions of state power which the latter had evolved either from Qur'anic doctrine or from the institutions of Byzantium or the Sasanid Empire. This state power was based on two power-wielding institutions : the learned institution (including formal religious advisers considered as state functionaries), and civil power represented by a military force attached to the sovereign. Thus the head arbiter's personal status is extended to include his agents, 'the men of the pen and the men of the sword'. Among other state prerogatives introduced by Idris II, we find a civil government represented by a wazir, the minting of coins, the

building of a capital, Fes, the application of the *dhimma* pact
and the levy of Qur'anic dues.

That the implementing of an effective doctrine of the state
and of the institutional means of its existence should have been
accepted by Moroccan society implies both national self-
consciousness and the recognition that this should be concretized outside tribal terms and by means of the dominant ideology.
So far, we may consider the situation of the sultan as the
ultimate stage in the evolution of the institution of arbitration
passing from a transtribal level to national existence through
a transcendental world-view. But this is also a situation
fraught with tension since the tribal system is at the same
time opposed to the concretization of effective leadership and
to the concentration of power in any single hand. This had to be
checked through manipulation of the arbiter network and
manipulation of the tribal pattern (notably through an extension of segmentary oppositions).

That, in fact, throughout this period the tribal cohesion of
the state was maintained points to the active role of tribal negotiators and their accepted integration into a hierarchized state
pattern, but no information on the subject is given by the
early Arab documents.

Proof of the manipulation of the tribal pattern is, on the
other hand, extant. Idris II had, in particular, recourse to
the creation of a privileged clientèle of his own, made up of
warrior contingents who were given land in exchange for
military service. They were Arabs called in from outside, and
notably from Spain. Idris II used this armed force to oppose
tribally based authority. This led to the general revolt of the
cAwraba in 807-8. They were defeated by Idris II and their
leader, Isḥaq, was executed. The resentment this caused
among Moroccans lasted centuries, as is evident from Ibn
Khaldun's account of the reign of Idris II: 'More than 500 warriors belonging to various Arab tribes of the Maghrib and
Spain, came to Idris and were under his command. They constituted a body of faithful servants and he placed his trust
in them and not in the Berbers. Through the help of these
contingents, he was able in large measure to develop his
authority'.(11) This lasting bitterness can be explained in
terms of the historical import of the event: the traditional
balance of power between tribes and arbiter was broken in
favour of the state. Moreover the particular form this took in
Morocco, whilst derived from the segmentary principle, constitutes a wide-scale manipulation of tensions in terms of ethnic
opposition - Arab versus Berber - which underlies, if not
Moroccan history where its importance is variable and generally
overestimated, at least the central government and its tribal
policy. It is no less significant, however, that tribal preponderance reasserted itself after the death of Idris II, but
at the cost of the unified nation state.

The next point is that the type of state power evolved out

of the Islamized institution of arbitration remained the model to which successive dynasties referred. Significantly the present reigning dynasty, that of the ^CAlawis, reasserts this. The early history of the ^CAlawi dynasty is connected with sharifian arbitration in the Tafilalt region. Mulay Al-Hasan bin Qasim is said to have come to Morocco in the second half of the thirteenth century, at the request of the inhabitants of Sijilmasa. A legend, later included in official chronicles, mentions the fact that the oases of the Tafilalt were unproductive and their date-palms barren, and that it was with a view to obtaining a divine remedy that a sharif from the Hijaz was sent for. Mulay Al-Hasan's arrival was thus associated with God's blessing witnessed to by the abundance of dates from then on. The rise of the Tafilalt sharifs to national status was effected on the basis of their predominant regional importance as an arbiter lineage. Their authority developed as the range of tribe-to-tribe negotiations extended. Of particular significance is the fact that their settlement in the Tafilalt coincides with the invasion of the region by Arab nomads, the Ma^Cqil who are of the same stock as the Banu Hilal tribes who swept through North Africa from the eleventh century onwards. Subsequently these Ma^Cqil Arabs were driven south into the Western Sahara. The ^CAlawis maintained their privileged connection with these groups who were later to constitute a military force which upheld the ^CAlawi bid for power and were incorporated into the new dynasty's army. Connected with this is the power and wealth acquired by the ^CAlawis as protectors of trade. The importance of trans-Saharan commerce from the sixteenth century onwards and the role of the nomad tribes in the desert where they could destroy or protect caravans at will, brought to the fore the holy lineages who could negotiate the necessary agreements. The rise to national importance of the ^CAlawis is upheld by the pattern of international trade and the safe connection the ^CAlawis could guarantee between the Sahara and the sea-coast. The pattern is itself characterized by a 'national' context which assumed its contemporary outlines in the sixteenth century, as a result of international relations with, on the one hand, a European domination of the seas and pressure along the Moroccan shores, and, on the other, a Western frontier established by the Ottoman Empire as the limit of its Algerian territories.

Let us now consider, with respect to the ^CAlawis, the particular image of itself which royalty projects. Outward signs are often revealing of attitudes, particularly the ones one wishes to impress on observers. This is also true of the ^CAlawi sultan, a hieratic figure swathed in white, surrounded by slave servants and soldiers, isolated from the crowd and further practising a form of reclusion in his private and part of his social life which are *ḥaram*. Thus we see him discarding those very attributes that had sometimes made his rise to power possible, namely dynamic leadership (including fighting), regional ties and

tribal support. As king he was posed in the non-connective
idiom of the traditional holy lineages as non-warring 'strangers'.
At the same time, however, we can note distinctive emblems
of sovereignty (which were often borrowed from the East, or
from the Ottoman Empire). These details, which range from the
royal parasol to particular phrases, constitute a complex aura
which in Morocco characterizes the *makhzan* or state. The king,
or sultan, both belongs to the institution of arbitration and has
a special position with respect to it, just as the body of arbiters as a whole are defined in contradistinction to the tribal
environment.

This is underscored by the *bay^{c}a*-s or acts of allegiance by
which each component group (tribes, towns, holy lineages)
recognizes the authority of a new sovereign. A bay'a reproduces
albeit in a more elaborate form, the pacts that were traditionally established between representatives of given tribes
and the holy lineage they appointed as their permanent arbiters.(12) It confers transtribal duties on the sharif. Reference
is made to his saintly origins and the blessing and prosperity
these are expected to bring. The specific tasks required of him
are then enumerated. They are never sectarian or defined in
terms of group interests but refer to the common weal and
Islamic justice. Thus we generally find the sovereign asked to
maintain the jihad, to ensure the safety of roads and sometimes
to do away with particular taxes on the grounds that they are
not in conformity with Islamic prescriptions. The document
ends with the signatures of the representatives of each tribal
or social group.(13)

The same attitude is upheld in the official expression of the
nation through the monarchy, be it in royal actions, speeches
or chronicles. This constitutes an official representation of
the makhzan at work in terms of a discourse posed as self-
sufficient but which, in fact, derives its significance from a
tribal reality which is never directly expressed and its evaluation in Islamic terms. Geertz aptly defines this as 'the doctrine
of the exemplary centre'. By this he means the notion that
'the king's court and capital, and at their axis, the king himself, form at once an image of divine order and a paradigm
for social order'.(14) A closer examination of the concepts
involved shows up their dependence on the two levels of
reality - political and ideological - which they seem, on the
surface, to evacuate. This specific discourse, which characterizes the monarchy's view of itself, reflects at the state level
the position of the arbiter active at the tribal level and yet
apparently uncommitted to it, and defines his autonomy in
terms of a political morality derived from the Islamic world-
view.

Abstract though the discourse be, its foundations are concrete and practical, namely the implementing of state authority.
The last point I wish to make is that this is largely dependent
on the institution of arbitration and involves the interaction

Figure 2.1 *Political concepts in Morocco*

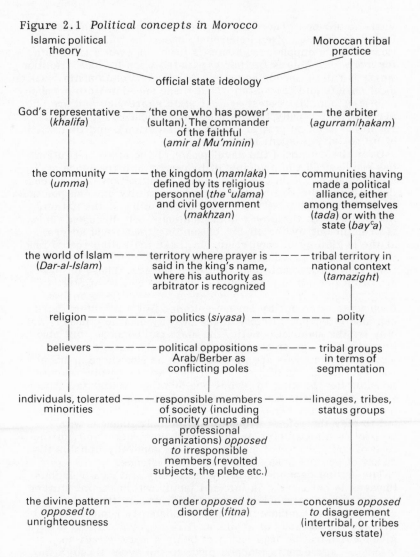

of levels of segmentation, more particularly, of course, in this context, interaction between local arbiters and the king as head of the institution.

The position of the king with respect to holy lineages is that of primus inter pares. This is overtly emphasized by mutual visits and gifts which have both a ceremonial importance and popular inferences, since royal tours - a characteristic manifestation of the king's effective presence - are marked by stop-overs at local religious establishments and notably by

visits to shrines. These are further recalled by architectural
traits since kings often generously order the building of a
mosque, or a cupola over a saint's tomb, or even a main gate
for a zawiya. This is further expatiated upon by local tradition
which is full of anecdotes as to a privileged relationship between
local sharifs and the sultan. That these anecdotes often embody
a form of popular protest against state supremacy and are not
necessarily factually true is immaterial. What counts is that
royalty is seen as part of the religious network and that much
of its activity is spent furthering this.

Over the centuries the development of the state institution
has emphasized the principle of hierarchy and therefore of
subordination within the institution of arbitration. The Islamic
definition of the role of the national community and the position
of the head arbiter as the symbol of the unity of the nation,
invest him with the power to authenticate holy lineages. This
is brought out by the custom of sending them royal letters
at the beginning of each reign. In these the sultan reconfirms
the status and privileges (tax-exemptions, benefits from
particular endowments, etc.) of each lineage. These letters
are often periodically reissued during the course of a reign.
They generally refer to precedent and explicitly reconfirm
documents made out by earlier sultans. But a reigning sharif
can also intervene directly in the destiny of a holy family, not
only by the material benefits the state can concede, but also
by upholding one or other branch of a holy lineage since
segmentary tensions are present there as elsewhere in tribal
society. The death of a *sayyid* or head of the family makes it
possible for the king to favour one or other candidate, especially in view of the fact that state tradition has it that he
should ratify the choice by royal decree. The king is further
led to play the role of protector of the holy lineages with
respect to his own civil or military administration and, in the
case of conflict, to act as mediator. He generally upholds the
claims of arbiter lineages in such circumstances.

The mutual dependence of the monarchy and local religious
lineages is not merely an internal factor within the institution.
It also has an external objective basis, namely the fact that
royal policy is fundamentally and consistently implemented
through the network of arbiters. Official royal activity always
gives a frustrating impression of being a mere parade to
officialize agreements reached prior to the event through the
more or less clandestine mediation of the saintly arbiters. I
illustrate this by three concrete examples taken from different
fields of policy implementing which can be considered as connected with state prerogative. The first is the problem of
population distribution. In Morocco the last major phase of
tribal redeployment occurred in the seventeenth century and
it was accompanied by political readjustments which brought
the ᶜAlawis to power. This was followed up by changes in the
arbitration network and an effort by the sultans to promote a

new tribal equilibrium. One of the major difficulties which the
new dynasty had to face was the presence of expansive tendencies in the Middle Atlas. The sovereign was thus led to
undertake a vast programme of settlement by bringing in tribal
contingents from the South and establishing them in the Atlas
where they could effectively by their presence neutralize the
motive force of local populations. The way this chequered
pattern was established can be studied through a zawiya text
which shows this as having been arranged by the descendants
of Sidi Bu Ya^cqub at Mulay Isma^cil's request.(15) This type of
joint action could obviously be studied on a wider scale, in
different regions and at different periods. A quite different
example but one that is of considerable import with respect to
the king's capacity to implement the nation's foreign policy,
is brought out by the situation that followed on the Spanish
occupation of Tetuan in 1860. To obtain the evacuation of the
foreign army the sultan agreed to pay a war indemnity which it
was generally supposed he would be unable to collect. And
yet much of the money was paid in by the tribes. This was in
fact negotiated by the holy lineages whom Sultan Sidi Muḥammad
had contacted. The way in which he formulated his appeal is
an illustration of the interconnection between royalty and
traditional holy lineages in tribal context:

> It is necessary to negotiate with men of religion among
> those populations as to the amount to be levied in each
> tribe. Undertake these negotiations with men who are known
> for their piety and who are knowledgeable as to the situ-
> ation of each tribe. Inform us in detail of their comments so
> that we can send orders to the tribes in consequence.(16)

A third and still different example is that of the Ma al-^cAynayn,
the most influential religious lineage of the Western Sahara,
with whom the ^cAlawi dynasty had close and constant links in
the difficult pre-colonial and colonial period.(17) We can see
here the way in which the religious network contributed to
the building up of national ties. Isolated examples such as
these do not serve merely to illustrate a point but rather to
show up permanent trends still largely operative even today.
Actual political activity in Morocco is, I would suggest, traditionally deflected towards a persistent tribal structure to
which the official royal stand is largely subservient.

Even if head and local arbiters are both committed to upholding the tribal pattern, this is obviously a tension fraught
relationship since the local arbiter's commitments are basically
local and the head arbiter's are national. This national viewpoint places the king in a position of superiority where he
tends constantly to manipulate and readjust the network of
zawiyas to consolidate state power. This can also be illustrated
with respect to the Middle Atlas region described above and
which ^cAlawi policy has constantly tended to isolate. This led

in early times to the establishment of a military cordon at the
foot of the mountain range. Parallel to this we can see royal
arbiter policy working to promote to regional and even national
importance holy lineages situated along this strategic line of
defence. A zawiya such as Buja^{c}d(18) owes its rise to fame to
royal favour and support. Not that the state has a free hand,
for even 'royal' zawiyas must, to uphold their position, express
the views of their clientele. If this ambiguous situation is not
kept under control, it may lead to direct confrontation. Buja^{c}d,
for example, was attacked and destroyed by the royal army in
1784-5, but soon regained favour because it occupies an indispensable niche in terms of tribal layout. In fact, a sovereign
can neither do away with given zawiyas nor promote new lineages ex nihilo. This can also be illustrated in this same strategic region of the Atlas since the ^{c}Alawis who, on coming to
power, had destroyed the arbiter lineage of Dila which had
rivalled their claim to national supremacy, were not
able to avoid the reinvesting of the tribal scene by other, often
recent lineages which posed as Dila's successors and the monarchy had to compose with the zawiyas of Sidi Bu Ya^{c}qub, the
Iḥanṣalen or the Imhiwash. Conversely, royal efforts to set up
a holy lineage in the region under one Sidi ^{c}Ali al-Filali was a
signal failure and the holy man disappeared from the tribal
scene. In other words royal manipulation of the arbiter network ·
is defined and limited by the tribal context.

The power and autonomy of the tribal structure are not the
only limits to royal power, nor is tribal support the only weapon
local arbiters have to resist state encroachments. Their capacity
to fight back is also illustrated by a particular characteristic
trait of North African society which they directly helped to
promote, namely Sufi orders. Mystical doctrines which have
played an important role in the Maghrib since the eleventh
century, have given rise to numerous associations of laymen who
are grouped around a spiritual guide (*shaykh*). A common set
of practices, meetings and spiritual retreats in lodges, and
obedience to the shaykh constitute the bond which binds initiated members (*ikhwan*) to their order (*ṭarīqa*).

The connection between Sufi orders and traditional centres of
arbitration is not immediately apparent but is nonetheless suggested by the very word zawiya and its Maghribi connotations.
In classical Arabic, the word simply means a 'corner', particularly the corner of a mosque where a teacher lectures to his
students. In rural Morocco it refers at one and the same time
to religious establishments having arbiter functions and to fraternity lodges. This ambiguity shows up a structural connection.
The shaykh whose message or mystical experience attracts disciples is more or less inevitably drawn into the network of holy
lineages. It is only within the religious compound of the rural
zawiya that his voice can be heard without provoking a social
scandal. He often makes use of the infrastructure provided by
local religious establishments and is upheld by the moral

authority of the holy lineages who, in turn, derive prestige
from his presence and teaching. Thus the lonely reformer more
often than not uses existing religious establishments to preach
his message. He may himself be a member of such a social group
or will come to be connected with it by adoption and marriage.
Even when this is not the case, we find that as the mystic's
influence grows, he is ever more often appealed to for mundane
advice. In other words he comes to perform the traditional role
of an arbiter. As the lodge becomes influential, we generally
find a sharing out of responsibilities with representatives of the
shaykh (members of his entourage or family) specializing in
mundane matters whilst the holy man concentrates on teaching
and prayer. A purely religious figure can thus himself be at
the origin of an arbiter lineage.

An order, in its efforts to become popular, is largely dependent on zawiya relays which can either block or pass on the
message and which are the institutional means through which
a local community is attracted to the movement. Significantly
rural zawiyas have not only chosen to act as transmitters but
have involved themselves directly in Sufi orders since holy
lineages are generally affiliated to one and the zawiya is thus
the seat of a lodge. Why should local lineages have chosen to
act as promoters of ṭariqas? In doing so they are probably
answering several social needs, particularly the deeply rooted
Islamic ideal for an egalitarian religious community living its
faith outside the commitments of lay society. Sufi orders cut
across the barriers of a society based on tribal ties or class
stratification. Consequently we find them becoming ever more
prevalent and important as society becomes more complex and
rigid. At the same time the development of intertribal relations,
be it in terms of trade or of labour migration, enhances the
role of lodges as places where *ikhwan*, whatever their origins,
can find a congenial resting-house, new friends, advice and
an introduction to local society. The religious lineages capi-
talize on these needs and by this means come to acquire a
private clientele that cuts across traditional social barriers.

This has obvious political overtones since spiritual leaders
thus have a lay following that can act as a pressure group on
the social scene. This further puts them in a privileged position to monitor social change and to appear as leaders of public
opinion. Orders thus push out into two different but complementary directions by, on the one hand, promoting predominant
nation-wide organizations whilst, on the other hand, founding
associations adapted to specific social groups. In Morocco these
two trends become apparent on the social scene from the seventeenth century onwards (and are therefore also contemporaneous
with ^CAlawi power). From the seventeenth century and throughout the eighteenth, we find mass adhesion of the great majority
of Morocco's zawiyas to the Naṣiriya order. This further establishes a link between towns and countryside since the intellectual urban elite is often connected with the lodges. The

Naṣirya is probably the most important national organization of
the period. In the nineteenth century, for reasons that would
warrant further study, there is a general switch-over to another
order, that of the Derqawa. The eighteenth century also saw
the creation or development of the ᶜAisawa and Ḥamadsha whose
membership comes essentially from a growing detribalized urban
subproletariat. At the end of the nineteenth century, an
'aristocratic' order, that of the Tijaniya, becomes a typical
feature of the makhzan and of the class of notables in general.
From the point of view of the network of holy lineages, manipulation of Sufi orders and their following constituted a wide-
scale power-stand from which they could hope to neutralize
growing state-power.

This is played out in a respective show of strength in which
manifestations of state power are opposed by religious leaders
with reference to popular opposition. The idiom of confrontation,
however, generally remains that of arbitration, namely religious
ideology. Both parties refer to the jihad, not only war against
the infidel but in its deeper meaning of the duty of Muslims to
reform their community; but whereas the Amir al-Muᵒminin
claims his right to 'do good and eradicate evil' even by force
and at the cost of human lives, religious leaders uphold reform
as a collective and popular undertaking. In preaching a return
to primitive Islamic purity they criticize the prevalent system
and sometimes the king himself. Our contemporary tendencies
to overestimate state-power should not blind us to the fact that
the popular appeal of fundamentalism which generally goes with
Sufi doctrines is present in most forms of organized political
opposition. The fact that such movements have often used
lodges as a political arena no less than the fact that an estimated 80 per cent of the male population has affiliations with a
lodge shows up the potential force which can be brought to
bear in a nation-wide confrontation.

Typically, however, the institution of arbitration generally
avoids open conflict, and this is also true of the king as head-
arbiter. The attitude of the monarchy towards Sufi orders has
consequently always been ambiguous and shifting. Whilst
officially ignoring them, it never cuts itself off entirely from
the possibility of counter-manipulation. We thus generally see
members of the royal entourage if not the king himself having
connections with ṭariqa leaders and sometimes upholding their
order for political reasons. Thus, to cite but one example, the
sovereigns at the beginning of the twentieth century supported
the ᶜAyniya both to further their Saharan policy and, perhaps,
to counterbalance the influence of other powerful orders. But
on the whole, the state tends to be hostile and has on occasions
fought them openly, as did Mulay Sliman in terms of Wahhabi
doctrines in the nineteenth century or Muḥammad V in the name
of *Istiqlal* at the turn of the twentieth.

If I have analysed in some detail the history of these religious
movements in modern Morocco it is because it summarizes and

highlights the conclusions this account of royalty leads me to
formulate. The modern state in Morocco as symbolized by a
sharifian dynasty may be seen as an ultimate development
in the power-stand established by tribal arbiters through
Islam. It implies a hierarchized body implementing state policy
through the network of holy lineages by means of the traditional forms of manipulation of public opinion and social structure which characterize the institution. Political confrontation
is thus deflected towards the network and derives its ideological basis from a religious reinterpretation of the tribal
system. With respect to the institution of arbitration the tensions are often apparent in terms of levels of segmentation:
that of the head arbiter who has recourse to those particular
attributes of power which are justified by the Islamic definition
of the head of state, later enlarged by modern attributes
(often derived from European models), whilst lower levels
appeal to popular following basically on the tribal mode but
increasingly through a wider popular opinion monitored
through affiliation to Sufi orders. The fact that these have
sometimes played a positive role, notably in organizing resistance to foreign encroachments (though not as successfully as
the Libyan Sanusiya) but have, at other times and notably
during the colonial period, used the wrong strategy and made
the wrong decisions, is here immaterial. What counts is the
capacity shown both to channel popular protest and to adapt
to social changes which include both a growing sense of the
nation as such and the evolution of society from a purely
tribal structure to one in which class stratification becomes
increasingly marked.

This in turn points to a further conclusion, namely that state
power and the institution of arbitration derive their durability
from the fact that they overlay the tribal structure and from
the permanent capacity they have shown in adhering to the
social pattern and monopolizing expressions of collective self-
consciousness. What the problem of tariqas shows up is something far more fundamental than Sufi doctrines or even
divergent conceptions of the inner jihad, namely the fact that
up to recent times the fundamental dialectics of state and
nation were played out in this field. The very means used by
the institution of arbitration in general and the monarchy in
particular to control and block fundamental political and social
contradictions - namely artificial stability through the neutraliz-
ation of contending forces on a segmentary basis - though
largely successful up to the present, create, beyond surface
inertia, explosive situations. These have in the past led to
national disruption and mass upheaval. The latest was that
which led to the establishment of the ᶜAlawi dynasty on the
basis of a new deployment of tribes and arbiters. The state
order, in spite of pressure due to the international context,
has survived to the present. It does not exclude further
upheavals. Whether they will be reinterpreted in those tradi-

tional terms which have up to now characterized Moroccan history or whether they will lead to radical social mutations is another question.

NOTES

1 Pierre Clastres, 'La Société contre l'état', Paris, 1974, and particularly Philosophie de la chefferie indienne, first published in 'L'Homme', II, 1, 1962.
2 David M. Hart, Segmentary Systems and the Role of 'Five-Fifths' in Tribal Morocco, 'Revue de l'Occident Musulman et de la Méditerranée', III, 1, 1967, and the present volume.
3 Sallust, 'Bellum Jugurthinum', cf. chapter XIII.
4 Robert Montagne, 'Les Berbères et le Makhzen dans le sud du Maroc. Essai sur la transformation politique du groupe chleuh', Paris, 1930.
5 Cit. by Joseph Chelhod, Ḳabila, in 'Encyclopedia of Islam', 2nd edn.
6 Cf. note 3.
7 Cf. Mohamed Hajji, 'L'Activité intellectuelle au Maroc à l'époque sa^{c}dide', Rabat, 1976, and Mohammed Lakhdar, 'La Vie littéraire au Maroc sous la dynastie ^{c}alawide', 1075-1311/1664-1894.
8 Muhammad al-Mukhtar al-Susi, 'Al-Ma^{c}sul', Casablanca, 1960-3, and 'Iligh qadiman wa hadithan', Rabat, 1966.
9 In his unpublished thesis, Contribution à l'histoire du Tafilalet. Aspects d'histoire économique et sociale du sud-est marocain aux 16e et 17e siècles à travers l'analyse de quatre documents inédits, 1977.
10 The Idrisids are the first national and independent Moroccan dynasty, but at a local level (Rif region) they were preceded by the Banu Ṣaliḥ who governed the region with the aid of a contingent of Arab warriors, by virtue of an *iqta^c* (concession) granted by the ^{c}Ummayyad *khalifa*. Little, however, is known about these rulers.
11 Ibn Khaldun, 'Histoire des Berbères', tr. de Slane, vol. II, p. 561.
12 As, for example, that between the descendants of Sidi Bu Ya^{c}qub and their clients. Cf. Captain Roger Henry, Notes sur les Ait Sidi Bou Yacoub, unpublished paper, CHEAM, no. 45, vol. 3, January 1937, p. 31 ff, text and genealogies. This is analysed in detail by Mezzine in his unpublished thesis, Contribution à l'histoire du Tafilalet.
13 A great number of such acts of allegiance have been published by ^{c}Abd al-Wahhab Al-Mansur in 'Al Watayq', Rabat, 1976, 4 vols, published.
14 Clifford Geertz, 'Islam Observed. Religious Development in Morocco and Indonesia', Chicago 1968 and 1971.
15 Reyniers, Un Document sur la politique de Moulay Isma^{c}il dans l'Atlas, 'Archives Marocaines', vol. XXVIII, Paris, 1931.

16 Letter from Sultan Sidi Muḥammad to Mulay ^CAbbas,
9 February 1861, quoted by Germain Ayache, in Aspects de
la crise financière au Maroc après l'expédition espagnole de
1860, 'Revue historique', October–December 1958, p. 8.
17 Cf. B.G. Martin, 'Muslim Brotherhoods in 19th-Century
Africa', Cambridge, 1976.
18 Cf. Dale Eickelman, 'Moroccan Islam', Austin and London,
1942.

3 SEGMENTARY SYSTEMS AND THE ROLE OF 'FIVE FIFTHS' IN TRIBAL MOROCCO

David M. Hart

The two articles presented here, the first a republication of a 1967 original and the second a much shorter 1978 addendum to it, and not previously published, may be considered as a unit and as at once an exercise both in structural theory (1967) and in historical methodology (1978). The ideology of 'five fifths' as a powerful segmentary concept which underpins the first article is shown in the second not only to have been fundamentally Islamic, but to have been a principle adapted by the Prophet himself, possibly even from a pre-Islamic prototype, toward the division of plunder captured in wars from his non-Muslim enemies. Hence its purpose was originally military and was associated, in one way or another, with the early conquests and expansion of Islam. Its subsequent proliferation as a diagnostic of certain specifically Moroccan tribal structures may be more difficult to explain (though it may well have had pre-Islamic roots there too); but the interesting fact is that in the Moroccan cases recounted here, the form of the phenomenon and of its power ideology for its possessor groups remained everywhere the same. This was so even though its function came to differ markedly, even radically, from one such possessor group to the next, which was generally spatially discontinuous with it.

But Islam was always present here, even at conclaves of lay tribesmen: for whether the concept was invoked to pay up or divide up a heavy fine for murder on a market day, a fine in which the top segments of a whole tribe theoretically participated, or to elect a top chief with, again, the participation, in theory, of every maximal tribal segment, there were always members of the local *baraka*-holding saintly lineage present, in their white robes, to officiate, to supervise and to see to it that the proceedings were carried out 'in the name of God, the Merciful, the Compassionate'. Not only this, but as the members of such lineages claimed and could demonstrate their genealogical links to the Prophet, they also, and equally demonstrably, claimed kinship with his most illustrious Moroccan descendant, the sultan (now king), the supreme arbiter of the nation. These considerations in themselves tie directly into the mainstream of tribal Islam and hence into the main theme of this symposium.

I

This paper is an attempt to examine certain aspects of the segmentary systems of Moroccan Muslim tribes, with particular
attention given to a specific and recurring segmentary theme
which obtrudes, here and there, all over the landscape of rural
Morocco. All the tribes which exhibit this phenomenon are, or
consider themselves to be, large and powerful; and the phenomenon itself is that they are divided into *khams khmas*, or 'five
fifths', five primary segments. These five segments, taken
together, constitute the totality of each tribe in question.
Although this sounds simple enough on the surface, there is
more to it than meets the eye. Some introductory remarks,
however, on the general nature of Moroccan tribes and of the
segmentary features of their social structure will not be inappropriate.

Although the situation has, in varying degrees for the regions
of Morocco concerned, become modified since the establishment
in that country of the joint Franco-Spanish protectorate (in
theory, in 1912, but not in effect until 1926 in the Rif Mountains,
and in 1933 in those of the Central Atlas), and even more so
since independence (1956), it is convenient, for our purposes
here, to regard pre-protectorate Morocco as being divided
according to three basic axes, none of which are or were
mutually exclusive: 1. an urban-tribal axis (rather than simply
urban-rural, for virtually everything which, prior to 1912, our
'zero point', was not urban was tribal); 2. an Arab-Berber axis
(essentially linguistic, and to some extent institutional, though
not at all structural), and 3. a *makhzan-siba* axis. This last
requires a brief contextual explanation.

Morocco has always been a monarchy (and in 1962 it became
a constitutional one), with a sultan (now king) at its head; and
all the inhabitants of the country have always acknowledged
him as their spiritual head. However, his temporal authority
only covered, before 1912, a fraction of the surface area of the
country, i.e. specifically, the cities and surrounding (coastal)
plains, whose inhabitants regularly paid taxes to him.(1) This
was the so-called *blad l-makhzan*, or 'government land'; and
opposed to it conceptually was the infinitely larger *blad-s-siba*
or 'land of dissidence', in large part made up of mountains
and deserts difficult of access, and entirely populated by
tribespeople, most of whom happened to be Berber-speaking.
The tribesmen of the 'land of dissidence' traditionally paid no
taxes to the central government (in the framework of option
discussed by Lahbabi, they could either opt in or opt out,(2)
despite constant, and (under strong sultans) even annual
tax-gathering expeditions, the soldiery of which was made up
of 'tame' tribes from the 'government land'). However, a famous
North African proverb says that 'Tunisia is a woman, Algeria
a man and Morocco a lion', and, as the lion's roar usually
emanated from the 'land of dissidence', the tax-gathering forces

of the government, in pre-protectorate times, were as often as
not defeated. The tribes existing in a state of *siba*, of dissidence, were indeed strong, hard and tough. What made them
so?

The general principles that underlie segmentary systems of
tribal organization have been too well elucidated by Professor
Evans-Pritchard and other social anthropologists, following
him, to need much further theoretical comment here,(3) but it
should be stressed that Moroccan tribes are highly agnatic
and highly segmentary in character. This is true whether one
is dealing with an Arabic-speaking *qbila*, a Rifian *dhaqbitsh*,
or a Berber *taqbilt* (all terms deriving from the same Arabic
root *q-b-1*) in the Atlas Mountains; all mean 'tribe' (though in
the last-mentioned case, often 'clan'), and all in general base
this meaning on the same underlying set of assumptions, which
I discuss here briefly before embarking upon my main theme.

Moroccan tribes tend to be structured according to either one
of two basic principles, that of 'common ancestorship' or that
of 'heterogeneous clans'. This fact needs in itself to be scru-
tinized more closely. Some tribes speak Arabic, some speak
Berber; but what, aside from linguistic differences, do they
have in common? The answer is: a very great deal. In conformity with the language difference, there are of course differences in (linguistic) nomenclature, i.e. an Arabic-speaking
tribe may be referred to as 'Ulad' or 'Bni X', 'children of' or
'sons of' X, whereas a Berber-speaking one may be referred
to as 'Ait', 'Aith' or 'Asht X', 'people of' X. These are small
differences, and the ultimate result is the same. By this, I
mean that X may refer either to a common patrilineal ancestor,
whether or not he be genealogically traceable, or to a place
(perhaps a point of origin). As amongst almost all Muslims,
descent is reckoned for all practical purpose through the male
line only; and all Muslim tribal groups known to any investigator undergo that process of subdivision through time and
space which is known to social anthropologists as 'segmentation'.

Segmentation is easily defined: each tribe, whether it bears
the name of a putative common ancestor or the name of a putative point of origin, is segmented into X number of clans
(seldom more than five – and here we begin to 'zero in' on our
subject). Each of these is in its turn segmented into Y number
of subclans; and each of these in its own turn is segmented
into Z number of agnatic or patrilineal lineages, which may
themselves segment again, and again, and again, down to the
level of the elementary or nuclear family of father, mother and
unmarried children. Furthermore, it is also a basic principle
of the system (although one which has in at least six Rifian
cases that I know of been violated) that although the descendants of two brothers, A and B, may fight against each other,
they will join together if attacked by the descendants of those
brothers' cousin C, because, although A, B and C all go back
ultimately to the same ancestor D, A and B are more closely

related to each other than either of them is to C.(4)

Each tribe, in good segmentary fashion, has a given name and a given territory; and each clan within the tribe has its corresponding name and sub-territory, so that the overall system of tribal land-ownership is in fact nothing but the segmentary system (conceived always in terms of time) flopped down spatially upon the ground.(5)

The linguistic axis of Arab-Berber, referred to above, cuts across certain features of the tribal systems: many if not most Arabic-speaking tribes consider themselves to be descended from common ancestors (as bedouin tribes, classically, do), but some (particularly in the Northwestern Jbala) are built up more on the toponymy principle, with heterogeneous clans merely having come in and having occupied territory which eventually became that of the tribe in question, under its present name. The same is true of Berber-speaking tribes: those in the Rif Mountains in the North and those in the Southwestern Atlas Mountains, Sus Valley and Anti-Atlas tend to be organized (to the extent to which, given our limited documentation, this fact can be generalized) on the heterogeneous and often toponymical clan principle – while those in the Middle and Central Atlas tend to be organized around the principle, real or putative, of common ancestorship. One can also make, in very general terms, an economic correlation here: the bulk of the tribes, whether Arabic or Berber-speaking, which are structured on the 'heterogeneous clan' principle are sedentary agriculturists who live the year round in fixed houses, while the bulk or those structured on the 'common ancestor' principle are either trans-humants or nomads. (By 'transhumants', I mean that they generally make two well-defined moves per year : up into the mountains to pasture their sheep and to live in tents in spring, and back down into the lower valleys, where their permanent houses are located, in the autumn.)

Another feature common to most, though not all, Moroccan tribes is (or was) the existence, in their midst, of resident holy men (most not only claiming descent from the Prophet but possessing genealogical evidence, either written in Arabic or in their heads, to back up their claim) who form lineages or even whole clans apart from but, at the same time, with the rest of the tribal community, and whose job is the arbitration of conflicts, both inside and outside the tribe. Such conflicts, in tribal Morocco before 1912, were very much the order of the day. (It can be, and has been, argued, that feuds and wars, far from promoting any disintegration of the tribal system provided in fact the main force which kept it going, a state of affairs which led French and Spanish investigators of a generation ago to categorize tribal systems as 'systems of organized anarchy' - not, perhaps, the right label, for, to my mind, at least, the term 'anarchy' implies a total lack of government; but they were nonetheless on the right track.) Again, a generalization can be made here : nomad and trans-human tribes tended to engage in intertribal warfare, while amongst sedentary tribes, feuds were generally intratribal in character. In the Rif, for example, each tribe was literally split in half, and when the two halves were not fighting against each other, feuding continued just as intensively on a lower segmentary level, amongst, for instance, the lineages of a single subclan. Not only this, but only the holier of the holy men abstained from fighting; the rank and file fought amongst themselves, although not, as a rule, with outsiders. And the holier holy men, in their white robes and the *baraka* emanating from their persons, the 'blessing-substance' given them by God to endow them with their ability as miracle-workers (an ability the lesser ones did not possess), lived up to the prestigious role and status ascribed to them by the (generally warring) lay community by seeing to it that feuds and wars were interrupted by seasonal truces for harvesting, etc., while at the same time receiving helpful 'perks' through annual offerings from their constituents as well as (in the Rif) a 'cut off the top' when fines for murder were imposed by the tribal council.

In some of these tribes (generally the Arabic-speaking ones, although with the exception, by and large, of the Northern-Jbala) power was traditionally more or less centralized and auto-cratic, and held in the hands of a single *qaid*, although a council usually acted as a brake on his possible abuses. In others (generally the Berber-speaking ones, with the notable exception of those tribes in the Western Atlas which came under the sway of the Glawi and the other 'Grand Qaids', and of the Rifians after the ascendance to power of 'Abd al-Krim), power was remarkably diffused; a system of superimposed representa-tive councils, on the different segmentary levels, was the rule; chiefs, where they existed (notably among Middle and Central Atlas transhumant tribes), could be thrown out of office if they proved unsatisfactory; and egalitarianism was very much the norm.

II

Into this generalized situation we may now introduce our main theme, the recurring feature of a basic segmentation, in certain Moroccan tribes, into *khams khmas* or 'five fifths'. I plan to discuss this for three well authenticated cases, the Aith Waryaghar of the Central Rif, the Ait ^{C}Atta of the Saharan slope of the Central Atlas and the Jbil Saghru (in both of which tribes I myself have done intensive fieldwork), and the Duk-kala of the Atlantic coastal plain (this case is derived from the existing literature).(6) These by no means exhaust the rostrum of tribal groups segmented in this manner, but whether they in fact can be said to represent 'type cases' on the one hand or merely one (heavy) end of the available spectrum on the other, our ethnographic knowledge is at present still too spotty to determine.

If, however, we compile a list of 'possibles' which may be segmented in this manner, it becomes indeed an impressive one : in the Northwestern Jbala, Bni Huzmar, Bni Gurfat, Ahl Srif, Bni Yisif, I-Khmas (perhaps by definition, in this case, although the definition here is not entirely in accordance with the present-day clan breakdown), Ghzawa and Bni Mstara;(7) in the Ghmara region, just east of the Jbala, Bni Silman and Bni Rzin;(8) and Sinhaja Srir group, just east of Ghmara and west of the Rifians Proper, Ktama.(9) In the Rif, aside from our Aith Waryaghar, there are also Igzinnayen (although accounts given me by informants in this tribe conflict), Axt Tuzin, Thimsaman, Aith Sa'id, Aith Wurishik, the five tribes of Iqar^{c}ayen,(10) and near Oujda, Ait Iznasen. Moving south, the Shawiya near Casablanca and the Sraghna near Marrakesh may represent examples,(11) aside from the Dukkala of the coastal plain; and in the foothills of the Middle Atlas, the Zimmur are also said to be one.(12) In the Middle Atlas itself, we have the five-tribe confederation of Ait Umala (Ishqirn, Ait Ishaq, Ait Wirra, Ait Umm l-Bakht, and Zayan,(13) the Ait Mgild, Ait Ndhir(14) and Ait Warayin;(15) and in the Central Atlas, aside from the Ait ^{c}Atta, the five-tribe confederation of Ait Yafalman (which was organised to fight against the Ait ^{c}Atta,(16) and the Ait Sukhman).(17) In the Sus, the twelve Haha tribes are each structured in this manner;(18) and in the Western Sahara, the Rgibat bedouin say that they have khmas khmas, but their actual segmentary system contradicts this statement, as I discovered personally.(19)

Many European writers on Moroccan tribes have tended to regard them as examples of what Gellner has recently called 'a kind of binary fission';(20) Gellner thinks, and I agree, that the number 'two' has no pre-eminence. Most of these authors have tended to confuse segmentary systems with a certain kind of alliance system found in parts of Berber Morocco (e.g. in the Rif and in the Western High Atlas, in its classic manifestations, though these themselves differ between the two regions). Binary fission, in its purely literal sense, does indeed exist in certain small Moroccan tribes (Tafarsith in the Eastern Rif being but one example, and here the two clans also corresponded to the two hostile moieties in the tribe); but its existence seems doubtful in larger tribes. 'Two' has no primacy in bigger tribes, but 'five' has; and it is not stretching the point to assert that the notion of khams khmas represents the quintessence of tribal social structure in Morocco.

We now come to the core of the argument : granted that certain Moroccan tribes are divided into five primary segments (call them 'clans', or whatever), what is the structural significance of this type of segmentation; what, in each case, is its function; and what finally, is the relationship between the two?

Here there are, very appropriately, five criteria of relevance, all of which fit the 'type cases' which will be described below.

(To what extent they fit the 'possible' tribal groups just mentioned, I cannot say, but it is reasonably safe to assume that
some of the criteria fit some of the 'possible' tribes.) These
criteria are as follows:
1. Any tribe segmented into five 'fifths' is explicitly regarded
to be such by its members, who are themselves thoroughly
conscious of the principle involved, and who articulate it as
such in their own self-conceptualizations, which are geared to
2. The idea that five 'fifths' indicates the strength and power
of any tribal group possessing them, and is thus a great source
of tribal pride.
3. In the ideal situation, the notion of 'five fifths', aside from
its structural relevance, always contains a functional relevance
as well, although the function in each individual case may, and
generally does, differ from tribe to tribe (or from region to
region).
4. The structural relevance of the principle is particularly
apparent in tribes which show, either within or outside their
boundaries, a combined discontinuity and reduplication of clan
segments on the territorial level. (By this, I mean that a given
clan, Bni or Ulad A or Ait B, of a tribe Bni or Ulad X or Ait Y,
is reproduced spatially, while maintaining its same name, in two
or more different places either within or outside the main bloc
of the tribal territory.)
5. This 'quintessential' principle given here as Point 5 subsumes all the others, and provides their referential articulation
with each other : the principle of khams khmas, by articulating
territorially discontinuous clans in and of a given tribe, tends
to produce, in each instance, not only concrete examples of
corporate tribal action, but to act as a brake on other, divisive
forces (which, in the Ait Waryaghar case, at least, are maxi-
mized) within the total sociopolitical structure of the tribe.

III

In the light of the above five criteria, we may now consider our
three 'type cases', two of which are 'Berber' and one, 'Arab'.

Case 1
The Aith Waryaghar of the Central Rif (who produced [C]Abd
al-Krim) are sedentary agriculturists, numbering, in 1960,
almost 76,000 in population; they live in fixed habitations but
in local communities which show an extreme degree of dispersion
of individual houses; and their response to poverty and
population pressure has traditionally been bloodfeuding, now
supplanted by labour migration. They are the biggest tribal
group in the Rif, and the only one in that region exhibiting
the phenomena of territorial discontinuity and reduplication
mentioned above, even though on the tribal level, as opposed
to that of the clan, they form a single bloc. This point has

already been mentioned by Montagne, (21) and both he and
Professor Coon, (22) equally, mention the existence of five
'fifths' in this tribe; and Coon's work has at least the merit of
implying the importance of this phenomenon in Rifian social
structure in general. Neither, however, discusses either the
structural or the functional relevance of the system, which I
shall do below.

The khams khmas of the Aith Waryaghar are as follows in
Figure 3.1:

Figure 3.1

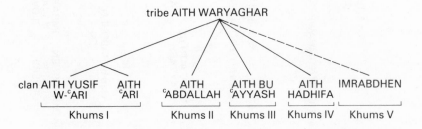

tribe AITH WARYAGHAR

clan AITH YUSIF   AITH   AITH   AITH BU   AITH   IMRABDHEN
W-^cARI   ^cARI   ^cABDALLAH   ^cAYYASH   HADHIFA

Khums I   Khums II   Khums III   Khums IV   Khums V

It is immediately discernible here that the correspondence
between clan (ar-rba^c, pl. r-$urbu^c$) and *khums* (sing. of *khmas*)
is only partial. It is complete in khmas II, III, IV and V (the
intrusive Imrabdhen, designated in Figure 3.1 by a dotted
line, who claim to be Idrisid *shurfa* and have an excellent, and
probably indeed impeccable, genealogy to back up their claim,
but who have no rights to an annual share in the 'box' of
Mulay Idris in Fez); but khums I is made up of two clans. The
further segmentation into subclans (equally, ar-rba^c), given
in Figure 3.2, indicates that the division into 'fifths' was
primarily a recombination of clans (and subclans) for political
purposes, especially for the collection, payment and distribution of tribal fines (*haqq*) which murderers had to pay to the
members of the clan or tribal council (the *imgharen* of the
aitharbi^c in), if they committed a murder in the market (*suq*)
on market day. Given the implicit lack of common ancestry (for
the tribal name is derived from that of a mountain in the massif
of the Jbil Hmam, the Mountain of Doves, the point of origin of
the tribe in the southernmost part of its territory), the division into 'fifths' was also designed, one may assume, with an
eye toward the reduction of conflicts which in this tribe were
invariably at a maximum; for the bloodfeud, in times past, was
the dominant social institution in this tribe. If feuds were
dormant, for example, on upper levels of segmentation, they
were active on lower ones; and we shall see further on how the
alliance structure quite cut across the khums-clan system.

The territorial system of the Aith Waryaghar is also characterized by the twin phenomena of territorial discontinuity and

Figure 3.2

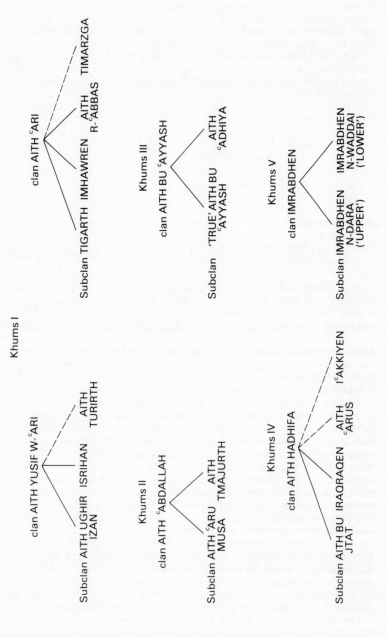

reduplication (which I have discussed in detail in another pub-
lication(23)); and it should be emphasized that in the Rif,
these phenomena exist only in Aith Waryaghar, among whom
each 'fifth' (or each clan, if the two should coincide) possesses
its principal territory in the mountains and enclaves in the
Plain of al-Husaima, or vice versa.(24) And in three 'fifths',
I, IV and V in Figure 3.1, we find, in fact, for each one,
two or more principal chunks of territory each clearly separated
from the other, within the framework of the total tribal land
as a whole.

The division into 'fifths' (and/or clans, as we have seen) is
further subsegmented into subclans, as in Figure 3.2.

Here we may note another phenomenon, although one that
is not necessarily peculiar to tribes divided into 'fifths' : that
of dominance and recessiveness of clan names. Though I have
commented upon this elsewhere,(25) no less than three instances
of this may be noted in Waryagharland : 1. in khums I, the two
subclans of True Aith Yusif w-CAri, as opposed to their
'brothers' of Aith Turirth (all three being territorially discontinuous from each other), and the three subclans of True Aith
CAri as opposed to their 'brothers' of Timarzga (with, again,
territorial discontinuity among all four); 2. in khums II, the
subclans of True Aith BuCAyyash and Aith CAdhiya (the first
is not territorially discontinuous, although the second is very
slightly so); and 3. in khums IV, the two subclans of True
Aith Hadhifa as opposed to their 'brothers' (*umathen*) of Aith
CArus and ICakkiyen (and in this case, the first two are not
discontinuous, but the second two are....And it might be noted
that the 'brotherhood' between clan groupings, 'brotherhood'
as opposed to actual descent from a common ancestor, is constantly referred to by Aith Waryaghar elders, perhaps even as
a sop to the investigator for being unable to trace common
descent!). The 'true' subclans, in a case of this kind, are
those which give their own names to those on the segmentary
level immediately above them, and it is, thus, they which are
dominant, in this pseudo-genetic sense, and the others, whose
names are only retained on *one* level, the lower one, which are
recessive. Furthermore, on the actual ground and territorial
level per se, there is yet additional territorial discontinuity
and reduplication of local communities (*r-udshur*, sing. *d-dshar*)
among, in particular, True Aith Yusif w-CAri and True Aith
CAri (the two having been hostile to each other in the traditional alliance system, with Aith Turirth having backed the
first group and Timarzga the second). And, finally, the intrusive Imrabdhen (allied, traditionally, through marriage to
Aith Yusif w-CAri) have two principal blocks of territory,
'Upper' and 'Lower'; but they also have many even more intrusive individual lineages (*dharfiqth*, pl. *dharfiqin*) dispersed
at strategic points throughout the tribal territory, among the
other clans. (It was these lineages, perhaps by their position
as much as by anything else, which provided the very small

minority of white-robed baraka-possessors and adjudicators of
disputes in the tribe; one man, and only one in a given 'holy'
lineage at a given time, held the miracle-working power of the
baraka, to be transmitted on his death to one of his sons,
while another man of the same lineage, generally his brother,
acted as arbitrator of conflicts. A sacred and profane division
of labour and power there was here - while all the other
Imrabdhen might just as well have been laymen, for they
eternally fought amongst themselves.)

Among the Aith Waryaghar, the segmentation into khams
khmas, 'five fifths', had its concrete expression - and we now
come to the question of function - in the division of the tribal
fine inflicted on a murderer : 2,000 duros hasani if he killed
someone in the market itself, and half of this sum, or 1,000
duros hasani, if he killed him on any path leading to the
market, on the day of the week that the market was held. The
money was divided into five equal parts amongst the *imgharen*,
the council-members, of each 'fifth', in order to keep the suq
or market as a place of peaceful commercial exchange. (Within
the 'fifths', ideally, and starting with khums I, for example,
that of Aith Yusif w-^{C}Ari and Aith ^{C}Ari, the first clan received
one half, and the second, the second half; then, from the first
half, one-fifth was given to Aith Turirth and the rest divided
in half between Aith Ughir Izan and Isrihan. In the second
clan of khums I, Aith ^{C}Ari, one-fifth was given to Timarzga,
and the rest divided into three equal parts among Tigarth,
Imhawren and Aith r-^{C}Abbas. In khums II, Aith ^{C}Abdallah,
their share was divided in half between the two constituent
subclans, and the same applied for khums III, Aith Bu ^{C}Ayyash,
and for khums V, Imrabdhen. In khums IV, Aith Hadifa, the
two subclans of True Aith Hadhifa received two-thirds, this
being divided in half between the two of them, while the remaining one-third went to Aith ^{C}Arus and I^{C}akkiyen; of this last,
Aith ^{C}Arus got two-thirds and I^{C}akkiyen the remaining third.)
If the murderer could not or did not pay, he had his house
burned down by the council members and also, if he did not
flee to another tribe entirely, or at least to another clan in his
own tribe, he always risked being killed by the agnates of his
victim. Thus the division of the fine functioned as a validation
of the system of 'five fifths', and of, in fact, the segmentary
system in general.

There was, however, another disruptive factor which could
and did come into play here : the *liff*-type alliance system,
which cut the tribe into two hostile moieties in such a way
which, in the Aith Waryaghar, did not correspond with the
division into 'fifths', and which, indeed, cut across it. This
cross-cutting process the 'fifths' as such tried to resolve
through pulling together in fine-sharing for murders on market
day, but the one always went against the grain of the other,
even so. The *liff* system, as it existed in Waryagharland, in
fact corresponded more closely to the system, division, and

distribution of subclans, as may be seen in Figure 3.3, and by
comparison with previous figures.

Figure 3.3

	LIFF A	*LIFF B*
Within:	Aith Yusif w-ᶜAri	Aith ᶜAri
	Aith Turirth	Timarzga
	True Aith Hadhifa	Aith ᶜAbdallah
	Aith ᶜArus	
	Iᶜakkiyen	
	True Aith Bu ᶜAyyash	Aith ᶜAdhiya
	Imrabdhen	
Without:	Ijaᶜunen, clan of	Ibuqquyen (tribe)
	Aith ᶜAmmarth	Truguth, clan
		of Thimsaman
		Axt ᶜAkki, clan
		of Axt Tuzin

Theoretically equal, these two liffs were in fact in disequili-
brium, as may be seen from Figure 3.3; and the limits of the
system (for all Rifian tribes, not only for Aith Waryaghar)
were in fact the limits of the tribe itself. And thus the whole
may be represented, as I have shown it elsewhere,(26) as a
series of interlocking concentric circles, quite unlike the chess-
board system propounded by Montagne for the tribes of the
Western Atlas. Neighbouring clans of neighbouring tribes
were sometimes implicated, giving 'secret' aid in arms and money
to the liff which they favoured in the warring tribe; but never
was a whole neighbouring tribe involved, as it also had its
own hostile moieties, organized in the same way. When there
was no full-scale internal tribal war, the smaller 'temporary'
liffs existing on the local level among, for instance, lineages
of a single subclan were invoked; and these often changed or
switched alliances, although the big liffs on the upper levels
(in the Waryaghar case, at least) apparently never did.

Nonetheless, rent though they were by internal feuds, the
Aith Waryaghar pulled together as one on three distinct occasions in their recorded history : 1. in 1908, against the army
of the Pretender Bu Hmara, whose own army they slaughtered on
the banks of the Nkur River; 2. in 1921-6, under ᶜAbd al-Krim
(who was responsible for changing much of their 'custom',
although his control of the tribe during the crucial years of
the war was based on the system of 'fifths' - which later
became too difficult for the Spaniards, who changed it administratively), and during the Rifian War against Spain and France;
and 3. in 1958-9, during their recent revolt.

It would thus appear, in the Aith Waryaghar case, that their
organization into 'five fifths' satisfies, and amply so, all the

criteria listed above : explicitness of the concept, pride and
strength, the relevance of function (fines for murder distributed five ways), territorial discontinuity and reduplication,
and the provision of an avenue toward corporate action when
necessary. And corporate action could and did happen, even
in a tribal group so utterly rent by inter- and intra-clan
feuding as the Aith Waryaghar. Except when, by force of circumstances, the Aith Waryaghar had to direct their excess fighting energies outwardly, their normal idea was always to kill
each other. They provided (prior to ᶜAbd al-Krim) an almost
classic example of the 'Neolithic' philosophy of 'Keep away from
my woman and get off my land!' (Woman first and land second).

Case II
The Ait ᶜAtta, numbering about 150,000 people spread out,
today, over three provinces in southern Morocco (Beni Mellal,
Warzazat and Ksar es-Souk) occupy an immense territory which
extends, in their idiom, from the holly-oaks of the Middle Atlas
(i.e. Ait ᶜAtta n-Umalu, discontinuous from the main body of
this supertribe, at Wawizaght near the Bin el Ouidane Dam)
down to the palms of the Sahara, from Wawizaght to Tawuz.
Like the Jbil Hmam heartland of the Aith Waryaghar (whence
the latter gradually spread, over the course of a millennium,
down to the Mediterranean), the Ait ᶜAtta also have a heartland,
the Jbil Saghru - the most treeless mountains in Morocco, more
so even than the Jbil Hmam of Waryagharland - whence they
radiated out in all directions, looking for pasture for their
sheep. Their radiation was much more recent, in time, than
that (as postulated) of the Aith Waryaghar : about the fifteenth
or sixteenth century A.D. They say that they started out as
pure nomads, but that they modified this way of life to transhumance (in a northerly direction, up into the Central Atlas,
for most ᶜAtta groups, although some transhume southward
into the desert) after adopting the several-story *qsur* of the
negroid Haratin of the pre-Saharan oases, whom they put to
work for them as irrigation experts and date cultivators. The
Haratin received one-fifth (the number is a very standard
agricultural one in Morocco, but suggestive all the same) of
the ᶜAtta crops in return for ᶜAtta protection : and, with
certain modifications, this métayage relationship still persists
today. And, contrary to the thesis advanced by Gerlings and
Jongmans,(27) the great majority of Ait ᶜAtta groups (with a
few notable exceptions : the Ait ᶜAtta n-Umala of Wawizaght,
the Ait Wallal of l-Qual'a Mguna, and the Ait Unir of Bu Maln
n-Dads, the last-mentioned group showing that very rare
phenomenon in ᶜAtta-land, of thoroughgoing Haratinization) are
still transhumants, and as much so as ever.
   Where the Ait ᶜAtta show a difference from the Aith Waryaghar,
however, lies in their structural conceptualization of themselves: they claim that they are all descended from a common
ancestor, Dadda (Grandfather) ᶜAtta, who was supposed to

have been killed in battle against Arab tribesmen on the Oued
Dra, and who is buried at Taqqat n-Iliktawn, near Tagunit, and
south of Zagora. But, in classic clan fashion, the Ait ᶜAtta of
today are unable to trace their descent back to Dadda ᶜAtta.
They resort, indeed, to justificatory legends about his forty
warlike sons, and the like, legends which also explain their
traditional hostility toward, in particular, the Ait Siddrat and
Ait Murghad tribes (and indeed toward the Ait Yafalman confederacy in general, formed at Murghad instigation for the purpose of combating the ᶜAtta), but equally their reverence for
two groups of *igurramen* or holy men, the Shurfa of Ulad Mulay
ᶜAbdallah bin l-Hsain, some of whom are resident in and south
of the Jbil Saghru, and, to the north in the Central Atlas, the
descendants of Sidi Saᶜid Ahansal. (With both these saints,
Mulay ᶜAbdallah bin l-Hsain in particular, Dadda ᶜAtta himself
was on very good terms, and the Ait ᶜAtta annually send a mule
caravan loaded with *ziyara* offerings to Mulay ᶜAbdallah's tomb
at Tamsluht, near Marrakesh; and it is those descendants of
Mulay ᶜAbdallah who, residing in the Jbil Saghru, act as guardians of the Ait ᶜAtta battle-flag.)

Perhaps this inability on their part to trace their descent from
Dadda ᶜAtta partially accounts for their segmentation into the
khams khmas of the Ait ᶜAtta, as in Figure 3.4:(28)

Figure 3.4

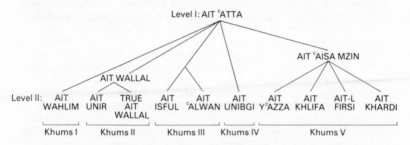

The function of the 'five fifths' of the Ait ᶜAtta, which, as
we shall see, show the twin phenomena of territorial discontinuity and reduplication to an extent probably unequalled in
tribal Morocco, was to provide a top chief (*amghar n-ufilla*)
for the whole of this supertribe.(29) This chief was, ideally,
elected annually, in the ᶜAtta heartland of the Jbil Saghru,
at a point near their 'capital' of Igharm Amazdar, where they
had their Supreme Court of Appeal (*l-istinaf*), and within the
limits of the *hurm* or 'sacred' territory of the tribe at large,
called Tafrawt n-Ait ᶜAtta, within which murder, even attempted murder, was expressly forbidden, under penalty of a
prohibitively heavy fine or banishment from the tribe. Chieftainship and the election of chiefs, not only for the Ait ᶜAtta
but for most Berber tribes in the region (though only the Ait

CAtta had a single top chief) reposed upon the twin principles
which Gellner(30) discovered near Zawiya Ahansal, which he
has labelled 'rotation and complementarity', and which he has
described extremely well, in general terms. I should, however,
like to add a temporal refinement to his classification and label
the phenomenon 'annual rotation and complementarity', as I
think this represents just a shade more closely the Berber
ideal of yearly elections.

The principle is easily broken down into its two component
elements. Insofar as that of rotation is concerned, let us keep
to our Ait CAtta example, with khmas or 'fifths' I, II, III, IV
and V. If, during one year, the chief comes from khums I,
the next year he will come from khums II, and the third year
from khums III, etc. in rotation. This is simple enough, but
in the Ait CAtta case (which Gellner's excellent proposition,
as stated, did not entirely provide for), there is a corollary
to it. This corollary comes into play when a khums is formed
by two, three or four (or even more) discrete clan groupings.
What happens here, ideally, is that when the turn of such a
khums arrives, in a given year, its member groups or clans
are 'mixed'. This is to say that if in one year the top chief
comes from True Ait Wallal (note the similar phenomena of clan
dominance and recessiveness as discussed for the Aith Waryaghar), he does not necessarily come from Ait Unir five years
later - he may come once again from Ait Wallal on that khums'
second time around. The principle of rotation, thus, does not
extend into each of the clans or groups comprising the khums
itself, but applies only to the khums, as a whole.

Now for 'complementarity', which answers the question of who
does the electing. If it is the turn of khums I to provide the
chief, the members of that khums, as potential imgharen, cannot vote. They sit in a circle and await the decision of the
other khmas, II, III, IV and V, who have removed themselves
from the scene in order to select, or elect, the man of their
choice from khums I. The next year, when it is the turn of
khums II, the members of II sit in a circle to await the verdict
of I, III, IV and V; and so on.

According to Spillmann,(31) the Ait CAtta had a top chief,
elected every year at Igharm Amazdar in the above manner,
until 1926, when the French conquest of their country (lasting
until 1933, and spearheaded by the Glawi), began; but his
statement to the effect that certain clans failed, for one reason
or another, to participate in the annual elections(32) is, according to my CAtta informants, seriously misleading, as it tends
to vitiate the highly segmentary theory behind the system.
By virtue of this theory - which CAtta themselves regard as
fact and as law - every man in this highly segmentary and
remarkably egalitarian society had the vote, and could become
top chief (much as 'Any American Can Become President'),
even individuals naturalized as Ait CAtta, from other tribes,
through sacrifice; and an electoral equilibrium obtained

throughout. This was so despite the fact, for example, that the Ait Wahlim and Ait Y^cazza consider themselves superior to the rest, and that they sneer in particular at the Ait Isful, whom they regard as illegitimate. Furthermore, a chief might in fact remain longer in office than his appointed time if he proved himself capable in war; conversely, if he showed himself a 'no-good', i.e. if his *aduku* or 'luck' (lit. 'slipper') was bad, impeachment was instant and a re-election was held at once.

Thus there was in fact no fixed time for election day, and in a society where diffusion of power was great as in this one, the elective body of councillors or *ajmu*^c always acted as an excellent check on any possible power abuses by a top chief. The ritual of election was also extremely interesting: one of the *shurfa* of Ulad Mulay Abdallah bin l-Hsain, who was present to give his sanction to the proceedings, together with the outgoing chief, placed a few blades of grass in the turban of the incoming chief, to insure a prosperous year, a good harvest and fat sheep. The sharif then gave the new chief a bowl of milk to drink; and as he drank it, the sharif pushed it into his face so that it ran all over his beard and shirt! Then he gave him some dates (and here we have the traditional Moroccan milk and dates ceremony); and finally, a little milk and one date was handed to every man present.

Unlike the Aith Waryaghar, the Ait ^cAtta were never permanently split into mutually hostile liffs – such liffs as did exist were purely *ad hoc*, although on one occasion, most of the ^cAtta were split in such a manner that a top chief, elected by rotation and complementarity, headed each liff. This, however, was the exception rather than the rule, as the ^cAtta themselves are quick to admit. Unlike the Aith Waryaghar, again, the hostilities of the Ait ^cAtta were primarily outwardly directed, toward neighbouring tribes, rather than turned in upon themselves.

However, given the highly segmentary character of ^cAtta society, lower chiefs (on the segmentary ladder), all again elected according to rotation and complementarity, existed on several levels at once. The khums itself, consisting of clans apt to be extremely dispersed territorially, had no chief – its job was to provide the top chief, and this was its function in the overall political system.

The 'rotation of wheels within wheels' within this system, as Gellner(33) calls it, is a complex problem, but it will be useful to look at one example of it in order to show how, mirroring the overall structure, local chiefs, or 'land chiefs' (*imgharen n-tmizar*, sing. *amghar n-tmazirt*) were elected. To this end, we further segment khums I, Ait Wahlim (Figure 3.5).

Figure 3.5

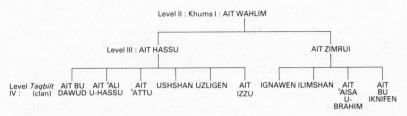

We continue this segmentation further, in the case of one *taqbilt*, or clan, Ilimshan (described as the toughest fighters of the Ait ^CAtta and 'the gasoline of the ^CAtta car', in their most descriptive imagery) (Figure 3.6):

Figure 3.6

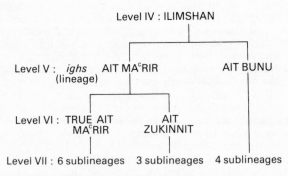

N.B. On Level VI, True Ait Ma^crir may be regarded as 'dominant', and Ait Zukinnit as 'recessive'.

And now to tie the foregoing into the chieftainship system see Figure 3.7.

All this may seem unduly complicated (and indeed it is!); but what it represents is a classic example of 'level-skipping' in which the ideal is that chiefs exist on one level and that they are elected on the next level down, which is devoid of chiefs itself. Inside arrows pointing upward indicate election; outside arrows pointing downward, and skipping levels, indicate the ratification by the chief on the level above of the choice of the lower-level chiefs two levels down. The *idbab n-imuren* (sing. *bab n-umur*), or local lineage representatives, on the lowest level, are not elected by rotation and complementarity but are directly nominated by the 'land chief'(34) three levels further up.

In this particular level-skipping instance, however, what is truly startling is its structural symmetry. To recapitulate this: chiefs exist on Level I, IV and VII with two levels between each

Figure 3.7

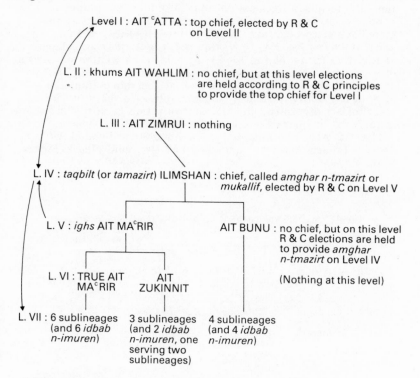

Total *idbab n-imuren* on Level VII for *taqbilt* Ilimshan on Level IV: 12.

of the first two. On the lower of these two levels, i.e. on III and VI, nothing happens, and these may be regarded as, perhaps, 'vestigial' from a structural point of view; but on the upper of these two levels, i.e. on II and V, although no chiefs exist here, elections are nonetheless held for the chiefs on I and IV. Then the top chief on Level I ratifies the election of the one on Level IV, who in turn nominates his *idbab n-imuren*, representing the localized lineages of the clan, on Level VII.

Not all variants of the system are as complicated or indeed as symmetrical as the previous example. The Ait Bu Iknifen of Imidar, near Tinghir, for instance, say that chiefs exist on *all* levels, and that only the top chief is elected by rotation and complementarity, all other lower ones being nominated by those above them. In other words, there is considerable variation and indeed ambiguity in informants' accounts.

I have mentioned that at Igharm Amazdar in the Saghru, the

Ait ^CAtta used to have their Supreme Court of Appeal, or *istinaf*.
Here the localized lineages not only provided the judges on the
bench, as it were, of this court, but they also acted as the
guardians of the *izirf* or Custom of the Ait ^CAtta, of the so-called
shrut n-khams kmas n-Ait ^CAtta, the 'regulations' or 'charter'
of the 'five fifths' of the Ait ^CAtta, said to be written on pieces
of camel skin. A quick look at the localized system of chieftainship at Igharm Amazdar, plus a look at the role of these lineages in the Court itself will perhaps epitomize the unity in
(territorial) diversity, and the centralization in diffusion, that
is (or was) so characteristic of the ^CAtta political system.

The Ait ^CAtta who inhabit Igharm Amazdar are called Ait
^CAisa n-Igharm Amazdar, and they had one 'land chief' (Figure
3.8):

Figure 3.8

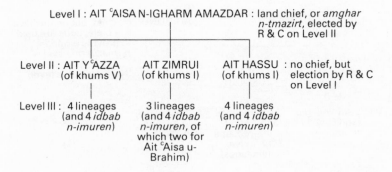

Level I : AIT ^cAISA N-IGHARM AMAZDAR : land chief, or *amghar
n-tmazirt*, elected by
R & C on Level II

Level II : AIT Y^cAZZA   AIT ZIMRUI   AIT HASSU   : no chief, but
(of khums V)   (of khums I)   (of khums I)   election by R & C
on Level I

Level III : 4 lineages   3 lineages   4 lineages
(and 4 *idbab*   (and 4 *idbab*   (and 4 *idbab*
n-imuren)   *n-imuren*, of   *n-imuren*)
which two for
Ait ^cAisa u-
Brahim)

Total *idbab n-imuren* on Level III: 12.

Several points may be noted here. First of all, of the localized
clans of Ait ^CAisa n-Igharm Amazdar, the first, Ait Y^cazza,
belongs to khums V and the other two, Ait Zimrui and Ait
Hassu, to khums I. In local communities (*timizar*, sing. *tamazirt*,
lit. 'land') throughout ^CAttaland, one finds a perpetual mixture
of 'fifths' which, however, becomes perfectly clearcut once one
reaches the level of the *taqbilt* or localized clan and once one
knows to which 'fifths' the clans in a given region belong (A
representative example is a community which I have studied in
depth, Usikis, north of the Gorge of the Dades River. This
community contains three clans, all of which belong to different
'fifths' - Ait Y^cazza to khums V, Ait Unibgi to khums IV, and
Ait Bu Iknifen to khums I, Ait Wahlim.)

All co-operate on the local level to elect local chiefs (by, of
course, rotation and complementarity); and in Figure 3.8,
four *idbab n-imuren*, it will be noted, are required for the
three lineages of Ait Zimrui because one of these lineages, Ait
^CAisa u-Brahim, needs two such representatives as it is larger

than the others. As noted also in Figure 3.8, the 'land chief'
of the Ait ^CAisa is elected on Level II, on which there is no
chief, to serve on Level I, after which he nominates the *idbab
n-imuren* of the various lineages on Level III - and here again,
of course, we may note an incipient tendency to skip levels.

The system on all levels is kept as much as possible in a state
of equilibrium, and the number of lineage representatives on
the lowest level is invariably an accurate reflection of the
numerical strength of the lineage in question. Thus, in a territorial sense, the 'fifths' of the Ait ^CAtta are all mixed up,
and any distributional or tribal map showing discontinuity and
reduplication of clans here and there, all over ^CAttaland,
immediately suggests why chiefs would not be adequate at the
khums level. The level of the local community was and is still
the most effective and viable unit to be represented by a
chief - and so it was, and still is by the *amghar n-tmazirt*, the
'chief of the land' (... and by his present successor, the
shaikh).

In all the foregoing respects, the Ait ^CAisa of Igharm Amazdar,
in good discontinuous ^CAtta fashion, are indeed prototypical.
They had, however, another function beside this, and one
unique to them, i.e. that of acting as members of the Supreme
Court of Appeal, as mentioned above (the Supreme Court building is today a rural school). We may now consider this aspect
of their political life and activity in context.

Trial by collective oath was, until 1956, the touchstone of the
judicial process among Berber tribes of the Central Atlas; but
a full discussion of this mode of trial is not germane to the issue
here. It should, however, be noted that, as a man accused of
a crime had to produce X number of cojurors from among his
own agnates (the number varying with the gravity of the
offence) to swear to his innocence, and that if any of these
men (knowing of their kinsman's guilt, for instance) failed to
turn up at the oath - a very public affair - the accused had
to pay the fine (in sheep) to the plaintiff. The point that such
a 'broken' or perjured oath illustrates, for example is, as
Gellner remarks,(35) not so much of supernatural sanction
(although this is how the tribesmen themselves tend to interpret
it) as that, in segmentary societies in general, conflict tends
to occur within segments as much as between them. And it was
at Igharm Amazdar that the nuances of trial by collective oath
were most highly developed, although this was not a mode of
proof invoked at the Supreme Court. Several other tribes in
the area had courts of appeal (all outlawed in 1956, at the same
time as collective oaths and the rescinding of the 'Berber
Dahir'), but none had a Supreme Court as the Ait ^CAtta had,
nor a capital, nor a top chief. And to Igharm Amazdar came
all the litigants and disputants from all over ^CAttaland who
were unable to resolve their differences of opinion at home.(36)

The court itself always had six regular members, called
variously *inahkamen*, *ti^Caqqidin* or *ait l-haqq* ('people of the

truth' - *haqq* here shows a semantic variation from the way in
which it is employed in Waryagharland) who were always
changed after each case. They always came, however, from the
localized lineages of the Ait ^CAisa n-Igharm Amazdar, and, in
this case, they were chosen by rotation and complementarity:
two from Ait Y^Cazza, two from Ait Hassu and two from Ait
Zimuri (of which one came from Ait Bu Iknifen, one of the
most ubiquitous clans in ^CAttaland, and one from Ait ^CAisa
u-Brahim). If the vote among the six men was three to three,
a dead heat, the vote of the current *amghar n-tmazirt* or land
chief would be solicited to tip the balance, one way or the
other, at four to three. (The matter could indeed become more
complicated than this: for instance, if the first set of six were
not agreed, six more were called in, and then if there was
still a disagreement, a final six, now making eighteen in all,
were brought in. If the vote was still nine to nine, then the
land chief would be asked to make it ten to nine by casting his
vote.)

These men had to know ^CAtta customary law (*izirf*) by heart,
as indeed all the Ait ^CAisa did, as any of them was liable to be
chosen as a member of the *ait l-haqq*. They were no 'better'
than any other Ait ^CAtta, given the extreme egalitarianism of
this tribal group; but it was through them, through the
Supreme Court, through the mere existence, even, of Igharm
Amazdar as their capital (although today it is a dilapidated
and tumble-down series of *qsur*, Ait ^CAtta still speak of it as
their 'United Nations', or, they say, 'London, Paris, Washing-
ton and Igharm Amazdar') and through a system of elections
by which chiefs existed on all the necessary segmentary levels,
from the bottom level of localized lineage *idbab n-imuren* right
up to the top chief of the whole supertribe, that the rationale
for the existence of 'five fifths' to elect the top chief provides
a magnificent annual example of corporate ^CAtta action.

As other neighbouring tribes grudgingly say, the Ait ^CAtta
are as numerous as flies; but none of these other tribes can
properly boast 'five fifths' or anything like the remarkable
structural cohesion which this concept gave to the political
system of the Ait ^CAtta.

Case III
This example, the Dukkala of the Atlantic Coastal Plains behind
El Jadida (Mazagan), will be infinitely shorter than the two
preceding ones, as my account here is based entirely on the
literature(37) and not upon personal knowledge of the group
in question. These people constitute the largest, by far, of
our three groups, with over 360,000 population in 1960; and
they are the only 'Arab' and Makhzan group so far discussed,
for the two previous cases have dealt entirely with Siba tribes.
Nonetheless, it would seem that even the Dukkala appear to
have been forced into the Makhzan mould only in the last
century.

Precision on the question of Dukkala origins is difficult –
about all that can be said is that the majority of them are
descended from the Banu Hilal, that immense wave of bedouin
which swept across North Africa starting in the mid-eleventh
century.(38) And like many or most of the Gharb and Atlantic
coastal tribes, the Dukkala persist today as sedentarized or
semi-sedentarized bedouin, living almost indiscriminately in
nwala-type huts and in tents. For them, animal husbandry
predominates over agriculture, in traditional bedouin style:
and they have numerous cattle and sheep as well as baggage
camels and horses. All the coastal tribes indulge heavily in
the *la^{c}b l-barud*, the 'powder-play' on horse-back (why it
should so often be rendered as 'fantasia' I have no idea), and
the Dukkala are no exception. And, as we shall see, their
horsemen had a functional role to play within the framework of
their segmentation into 'five fifths', khams khmas, as in Figure
3.9:

Figure 3.9

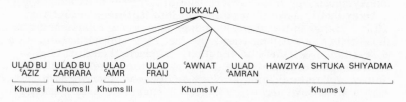

These nine clans or tribes in Figure 3.9 are probably fairly
heterogeneous (as the available accounts are very silent on the
subject of common ancestorship), while a tenth, Qwasim, which
does not fit into the khams khmas schematization, is a *shurfa*
or murabitic group whose lineages are disseminated in small
pockets all over Dukkalaland, like those of the Imbrabdhen in
Ait Waryaghar. Unlike the Waryaghar Imrabdhen, however,
they do not have any principal blocs of territory; their dis-
semination, and hence discontinuity and reduplication, is
absolutely complete. The available tribal maps do not indicate
discontinuity or reduplication for any of the other Dukkala
groups; but the internal clan and lineage listing do.(39) (Ulad
Hamdan lineage, for instance, being reduplicated, in both of
the two clans, within the Ulad Fraij.)
In the Dukkala case, the 'five fifths' seem to have been
imposed (as among the Zimmur, but in this latter case with far
less success, and hence the less functional significance) 'according to a *qa^{c}ida* or tradition of the Makhzan', by the government,
for two purposes: tax-collection and the levying of *harzas*,
soldiery for military expeditions (generally into *siba* territory).
Each khums had to pay the Makhzan a fixed amount of *mitqals*
in cash, presumably annually, and to furnish a standard number

of *khayyala* or horsemen, who were equipped and armed at tribal, not government, expense.

Michaux-Bellaire notes that the division into khams khmas was abandoned under the protectorate (as it was among the Ait ᶜAtta, and among the Aith Waryaghar under Spanish admini-stration) as it 'did not correspond to administrative reality'.(40) Nonetheless, at least one educated Dukkali has assured me that khams khmas is still considered as a guiding structural prin-ciple by his people. If this is the case, then surely it must in all likelihood represent just as much a local structural arrange-ment as one imposed from without. Only proper fieldwork will show whether this is, or is not, so; and it may now be too late. Even so, however, it is my contention that, according to the principles which I have set up in this paper, the Dukkala satisfy all the criteria of (to coin a word) 'fifthness', and the same criteria as satisfied by the other two cases. The fact that the Aith Waryaghar and the Ait ᶜAtta are both 'Berber' and that both fell into the region of *siba*, while the Dukkala are 'Arab' and fell into that of *makhzan*, I regard as being of purely secondary importance in the present context.

An explicitly avowed organization into 'fifths'; the fact that 'fifths' are an index of pride, power and power relationships to those tribes possessing them; the fact that such an organization always has a well-defined function, different though this may be from one possessor tribe to the next; the territorial discon-tinuity and reduplication of clans or lineages which promote such a structural arrangement (or, perhaps, re-arrangement); and the corporate tribal action toward which the system is essentially oriented: these are at least certain considerations to be looked for. I feel that they are all valid criteria for the study of this particular phenomenon which occurs and recurs in the segmentary systems of Moroccan tribes. There may be others, just as there may be many more Moroccan tribes struc-tured into 'fifths', which fit the specifications herewith discus-sed; and the possible discovery of such tribes and the delinea-tion and application of the relevant principles in such new cases as come to light is, I think, a 'quintessential' point worthy of consideration by future anthropologists who elect to work among the (changing) tribes of the Maghrib.

ADDENDUM: SEGMENTARY SYSTEMS AND THE ROLE OF 'FIVE FIFTHS' REVISITED AND UPDATED

After re-reading my original article, Segmentary Systems and the Role of 'Five Fifths' in Tribal Morocco, over a decade after it was published, and after giving the matter careful thought, I decided (as of the end of 1978) that the most effective way to bring it up to date was not by revising it, but simply by appending an addendum, which is presented herewith. The reasons for this are threefold, and interrelated: (1) a wish to assess further information on the subject which has come to my attention since the publication of the original in 1967; (2) an admission that, in the light of subsequent research and publication by other scholars,(41) some of my ideas about the contours and configurations of the material as presented in the original article have become considerably modified; and (3) my conviction that my core ideas about the structural and ideological (though today only historical) validity of the khams khmas or 'five fifths' principle as operative in a segmentary and tribal context - even though in some cases this context itself may be modified as well - still hold good. In addition, and in the light of this last reason, a further and fourth case study, that of the Dawi Mani' of southeastern Morocco and southwestern Algeria, will be added (in the light of material presented by Ross Dunn(42)) to the three cases already documented in the original. These, then, seem sufficient grounds for the inclusion of a postscript rather than an amendment, while an out-and-out revision, I feel, is neither needed nor called for.

Nonetheless, before we embark on any of the above, one sin of omission, with respect to the original article (and one which at the time was quite deliberate, given my more rigid preoccupation with strictly structural-functional problems then than now), should be rectified: a consideration of what is known about the origin of the concept. The fact is that not only is the whole question of khams khmas one of very respectable antiquity in Islam; it is, indeed, even pre-Islamic, at least in the Maghrib, which again draws attention to its very deep roots there. This antiquity may of course be purely coincidental, but I am by no means convinced that such is the case. The specific reference in question is, as it happens, one which has survived only in Latin rather than in Berber: to the Quinquegentanei or 'five tribes' of the Algerian Jurjura Mountains (present-day Kabylia) who steadfastly resisted, in the third and fourth centuries A.D., all attempts by the Romans to colonize them; and indeed, despite the collective Latin appellation of the group as a whole, one of these 'five tribes' bore a name virtually identical with that of a major Kabyle grouping at the present day, the Iflisen (rendered in Latin as Isaflenses).(43) But the fact that the concept was also incorporated into the *sunna* or Custom of Islam at a very early stage is also apparent from the practice by the Prophet's Companions in Medina of setting aside, for him alone, one-fifth of all the spoils taken by the Muslims in any given battle, even though he himself is held to have waived this privilege originally.(44) And that the concept was known in Morocco, during Almoravid times, as *takhmis al-barbar*, 'the five-fold division of the Berbers', is also clear, although whether it represented the way in which spoils were distributed or the way in which troops were organized is less so.(45)

These are attestations or signposts rather than explanations; but there would also seem to be little doubt about the linkage of the concept with the five fingers of the human hand, in particular when these are employed with palm forward and uppermost in order to ward off the evil eye. This is of course the *khamsa fi 'ainik* or 'five (fingers) in your eye' manifestation or syndrome so thoroughly discussed by Westermarck,(46) that which is coupled with the ubiquitous wearing and use by North African women of the *khumsa*. The latter is a metal amulet of a highly stylized human hand with five fingers, in which, generally, the thumb and fifth finger are of equal length and are very short, while the index, third and fourth fingers, also of equal length, are much longer. Indeed, the *khumsa* itself also clearly antedates Islam in the Maghrib, for the emblem of a benedictional and protective five-fingered hand has been frequently found in association with Phoenician and Punic burial monuments and stelae at Carthage. Whether, however, it was a Carthaginian 'original' may well be open to question.(47)

Now that this has been said, we may proceed with the first of the three points made at the outset of this addendum, that of simple updating of the material. As noted in the original article, the list of Moroccan tribal groupings claiming a khams khmas-type organization was in no way to be regarded as exhaustive; and neither are the subsequent additions given here to be so construed, even as 'epiphenomena',(48) despite the fact that the pre-Islamic Quinquegentanei of Algeria, the Almoravid *takhmis al-barbar*, and the Tashumsha of Mauritania, as well as Prophetic tradition, all provide historical indications that the baseline of the concept is not merely or only to be found within the territorial bounds of Morocco, as I had originally surmised. Indeed, only a very few other such groups have come to my attention through subsequent perusal of the literature since Segmentary Systems and the Role of 'Five Fifths' in Tribal Morocco originally appeared.

The first of these is the CAbda, southern neighbours of the Dukkala (Case III in the original paper), among whom the khams khmas concept, as attested by Aubin,(49) may simply be regarded as a carbon copy of the Dukkala case: for the makhzan-imposed levying, on command, of either five units of horsemen or five units of group taxation. A second is that of the Berber (Tashilhit)-speaking Msfiwa of the foothills of the Western High Atlas, as attested by Lafuente,(50) although in this instance, again, as in so many others cited in my original paper, we are left without a clue as to what either the original function of the institution may have been or as to what it may have evolved into at a later date. Hence the issue remains conjectural and unresolved, although it is clear from the overall context that in any given instance, including all those discussed in the original article, the khams khmas concept could have or have had only one function at a time. A third is that of the Arabic-speaking Rahamna north of Marrakesh, as attested

recently by Hoover;(51) and this is a very interesting and possibly unique case in which not only was the category one which
was makhzan-imposed but one in which, for a variety of reasons,
only one khums, the Berabesh, remained constant, while the
other four, on the eve of the French protectorate, were in a
continual process of fluctuation, shift, realignment and change.
And a fourth, that of the Dawi Mani', both as noted in the
original paper and as recently attested in far more detail by
Dunn,(52) will be dealt with presently as Case IV.

The second point, perhaps more fundamental than the first,
may now be considered. This is my admission that not only
have some of the contours of the material changed, in my view,
since the publication of my original paper, but it also entails
my recognition of the fact that it is now evident, in the light
of subsequent research, that by no means all Moroccan tribes
(or perhaps 'named groups', as this involves differing interpretations of the *qabila*-concept which were both beyond the
scope of my original paper and beyond that of this addendum)
are or were organized according to recognizably segmentary
principles, even before the imposition of the two protectorates.
First, what I mean specifically by 'changing contours' is that
my original three-pronged assumption based on a set of binary
opposites (urban-rural/tribal, Arab-Berber and makhzan-siba)
has now become blunted in the light of interim findings,(53)
the point being that none of these dichotomies is as sharply
defined or as closed-circuited as either the earlier French
research or, inter alia, my own, would have led us to believe.
On the other hand, a correspondingly greater open-endedness
in terms of these matters has also opened the door to a certain
degree of dialectic, hence providing room for negotiation. I
would still strongly echo Gellner's statement, as I did in my
original paper, about the number two having no pre-eminence;
and I now realize that to take this to its logical conclusion is,
of course, to scrap the notion of binary opposites as a modus
operandi. Recent research has shown the categorization of
'urban' and 'rural/tribal' to represent not a dichotomy but a
continuum, while on linguistic grounds it is not only clear that
any 'Berberistan' (or should one say *'Tamazirt n-Imazighen'*?)
issue has not only never posed a political problem in Morocco
but that it probably never will: for in the mountainous parts of
the country, Berber becomes ever-increasingly the language of
the home, while all citizens learn Arabic. In addition, the whole
recent emphasis on regional particularism and regional bargain-
ing positions vis-à-vis the centre has pushed the whole makhzan-
siba issue into the background - to become, in effect, one of the
dead horses of colonialism, and hence hardly worth flog-
ging.(54)

Secondly, it seems clear today that a truly segmentary tribal
organization in Morocco existed either only or optimally in those
areas of the country which were furthest removed from the
effective economic and political (though not spiritual) authority

of the sultan and the makhzan. That these areas happened also for the most part to be ones of Berber speech is of less importance: what is paramount is that segmentary structures, with their resulting diffusion of power in equal doses along segmentary lines, worked most effectively where sultanic control and, consequently, centralization of power, were minimal. Recent researches have not only revealed the western half of the northern zone, the Jbala as opposed to the Rif, to have been non-segmentary,(55) but also, and not unexpectedly, the Atlantic coastal plain and its immediate hinterland,(56) while, as already hinted at in my 1967 paper, even a number of Middle Atlas tribes fell into this category.(57) So all of this, in effect, helps to narrow down the field.

However, and here we come to our third and final point, this is not to say that the existence of a named segmentary group does not or did not preclude the fact that this group may have possessed an overarching organization along 'five fifths' or khams khmas lines. To the contrary, the available evidence points to the fact that there were numerous such groups that did possess it, the Zimmur, the Dukkala (Case III in the original article) and the ᶜAbda all being cases in point. But in these instances the fact remains that for whatever the reason, whether for tax-gathering purposes or for raising military or cavalry contingents, the organization was makhzan-imposed. And here we have a fundamental difference with those cases, as among the Aith Waryaghar of the Central Rif and the Ait ᶜAtta of the Saghru (Cases I and II in the original article), in which the concept was very clearly self-imposed, i.e. by the group itself, and for itself, so as to improve the efficiency of its own internal functioning. (Whether or not the model of choice was makhzan-inspired - which in these two instances was patently not the case - is of entirely secondary importance, at least in the present context.)

That this internal functioning was segmentary in nature there is no doubt, at least in my mind. The fact that the internal mechanisms of these tribes were couched in the overall framework of khams khmas rather than in those, let us say, of *zuj nsas*, 'two halves', *tlata tulutat*, 'three thirds', *arb'a rbu'a*, 'four fourths', or even *sitta sudusat* (or *sitta sdas*), 'six sixths', may possibly raise a philosophical issue; but it leaves us in no doubt, once again, as to the conceptual efficacy of the power ideology involved. In a segmentary context the self-imposition, by the group concerned, of the khams khmas or 'five fifths' concept is of crucial importance, again a point which was perhaps not sufficiently highlighted in the original article. It is a point that contributes actively to the 'quintessence' of the system as a whole, and to my conviction that this 'quintessence' still holds good, from the standpoints of form, content, structure and function.

With the above in mind we may now turn to the Dawi Mani' of southeastern Morocco as Case IV.

Case IV
The Dawi Mani', a nomadic and Arabic-speaking tribe of nomads
and caravaneers descended ultimately from the Ma'qil and more
immediately from a putative common ancestor named al-Mani',
numbered about 15,000 at the end of the nineteenth century.
(Their number as of the 1960 Moroccan census was indeter-
minate and unreliable, because many of them were by then
within the borders of Algeria, and were scattered.) In the last
century, they occupied a wide band of pre-Saharan territory
stretching from the Wad Zusfana in the east to the Tafilalt in
the west. But theirs was evidently a west-east migration toward
the Wad Gir and the Wad Zusfana, in present-day Algerian
territory; and as they are near neighbours of the Ait 'Atta,
and specifically of the Ait Khabbash subclan in the Tafilalt, it
is quite possible that they took the concept of khams khmas
from the latter and adapted it to their own circumstances. At
any rate, Dunn makes it clear that the notion came to be
oriented towards their military expansion and to acquire an
important corporate significance. He gives the Dawi Mani' paradigm of 'five fifths' as in Figure 3.10:(58)

Figure 3.10

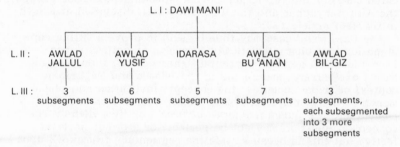

Each of these 'fifths' had a *qaid* as permanent leader, and
in warfare its members fought corporately under his leadership
and under that of the shaikh, an ad hoc leader elected for the
duration of the crisis. Not only this, but Dawi Mani' belief
held that the success of any such endeavour resided in the fact
of all five 'fifths' operating in concert. Any group or individual
failing to appear when summoned by the tribal police, called
here *aitarba'in* (which in this instance, unlike that of the
Rifians, whether of the Aith Waryaghar or elsewhere, may
literally have meant 'people of the forty'); and any victory
against another tribe was followed up by a proportionate distribution of the spoils among the 'fifths' according to the number
of participants provided by each one.
But from an originally military function, the institution of
khams khmas among the Dawi Mani' came by the late nineteenth
century to acquire one that was largely economic: the annual
reorganization of arable land in the flood plain of the Wad Gir,

near ᶜAbadla. The flooding took (and takes) place each year
between November and December, and the harvesting between
April and June; and as many as 6,000 hectares could be irrigated. As indicated, reapportionment according to the 'fifths'
changed each year, and even though another tribe, the Awlad
Jarir, came to be considered by the nineteenth century as a
sixth (and accreted) khums of the Dawi Mani' for purely military reasons, Dunn makes it clear that they did not share
rights to cultivate in the ᶜAbadla Plain.

Although further details may be found in Dunn's study, what
is of interest to us here is that the annual call to plough, sow
and harvest together acted as a kind of centripetal force on the
Dawi Mani' as against any further centrifugal expansion: for
almost the entire tribe appeared, in order to act corporately
in what had now become an agricultural and an economic context:
that of sowing grain, harvesting it, threshing it and storing
it in underground silos.(59) In this context, it seems, the
Dawi Mani' felt that a sixth 'fifth' was not needed. Hence their
original and self-imposed ideology of khams khmas or 'five
fifths' was as well preserved as a structural mechanism for
corporate action, internal to themselves and external with
respect to outside tribes, as it was in the equally well-authenti-
cated cases of the two larger Berber-speaking possessor groups,
the Aith Waryaghar and the Ait ᶜAtta, both discussed at length
in the 1967 article.(60)

The Dawi Mani' case may thus be said to prove a fitting cap-
stone for that characteristically Moroccan structural super-
imposition on a general segmentary theme often, though by no
means exclusively, manifested in the Islamic and Maghribine
context of tribal societies: the concept, institution and phenomenon of the principle of khams khmas - for the classically
minded and the purists, *khamsa akhmas* - or 'five fifths'. The
concept in question may not be perfect, or may not work perfectly; but this is because, like the segmentary framework upon
which it rests or is superimposed, it represents not an article
of faith (although it can certainly come to act as one of ideology)
but a structural strategy. As such, it has usually or often
been translated into a kind of economic, political or military
statement about the tribes which have or had it and which still
point to this fact with pride, even though in the kaleidoscopic
social change of Maghrib today the notion of khams khmas may
now only be turning into an increasingly dim memory.

NOTES

1 For an interesting discussion on this problem as a situation
  of 'social contract', see Lahbabi (1958).
2 Ibid.
3 Cf. Evans-Pritchard (1940) passim, as well as Fortes and
  Evans-Pritchard (1940). For more recent and succinct

statements, cf. Bohannan (1963); and Beattie (1963); and
Lienhardt (1964), pp. 71, sq. Also, cf. the articles
Lineage and Segmentation by Middleton (1964). None the
less, Durkheim (1893), clearly enunciates some of the
'first principles' of segmentary theory, and this in connection with the Berber-speaking Kabyles of Algeria!

N.B. This paper was completed for publication early in
1965. However, as of 1967, it may prove to be that not all
Moroccan tribes are segmentary. The researches of Dr
Clifford Geertz and of Mr Lawrence Rosen, of the University
of Chicago, on the Ait Youssi tribe near Sefrou would
appear to indicate a 'fission-fusion' process within this
group (which appears to be 'segmented' rather than 'segmentary' as such), determined at least in part by the
easy acquisition by strangers of tribal lands (and hence
of tribal *droit de cité*) through purchase. This process
seems also to be a result of existence of horizontally (rather
than vertically) structured social units which are, in turn,
geographically rather than genealogically based. Mr Rosen
(personal communication, 1966) thinks at present that such
may prove to be the case for most Middle Atlas Berber
tribes, none of which, to my knowledge, exhibit the
structural feature of khams khmas or 'five fifths', which
is so crucial to my argument in this article. (Contrary to
what I suggest in note 13, I discovered in mid-1965 that
the Zayan are not organized into 'fifths', and that their
fifteen clans are both entirely heterogeneous in composition
and geographical in base, rather as Rosen would suggest
for the Ait Youssi.)

4 Principles exist, however, to be violated, and I know of at
least six cases in the Rifian tribe of Aith Waryaghar in
which full brothers, by father and mother, were pitted
against each other to the death, as indicated above.

5 Clan, subclan, lineage and sublineage, and whatever labels
one wishes to give to such unity, almost invariably form
continua in Moroccan tribal areas. I define 'clan' as the
maximal segment of any tribe or tribal group whose members say 'We are all descended from X', or 'We all came from
Place Y', but who are unable to trace their genealogical
connection to X or to take it back to Place Y except in a
general kind of way. A 'subclan' is a unit, defined in
exactly the same way, within a clan – and any clan may
have two or more subclans. On the other hand when one
reaches the level of the 'lineage', further down, this unit
may be defined as the largest unilateral descent group (in
this case, of course, unilateral means agnatic) whose
members can and do trace their ascent to a common agnatic
ancestor, through X number (usually 4 or 5) generational
links – and the 'sublineage' is constituted by each of the
lineage branches, generally descended from the sons of
the original founder of the lineage. In any segmentary

system (and the Moroccan system is no exception) the
terms, Arabic or, Berber, by which given social units are
designated are far fewer than the actual number of segmentary levels themselves (I, II, III, IV, V, etc., starting
from the tribe to the clan and then on down), so that a local
term often covers several units, on neighbouring levels
up and down, at once, and thus attests to the essential
fluidity and implied continuity of the system. I say 'implied'
because it is a curious fact that the names given to segments remain fixed and immutable through time, illogical
though this may seem or be.

6 Cf. Michaux-Bellaire (1932), p. 163.
7 This listing is taken from Capdequi Y Brieu (1923), and
from Alta Comisaria de Espana en Marruecos (1955), plus
tribal listing in Arabic under the same auspices. This work
is henceforth referred to simply as 'Nombres'.
   Also in the southwestern Jbala, the tribe of Bni Zarwal,
and in the southeast, those of both Branis and Dsul fall
into this category. I am indebted to Mr Lawrence Rosen for
calling my attention to the first-mentioned; for the last two,
cf. Trenga (1916).
8 Cf. 'Nombres'.
9 Cf. 'Nombres'.
10 Cf. 'Nombres'.
11 Cf. Protectorat de la République Française au Maroc,
Secrétariat Général du Protectorat, Service du Travail et
des Questions Sociales (1939). This work is henceforth
referred to as 'Répertoire'.
   The Sraghna case is confirmed by Julien Couleau (1968),
pp. 61-2.
12 Querleux (1915), pp. 13-14; Michaux-Bellaire (1920),
p. 198. Cf. also Marcel Lesne, 'Histoire d'un Groupement
Berbère: les Zemmour'. Thèse complémentaire pour le
doctorat présentée à la Faculté des Lettres et Sciences
Humaines à Paris, 1959, p. 47. In the Zimmur case, however, the division into khams khmas seems to have been
effected by the government of pre-protectorate Morocco
for taxgathering purposes (not always successful): but the
evidence is not entirely clear in this case.
13 Cf. 'Répertoire'. Whether the Zayan themselves constitute
such a group I have no idea although Aspinion (1946),
p. 20, implies that they do.
14 Cf. Abès (1918), p. 16, who says they are divided into
two *nisfs* (halves) of five *khmas* each.
15 Cf. 'Répertoire', for Ait Warayin and Ait Mgild.
16 Cf. Bousquet (1956), pp. 113-230. My reference is to
p. 114.
17 From my own field notes, 1959-61.
18 Montagne (1930), p. 155.
19 Cf. Hart (1962), pp. 515-27.
   Some Rgibat say that in their case the khams khmas are

the five countries over which they roam: Morocco, Algeria, the Spanish Sahara, Mauritania and the Sudan; but this is probably an a posteriori explanation.

I have also been informed by Mr Ross Dunn that Captain Jigue in a CHEAM paper reports the Dwi Mni' of the Algero-Moroccan 'confins' region as having a system of five fifths, apparently in this case for purpose of dividing up agricultural land in the Ghir Valley.

20 Gellner (1973).

21 Montagne (1930), note 2, pp. 175-6.

22 Coon (1931), p. 92. Coon's listing of the 'fifths' of Aith Waryaghar, as of Igzinnayen and Thimsaman, however, is wrong in detail on all three; and his functional analysis of the 'fifth' situation in the last mentioned tribe is wrong as well. As I have said, I do not regard Igzinnayen, Thimsaman or Axt Tuzin (not cited by Coon in this connection) as 'type cases'; on Iqar'ayen, which Coon also gives as an example, I cannot properly judge.

23 Cf. Hart (1970b).

24 Aith Waryaghar say that only 'true' Waryaghar clans and lineages which live in the plain have 'brothers' in the Jbil Hmam. The Mountain of Doves (1,930 metres at its highest point, the tomb of the most major tribal saint, Sidi Bu Khiyar, who was not a member of the 'fifth' of Imrabdhen, but a stranger – and hence his holiness), in Timarzga, the southernmost part of the tribal territory; and, of course, vice versa. All true Waryaghar identify with the Jbil Hmam.

25 Cf. note 23.

26 Cf. note 23.

27 Jager Gerlings and Jongmans (1955). The thesis of this work, the coverage of which is extremely superficial, is contained in its title.

28 An extremely accurate breakdown of [C]Atta segmentation, with which my own data only disagree in a few very small particulars, is given in Spillmann (1936), pp. 73-98; and a second good published account, complied by de Monts de Savasse, appears as Appendix no. 7 in Jager Gerlings and Jongmans (1955), pp. 73-5. Spillmann's book, despite numerous defects and inaccuracies in detail, is nonetheless the best available introduction to Ait [C]Atta society and culture thus far. His skeleton of the system of khams khmas is excellent, for instance, but he was only dimly aware of the function of these 'five fifths' – and one looks in vain in his book for any treatment of other crucial sociopolitical institutions, such as, for instance, the collective oath.

29 There is no single term in Berber to denote the totality of Ait [C]Atta or any other such top-level grouping; and as the [C]Atta at least, all claim descent from a single ancestor (whether real or putative does not matter here). I prefer the designation 'supertribe' to the usual French-employed

term 'confederacy', although the latter applies very justly
to the Ait Yafalman. Below the top 'supertribal' level, for
the ^{C}Atta, there is of course the khums, and below this the
taqbilt, pl. *tiqbilin*, which I here label 'clan'; and then
several levels of *ighsan* (sing. *ighs*. lit. 'bone'), or agnatic
lineages. Again here, terminology of social units is fluid.

30 Cf. Gellner (1963), pp. 145-58, and more particularly his
more recent article (1973), p. 5. Some of the 'lay' tribes
of the area (e.g. the Ait Hadiddu of the Ait Yafalman confederacy, and the Ait Siddrat) do not observe this type of
election, but, to my knowledge, all the rest do. A good
many French authors have spoken of the 'rotational' aspects
of the question, but only Gellner discovered 'complementarity', and how the two principles form part of a single
and functional whole.

31 Spillmann (1936), p. 61.

32 Ibid., p. 57.

33 Gellner (1973).

34 All the tribes in the Central Atlas region, including Ait
^{C}Atta, had other kinds of chiefs - 'transhumance chiefs',
'storehouse chiefs', 'market chiefs', etc - for different
reasons and different functions, but these were usually
appointed by the 'land chiefs' of the district, not elected
by rotation and complementarity.

N.B. In late 1966, well after the completion of this paper
for publication, a question of some importance occurred to
me, one to which the answer still seems elusive: what is
the real function and/or utility of all the 'frills' involved
in the recurrent phenomena of 'level-skipping' and/or
'leap-frogging' which so often characterize the election of
chiefs by the twin processes of rotation and complementarity? It is of course argued by Berbers that when chiefs
exist and act at the odd-numbered levels of segmentation,
they are elected by their constituents on the even-numbered
levels, and that thus participation in the system, in one
way or another, occurs at all levels and is open to all
members of the group or groups concerned. Nonetheless,
the query remains as to whether or not simple ratification
on all but the top level (as amongst the Ait Bu Iknifen of
Imidar) could not really have served the same purpose. In
other words, from a Malinowskian standpoint, what is the
need for all these structural embellishments? This is, of
course, a 're-thinking' of my own field data on my part,
and it can indeed be argued that these embellishments
represent variations in the overall 'structural model' (if
there *is* an overall structural model); but the matter is
genuinely puzzling, even so. Considerations of space
prevent any discussion of the system as it existed amongst
the Ait ^{C}Abdi (Ait Sukhman) of the Kusar Plateau in the
Central Atlas, for example; but their particular version of
rotation and complementarity is far and away the most

complex one that I have yet encountered, far more than any
of the ^CAtta versions. Dr Ernest Gellner of the London
School of Economics has previously reached similar conclusions, based on his own research amongst them.

35 Gellner, pp. 7-8.

36 There was an intermediary court at Tiraf n-Ait ^CAlwan,
near Tagunit, as well, at which, also, in the unlikely event
that a case could not be resolved at Igharm Amazdar, a
final verdict was rendered; but to discuss this and many
other peripheral problems in full would be to complicate the
issue unnecessarily for the purposes of this paper.

37 Cf. note 6.

38 For an excellent discussion of the Arabization of the North
African countryside, cf. William Marçais (1961a),
pp. 171-92.

39 Michaux-Bellaire (1932), pp. 167-171.

40 Ibid., p. 163. It is also worth noting that the work of
Michaux-Bellaire and of a good many of his French successors gives the impression (an erroneous one) that the
system of khams khmas was exclusively a makhzan-imposed
structure. How could this have possibly been the case for
the Ait ^CAtta and Aith Waryaghar, both of which groups
were fully in *siba* until pacification? The fact of makhzan
imposition of the system of 'five fifths' represents only one
possibility on the available spectrum. That there are others
I have already demonstrated. It might, however, have been
the case that in the makhzan-imposed examples the idea was
taken from tribes in *siba* and turned into an instrument of
more effective control.

41 Notably Burke (1976); Dunn (1977); and Laroui (1977). In
Laroui's case, however, if it is true that, as a number of
observers of the Moroccan scene have noted, he is ultimately an étatiste and an apologist for the makhzan, then
it follows that he places greatest primacy and reliance upon
source materials that are written and in Arabic, as he has
himself proclaimed often enough. But it also follows, ipso
facto and by definition, that sources that are oral Berber
and tribal either fall outside his arena of competence or
that he sees fit, deliberately, to ignore them. Cf. also the
interesting review of Laroui by Joffé (1979).
   I would also call attention to the interim publication of a
major work of my own: Hart (1976b), especially chapters
10 and 11, pp. 235-78, 279-312. In this book the traditional
five-way division of the *haqq*, the tribal and/or market
fine for murder, is spelled out in full.

42 Dunn (1977), pp. 50-67.

43 As I have already acknowledged in previous publications,
I am indebted to Prof. Lionel Galand for calling this point
to my attention. Cf. his article Les Quinquegentanei
(Galand, 1970). For further details cf. Boulifa (1925),
pp. 10-13. The only surviving usage of the concept which

is demonstrably Berber from a linguistic standpoint seems
to be that of the group name Tashumsha among the Znaga-
speaking *zwaya* or 'clerical' tribes of the Gibla in southern
Mauritania. Cf. Miské (1970), p. 108. In this case as well,
one tradition attributes a common ancestor to all five clans,
but the ties between clans become very distended with
time; another, given me in Mauritania in 1973 by Shaikh
Mukhtar wuld Hamidun and Thomas Whitcomb, has it that
they are descended from five unrelated men, but that each
clan acquired a great many lineages through accretion,
over time, and that in this case a true khams khmas
principle was obviously not operative, or became inoperative in due course.

44 Watt (1961), pp. 110-11, and Watt (1956), p. 89. Over
twelve centuries later, Muhammad Ahmad, the Sudanese
Mahdi, did the same, although warning his companions not
to be fraudulent with the booty. Cf. Shaked (1978),
p. 99.

45 Abu l-ᶜAbbas Ahmad bin Muhammad Ibn 'Idhari, Al-Bayan
al-Mughrib fi Ajbar Muluk al-Andalus wa l-Maghrib, in
Ambrosio Huici Miranda, Un Fragmento Inedito de Ibn
'Idhari sobre los Almoravides, 'Hespéris-Tamuda', II, 1,
1961, p. 49. I am indebted to Thomas Whitcomb for bringing to my attention both this source and another by Hermann
von Wissmann, art. Badw. In the latter the author notes
from certain pre-Islamic and Epigraphic South Arabian
inscriptions that the root *kh-m-y-s* (*khumays*, no doubt
derived from *khums*) referred to a regular army while
a'rab referred to bedouin contingents mounted on camels
or on horseback during the conflicts in southern Arabia in
the second century A.D.

46 Westermarck (1926), pp. 445-78.

47 Harden (1963), p. 88.

48 As for instance among the Apache as suggested by Kaut
(1974), pp. 45-70.

49 Aubin (Descos) (1906), p. 23.

50 Lafuente (1968), pp. 71-116, esp. pp. 78-9.

51 Hoover (1978), pp. 62-5, 155-8.

52 Cf. note 42.

53 Cf. in particular Burke (1973), pp. 175-200. Certain other
papers in the same symposium, although not my own (Hart
1973), reach substantially the same conclusion.

54 It may be claimed by some that I am here merely substi-
tuting a concept of quintessence (in its original meaning
of fiveness) for the one of binarism which was so favoured
by the French. I do not think so, for the very good reason
that binarism does not enter conscious thought in Morocco,
whereas quintessence most certainly does - in the formerly
tribal countryside, in any case.

55 Cf. the work of Mr Henry Munson, Jr., in the Bni Msawwar
of the northwestern Jbala as well as that of Mr E.G.H. Joffé

in the southern Jbala around Wazzan.
56 Cf. Eickelman (1976), pp. 105-21.
57 Cf., *inter alia*, Vinogradov (1974), pp. 51-78. However,
   in this particular case, the Ait Ndhir may well have been
   an eighteenth-century makhzan creation in the first place;
   and the implications of this fact are not fully explored in
   the work in question.
58 Ibid., p. 53.
59 Ibid., p. 56.
60 For further information of relevance, cf. Hart (1970a);
   Hart (1970b), vol. 2, pp.3-75; Hart (1973); Hart (1975);
   Hart (1976a); Hart (1976b); Hart (1977), pp. 75-105.

BIBLIOGRAPHY

Abd el-Krim et la République du Rif (1976), Actes du Colloque
   International d'Etudes Historiques et Sociologiques, 18-20
   Janvier 1973, Paris: François Maspéro.
Abès, M. (1918 reprint) Les Aith Ndhir, 'Archives Berbères',
   Paris: Ernest Leroux.
Alta Comisaria de España en Marruecos (1955) 'Nombres de los
   Musulmanes Habitantes en la zona de Protectorado de España
   en Marruecos: Territorios, Kabilas, Fracciones y Poblados
   de la Misma', Tetuan.
Aubin (Descos), Eugène (1906) 'Morocco of Today', London:
   Dent, and New York: Dutton.
Aspinion, (Cmdt.) Robert (1946) 'Contribution à l'Etude du
   Droit Coutumier Berbère Marocain: Etude sur les Coutumes
   des Tribus Zayan', 2nd ed. Casablanca: Ed. Moynier.
Beattie, John (1963) 'Other Cultures', London: Cohen & West.
Bohannan, Paul (1963) 'Social Anthropology', New York: Holt
   Rinehart & Winston.
Boulifa, Saîd A. (1925) 'Le Djurdjura à Travers l'Histoire:
   Organisation et Indépendance des Zouaoua (Grande Kabylie)',
   Algiers: J. Bringau.
Bousquet, Georges-Henri (1956) Le Droit Coutumier des Ait
   Haddidou de l'Assif Melloul et de l'Isellatène, 'Annales de
   l'Institut d'Etudes Orientales à Alger', t. XIV, pp. 113-230.
Burke, Edmund, III (1973) The Image of the Moroccan State
   in French Ethnological Literature: A New Look at the Origins
   of Lyautey's Berber Policy, in Ernest Gellner and Charles
   Micaud, eds, 'Arabs and Berbers: From Tribe to Nation in
   North Africa', London: Duckworth, and Lexington, Mass.:
   Heath, pp. 175-200.
Burke, Edmund, III (1976) 'Prelude to Protectorate in Morocco:
   Precolonial Protest and Resistance, 1860-1912', Chicago:
   University of Chicago Press.
Capdequi y Brieu, Mauricio (1923) 'Yebala: Apuntes sobre la
   Zona Occidental del Protectorado Marroqui Espanol', Madrid:
   Editorial San Fernando.

Coon, Carleton Stevens (1931) 'Tribes of the Rif', Harvard
    African Studies, vol. IX, Cambridge, Mass.: Peabody
    Museum.
Couleau, Julien (1968) 'La Paysonnerie Marocaine', Paris:
    Editions du Centre National de la Recherche Scientifique
Dunn, Ross E. (1977) 'Resistance in the Desert: Moroccan
    Responses to French Imperialism, 1881-1912', London:
    Croom Helm, and Madison: University of Wisconsin Press.
Durkheim, Emile (1960) 'De la Division du Travail Social'
    (1893), 7th edn, Paris: Presses Universitaires de France.
Eickelman, Dale F. (1976) 'Moroccan Islam: Tradition and
    Society in a Pilgrimage Center', Modern Middle East Series,
    no. 1, Austin & London: University of Texas Press.
Evans-Pritchard, E.E. (1940) 'The Nuer: A Description of the
    Modes of Livelihood and Political Institutions of a Nilotic
    People', Oxford: Clarendon Press.
Fortes, M., and E.E. Evans-Pritchard (1940) 'African Political
    System', Oxford and London, International African Institute.
Galand, Lionel (1970) Les Quinquegentanei, 'Bulletin de
    l'Archéologie Algérienne', IV.
Gellner, Ernest (1963) Saints of the Atlas, in Julian Pitt-Rivers,
    ed., 'Mediterranean Countrymen', Paris and The Hague:
    Mouton, pp. 145-58.
Gellner, Ernest (1969) 'Saints of the Atlas', London: Weidenfeld
    & Nicolson, and Chicago: University of Chicago Press.
Gellner, Ernest (1973) Political and Religious Organisation of
    the Berbers of the Central High Atlas, in Ernest Gellner and
    Charles Micaud, eds, 'Arabs and Berbers: From Tribe to
    Nation in North Africa', London: Duckworth, and Lexington,
    Mass.: Heath, pp. 59-66.
Gellner, Ernest and Charles Micaud, eds (1973) 'Arabs and
    Berbers: From Tribe to Nation in North Africa', London:
    Duckworth, and Lexington, Mass.: Heath.
Gould, Julius and William J. Kolb, eds (1964) 'Dictionary of the
    Social Sciences', London: Tavistock.
Harden, Donald (1963) 'The Phoenicians', London: Thames &
    Hudson.
Hart, David Montgomery (1962) The Social Structure of the
    Rgibat Bedouins of the Western Sahara, 'Middle East Journal',
    XVI, 4, pp. 515-27.
Hart, David Montgomery (1970a) Conflicting Models of a Berber
    Tribal Structure in the Moroccan Rif: the Segmentary and
    Alliance Systems of the Aith Waryaghar, 'Revue de l'Occident
    Musulman et de la Méditerranée', VII, 1, pp. 93-9.
Hart, David Montgomery (1970b) Clan, Lineage, Local Com-
    munity and the Feud in a Rifian Tribe, in Louise E. Sweet,
    ed., 'Peoples and Cultures of the Middle East: An Anth-
    ropological Reader', 2 vols, New York: Natural History Press,
    vol. 2, pp. 3-75.
Hart, David Montgomery (1973) The Tribe in Modern Morocco:
    Two Case Studies, in Ernest Gellner and Charles Micaud,

eds, 'Arabs and Berbers: From Tribe to Nation in North Africa', London: Duckworth, and Lexington, Mass.: Heath, pp. 25-58.

Hart, David Montgomery (translator and editor) (1975), 'Emilio Blanco Izaga: Colonel in the Rif', Ethnography Series, HRAFlex Books MX3-001, New Haven: Human Relations Area Files, 2 vols.

Hart, David Montgomery (1976a) De 'Ripublik' à 'République': Les Institutions Sociopolitiques Rifaines et les Réformes d'Abd el-Krim, in 'Abd el-Krim et la République du Rif', Colloque International d'Etudes Historiques et Sociologiques, 18-20 Janvier 1973, Paris: François Maspéro, pp. 33-45.

Hart, David Montgomery (1976b) 'The Aith Waryaghar of the Moroccan Rif: An Ethnography and History', Viking Fund Publications in Anthropology, no. 55, Tucson: University of Arizona Press.

Hart, David Montgomery (1977) Assu u-Ba Slam (1890-1960): De la Résistance à la 'Pacification' au Maroc (Essai d'Anthropologie Sociale), 'Les Africains', tome V, Paris: Editions Jeune Afrique, pp. 75-105.

Huici Miranda, Ambrosio (1961) Un Fragmento Inédito de Ibn Idhari sobre los Almoràvides, 'Hespéris-Tamuda', II, 1, p. 49.

Hoover, Ellen Titus (1978) 'Between Competing Worlds: The Rehamna of Morocco on the Eve of the French Protectorate', Ph. D. dissertation, Yale University.

Jager Gerlings, J.H., and D.G. Jongmans (1955) 'The Ait Atta: From Nomadic to Settled Life', Royal Tropical Institute, Dept of Physical and Cultural Anthropology, no. 50, Amsterdam.

Joffé, E.G.H. (1979) review of Abdallah Laroui, La Naissance du Nationalisme Marocain, 1830-1912, in 'Journal of African History', XXII, 2.

Kaut, Charles (1974) The Clan System as an Epiphenomenal Element of Western Apache Social Organization, 'Ethnology', XIII, 1, pp. 45-70.

Lafuente, M. (1968) La Vie Humaine dans un Groupement Berbère du Haut Atlas de Marrakech: les Ait Oucheg, 'Revue de Géographie du Maroc', no. 14, pp. 71-116.

Lahbabi, Mohammed (1958) 'Le Gouvernement Marocain à l'Aube du XXe Siècle', Rabat: Editions Techniques Nord-Africaines.

Laroui, Abdallah (1977) 'La Naissance du Nationalisme Marocain, 1830-1912', Textes à l'Appui, Paris: François Maspero.

Lesne, Marcel (1966/7) Les Zemmour: Essai d'Histoire Tribale, 'Revue de l'Occident Musulman et de la Méditerranée', II, 2, 1966, pp. 111-54; III, 1, 1967, pp. 97-132; IV, 2, 1967, pp. 31-80.

Lienhardt, Godfrey (1964) 'Social Anthropology', Oxford: Oxford University Press.

Marçais, William (1961a) Comment l'Afrique du Nord a été Arabisée, in William Marçais, 'Articles et Conférences',

Publications de l'Institut d'Etudes Orientales à Alger, XXI,
Paris: Adrien-Maisonneuve, pp. 171-92.

Marçais, William (1961b) 'Articles et Conférences', Publications
de l'Institut d'Etudes Orientales à Alger, XXI, Paris: Adrien-
Maisonneuve.

Michaux-Bellaire, Edouard (1920) 'Villes et Tribus du Maroc',
vol. V: 'Rabat et sa Région', tome III: 'Les Tribus', Paris:
Ernest Lerous.

Michaux-Bellaire, Edouard (1932) 'Villes et Tribus du Maroc',
vol. X, tome I: 'Les Doukkala', Paris: Ernest Leroux.

Middleton, John (1964) art. Lineage, in Julius Gould and
William J. Kolb, eds, 'Dictionary of the Social Sciences',
London: Tavistock, pp. 391-2.

Middleton, John (1964b) art. Segment(ation), in Julius Gould
and William J. Kolb, eds, 'Dictionary of the Social Sciences',
London: Tavistock, pp. 627-8.

Miské, Ahmed-Baba (1970) 'Al-Wasit: Tableau de la Mauritanie
au Début du XXe Siècle', Paris: Klincksieck.

Montagne, Robert (1930) 'Les Berbéres et le Makhzen dans le
Sud du Maroc: Essai sur la Transformation Politique des
Berbères Sédentaires (Groupe Chleuh)', Paris: Félix Alcan.

de Monts de Savasse (Capt. R. (1955), Appendix to J.H. Jager
Gerlings and D.G. Jongmans, 'The Ait Atta: From Nomadic to
Settled Life', Royal Tropical Institute, Dept. of Physical and
Cultural Anthropology, no. 50, Amsterdam.

Pitt-Rivers, Julian, ed. (1963) 'Mediterranean Countrymen',
Paris and The Hague: Mouton.

Protectorat de la République Française au Maroc. Sécrétariat
Général du Protectorat, Service du Travail et des Questions
Sociales (1939) 'Répertoire Alphabétique des Confédérations
de Tribus, des Tribus, des Fractions de Tribus et des
Agglomerations de la Zone Française de l'Empire Chérifien,
au 1er Novembre 1939', Casablanca: Imprimeries Réunies
(Vigie Marocaine et Petit Marocain).

Querleux (Capt.) (1915 reprint), Les Zemmour, 'Archives
Berbères', I, 2, Paris: Ernest Leroux.

Shaked, Haim (1978) 'The Life of the Sudanese Mahdi', New
Brunswick, New Jersey: Transaction Books.

Spillmann (Capt.) Georges (1936) 'Les Ait Atta du Sahara et la
Pacification du Haut-Dra', Publications de l'Institut des
Hautes Etudes Marocaines, XXIX, Rabat: Félix Moncho.

Trenga, G. (1916) Les Branès, 'Archives Berbères', vol. 1,
no. 3, pp. 200-18.

Vinogradov, Amal Rassam (1974) 'The Ait Ndhir of Morocco',
Museum of Anthropology, University of Michigan, Publication
no. 55, Ann Arbor: University of Michigan Press.

Watt, William Montgomery (1956) 'Muhammad at Medina', Oxford:
Clarendon Press.

Watt, William Montgomery (1961) 'Muhammad: Prophet and
Statesman', Oxford: Oxford University Press.

Westermarck, Edward (1926) 'Ritual and Belief in Morocco',

2 vols, London: Macmillan.

Wissmann, Hermann von, art. Badw, in 'Encyclopédie de l'Islam', tome I, p. 910.

4 CULTURAL RESISTANCE AND RELIGIOUS LEGITIMACY IN COLONIAL ALGERIA *

Fanny Colonna

The study of the part played by religious forces in the resistance to colonisation in Algeria raises questions concerning religious movements with conspicuous political roles, in other words questions about the relation between the political and the religious spheres. In the nineteenth century, these movements consisted of marabouts – holy men, dervishes – and brotherhoods, and in the twentieth century, of Reformism, that is the Salafiyya movement. Since the days of Marx and Weber it surprises no one that every religious movement also fulfils social and political functions, that it expresses, as Engels said, very definite class interests. But the specific nature of these movements raises special difficulties:

One approach involves treating them in a general way – as is most common in the study of messianisms(1) – as the total reaction, of an entire society, to external aggression. In these cases, it is the reactive character, the relation between aggression and response, which is stressed. This relationship is particularly visible, for instance, in the messianisms invoking Christian themes, for instance in the Congo.

The weakness of this approach is that, concentrating on the external functions of the movement, it fails to analyse its internal functions. It does so because it refuses to see that every religious reaction (just as every political one), far from being a total reaction of a total society, is always the reaction of a specific group, or a coalition of groups, and that at the same time as it fulfills certain functions of defence, it also and necessarily constitutes an internal 'settlement of accounts'. It is for this reason that the typological researches which try to select a series of religious reactions and in effect treat these as myths are so unsatisfactory; they forget that even the science of myths presupposes an intimate knowledge of the groups that produced them. (2) The establishing of the relation between the resistance movements and their social base, which is always done for political movements, is seldom made clearly for religious movements; and above all, it is almost never done thoroughly. Consider the following:

1 When the counter-strategies to imperialism of colonised lands are analysed, it is plain that they are diverse (political, cultural, economic), but the question is not raised: may they not

*The author wishes to thank Ernest Gellner for his help in preparing the English version of this text, first published in 1974.

express the strategies of groups that are mutually hostile, and hence, may they not be mutually incompatible?

2 The second danger, the obverse of the first, consists of seeing the religious character of these movements as nothing but a camouflage of the class struggle. If one interprets the most down-to-earth writings of Engels in a reductivist manner and for reductivist ends, no doubt one can indulge in a jolly game of producing social explanations for these movements. But in doing this, one abandons any serious attempt to explain why indeed these are religious movements rather than political ones, and what they owe to this specifically religious character.

Algeria is precisely a good specimen for the interpretation of religious movements as religious movements, in as far as the present central importance of religion in social and political life is, as we shall see, linked to religious factors operating during the colonial period. This has happened, it seems to us, not directly, as is the case in other countries where religious forces seize power, but indirectly: religious factors have succeeded in creating an autonomous religious sphere.

Hence the real question is not so much about the role of the religious forces in the resistance to colonisation as (1) the effects of the colonial situation on the relationship of various religious forces to each other, and to political forces, and (2) the consequences of the changes which took place during the colonial period in the present constitution of the religious sphere, and in its relationships to political authority.

This formulation leads to the decision to speak only of religious forces, and to ignore the role, which is considerable, of Islam as an ideology in the anti-colonial resistance. It is known in Algeria that all parties, and virtually all movements, have used Islam at one stage or another of their development. No doubt this is itself an interesting sign, but it does seriously complicate the problem.

I ECSTATIC AND PURITAN FORMS OF RESISTANCE

In Algeria, French colonial domination saw two kinds of religious forces rising up against it: the brotherhoods and the *mrabtin* (roughly, living saints) in the nineteenth century, and the Reformist ^{c}*ulama* (religious scholars) in the twentieth.(3) It is important to note a feature which distinguishes these movements from others provoked elsewhere by colonisation:(4) these are not new religious forms. The coexistence of scripturalist currents is evident from the very beginnings of Islam, as is the often virulent struggle for influence between the doctors (^{c}*ulama*) on the one hand, and the representatives of the religious orders on the other.(5) Algeria was no exception, and these two tendencies had been locally present for centuries.

A Ecstatic religion (Sufis)
It is a kind of misuse of language to use the same word to
describe extremely diverse things - but in this case orientalists
and anthropologists merely follow popular usage. In Arabic,
the generic term for describing Muslim mysticism - Sufi - evokes
a memory of great intellectual giants such as Ibn al-^CArabi or
al-Ghazzali, but it also suggests primitive folk religion with its
amulets, exotic ceremonies and half illiterate 'saints'. The confusion is inevitable, and Muslim mysticism or sufism always
contained both elements, a sophisticated intellectualism in a
framework of esoteric doctrines, as well as simple-minded
manifestations of folk religion.(6) In Algeria the term designates
tribal groups organised around a holy lineage, practising an
annual cult of the ancestor tied to the seasonal cycle,(7) as
well as extensive mystical brotherhoods whose area of recruitment extends beyond North Africa, and which are both hier-
archic and egalitarian, i.e. based on freely chosen membership
rather than birth but well organised and managed by an elected
shaikh.(8) It is essential to note that both these types of
groupings claim to be within strict Sunni orthodoxy, even if
they are accused of heresy by the urban doctors.
   As stated, the maraboutic grouping is an element of the
tribal structure, within which it functions not only as a means
of religious organisation but also of social organisation. The
holy lineages act as economic and political mediators between
other lineages and between tribes.(9) By contrast the order
organisation cuts across tribes and states, and one might even
say that in a certain way it is anti-tribal.(10) Whilst it is of
course a religious community, it also acts as a freemasonry with
economic and other secular purposes.(11)
   Although the great sharifian families (i.e. such as claim descent from the Prophet) took part in resistance in various forms
till the end of the nineteenth century, maraboutic organisation
was quickly subjected to the effects of colonisation, and its
disintegration followed that of tribal society.(12) By contrast
the orders played an increasing part in religious and more
generally cultural resistance, and also on occasion in military
resistance. In effect, the clerkly calling is not warlike in Islam,
but in the case of holy war even the clerics are obliged to take
up arms. Finally, if during the first twenty years of colonisation the activity of the religious orders was mainly that of its
high dignitaries, from 1850 onwards one may say that it became
above all activity of the petty clergy; thenceforth this was the
only activity which was possible, but it was also to be extremely
effective for at least half a century. As is known, Amir ^CAbdal-
Qadir was the son of a shaikh of the Qadiriya order, and
Mohammad bin ^CAbdallah, better known as Bu Ma^Cza, who led a
revolt in the Dahra region,(13) was of the Tayyibiya order,
and the sharif Bu Baghla and Si Saddiq Bil Hajj, leaders of
the insurrections of 1850 and 1859 in Kabylia, were affiliated to
the Rahmaniya.(14) Finally Shaikh al-Haddad, who provided

crucial help for al-Muqqrani during the insurrection of 1871, was one of the two shiyukh of the Rahmaniya.(15)

Seeing them in perspective after a century and a half, in relation to the events of the time and to their first chroniclers (Neveu, Rinn, Richard, to name only the best), the religious orders of the nineteenth century appear as a species of religious confederacy, equipped with mutually diffentiated ideologies (even though all of them are attached to Sufi Islam), able to 'raise' thousands of warriors, but also of assembling hundreds of scholars, and even of devising and implementing extremely complex strategies, sometimes in conflict with each other.(16) Toward the middle of the century, after it became clear that military action was no longer possible, the orders continued to carry on a kind of psychological campaign, having previously been the motive force of something which was very close to revolutionary war (fomenting uprisings everywhere so as to exhaust and rout the enemy):

'Every *talib* (Qur'anic teacher) in Algeria signs up as a "brother" in a religious order', wrote Y. Turin. 'These orders have connections and contacts with a whole set of lodges, related to each other and dispersed as far as Morocco, Tunis, and Tripoli. The influence of such a personage is far greater than that of a mere village teacher: he is teacher and vicar all at once ... because he knows how to write, he is often involved in family affairs. Because he can read, it is he who deciphers the notes from the district officer for the shaikh. He is not just the learned man, but the only learned man, the light and oracle of the tribe.'(17)

Spied on by the army, economically anaemic, greatly reduced in their intellectual importance, the *zawiyas* (lodges), local bases of the orders, became mere dispensaries of rumours, the inspiration of opposition against the school brought in by the colonial administration, against attempts at preventive medicine and the establishment of civil registration, in other words against all measures aimed at establishing effective administrative controls.

B Scripturalist religion: the reformist ᶜ*ulama*
The resistance of the brotherhoods exhausted itself at the end of the century. The colonial school, medicine and adminstration all prevailed – we shall see later just by what means. However, twenty years after the start of the century a new movement takes over. At first sight at least everything about the Reformist Movement stands in contrast to the religious forces which were described above. The brotherhoods were legion (Rinn, in 'Marabouts et Khouan', describes nineteen main ones, not counting secondary branches, at the end of the nineteenth century), as were the maraboutic lineages (which no doubt could be counted in their hundreds). By contrast the ambition of the ᶜulama was to create a single movement, which would unite under the banner of one doctrine all the theological schools and even incorporate schismatic tendencies.(18) The social basis of the

movement is urban and bourgeois: Bin Badis, its main leader,
is the offspring of an old and rich family from Constantine,
and he as well as his main disciples (al-CUqbi, Ibrahimi) were
trained in a scriptural manner in Arabic universities of Tunisia
or the Middle East. Though their Association conquers a large
number of semi-urban agglomerations (amongst many others,
Mila, Setif, Laghouat, Nedroma), it nevertheless always retains
an urban style and clientele, made up of large and small traders,
artisans and middle-range officials.

Ideologically, Bin Badis and his disciples consciously derive
from Near Eastern Reformism, and in particular the Salafiya
movement: their masters are Muhammad CAbduh and Rashid
Rida.(19) Being an insistence on the return to the tradition of
Muhammad and the teaching of the ancients (Salaf), Algerian
reformism was bound to struggle on two fronts, against the
'ossified conservatives and the repudiators' (the former being
Mrabtin, taken as representatives of Sufism, and the latter
the 'emancipated' and the 'assimilators', such as the members
of the Mouvement Jeune Algérien).(20) Against the former,
it preached the emulation of historic models (Salaf), well-based
on the orthodox tradition, in contrast to those of the living
or legendary saints. At the same time it exhorted the Algerians
to see Islam as a religion-for-this-world, which obliges the
faithful to take part in social and political life, and to acquire
the new techniques which are needed for the protection and
progress of the community.(21) In opposition to the mystic
doctrines of the brotherhoods, the reformists rehabilitated
money and efficiency, denounced the wastage of time, and any
conspicuous consumption: here one can discern a puritan ethic,
a kind of Calvinism.

Against the threat of assimilation by western culture, the
Badisian Culama built up a powerful tool which, even if it did
not prove as effective as they expected, yet helped completely
to transform the cultural condition of Algeria between the two
wars (1920-40). Their network of private schools, cultural
circles and youth movements rapidly extended itself over the
country and affected, at least superficially, a good proportion
of youth, other than that which was purely rural.

The co-ordinated action of these scholastic and cultural
networks, the preaching in the mosques, and above all the
reformist press in Arabic, had a considerable impact on Algerian
society and played an important part in the growth of nationalist feeling in Algeria.(22) By its sheer existence, it challenged
the linguistic monopoly of the French language, and the control
of the religious apparatus. If it unmasked the cultural domination without yet, as we shall show later, being able to overcome
it, this was because the real conflict took place at the political
and economic levels, and not at the cultural one.

C Religious movements or political parties?
Unlike the religious orders of the nineteenth century, the

^culama never carried out direct political action, and still less any military action. Yet the temptation to interpret their movement as a political party is great, greater than is the case for their nineteenth-century predecessors. All the same it was not a political party: its message, its aims, and above all its enemies were religious. The men who composed it saw themselves and were seen as clerics, as 'guardians of faith' ('El Nadjah', 1938), and not as political militants. One cannot really claim that the movement changed its nature or its sphere of action from the fact that after the Muslim Congress of 1936, and till the death of Bin Badis in 1940, political themes became more prominent in its press. The politicisation of the ^culama, the consequence of the this-worldly vocation of the new faith, was closely tied to the debate concerning the problem of personal (legal) status. This was the issue of the loss of Muslim legal status through the acquisition of French citizenship, and hence was linked to the crisis of identity, religious and cultural as much as political. As for the brotherhoods, these must be seen in the proper light: it is true that they played a political and even military role, preparing risings, carrying out intelligence, just as peasant wars were indeed wars, and Thomas Munzer was an agitator. Nevertheless they remained religious movements – as were the peasant wars – in as far as they made use of religious means and codes (calls to the holy war, prophecy, eschatology) in a non-instrumental manner: it was a common set of religious ideas, the faith in a shared dogma with very definite secular implications, which enabled leaders and simple warriors to conduct a war of liberation as a war of religion.(23)

The question of the precise nature of the religious movements which visibly perform a political role cannot be evaded. Algerian Reformism is indeed contemporary with movements which overtly present themselves as political or at least as secular: such as the Mouvement Jeune Algérien, or the Voix des Humbles, and a little later the Étoile Nord Africaine.(24) Similarly, the insurrection of 1871 in its beginnings and the practice of al-Muqqrani were indisputably secular. It was only in its second stage, with the participation of Shaikh al-Haddad, that the movement became religious.(25) Thus there existed in the twentieth century, and even in the nineteenth, a secular resistance which is independent of the clerics. The issue clearly arises from the situation, once we reject the orientalist or islamological conception of the involvement of religion and politics in Muslim societies and hence of the concomitance of religious and political movements. For the answer in terms of 'social base' also is not satisfactory. In any case it is not simple. To take an example: the traditional bourgeoisie of Constantine which found expression at the end of the nineteenth century in the activity of local political notables, and which at that stage still seemed homogeneous,(26) in due course produced both the Reformist movement in the person of Bin Badis, and the Fédération des Élus, a modernist grouping which, as its name implies, undertook political activity of the legislative kind within the colonial framework.(27) How should one account for these divergent choices, laden with consequences for nationalist strategy, and for Algerian social stratification? No doubt one must invoke the rivalry of diverse segments within that bourgeoisie. We know nothing of the underlying principles of those oppositions, but it is important to note that they must have existed. The fact that Algeria lacked a political party representing the traditional bourgeoisie, and comparable to the Old Destour party in Tunisia,(28) may wrongly tempt one into overestimating the political character of Bin Badis's movement. On the contrary, the correct question is - why was such a party absent? Why did the bourgeois movement of 1887, in Mustafa Lacheraf's words, 'split in two'? What retardation or regression prevented the urban elites from doing anything other than either handling the political problems of their society in a foreign idiom (the ideology of 1789 and of the Declaration of the Rights of Man), or of insisting on the integrity of their national culture in an exclusively religious idiom? For lack of a sufficiently intimate knowledge of the social history of Algeria, we can only raise these questions; we cannot answer them.

II TWO ENEMIES, TWO SOCIETIES

It is no accident that in colonial Algeria, Sufism was the expression of tribal resistance, and Reformism of urban bourgeois resistance. Similarly it is no accident that the latter replaced the former at a given moment of colonial history. There are in our view reasons for these facts:

- the type of colonial aggression was very different before and after 1880;
- the condition of Algerian society, which was profoundly transformed under the impact of colonialism. In particular, the balance of forces within that society changed - for even in a conquered and crushed society, there exists a balance of forces.

A The threat of arms and the threat of law
There is no harm at this stage in following temporarily the example of the 'reactionists', in other words adopting a culturalist viewpoint and to seeking the key to the varieties of religious resistance in the differences of style in colonial aggression.

Until about 1870,(29) French intrusion in Algeria was above all military, incoherent, unpredictable, and left the Algerians with the impression that it was ephemeral. Apart from certain exceptions in time (1858-60) or in space (mainly the towns), the country was absorbed by war, or rather a series of wars, and was the object of military domination, that of the Bureaux Arabes, which practised indirect rule. The danger which this

conquest constituted, great though it was seen to be by men
such as ^cAbdal-Qadir or Ahmad Bey, yet did not seem to strike
the rest of Algerian society as something fundamentally new or
unmanageable. Basically, those rough-neck generals, who
indulged in raids and in smoking out their enemies, who signed
spurious treaties or traded in arms with their enemies, were
altogether in the good North African tradition. Algerian society
reacted to them in the same way as it had done to the Christian
Reconquista of the sixteenth century,(30) or to the Ottoman
conquest later: in part by the resistance of the aristocracy of
shurfa (descendants of the Prophet), and above all of the
religious orders. An aggression which seemed to be directed at
local groups, and to be devoid of any visible overall strategy,
provoked a traditional or classical reaction, which was itself a
reaction of groups (tribes or brotherhoods).(31) Colonial policy
in the proper sense of the word did not appear on the scene
till later, after 1871.(32) It was in effect during the aftermath
of the failure of the great insurrection of 1871 that, for the
first time, a coherent colonial policy, officially assimilationist,
and in fact profoundly destructive, was implemented under the
influence of the settlers. It was then that one saw the application of a whole series of measures with converging effects: the
land tenure laws of 1873 and 1887, following the decrees of
1863, aimed at the breakup of 'native' property and at the collapse of tribal structures, the extension of civilian administration which subjected a large part of the native population to
the power of the settlers, increase of native taxation, abolition
of traditional justice, persecution of the holy lodges, and the
establishment of an 'official' clergy, controlled by the state. To
this one must add the establishment in 1881 of a Natives' Status,
which was a special jurisdiction allowing convictions for 'specifically native' offences, the establishment of civilian registration
for Muslims, openly presented as a 'denationalisation' measure,
and finally the massive Gallicisation of place names aimed at a
kind of transformation of the social landscape.(33) These assimilationist measures, for the first time numerous and coherent,
reinforced the disaster begun by the repression and confis-
cation which followed the insurrection of 1871. Thus one can
place between 1870 and 1880 the destruction of the economic
and social base of traditional society, of its system of land
tenure and of its aristocracy.(34) The reaction of the reformist
^culama, organised, almost bureaucratic, was that of a society
which has passed from the tribal stage to that of a nation
divided into classes. It was reacting to a definite scheme, that
of the settlers, in a struggle in which the stakes were the
seizure of its own economic base, the destruction of its social
organisation, and the elimination of its own culture. The reaction was simultaneously new, through its modernist style, and
in particular by its content, and yet it also had a 'déjà vu'
character: the ^culama played an important part before and
indeed throughout Muslim history.

This repetition of an old theme makes possible another interpretation of Reformism: historically, the ^{C}ulama also reached
the height of their influence when the state was strong and
centralised and the towns prosperous (Turkey in the eighteenth
century, or Tunisia at the beginning of the nineteenth for
example).(35) For the rise of Bin Badis's movement does indeed
coincide with the marked urbanisation and an undeniable con-
solidation of the central power, though French and Turkish
centralisms have nothing in common. It may be that the dis-
astrous circumstances brought about by colonisation for
Algerian society as a whole were, relatively speaking, more
favourable to the growth of a body of scholars and a scripturalist movement than those which, for example, prevailed in the
Regency of Tunis. The account of the social base of the two
movements will enable us to return to this point.

B From a segmentary to a class society
If religious resistance changed in style it was not only because
colonial aggression changed in character, but also because
Algerian society was radically transformed, and, after the passage of half a century, it was no longer the same groups that
expressed themselves through the religious message. It was
only within the religious sphere that both owing to colonisation
but also no doubt because of the historic stage of the society
itself, class conflict could express itself. Only Sufi resistance
manifested itself in the nineteenth century, because only tribal
Algeria was at that stage capable of a reaction to the conquest.
The towns had been destroyed or occupied by the French; the
townsmen, reduced to naught, had either fled or were ruined.(36) Moreover, there are various signs suggesting that
the urban bourgeoisie was numerically unimportant, economically weak, politically feeble already under the Turks.(37)
Under such conditions, it is not surprising that its role in the
resistance to the French and in religious resistance in particular
had been negligible. The Islam of the brotherhoods is well
adapted to what was then the non-urban world; the co-existence
of tribes led either by *jwad*-s (war chiefs) or by *mrabtin* (religious chiefs), and linked by those vast religious parties the
brotherhoods. The complex tissue of nineteenth-century risings,
from ^{C}Abdal-Qadir to al-Muqqrani, conveys the rivalries and the
alliances of those three dominant and competitive elements of
the tribal world.(38) This tribal world does, of course, have
relations with the urban world. All in all these indicate domination by the cities and the Regency, but the French conquest
totally overturned this particular balance.

When, half a century later, colonisation had broken up this
tribal society, had created or re-created the towns and initiated
a class stratification, some new solution had to be found. The
brotherhoods, even if they continued to exist, became all at
once anachronistic, and politically and socially ineffective.(39)
Just as the fragmented reaction of the brotherhoods was adapted

to a society fragmented into tribes, so the new conditions brought about by colonisation made both necessary and possible the establishment of an overall movement, at the level of the country as a whole, capable of organising isolated individuals, without a tribal framework, through a puritan and individualistic religion, and also capable of borrowing the colonisers' organisational models. In both cases, religion remained the only principle of unitary organisation(40) against colonisation, and it acted through a religious code, as in each case a centralist political tradition was lacking.(41)

C The new balance of power

Whilst providing the best or only available reaction at a given stage, each of the two movements corresponded to a balance of forces within Algerian society itself and within its religious sphere: the increasing importance of the movements of brotherhoods during the nineteenth century was linked, paradoxically, on the one hand to the elimination of the towns and on the other to the disintegration of tribal society.(42) In the one case, the competition by the body of scholars closer to orthodoxy now disappeared, and in the other, the hereditary and unquestioned prestige of the holy lineages maintained itself. But in any case, it was a class of local notables with a good tribal basis which represented the orders. The struggles between brotherhoods and marabouts reflect only the struggles of factions within the tribal world.(43) The emergence of Reformism clearly expressed the restoration of an urban bourgeoisie and its determination to recover its place in society, or perhaps to secure a position it had never previously possessed.(44) Even if, owing no doubt to the colonial situation, the movement was not accompanied by the economic success which one might expect from the carriers of the puritan ethic, one cannot fail to see in this movement the expression of the rising bourgoisie. Hence it is not surprising that its class enemies came from the tribal aristocracy. Yet as they were a religious movement, the reformists never attacked tribal aristocracy except by way of attacks on maraboutism and on the brotherhoods. This was so not for tactical reasons but because the confrontation in effect took place within the religious sphere, and it was only in this form that the society could formally express itself. They also conducted a parallel struggle against the 'mercenary clerics' trained, placed, and paid by the colonial power,(45) against the culture-eroding colonial education, against the obscurantist education by the holy lodges, and the superstitious perversions of the creed transmitted by the brotherhoods. Nevertheless, as each 'religion' had its own favourite catchment area it seems that the sphere of their competition was above all the intermediate zone between them, i.e. the new urban centres and townships established by colonisation. Moreover the existence of a semi-urban and in effect semi-rural clientele is one of the characteristic traits of Algerian and perhaps all North African scripturalism. Just as religious forces attained political ends in their struggle against the invader, so similarly, and for the same reasons, class conflicts found their expression in the religious sphere, and were fought out between religious forces and for religious stakes. The reasons why external resistance and internal conflict both found religious expression are the absence of an internal political sphere, and the social and cultural 'backwardness'.(46) But unlike the resistance to the coloniser which expressed itself in both religious and political terms, the conflict between the bourgeoisie and the landed aristocracy seemed unable to find any but religious expression: it seems to find no other formal articulation. This is even more true of the conflict between the traditional and modernist bourgeoisie. In any case there were probably no internal struggles more violent prior to 1954 than those between the Reformers and, on one front, the marabouts, and on the other, the 'evolués'. One thing is certain: the society as a whole and the participants themselves saw in it nothing but 'violent theological disputes'. Internal dissent, shunned as scandalous when the society as a whole is in a state of subjection, can only be allowed about vital questions which concern the very existence of the society, that is questions of faith.

III   THE ESTABLISHMENT OF A UNIFIED RELIGIOUS SPHERE

The change in religious leadership which can be seen in Algeria between the nineteenth and twentieth centuries is not a special case of that oscillation between ecstatic and puritan Islam described by E. Gellner.(47) According to that author, who takes over and applies to Islam a scheme elaborated by David Hume in his 'Natural History of Religion', the succession of religious movements in Islam can be compared to a kind of pendulum, swinging from a kind of Right (ecstatic religion, strongly hierarchical, with charisma) to a kind of Left (scripturalism, puritanism, egalitarianism, based on communal consensus). One could also translate this into Weberian terms: within Islam, Sufism fulfils a prophetic role, competing with the priesthood which is the guardian of orthodoxy (the ^culama), sometimes combated by it, and sometimes incorporated by it.(48) Contrary to this 'classical' structure, the historic process observed in Algeria towards 1920 is irreversible. The pendulum comes to a halt on the Left: Reformism acquires religious legitimacy for itself and outlaws ecstatic religion.

A The conquest of religious legitimacy
What has happened? In this struggle, the existence of the colonial context, of which one may seem to have lost sight, is decisive. History shows that, theologically speaking, no victory is possible. In fact, the very idea of a 'theological victory', independent of the operation of the social forces involved, is an

absurdity from a sociological viewpoint. The various stages of
the conflict are ever linked to the political power game. In the
case of colonial Algeria the political factor intervenes negatively.
As it was easy enough to prove that on occasion, at various
given places and times, the religious aristocracy and the orders
had compromised with the colonial administration, and as in any
case it was clear that neither the one nor the other was able
to arrest an educational, legal, religious policy that was perilous
for the nation, the Reformist movement soon came to appear as
the only defender of Islam and of Arabic culture. Correspondingly, the brotherhoods and the marabouts were not merely
eliminated from the game, but outlawed, because they had
betrayed Islam (by encouraging superstition) and the nation
(by dealing with the invader). This condition lasted as long as
the colonial period. In effect, there was no reason to question
it, as long as the colonial situation lasted. With Independence,
a new situation might have arisen had the state chosen to be
neutral in this conflict. But the state did take sides by endowing
Algeria with an established religion by the constitution of 1963,
by turning Bin Badis into a national hero and finally by adopting the ideology and aims of the Reformist movement (Islamisation and Arabising of the country). Thereafter, the religious
pattern which began in 1920 was consecrated and reinforced.

The consequence of the outlawing of the orders and marabouts and the unconditional legitimation of the Reformers was
in effect the establishment of a unified and organised religious
sphere, within which Reformism, having once - roughly from
1920 to 1930 - fulfilled the role of prophecy, now fulfilled that of
priesthood, that is, of the established religion. At the same
time, Sufi religion was demoted from the rank of prophecy, which
it traditionally possessed, to that of magic - as an objective
profanation of religious (and political) orthodoxy.(49) Thus
the relationship between orthodox and Sufi Islam, the faith of
cities and the faith of tribes, which had once been in competi-
tion(50) now became, through the colonial distortion of the
classic pattern of religious forces, a matter of institutionalised
domination. In his 'Contribution to the History of Primitive
Christianity',(51) Engels remarked in 1894 that 'the risings
in the Muslim world, notably in Africa, constitute a curious
contrast ... [with Christian risings]. These movements spring
from economic causes', he continues, 'even if they have religious camouflage.(52) But even if they succeed, they leave the
economic conditions intact. Thus nothing has changed, and
the clash becomes recurrent.' It is this cyclical pattern (which
exemplifies equally well the three generation theory of Ibn
Khaldun and the pendulum of Ernest Gellner) which Algerian
history now overcame through colonisation, both because this
was no longer a country of 'towns and tribes' but a class
society, and because a position of dominance permitted the use
of political means (the discrediting of one of the parties in
question) for religious ends (conquest of legitimacy). For once,

politics was not conducted through religious means but in an
openly political way. If the scheme described by Engels –
possibly taken from Ibn Khaldun(53) – could last so long it
was because historically religious monopoly was not possible in
Muslim countries and hence there was no unified religious
sphere. The coexistence of towns and tribes, interdependent
yet in permanent opposition, did not allow the establishment of
a single religious authority, just as the central state never
really controlled all the tribes. Probably, the holy lineages were
what made visible and credible the incorporation of tribes in
universal Islam,(54) whereas the brotherhoods made possible
the mobilisation of a set of tribes for centralised ends (though
not necessarily urban ones, as is shown by the case of ᶜAbdal-
Qadir), a mobilisation which was always legitimated in religious
terms. But the religious and political problems of the tribes
were as much beyond the reach of the ᶜulama as they were
beyond that of the central state. It is ecstatic Islam which
provided solutions for them. Thus there was no question of
eliminating it completely. Moreover the two equations, 'ecstatic
religion is tribal' and 'scriptural religion is urban', are the
effect rather than the cause of this organisation of the religious
sphere. In effect, in the nineteenth century one observes, at
least in Tunisia and Morocco,(55) that almost all the ᶜulama,
like, for that matter, the personnel of the central state, were
members of brotherhoods. This confused situation indicates
at least two things: (a) that the brotherhoods occupied an
inherently ambiguous position, being leagues that were neither
tribal nor scripturalist and (b) that given the lack of a well-
organised religious sphere there was nothing to prevent one
belonging at the same time to two diverse and even hostile
religious systems, which also suggests that these systems were
not always hostile, but only became so when the scripturalist
establishment was strong, as was the case in the Ottoman
Empire, or in twentieth-century Algeria. By radically changing
the Algerian social structure, and in particular by modifying
urban/tribal relations, colonisation made possible a ranking in
the religious sphere. It also did so because it eliminated the
integrative role of ecstatic religion: education on the one hand,
and a struggle against the invader on the other, took over
this task.

B Autonomy of the religious sphere
What happened in the religious sphere is thus the consequence
of what happened in the rest of society: a change in tribal/
urban relations, the establishment of a strong central power,
and finally the emergence of one or even of a number of bourgeoisies. All the same, the total success of the urban bourgeoisie in the religious sphere, its partial but nevertheless
significant success in the cultural and especially the scholastic
sphere, did not have their counterparts in the economic and
political spheres. The cause of this lies not merely in the control

of the economy by the dominant colonial class, but also in the existence of another and modernist bourgeoisie, educated in colonial schools, which soon monopolised the liberal professions, and whose sons were destined to be the technocrats of independent Algeria.(56) This is something which was to have weighty consequences. In the sphere of language, Arabic, even though rehabilitated by the efforts of the movement, and restored to the front rank in the nationalist ideology and in the minds of most Algerians, could not replace French, either during the colonial period or even thereafter, at least from the viewpoint of social usefulness. As for the scholastic establishments controlled by the movement, they were unable, either by their recruitment or by the standing of the positions to which they gave access, to compete in any serious way with the colonial establishments. They were composed almost exclusively of primary schools providing literary and religious rather than scientific training, and they recruited mainly from the middle and lower classes of towns and townships, and from families which had never had any contact with the colonial system of education. Moreover it was almost impossible, prior to independence, to move from one system to the other. Finally the control over the attribution of paper qualifications and of employment, exercised by the colonial power, ensured that the jobs to which these schools led were less well paid, and in many cases less prestigious than those to which it was possible to aspire if one had gained entry to the colonial system.

Thus in the end the Reformers attained only part of their manifest aims, namely the conquest of religious legitimacy. But they failed to attain their latent aim, namely the conquest of economic and/or social power for the traditional bourgeoisie. This apparent contradiction is made possible by the establishment of an autonomous religious sphere, whose logic is not always the same as that which governs other sectors of social life.

It is this autonomy which, in our view, makes possible the role of religion in the present social structure. The use of a 'neutral' medium or pantheon, or in any case of one which can be progressively neutralised, is clearly a very significant support for any authority, whatever it may be. Of course, in sociology and in politics, autonomy does not necessarily mean independence: a neutral and autonomous religious sphere can be perfectly well dominated by political authority, which is what seems to be the case.

In brief, though the power structure in the religious sphere is closely linked to the historic transformations of the various groups, it would be altogether mistaken to see them as a mere reflection of the relations these groups have with each other. The religious sphere constitutes a kind of imaginary projection, the fantasy of the commercial bourgeoisie.

C The consequences of the fantasy

This has two sets of consequences, those which were expected and those which were not.

It is not surprising (though it was not inevitable) that the nationalised and centrally planned economic power should be in the hands of a group of 'specialists' (engineers, planners, academics) who possess European paper qualifications, and who inherit the cultural capital accumulated by an 'evolué' bourgeoisie, produced by colonisation.

But what was already less predictable was the division of labour between modernists and traditionalists, that is to say those who possess a Gallic cultural capital, and those who possess an Arabic one, the latter acquiring control of religion, justice and education as well as a part of administration. Hence the current importance of the linguistic conflicts in Algeria which are, in effect, struggles between factions of the ruling class for the control of executive power (which is always strategically crucial in an underdeveloped country). Of course, these repercussions of the fantasy are a consequence of the specific character of this state, and like the other repercussions which are to be described below, were initially simply one amongst the available options, and incidentally, they were independent of each other.

The existence of an established religion, mentioned in the Constitution, and the ex post facto exaggeration of the historic importance of the Reformists (the hagiography of Bin Badis), as well as the creation of a Ministry of Traditional Education and of Religion, on the Moroccan model, responsible for all that concerns religion (the independent schools, the nomination and control of religious officials), gives the state a complete hold over the religious means of production, similar to that which it exercises over the economic means of production. This no doubt is the least anticipated consequence of the fantasy of the bourgeoisie. The fact that the Reformist movement emerged and grew within the religious sphere, in other words, that it was at no point of the struggle an effective rival to any of the groups which constituted the FLN in 1954, is probably a precondition of this situation. The established religion is not merely a means of controlling the religious output, but also constitutes an important means for the manipulation and imposition of symbols. It is incidentally striking to note that the progress of Islamisation accompanies and reinforces (as well as being reinforced by) the strengthening of local administration.

In this respect, Algerian policy displays great sociological insight, which more modernist Muslim countries have not always possessed, to cite Tunisia or Ataturk's Turkey as examples.(57) Thus in Turkey, one could see the installation of a State religion (despite the desire to destroy the Ottoman religious establishment), through the creation of a General Directorate of Religious Affairs, with a body of religious officials - but this was unable to perform an integrative role, which in any case the state did not expect from it. The legal or formal elimination of ecstatic religion simply cut off the modernised cities from the countryside, especially in the East of the country. By contrast, in Algeria, the symbolic outlawing of ecstatic religion was not accompanied by any kind of judicial coercion. Despite a significant spontaneous revival of the activities of marabouts and orders,(58) everything seems to indicate the advance of the official religion, geographically socially and in authority, even in the non-urban zones and in the poorer urban districts. The impact of the state and that of puritan religion advance hand in hand.

As there is no doubt that a puritan Islam, in its Reformist form, is an ideology favourable to the development of a modern and centralist state, to ethical and technical rationalisation,(59) it may be that thanks to religion, and by a truly Weberian paradox, Algeria will be a successful variant of Turkey. The importance of religion in contemporary Algeria leads us not merely to history (in various senses), but also to the function of religion. There is a parallel between this socialist republic and that most dynamic of nineteenth-century entrepreneurial bourgeoisies, the English: 'one can explain its religious leanings', as Engels observes in 'Socialism, Utopian and Scientific'.

NOTES

1 Cf., for example, G. Balandier, 'Sociologie actuelle de l'Afrique Noire', Paris: PUF, 1955, V. Lanternari, 'Les Mouvements religieux des Peuples opprimés', Paris: Maspéro, 1962 (first Italian edn, 1960), M. Sinda, 'Les Messianismes congolais', Paris: Payot, 1972.
2 Cf., for example H. Desroches, 'Dieu d'Hommes, Dictionnaire des messianismes et millénarismes de l'aire chrétienne', Paris: 1969, W. Muhlman, 'Messianismes révolutionnaires du Tiers Monde', Paris: Gallimard, 1968 (first German edn, 1961), A. Fernandez, African Religious Movements, in 'Sociology of Religion', ed. R. Robertson, London: Penguin, 1969.
3 A slight qualification is required. It would not be accurate to say that brotherhoods and holy men played no part in resistance in the twentieth century. It is simply that they acted differently from the way they had acted in the nineteenth century, and also in a way different from that of the ^culama at the same time.
4 Cf., for example, works already cited in note 1, and also P. Worsley, 'The Trumpet shall Sound', London: Paladin, 1970 (first edn 1957). Certain new cults emerge from the post-Independence conflicts. Cf. G. Althabe, 'Oppression et Libération dans l'Imaginaire', Paris: Maspéro, 1969.
5 Dugat, 'Histoire des Philosophes et des Théologiens

musulmans', Paris: 1880, Rinn, 'Marabouts et Khouan', Algiers: Jourdan, 1884, chapter VIII.

6 L.C. Brown, The Religious Establishment in Husainid Tunisia, in 'Scholars, Saints and Sufis', ed. N.R. Keddie, Berkeley: University of California Press, 1972, p. 79.

7 Cf. A. Berque, Essai d'une Bibliographie critique des Confréries musulmanes algériennes, in 'Bulletin de la Société d'Archéologie et de Géographie d'Oran', 1919, T. XXXIX, p. 208.

8 Cf. Rinn, op. cit., chapters V, VI, VII. According to Rinn, three elements are essential for a brotherhood: link with orthodoxy, expressed by a chain of holy men leading back to the Prophet; the existence of a written body of rules and prayers, specific to the brotherhood in question; and finally a hierarchical organisation, encompassing, from top to bottom, a shaikh, moqqadem-s and the mass of khouan.

9 On this point see E. Gellner, 'Saints of the Atlas', London: Weidenfeld & Nicolson, 1969. The type of organisation specified in this work for Morocco also operates in Algeria, where however it has never been so well described.

10 Cf. E. Gellner, Doctor and Saint, in 'Scholars, Saints and Sufis', op. cit., p. 325, and L. Valensi, 'Le Maghreb avant la Prise d'Alger', Paris: Flammarion, 1969.

11 Cf. A. Berque, op. cit., pp. 207 and 224.

12 Maraboutism has remained alive in the regions not much affected by colonisation, directly or indirectly, such as for instance in the western Sahara.

13 Cf. Richard, 'Etude sur l'Insurrection du Dahra', Algiers, 1846.

14 Cf. Hanoteau et Letourneux, 'La Kabylie et les Coutumes Kabyles', Algiers: Jourdan, 1880.

15 Cf. Rinn, 'Histoire de l'Insurrection de 1871 en Algérie', Algiers: Jourdan, 1882.

16 On this point, see A. Nadir, Les Ordres religieux et la Conquête française, in 'Revue Algérienne des Sciences Juridiques, Economiques et Politiques', vol. IX, no. 4, December 1972.

17 'Affrontements culturels dans l'Algérie coloniale, Ecoles, Médicines, religion, 1840-1880', Paris: Maspéro, 1971.

18 As is well known, Sunni orthodoxy recognises the existence of four schools of law (rites): Maliki, Hanafi, Shafi[c], Hanbali. The most common in North Africa is the Maliki rite. As for sects, the only one represented to any significant extent in Algeria is the Kharijite one (with the Bni Mzab). Bin Badis desired and specially valued a dialogue with this community. Cf. A. Merad, 'Le Réformisme musulman en Algérie de 1925 à 1940', Paris: Mouton, 1967, p. 222. Also, the reformers proclaimed the unity of the Faith and stressed the links forged by history, in opposition to ethnic divisions.

19 Concerning the Reform movement in the Near East, see
   Henri Laoust, 'Les Schismes dans l'Islam', Paris: Payot,
   1965, chapter XI.
20 Taken from the title of an article in 'El Shihab', a reformist
   journal, entitled Between the rigid Conservatives and
   those who repudiate, May 1931, p. 322.
21 Cf. 'El Shihab', November 1933, p. 472, and January 1937,
   p. 477.
22 One can gauge this indirectly from the religious consensus
   observable today amongst the political and military elites,
   with their very diverse origins and backgrounds.
23 M.E. Spiro, criticising E. Leach's analysis of Kachin religion ('Political Systems of Highland Burma') writes in
   Religion: Problems of Definition and Explanation in 'Essays
   in Religious Anthropology' (1966, taken from French
   translation, Paris: Gallimard, 1972): 'In effect it is only
   because the Kachin believe that the verbal symbol "Nat"
   represents a real being – and not simply a social structural
   symbol – that they are able to manipulate this belief for
   political ends.' See also P. Bourdieu, Genèse et Structure
   du Champ religieux, in 'Revue Française de Sociologie',
   XII, 1971: '... the categories of theological thought are
   that which makes it impossible to conceive and to carry on
   a class war as such, whilst allowing it to be conceived and
   conducted as a war of religion'.
24 Cf; C.A. Julien, 'L'Afrique du Nord en Marche', Paris:
   Julliad, 1952.
25 Cf. Rinn, 'Histoire de l'Insurrection de 1871', op. cit.
26 On this subject, see Mostafa Lacheraf, 'Algérie, Nation et
   Sociéte', Paris: Maspéro, 1965, chapter 6: Résistance
   urbaine et lutte nationale depuis 1830, esp. pp. 185-92.
27 Cf. 'L'Afrique du Nord en Marche', cited above.
28 Concerning the relations between the Young Tunisians, the
   Old Destour party, the New Destour Party, and the
   Reformists in Tunisia, see A. Zghal, The reactivation of
   Tradition in a post-traditional Society, 'Daedalus', winter
   1973, pp. 225-52.
29 Concerning the first stage of the conquest, 'the Algeria of
   the soldiers', see C.A. Julien, 'Histoire de l'Algérie contemporaine', T.I, Les conquêtes et les débuts de la Colonisation, Paris: PUF, 1964. See also the summary provided by
   Ch. R. Ageron, 'Histoire de l'Algérie contemporaine
   (1830-1964)', Paris: PUF (Que sais-je), 1964.
30 See C.A. Julien, above, and also A. Nadir, op. cit.
31 The great risings of the Aures (1859), of Hodna (1860), of
   the Oulad Sidi Shaikh (1864), indicate precisely that all
   did not seem lost, and that local groups still believed in
   armed resistance.
32 'The Algerian problem was distorted from the day Algeria
   was called a colony', Napoleon III apparently said in 1860.
   (Cf. Ch. R. Ageron, op. cit., p. 31.) In other words,

till the fall of the Second Empire, the very principle of colonisation was not accepted.

33 On the totality of these measures and the colonial policy between 1871 and 1896, see Ch. R. Ageron, vol. I, 'Les Algériens musulmans et la France', Paris: PUF, 1968, and also Ageron, 'Histoire de l'Algérie contemporaine', op. cit., pp. 45-71.

34 On the economic and social consequences of the great land tenure laws of the end of the nineteenth century, see André Nouschi, 'Enquête sur le niveau de vie des populations rurales constantinoises de la conquête jusqu'en 1919', Tunis, 1961 (Thèse de Lettres).

35 Cf. 'Scholars, Saints and Sufis', cited above, part I: Scholars: the Ulama.

36 Cf. M. Lacheraf, 'Algérie, Nation et Sociéte', op. cit., p. 158 et seq. See also Malek Bannabi, 'Mémoires d'un Témoin du Siècle', Algiers: SNED, 1965. (This volume concerns Constantine in particular.)

37 Cf. A. Berque, La bourgeoisie algérienne, in 'Hespéris', 1948.

38 Cf. A. Nadir, op. cit.

39 Cf. A. Merad, op. cit., Chapter III, part 2.

40 It was not till 1954 that a Front (the FLN) took the initiative of united action against the coloniser.

41 Likewise, one can see the role of the Catholic Church in Malta or Ireland in a similar light. This 'political' function of the Church in a local context is particularly well studied in the work of J. Boissevain, 'Saints and Fireworks', London: Athlone Press, 1965.

42 Cf. A. Berque, 'Bibliographie sur les Confréries', cited above, and also A. Nadir, op. cit., p. 824.

43 Perhaps this was a matter of conflict between investment in culture and landed property, or between senior and junior branches of a lineage. We know too little about the recruitment of the brotherhoods to be able to say with confidence. Perhaps it was also a conflict between clerics-by-birth and clerics-by-scholastic-achievement.

44 Cf. A. Berque, 'Hespéris', op. cit.

45 Whilst Muslim 'clergy' is in principle elective, unremunerated and independent of political authority, Rinn writes (op. cit., p. 103): '... every Muslim priest (sic) paid and protected by central authority, thereby places himself in a false position - for, with the Koran in its hand, priesthood takes precedence over temporal sovereignty.'

46 Engels wrote, in the 'Peasant War': 'The Middle Ages retained from the lost old world nothing but Christianity, as well as some half-destroyed towns, deprived of all their civilisation. The result was that, as in all primitive stages of development, the priests obtained a monopoly of intellectual culture, and culture itself assumed a theological character.' (Quoted from French edn, Editions Sociales,

pp. 99-100.) The use of such purely evolutionist schemata
is never satisfactory. Nevertheless a comparison with
Tunisia, such as we have attempted above, suggests that
we are here dealing with a regression.

47 Cf. Pendulum Swing Theory of Islam, in 'Sociology of
Religion', op. cit., and Post-traditional forms of Islam;
the Turf and Trade, and Votes and Peanuts, in 'Daedalus',
winter 1973.

48 Cf. Max Weber, 'The Sociology of Religion', London:
Methuen, 1966. P. Bourdieu, Une interprétation de la
théorie de la religion selon Max Weber, 'Archives Européennes de Sociologie', XII: I, 1971.

49 On the distinction between magic as deliberate profanation
or inverse religion, and magic as objective profanation or
displaced/dominated religion, see P. Bourdieu, Genèse et
Structure du champ religieux, 'Revue Française de Sociologie', XII, 1971, pp. 308 and 309.

50 There was competing preaching of the towns to the tribes,
for example during the maraboutic wave of the sixteenth
century, of the tribes towards the towns as in the case of
the Almoravides, the Almohades, or of the Mahdi of Khartoum (1881-5).

51 Marx and Engels, 'On Religion' (quoted from French edn
'Sur la Religion', Paris: Editions Sociales, 1972, pp. 311
and 312).

52 The hypothesis of 'camouflage' (as contrasted with a code
familiar to all) is perhaps even more implausible for Muslim
societies than for Christian ones.

53 This seems very likely, in the light of the note: 'At the
end of a hundred years they (the bedouin) find themselves
in precisely the same condition as the others (the towns-
folk). A new purification is necessary, and a new Mahdi
emerges. The game restarts.' A French translation of Ibn
Khaldun was available at the time when Engels wrote these
lines (1894), namely that of de Slane (1862-8).

54 Cf. E. Gellner, Doctor and Saint, in N. Keddie, op. cit.

55 Cf. L.C. Brown, The Religious Establishment in Husainid
Tunisia, cited above, and E. Burke III, The Moroccan
Ulama, 1860-1912, an Introduction, in the same volume.

56 In the previous generation, this group found political
expression in the UDMA with Ferhat Abbas, and in the
succeeding generation it finds its home within the framework of the nationalised corporations and of central
planning.

57 For Tunisia, see the article by A. Zghal, in 'Daedalus',
cited above. For Turkey, see N. Yalman, Islamic Reform
and the Mystic Tradition in Eastern Turkey, in 'Archives
Européennes de Sociologie', X: I, 1969.

58 This remains to be analysed properly. One can already see
its outlines. All the same, one ought to be able to understand the services performed for the symbolic order by

subordinated religion which accepts such a status. Similiar
re-activations can be observed in Egypt (cf. Morroe Berger,
'Islam in Egypt Today', Cambridge University Press, 1970)
and in Tunisia (cf. S. Ferchiou, Zarda ou la fête mara-
boutique en Tunisie, paper presented to the 'Ist Congress
for the Study of Mediterranean Cultures under Arabo-
Berber Influence', Malta, April 1972, proceedings due to
be published by SNED, Algiers, and in 'L'Homme', XII,
no. 3, 1972).

59 This can be exemplified for instance in the Tafsir (Koranic
commentary) of Bin Badis, Cf; A; Merad, 'Bin Badis,
Commentateur du Coran', Algiers: SNED, 1972.

5   SUFISM IN SOMALILAND: A STUDY IN TRIBAL ISLAM
I.M. Lewis

PART I

INTRODUCTION

A description and analysis of religion have now come to be
regarded as essential components in any satisfactory study of
society. In no case, probably, is this more necessary than in
that of an Islamic people where the study of Islam tends to
throw as much light on the social structure as the study of
the social structure does upon religion. This close interdependence has always been particularly clear in Muslim societies with a state-like structure where the Sharī'a (the religious
law in the widest sense) has had a wide field of application,
although, of course, with the progressive Westernization of
the Islamic world the gap between the spiritual and temporal
realms is again widening (cf. Gibb, 1947; Milliot, 1949; Fakhry,
1954). But the conformity of social and religious structure is
equally far-reaching in a tribal Muslim society although it may
not at first sight appear so.(2) Somali society is a case in point.
This essay sets out to examine the role of Sufism in the social
structure of the Somali and is designed to elucidate the nature
and function of Somali genealogies.

It is unnecessary here to justify the ethnic classification
'South-Eastern Cushites' which embraces the Somali, Afar,
Saho, Galla, and Beja, and which rests upon similarities in
material and social culture, including religion, and upon physical and linguistic affinities, and certainly in the case of the
first four, upon traditions of common origin.(3) I assume here
that the pre-Islamic religion of the Somali was that of a Cushitic
Sky God (Waaq), and that the present Muslim structure of
Somali society owes much to the interpretation of Islam in terms
of Cushitic belief. It follows that it should be possible to relate
the social functions of present-day Somali Sufism to syncretism
between the two religions. There are still a few tribes (e.g.
some of the Dir and Hawiye) who retain much of their Cushitic
culture correspondingly little modified. Again among some of
the southern tribes of Somalia, especially those of the Hawiye
tribal family, certain features of Cushitic religion still survive,
as will be shown, and much of the terminology and beliefs
of Cushitic religion persist and are applied to Islam. In
interpreting Cushitic belief and practice in their present form

127

among the Somali, the wider literature describing the religion
of the Afar, Saho, and Galla has been drawn upon, but I do not
deduce from Cushitic religion in general any belief or custom
for whose independent existence among the Somali there is not
ample evidence. It is not implied that all those features of
Somali social structure whose interaction with Islam is considered
are necessarily typically Cushitic, but simply that in the pre
Islamic state of Somali society they were related to Cushitic
institutions.

We shall deal particularly with Sufism and examine the way
in which its social organization, political, and religious structure are associated with the *baraka* of Ṣūfī shaikhs and their
personal genealogies which trace religious power to the lineage
of the Prophet Muhammad. It will be argued that the genealogical canalization of divine grace (*baraka*) dependent upon connexion with Muhammad's clan of Quraysh finds close parallels
in the social and religious functions of Somali tribal genealogies
(*abtirsiinyo*). These similarities in function between Arabian
genealogies in Sufism and genealogies in the traditional (pre-
Islamic) social order account for the ease with which the genealogies of Ṣūfī shaikhs are absorbed amongst the Somali and
underlie the Somali claim to descent from the Prophet. Such an
interpretation, it will be noticed, does not depend upon the
validity of the preceding assumptions on the nature of Cushitic
religion, but, since these seem well established it is relevant
to consider the incorporation of Ṣūfī genealogies(4) into the
Somali lineage structure in relation to them. The religious functions of Somali genealogies which centre in sacrifice at the
tombs of eponymous ancestors are, in the pre-Islamic state of
Somali society intrinsically a part of Cushitic religion and knowledge of the larger hierarchy of Cushitic spirit-refractions does,
I think, throw light upon the nature of sacrifice to the dead
and leads to some elucidation of the religious concepts attached
to Somali genealogies. Thus it is proposed (1) that Ṣūfī genealogies are adopted due to the close resemblances in their religious and political functions to Somali tribal genealogies, and
that (2) this assimilation corresponds to underlying similarities
in the Cushitic and Sūfi religious concepts which attach to
genealogies.

I PRELIMINARY

Some 4,000,000 in number, the Somali occupy the territories of
the Republic of Djibouti, eastern Ethiopia, the Somali Democratic Republic and the North Eastern Region of Kenya. They
are essentially nomadic pastoralists owning in abundance
sheep, goats, cattle, and camels used for milking and the
transport of the nomad's hut and possessions. In some parts
of southern Somalia oxen replace camels as burden animals.

Some temporary cultivation is practised, but as a whole,
there is little permanent cultivation in the barren pastureland
of the north. In the south, however, arable land occurs along
the courses of the two rivers which water Somalia (the Shebelle
and the Juba), and in the hinterland between them. Here
enclaved settlements of Negroes, Bantu and others, are engaged
in permanent cultivation, and some Somali tribes, especially
those of the Sab family, have adopted a sedentary mode of life.
Mixed farming is characteristic of this region, and, under the
stimulus of administrative development, there is an increasing
tendency for nomadism and transhumance to give place eventually to fixed-cultivation.

The Somali nation comprises two main subdivisions, the
'Soomaali' and the 'Sab'.(5) The Sab tribes form an extensive
wedge of cultivators between the rivers of Somalia and separate
the nomads of northern Somaliland from those of the south.
The 'Soomaali', who are numerically superior, despite the 'Sab'
for their sedentary way of life, for their obscure origins (Galla
and Negroid admixture is pronounced), and for their mixed
genealogies. Nevertheless, Sab are included in the designation
'Soomaali' by outsiders, in much the same way as the inhabitants
of the British Isles are frequently indiscriminately referred to
as 'English'. Within the Somali nation, Soomaali and Sab are
differentiated although there is an increasing tendency for the
Soomaali/Sab cleavage to be ignored in the rising tide of Somali
nationalism. Urbanized and Westernized Somali maintain that
discrimination is 'old-fashioned', that it is contrary to the
injunctions of the Prophet, and that it undermines the unity of
the Somali people. In practice and actual social relations, however, these ideals are often betrayed, which serves to indicate
how deeply engrained the traditional Somali social order is.
Still, within Somaliland, the cleavage remains the primary subdivision of the Somali nation, and in the rest of this paper(6)
I shall use the term 'Somali'(7) to include the Sab except where
a distinction is expressly stated. Each comprises a vast segmentary system of units which may be classified as: tribal
families (of which there are seven: Dir, Hawiye, Pre-Hawiye,
Ishaaq, Daarood, Digil, and Rahanwiin), confederacies, sub-
confederacies, tribes, and tribal sections. This terminology
which I have elsewhere described (Lewis, 1955, pp. 14-40) is
illustrated in Figure 5.1.

The tribe stands out as a clearly defined unit which embraces
the most generally effective social solidarity. Livestock-theft and
war characterize the relations between tribes, and intertribal
hostility is frequently of long standing. Internally the tribe
tends to be divided by feud amongst its fractions. Within the
tribe, however, homicide is normally settled peaceably by payment of blood-compensation. With the extended enforcement of
the European administrative system tribes are now also, whenever possible, obliged to settle their differences by payment
of compensation in place of further fighting. The obligations

Figure 5.1 Condensed genealogy of the Somali nation, representing segmentation into social groups, with specimen segmentation of one tribal family, the Daarood (Lewis, 1955, p. 15)

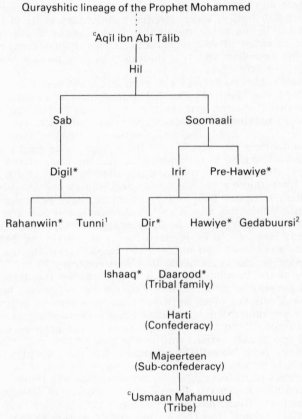

Qurayshitic lineage of the Prophet Mohammed

ᶜAqīl ibn Abī Tālib

Hil

Sab — Soomaali

Digil* — Irir — Pre-Hawiye*

Rahanwiin*   Tunni¹   Dir*   Hawiye*   Gedabuursi²

Ishaaq*   Daarood*
(Tribal family)

Harti
(Confederacy)

Majeerteen
(Sub-confederacy)

ᶜUsmaan Maḥamuud
(Tribe)

* Somali tribal families.
¹ The Tunni are a tribal confederacy rather than a tribal family.
² The Gedabuursi are of uncertain affiliation, they may belong to the Dir tribal family.

entailed by tribal membership are clearly formulated in the procedure for the adoption of strangers,(8) who undertake to share tribal responsibility in payment and receipt of blood-price and in other matters. In essence the tribe is of one blood, and it is, in short, a social, territorial, political, and to some extent religious unit closely similar to that of the Nuer (Evans-Pritchard, 1940) or of the Arab bedouin (Jaussen, 1908). It is not, however, entirely exogamous.(9) Like the total Somali society of which it is the microcosm, the tribe constitutes a balanced system of sections of various orders of segmentation. In some cases there may be no more than three orders of segmentation within the tribe, but in most cases there are at least four, for some tribes boast as many as 100,000 members. The average, however, seems to be about 20,000 tribesmen It will be seen that the Somali tribe is a relatively large unit, with a fairly high degree of internal segmentation.

In each political unit from the basic group of closely related families to the tribal confederacy, the elders constitute a council representative of the group's interests and convened by a political figurehead. In the tradition of the medieval period when the petty Muslim sultanates of southern Eritrea and north-western Ethiopia engaged Christian Ethiopia in war, chiefs are styled both by the Somali and by the Administrations as 'Sultan'. But this title does not imply that its incumbents wield authority over a centralized state and is not to be understood in the classical Muslim sense.(10) Normally the tribe recognizes a chieftain (called variously *boqor, garaad, ugaas*), as president of the tribal council. Yet not every tribe owns a common chief. In effect, a chief's authority derives from the structural situation - from the circumstances of tribal allegiance - and fluctuates with it. His power depends largely upon his personality. Thus the position of the Somali chief is closely similar to that of an Arabian shaikh (Montagne, 1947, p. 59).

Considerable religious power attaches to a chief. In the past chieftaincy seems to have been connected with rainmaking, and there is evidence that this function is still retained amongst the less Islamized tribes of the north-west corner of British Somaliland and of certain parts of Somalia. In many cases, the chief still conducts periodical rainmaking ceremonies (*roobdoon* 'seeking water') and the great rite (*lak*) performed in Somalia to mark the onset of the main rains. The chief's glance is referred to as 'the burning eye' (*il kulul*) and his person is so strongly endowed with power that among some closely related tribes it is usual for a visiting chief to avoid a face to face encounter with his equivalent and to be greeted indirectly by a representative. Consequent upon his special relation with God, a chief can call down blessing or misfortune upon his people and their stock. From the structural point of view, his most important function is to preside at the ceremonies which are held at the tombs of the eponymous tribal ancestors in commemoration of them. Each tribal section celebrates its founder at his shrine, offering up its own particular form of sacrifice(11) (Cerulli, 1923, p. 7). Where a hereditary chief is recognized members of his family (called *Gob*) represent him at sacrifices performed by the heads of subsidiary tribal fractions. In the case of tribal confederacies with a chiefly lineage

the same procedure is followed in the ceremonies of component
tribes. It is this duty more than any other which establishes
the sanctity of a hereditary chief, for, when he represents
his people in sacrifice at the eponymous ancestor's shrine, it is
his own lineal ancestor whom he commemorates before God. He,
the living representative of the founding ancestors, is the
closest descendant of those whom he celebrates on behalf of
his tribe. Generations later, he in his turn will be regarded as
an eponymous founder and will be commemorated in sacrifice
by his descendants on behalf of their tribesmen. In the traditional accounts of war and migration it is always the religious
aspects of leadership which are signalled out and held to be
responsible for the success of one group at the expense of
another. The fortunes of war are to some extent regarded as
a reflection of ritual efficacy.

On the political side again, there is no specifically constituted police organization to enforce the decisions which are
arrived at by the chief in council, except of course in the
pseudo-sultanates which have remained a legacy from earlier
times, in some parts of Somalia (Cerulli, 1919, pp. 46 ff).

The Somali lineage system

The emphasis placed by Somali upon descent has already been
indicated. In fact, the key to an understanding of Somali social
structure lies in the functions exercised by genealogies
(abtirsiinyo). Corresponding to the segmentary tribal system
described is an equally highly segmented lineage system, different orders of fragmentation and aggregation in which are
co-ordinate with equivalent levels of segmentation in the tribal
system. The total genealogical tree of the Somali nation represents the unity of all its component parts: tribal families,
confederacies, sub-confederacies, tribes, and tribal sections.
Social propinquity is expressed in terms of agnatic kinship.
The relations between groups of every order are in genealogical idiom expressed as relationships between eponymous
ancestors. At a higher level than the tertiary tribal section,
or, perhaps in some cases the secondary, such postulated kinship is largely fictitious, of course. Nevertheless it is the
principle which Somali assume to underlie social relationship.
The basis of political action is the agnatic lineage system -
its religious significance relates to the eponymous ancestors
to which it refers, and who are celebrated in the sacrifices
performed at their tombs. Such is the traditional social system
associated with nomadism and preserved where nomadism still
prevails. In the south, however, where sedentary cultivation
is replacing nomadism, the relations between territorial groups
cease to be always expressible in terms of descent. Here the
lineage system is disintegrating. The process of change is
gradual; at first territorial units form having a mixed clan or
lineage structure in which the political unit is co-ordinate with
a dominant clan or lineage. With subsequent development and

the continued settlement in the same territorial unit of increasing numbers of immigrants of heterogeneous clan origin, the
agnatic lineage structure becomes so distorted and confused
that the segmentation of the dominant lineage no longer represents territorial distribution and ceases to have political functions. The principle that neighbours must be agnatic kinsmen,
that territorial proximity implies genealogical propinquity, no
longer holds. Such disorganization is particularly characteristic
of the agricultural tribes of the Sab family. It is important,
however, to observe that although the characteristic social
unit of these regions is an agricultural settlement or 'mixed-
village' (Lewis, 1955, p. 95) with rudimentary state-like
political organization in which lineages have no political significance, agnatic kinship may still be applied at a higher level
to describe the relations between larger territorial aggregates
such as tribes or tribal confederacies. It is certainly still in
terms of agnatic kinship, for example, that the relations
between tribal families are described although relations among
the component units within the Sab family are not at all levels
represented genealogically. There is thus a certain inconsist-
ency in the organization of political relations at different levels
of the political structure. The lineage system which is the
fundamental principle is superseded amongst the smaller units
of the Sab, but retains its functions amongst those of a higher
order and referring to the tribal families knits the Somali
people together as the issue of the Prophet's lineage.

There are, as has been mentioned, seven tribal families - Dir,
Pre-Hawiye, Hawiye, Daarood, and Isħaaq of the 'Soomaali'
group; and Digil and Rahanwiin of the 'Sab'. Today there are
few Dir tribes and their importance lies rather in having given
rise, through the intermarriage of Dir's daughters with immigrant Arabs, to the great Isħaaq and Daarood tribal families.
Isħaaq and Daarood reached the Somali coast at a date which
has not yet been historically established but which tradition
places between the Hejira and the fifteenth century (Lewis,
1955, pp. 15-9, 23-4).

Traditions of Arabian descent are especially strong amongst
the Isħaaq and Daarood, but are held independently by the
Hawiye and Dir and even by many of the Sab tribes who, as it
happens, have as good claims to Arabian descent as their
northern Somali neighbours (the Dir, Isħaaq, Daarood, and
Hawiye), who hold them in such contempt. All tribal families
can establish connexion with each other without going as far
back as the Prophet's lineage, but the breach between 'Soomaali' and 'Sab' is only bridged by tracing descent to the Qurayshitic line of Muhammad. Only at this level of inclusiveness
are the Soomaali and Sab joined as the Somali nation, and it is
in this context especially that the Somali consider themselves
the children of the Prophet. For this solidarity transcends all
sectional interests and divisions, including that between
Soomaali and Sab and represents a real consciousness of common

nationality and religion. Individual genealogies (*abtirsiinyo*)
trace ascent through the hierarchy of social units from the
smallest tribal section to the tribal family, through the primary
bifurcation of Soomaali/Sab, through the Prophet's descendants,
and culminate finally in Muhammad, although they often extend
beyond this to include the Prophet's ancestors and resemble
typical Arabian genealogies (cf. Wüstenfeld, 1853). Usually
Somali genealogies are imperfectly Arabized (Islamized) and
contain a mixture of Cushitic and Arabic names indicative of
the absorption of Arab genealogies. Unless, however, Somali
wish to emphasize their exclusiveness with respect to other
peoples, that is when only relations between Somali are in question, the genealogies given stop at Soomaali or Sab and comprise
between 22 and 30 names. At their greatest extension, genealogies representing political and religious connexion are drawn
out to embrace the Prophet and his lineage.

Figure 5.2 (after Colucci, 1924, p. 26)

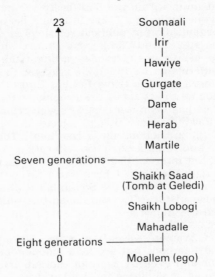

II ISLAM

Relations with Arabia: the introduction of Islam
The historical foundations for the contemporary claim to descent
from the Prophet lie in the existence of relations between
Somaliland and Arabia from the earliest times. Immigration from
and to Arabia has always been and still is a constant feature of
Somali life. There has always been a considerable floating
population of Arabs in various stages of absorption among the

Somali. Moreover, there is little doubt that Islam reached
Somaliland shortly after the Hejira and its establishment is
recorded by Arab writers of the ninth and tenth centuries.
The coastal commercial colonies which had been founded by the
Himyarite Kingdom before Islam eventually developed into the
small Muslim states of Zeila (in its widest extension known as
Adal) in British Somaliland, and of Mogadishu in Somalia.
These were ruled by local dynasties of Somalized Arabs or
Arabized Somalis. The history of Zeila has been adequately
described by Trimingham (1952, pp. 55 ff) and need be no
more than summarized here. Cerulli's research (Cerulli, 1924,
1927) shows that from the beginning of the tenth until half-way
through the thirteenth century Mogadishu was functioning as
a trading colony which comprised a federation of Arabian tribes.
Persians also played some part in its early history. The Arab
settlers had elected chiefs and acknowledged the religious and
jural authority of one lineage, the Qaḥtān ibn Wā'il. In the
course of time Somali influence increased and from a loose federation of Arab-Somali peoples, a sultanate with a local dynasty
(the Muẓaffar) emerged in the thirteenth century. The Muẓaffar
sultanate flourished in the thirteenth and fourteenth centuries
and by this time Shangānī and Ḥamarwein, the two halves of
the town of Mogadishu, were firmly established and Ḥamarwein
was dominant. This dynasty survived into the sixteenth century
when the sultanate declined as a commercial centre and reverted
to a hegemony of small townships. At the same time Mogadishu
was under pressure from tribes of the Hawiye tribal family who
were advancing southwards through Somalia. By the second
half of the eighteenth century Somalis had gained control of
Shangānī and imposed their imām as ruler of Mogadishu. Portuguese and British colonization contributed to the final collapse
of the sultanate. In the seventeenth century the town had been
occupied by the Imām of Oman for a short space, and remained
after his withdrawal in vague dependence to him. With the
division of the Muscat State early in the nineteenth century,
Mogadishu was allotted to the Sultan of Zanzibar, who attempted
to secure a more binding dependence by establishing military
garrisons along the coast. Almost immediately after, these were
sold to Italy and Mogadishu became part of the former Italian
colony of Somalia.

Southern Ethiopia supplied Zeila with its trade and the town
reached its greatest heights in the fourteenth century, but
began to decline after Ahmad Granhe's celebrated campaigns
against Christian Ethiopia in the sixteenth century. Its history
was from the beginning the chronicle of a series of wars
against the Ethiopian infidels waged in alliance with the other
petty Muslim states of southern Eritrea and north-eastern
Ethiopia. Mogadishu, as we have seen, had a shorter period
of prosperity in the fourteenth century and then declined
fairly rapidly under the joint pressure of nomadic incursions
from the interior and the influence of external colonization.

Such centres as these had an important effect in the development of Islam among the Somali. With the Arabian colonies
firmly entrenched in the other trading ports they provided a
foothold from which Islam spread amongst the nomads of the
interior.(12)

Sufism among the Somali
The Somali are orthodox Sunnis and adherents of the Shafi'ite
rite of the Sharī'a. Sufism is well developed and the remainder
of this paper will deal with the role of Sufism in Somali society.
As is well known, this revitalizing current arose in Islam
between the ninth and tenth centuries, attaining in its classical
form its aesthetic and theological climax in the twelfth and
thirteenth centuries. True Sufism is now considered by some
authorities to be in decadence (Arberry, 1950). In Somaliland
after a period of great activity and general expansion up till
the 1930s, the Dervish movement seems to be on the wane,
although it is extremely difficult to assess its true importance
at the present day. Tribal Sufism has always tended to form a
conservative barrier against European administration and
many of its adherents have strongly opposed the extension of
education lest it should undermine their authority. Administrative hostility, real or imagined, has reinforced the esoteric
and clandestine character of Ṣūfī practice and made it all the
more difficult to estimate its true significance. However, it is
not difficult to study its functional importance as a movement
in the social structure of Somali society, for whatever its
present number of adherents, it has left an indelible impression,
as will be seen.
    The adherents of Sufism belong to the congregations or com-
munities, in many Muslim countries known as *zāwiya*, in Somaliland as *jamā'a*, of the various Orders (*tarīqa*, 'The Way') into
which the movement is divided according to the doctrines and
services (*dhikr*) ordained by the founders of Orders. *Tarīqa*
means 'path' in the sense of the Way to follow in the search for
righteousness and the Way to God. The end of the tarīqa is
ma'rifa, absorption in God (gnosis). Those who have travelled
furthest, through virtue, the practice of devotion, and the
grace which God has vouchsafed them are nearest Him. As the
Path is traversed successive steps of the way are demarcated
as 'stations' or 'states'. These are discussed below. For his
godliness and virtue the founder of each Order is held to be
closer to God and to exemplify in his teaching and life the
True Path which it behoves the zealous to follow. The founder
is a guide who through his particular qualities of devotion, and
by his special virtue including the grace (baraka) bestowed
upon him by God, leads his disciples towards God. His baraka
passes to those who follow in his Path and dedicate their lives
to his example. Each Order is distinguished by the specific
discipline which its founder has established as the True Path.
Since there is no God but Allah and Muhammad is His Prophet,

religious prestige is a function of connexion with the Prophet's
Qurayshitic lineage. Thus those in whose blood (recorded in
personal genealogies) the Prophet's grace (baraka) flows are
eminently suitable for election to the office of head (*khalīfa*) of
an Order or of a congregation (shaikh). Shaikhs and khalīfas,
as also the founders of the Orders themselves, have personal
genealogies tracing descent from ancestors connected with
Muhammad. To what extent such claims are historically true is
in the present context irrelevant. The tradition is that descent
from Quraysh entitles to religious office and that to be a Sūfī
shaikh or khalīfa implies such descent. Thus in their furthest
extension the personal genealogies of the founders of Orders
and of their local representatives, shaikhs and khalīfas, reach
back to the Prophet's lineage. According to the lineage principle
in terms of which relationships in Somaliland are understood
each *jamā'a* is identified with the genealogy of its khalīfa or
shaikh. The consequences of this in the total genealogical
structure of Somali society will shortly be seen. Within each
ṭariqa the authority of the incumbent of the office of regional
khalīfa is founded upon a chain of tradition which has two
branches. Unlike his personal genealogy, these attach to the
office, not to the person. The *silsilat al-baraka* (chain of benediction) traces the chain of grace which unfolds from the
founder of the Order through his successive disciples down to
the present incumbent of the office of khalīfa. The *silsilat al-
wird*, the other branch, connects the founder with the Prophet,
and, through his mediation, with Allah. The *silsila* (lit. 'chain')
consists of a list of names through which spiritual affiliation is
traced and in some ways resembles a genealogy. It is quite
separate, however, from the shaikh's personal genealogy although that also is regarded as endowed with power.

In initiation (*wird*), the covenant (*ᶜahd*) of the ṭariqa is
administered to the novice by the head of the community in a
formal ceremony at which the service (*dhikr*) pertaining to the
Order is celebrated (for a description, see Robecchi-Bricchetti,
1899, p. 423; Trimingham, 1952, p. 237). The novice swears
to accept the khalīfa as his guide and spiritual director through
the baraka of the founder. He is then instructed in the performance of prayer-tasks (called variously *awrād, ahzāb*, and
rawātib), and is provided with a prayer-mat to carry upon his
shoulder, a vessel for ablution, and a rosary (*tusbaḥ*) to finger
as he recites his prayers. Somali ṭariqas are characterized by
fewer stages in the novice's progress towards illumination than
were customary in classical Sufism (see on this point, Arberry,
1950, pp. 74 ff). At first the novice is styled 'aspirant' (*murid*)
but also referred to by his brethren (*ᶜikhwān*) as 'brother'.
The majority of initiates never proceed beyond this stage. *Quṭb*,
which is the next step, requires a certain degree of mystical
perfection but is not comparable to the *quṭb* of literary Sufism.
Each successive step becomes increasingly difficult, and *al-
wāṣil* the next grade, signifying union with God after long strife

(i.e. the attainment of gnosis), corresponds to induction to the leadership of a fraternity. *Al-maddād*, the final goal, is attained by few pilgrims indeed, for it is that reached usually only by the founders of the Orders themselves.

Membership of the community does not imply celibacy; adherents live with their families in the community. Women have their own ṭariqas where they participate in the services in the name of the Prophet's daughter, Fātima, whom they regard as the founder of women's Orders. Female adherents are veiled (the veil is not normally worn by women in Somaliland), and are generally more amply clad than other Somali women. But for them also there is no embargo on marriage. There are always many people who although not formally admitted to an Order and not living in the community, follow the public ceremonies while ignorant of their esoteric content. Acknowledging the piety and religious powers of the founder whom they venerate as a saint, they regularly call upon his followers whom they regard as similarly endowed to act as mediators in disputes. Many of the brethren thus fulfil the functions of *qāḍis* and this is one of the many ways in which the sphere of interest of the Ṣūfī community encroaches upon that of the tribal structure. Tribesmen turn to the head of the jamā'a for assistance and counsel, to the neglect of the tribal authorities. This is one instance of a wide and far-reaching conflict between Sufism on the one hand and the tribal organization on the other which we shall consider in some detail below.

Somali ṭariqas

The three most prominent ṭariqas in Somaliland are in the order of their introduction, the Qadiriya, the Aḥmadiya, and the Saaliḥiya. The Rifāᶜiyya ṭariqa is represented amongst Arab settlers but is not widely distributed or important. In the south the Order's main centres are the coastal towns of Mogadishu and Merka: there are also some adherents in the British Protectorate. The Qadiriya, the oldest Ṣūfī Order in Islam, was introduced into Harar in the fifteenth century by Sharīf Abū Bakr ibn ᶜAbd Allāh al-ᶜAydarūs (known as al-Quṭb ar-Rabbānī, 'The Divine Axis'), who died in 1508-9 (A.H. 914). Abū Bakr is probably the best-known Shafiᶜite saint in southern Arabia where he is called al-ᶜAdani(13) and his mosque is the most famous in Aden.(14) The Qadiriya became the official Order of Harar and has considerable influence in the surrounding country. To the south the Order does not appear to have acquired much importance in the interior of Somalia until the beginning of the nineteenth century when the settlement of Bardera, known locally as jamāha, was founded on the Juba river. The Qadiriya has a high reputation for orthodoxy, is on the whole literary rather than propagandist, and is said to maintain a higher standard of Islamic instruction than its rivals. The Aḥmadiya, and the derivative Saaliḥiya, were both introduced into southern Somalia towards the close of the last century,

although the Aḥmadiya may have entered British Somaliland
somewhat earlier. This Order was founded by Sayyid Aḥmad ibn
Idrīs al-Fāsī (1760-1837) of Makkah (Mecca) and brought to Somalia by Shaikh ᶜAlī Maye Durogba of Merka. Muhammad ibn Sālih,
in 1887, founded by the Saaliḥiya as an offshoot of the Rashidiya
founded by Ahmad ibn Idris's pupil Ibrāhim al-Rashid (Cerulli,
1923, pp. 11, 12; Trimingham, 1952, pp. 235-6). The principal
Saaliḥiya proselytizer in Somalia was Shaikh Muḥammad Gūlēd,
a former slave, who launched the Order there by the foundation of a community among the Shidle (a Negroid people occupying the mid-reaches of the Shebelle river, see Lewis, 1955,
p. 41). Muḥammad Gūlēd died in 1918 and his tomb is at Miṣra
(named after Cairo, Miṣra in Somali), one of the communities
which he had established among the Shidle. The Order's strong-
hold is in Somalia but there are some communities in British
Somaliland. According to Cerulli (1923, pp. 14, 18) the Saaliḥiya is strongly propagandist and inferior to the Qadiriya in
mysticism and teaching. In the past it has been closely associated with Somali nationalism and the two rebellions of this
century have taken place under its mantle and in its name. The
more important rising was that led by Muḥammad b. ᶜAbd Allāh
(born about 1865) of the Habr Suleemaan Ogaadeen tribe, who
made several pilgrimages to Makkah (1890-9), and joining the
Saaliḥiya, sought to attract the northern Somali to this Order.
He founded several communities and in 1895 proclaimed himself
khalifa designate in Somaliland. In 1899, having marshalled widespread support, Sayyid Muḥammad initiated the jihād against all
infidels. He was repudiated by the leader of the Saaliḥiya in
Makkah and from 1900 to 1904 British forces, with from time to
time half-hearted Ethiopian and nominal Italian support, conducted four major campaigns aginst him. His power was
continually diminished but the rebellion was never decisively
crushed and dragged on until 1920 when the Sayyid died.

The Aḥmadiya with the smallest number of adherents of the
three Orders is said to concentrate more on teaching than the
Saaliḥiya (Cerulli, 1923, pp. 12 ff). Both Orders are for the
most part distributed in cultivating villages along the two rivers
of Somalia and in the fertile land between them. Qadiriya congregations, on the other hand, are more usually dispersed
amongst tribes and do not form autonomous settlements of
cultivators. This, naturally, is particularly the case in the
north where there is little arable land.

Where the congregation forms a stable cultivating settlement,
the land, which has been acquired through adoption into a host
tribe, is the collective property of the community and is divided
among the affiliates by their shaikh. Continuity of tenure
depends upon the maintenance of satisfactory relations with the
tribe of adoption and the regular fulfilment of the various
obligations which adoption imposes. Tenure is precarious and
is in theory at any time revocable by the ceding tribe. It follows that the individual holdings obtained by affiliates are not

automatically inheritable; absolute rights to land or crops are
never obtained by members of the community. If a member
leaves he relinquishes all rights to his holding and probably
his crops also, although he may sometimes be allowed a portion
of the harvest. The fields are worked collectively so that the
harvest in each brother's holding represents the collective
labour of the community. Part of the harvest is used to maintain the funds of the jamāᶜa, which also depend upon gifts
made by tribesmen and payments for ritual or religious services
performed by affiliates. Liabilities met from these general funds
consist of aid to the poor, assistance of pilgrims to Makkah
and expenses connected with missionary work and the various
dues payable to the tribe of adoption. As far as the host tribe
is concerned the jamāᶜa acts as a tribal section subject to the
same privileges and duties as are other sections of the tribe.
Congregations act as training centres for the devouts (wadaad),(15) usually described as 'bush teachers' or 'bush preach-
ers', who wander from camp to camp through the bush, stop-
ping now and then to hold classes where at least some rudimentary knowledge of theology is imparted. In these transitory
bush schools children are taught prayers and verses from the
Qur'an and generally acquire the ability to read and write
Arabic. Children receive a thorough grounding in the Qur'an
and their familiarity with Qur'anic texts remains with them
throughout their lives. Wadaad are also important as acting in
the capacity of unofficial qāḍīs administering the Sharī'a to
the extent to which its competence is recognized by tribal
authorities, i.e. in matrimonial affairs, inheritance of property,
contract, mortgage, etc., and assessment of the requisite compensation for injuries.(16) In intertribal politics they have
little authority to award decisions, and where their recom-
mendations conflict with tribal interests they are normally
ignored for wadaad here act as mediators rather than as arbitrators. It is probably through the wadaad who issue from
the jamaᶜa communities that Sufism exerts its greatest influence
in Somali social structure. The parent communities themselves
are essentially centres of mystical devotion and have produced
a considerable Arab-Somali religious literature written mainly
in Arabic but in some cases in Somali transcribed in an adaptation of Arabic script.(17) It is probable also that Ṣūfī works
are to be found in Somali oral literature and research should be
directed to discovering to what extent this is the case. Mysticism is adopted as a means to union with God (gnosis); Somali
Sufistic literature treats of divine ecstasy and is similar to
Ṣūfī writing in general. An interesting example is an unpublished manuscript called tawassul ash-shaikh Awês written by
Shaikh Awês,(18) which consists of a collection of songs for
dhikr. Where such works are biographical, as for example in
the autobiography of Shaikh ᶜAli Maye Durogba,(19) they
contain an account of the author's justification to claim descent
from Quraysh. Almost all such works include a section in which

the author's claims to Qurayshitic descent are set forth. Perhaps the most important of Somali Ṣūfī literature is a collection of works by Ḥaaji ᶜAbdullāhi Yūsif published under the title *al-majmuᶜat al-mubaraka*.(20) Ḥaaji ᶜAbdullāhi of the Qadiriya tariqa was a member of a group of shaikhs (known as Ashraf),(21) attached to the Majeerteen tribes of the Daarood tribal family; his work is analysed by Cerulli (1923, pp. 13-14, 22-5).

The cult of saints
An important feature of the Ṣūfī communities lies in the extent to which their founders are venerated. The local founders of Orders and congregations (jamāᶜa) are often sanctified after their death. Their veneration gives rise to cults which overshadow the devotion due to the true founder of the ṭariqa and even of the Prophet Muhammad. Their tombs become shrines (*gashin* in Somalia), tended by a small body of followers or the descendants of the shaikh and those who have inherited his baraka. To the shrines come the members of the Order as well as local tribesmen who are not initiates, to make sacrifice as occasion demands, and to take part in the annual pilgrimage to the shrine of the saint on the aniversary of his death. Outstanding events in his life are similarly celebrated. Muslim saint-days which have no connexion with indigenous saints are unpopular, especially in the interior. But to the extent to which the Qadiriya Order is followed emphasis has been given to the saint-day (*mawlid*) of the founder al-Jilāni, although even this festival enjoys only limited observance. Saints are not always associated with a particular congregation or Order. Many are ubiquitous, and common to several Orders, share the same veneration within the religion of the country. They are venerated for particular qualities. One of the most popular in Somalia, Saint Au Ḥiltir (a name suggestive of non-Islamic origin) is regarded as the protector of man from the attacks of crocodiles; another, Saint Au Mād, is recognized by tribes of the Rahanwiin tribal-family as the guardian of the harvest.

Tombs are scattered all over Somaliland and many, certainly, commemorate pre-Islamic figures who have been assimilated in Islam. Some of the families acting as the custodians of their ancestors' shrines have developed into small clans, usually dispersed; others have lost all autonomy and are scattered as holy men (wadaad) proselytizing and teaching. Others again remain attached to a particular tribe as the holders of a hereditary office of qāḍī. Such, for example, is the case with the seven lineages of the Gasar Gudda tribe of Lugh-Ferrandi in Somalia, where the office of tribal chief rotates among six lineages, while that of qāḍī is invested in the seventh, the Rer Dulca Mado (Ferrandi, 1903, pp. 213, 262 ff; Lewis, 1953, p. 115). This represents one of the possible conclusions in the history of a saintly family attached initially to a tribe in clientship, where the religious group has worked its way into

the lineage structure of the tribe and established a permanent
position. A good example of a dispersed clan venerated for their
baraka are the Rer Sheik Mumin whose ancestor's shrine is at
Bur Hakaba among the Elai of southern Somalia. Their influence
extends throughout the entire Rahanwiin tribal-family and tribute is paid to them on account of their reputation as sorcerers
(Ferrandi, 1903, pp. 138-9, 242-3). Ferrandi describes them
unflatteringly as a gang of robbers implicated in cattle raiding
and profiting by their ancestor's sanctity to impress and exploit
ignorant people. A similar dispersed shaikhly group are the
Aw Qutub of the British Protectorate whom Burton (1894, I,
p. 193) described as the descendants of Au Quṭb ibn Faqih
CUmar who was then claimed to have crossed from the Hijaz
'ten generations ago' and to have settled with his six sons in
Somaliland. The Aw Qutub are widely scattered and are found
as far south as the Ogaden. They have the title *Shakyash* which
Burton translates 'reverend'. In fact, such families of Arabian
origin are found all over Somaliland and are often rapidly assimilated in the Somali social structure where their members
enjoy high prestige (cf. Cerulli, 1926).

The role of Sufism in the social structure
We may now consider the position held by Ṣūfī ṭariqas and congregations or communities in the social structure. It is obvious
that for the total social structure the fraternities provide potential channels of alliance amongst warring tribes separated by
the very nature of the tribe. For the communities, economic
and political entities though they may be, and often themselves
at enmity even within the same Order, are bound together
through community of religious purpose. They aim at the
development and diffusion of Islam. Such were the ideals so
successfully translated into a transcendental movement ignoring
the narrow bonds of tribalism by the Saaliħiya Sayyid ħaaji
Muḥammad b. CAbd Allāh. His campaign is an illustration of
the potentialities which the ṭariqa organization offers for the
extension of national unity when a sufficiently great figure
emerges to inspire such feeling. Now, as elsewhere in Islam,
the new urban politial parties seem to have their roots in the
ṭariqa organization and to be a development from it.(22) Transtribal nationalist aspirations which previously found some outlet
in it are now promoted by political associations, the strongest
of which in the late 1950s was the Somali Youth League (SYL).
Within the tribal structure individual communities exercise
considerable influence, and it is this aspect of their social
functions which I wish particularly to consider. As we have
seen, among the nomads and especially in the north of Somaliland where there is little or no arable land, communities cannot
generally form cultivating settlements as they do in the less
barren south. They cannot therefore so easily exist as independent autonomous local groups. Among the southern cultivating
tribes (the Sab) settled cultivating communities occupy an

interstitial position on the ground. As social entities they are
accordingly in a better position to develop into units independent of tribal allegiance and to play an interstitial role in the
social structure. This naturally has important consequences
in the lineage structure. To take an example. The Qadiriya
community of Bardera (known locally as the jamāha) was
founded on the Juba river at the beginning of the nineteenth
century by Shaikh Ali Kurre, a Rahanwiin tribesman. New
settlements quickly sprang up round the mother community.
The affiliates were faced with considerable hostility from the
surrounding tribes. They fought the Galla Boran, the Gasar
Gudda (Somali Rahanwiin) who were successfully defeated and
their centre Lugh-Ferrandi destroyed, and, finally, the people
of Bardera extended their sway to the coast subjecting the
villages of Baidoa, Molimat, and the coastal town of Brava. Thus
they established dominion over all tribes of the Rahanwiin tribal
family. Retribution, however, was to follow. The Rahanwiin
recovered strength under the leadership of the Sultan of the
Geledi (then a powerful Rahanwiin tribe), and after a series of
battles besieged and destroyed Bardera in 1843. For some
years Bardera lay deserted but began to rise again with the
foundation of a new community by Shaikh Muhammad Eden of
the Elai. By 1924 it was possible for Colucci (1924, p. 264) to
describe the new centre in the following terms: 'The settlements
of Bardera constitute a truly independent territorial group freed
from all adherence to the tribes from whom the original grants
of land were obtained.'

Adoption
All communities originally enter the tribal structure through an
act of adoption. Genealogically this implies incorporation into a
lineage. Colucci (1924, pp. 78 ff) has drawn attention to the
frequent occurrence in tribal genealogies of names signifying
'holy', 'religious', 'saintly', etc., which denote the attachment
to tribal units of Şūfī communities or groups of holy men celebrated for their baraka. Such titles are: *shaikhal, ashraf, faqīr,
fogi, faqīh, ħaaji, hashya,* and other synonyms not noticed by
Colucci. The fact that some tribal families, especially those
with particularly strong traditions of Arabian descent such as
the Isħaaq and Daarood of northern Somaliland are often referred to as 'ħaaji' or 'hashya'(23) indicates that they are in some
sense regarded as sanctified. This is an illustration of the
extent to which religion is identified with tribal structure among
the northern nomads. We shall return to this point later. In the
genealogies of the southern cultivating tribes (the Sab), however, such words tend to occur in the lower portions of tribal
genealogies. Sometimes their occurrence indicates fairly feeble
ties of attachment between adopting tribe and priestly section.
In other cases where the attachment is more tenuous these
titles represent extraneous aggregates, often of long standing.
As examples of dispersed clans of holy men we have already

considered the Rer Shaikh Mumin among the Rahanwiin and the
Rer Aw Qutub of British Somaliland. Both are typical representatives of this class. The Shaikhal Lobogi section of the
Herab tribe of Somalia are, on the other hand, a good example
of a religious group or community firmly assimilated to the
tribe of adoption (see genealogy above, p. 134). Shaikh
Lobogi, the eponymous ancestor of the group, is a descendent
of Shaikh Saad whose tomb is at Geledi in Somalia. Groups
which have not achieved such firm integration in the tribal
structure or assimilation in the lineage structure, are the Ashraf
among the Saraman tribal cluster,(24) the Walamoji among the
Elai,(25) and the Waaqbarre among the Dabarre tribe.

The Ashraf rose to power in a manner typical of such groups,
they acted as mediators in a series of disputes amongst the
Saraman tribes which concluded in the expulsion of one, the
Harau, and the division of another, the Lisan, into two new
tribes, the Lisan Horsi and the Lisan Barre. At Saraman, the
Ashraf are known as the 'Three Feet' and take part in tribal
councils as arbitrators and peace-makers. There are many
religious clans known as Ashraf in Somaliland, and no doubt
some of them derive ultimately from immigrant Ashrāf. In view
of the importance of Mogadishu as a centre in the diffusion of
Islam it may well be that the Sharifs at present living in the
Shangānī quarter of Mogadishu who are of the Bā ᶜAlwī clan of
Hadramaut,(26) and who settled in Somaliland in the seventeenth century, may constitute one of the original nuclei from
which Ashrāf blood has spread.

The Walamoji wield considerable influence in Elai politics
through the high prestige which they enjoy as men of religion.
They claim to have accompanied the Elai in their wanderings
before they reached their present territory, but they only
recently became the official shaikhs of the Elai after they had
ousted another religious group – the 'Rer Fogi'. The founder
is said to be of Galla Arussi origin, but as in the case of all
religious sections they have vague traditions of descent from
Quraysh which they exploit to the full. The Walamoji have
considerable autonomy and are segmented into primary,
secondary, and tertiary divisions (Colucci, 1924, p. 141).

The Waaqbarre, who are attached to the Dabarre tribe, comprise three sections and have mixed traditions of connexion
with the Galla Arussi and descent from a 'Great Arabian Shaikh'.

As is clear from the foregoing many ṭarīqa communities degen-
erate into groups of *wadaad* (see above, p. 140) clustered round
the shrine of their founder. Again there is the constant factor
of the immigration of Arabian families of devouts and their
Somali descendants who may have no direct affiliation with a
particular ṭarīqa. The complete picture is intricate and complex;
it is not always possible to establish the ṭarīqa affiliations of
religious groups with a Sufistic organization. Certainly it is
often difficult to discover to which of the three – ṭarīqa communities, shaikhly families, or Arabian immigrants – particular

names in tribal genealogies actually refer. There is no doubt
that in many cases all are confused. They have in common an
association with baraka. It seems, however, that apart from
Arabian families venerated for their name and piety and not
necessarily Ṣūfīs in the strict sense, it may generally be inferred that the primary units are ṭarīqa communities. This sup-
position is supported by the fact that Arabian immigrants whose
genealogies show connexion with Quraysh and consequently
endowment with baraka are venerated in the same manner as
Ṣūfī saints and their cults are absorbed in the overriding
ṭarīqa organization. It is with ṭarīqa and jamā'a that we are
primarily concerned.

The land necessary for the foundation of a jamā'a is sometimes
made readily accessible through the nomad's lack of interest in
and contempt for cultivation. Often it was obtained as a result
of skilful intervention in tribal disputes over land. Contested
areas of arable land bordering tribal territory were ceded to
astute shaikhs who were thereby enabled to establish jamā'as.
At the same time the creation of these farming settlements contributed to the demarcation and definition of rigorous tribal
boundaries (Lewis, 1955, pp. 43 ff, 143). Thus, for example,
a chain of communities marking the principal watering-places
and boundaries between tribes was set up along the Shebelle
river from Afgoi to Mahaddei (Cerulli, 1923, p. 26). For this
reason it is appropriate to describe Ṣūfi jamā'as in southern
Somalia as forming enclaves amongst tribes and occupying an
interstitial territorial position analogous to their role in intertribal politics.

The community's lands are acquired through adoption into
a host tribe. Adoption within the tribal and lineage structure
(if this is still functioning) places the head of the community
and his followers in the initially inferior status of clients, subservient to the tribal elders and chief. At this stage the burden
of the conflict between tribal custom (ḥeer, *tastuur*) on the
one hand, and the Sharī'a on the other, seems to lie against
the Ṣūfī community. For the members of the jamā'a are subject
to conflicting loyalties. The Islamic code which should rigorously
govern their internal affairs cannot always be enforced in their
relations with the tribesmen upon whom they are in dependence.
Should tension between tribe and community reach a high pitch
the community is in danger of losing its tenancy. However,
such is the strength of tradition that in the hands of a wise
shaikh skilful in the maintenance of good relations with his
tribe of adoption, tenancy easily lapses into ownership. Tenure
has given rise to absolute possession. Rights to land may never
be challenged, and the jamā'a may achieve sufficient power to
free itself completely from tribal allegiance. Such is the case
of Bardera (above, p. 138).

With the high premium which the increasing adoption of agriculture has caused to be set upon land, disputes over possession are common. But rivalry over land for cultivation is only

one among many likely points at issue between a Ṣūfī community
and its tribe of adoption. In addition to the general dis-harmony
between tribal custom and the Shari'a, the interference of
shaikhs in tribal politics, and the passing of religious leadership from tribe to jamā'a, tribal sanctions would seem to be
weakened by the asylum offered in jamā'as to defaulters from
tribal justice. At the same time a variety of factors encourage
the growth of Ṣūfī farming communities. The opportunities
which a stable existence in agricultural settlements affords,
together with the greater stability of tribal relations among the
sedentary cultivators or only part-transhumant tribes of Somalia, attracts dispossessed people, many of whom are of servile
origin, and promotes the further development of agriculture.
The soil is favourable, there is administrative encouragement
to cultivate - and many settlers are by nature cultivators -
and the Shari'a, more thoroughly applied here, provides an
essentially urban code whose juridicial ordinances are more
appropriate to farming settlements than they are to nomadic
tribal society. All these factors are contributory to the disintegration of the lineage structure as well as to the formation
of jamā'a farms. It is not surprising then that there is a constant drift towards the religious settlements and away from
the tribes: that it is no greater must be ascribed to the nomad's
contempt of cultivation and those who practise it.

When these factors are considered it is clear that there are
many opportunities for friction between tribe and adopted community. In all disputes the procedure followed is the same: the
tribe claiming the land occupied by the community seeks to
abrogate the mandate by which it is alleged to have been ceded.
The conflicts which ensue are usually resolved by the intervention of the administration. A typical example of the type of
dispute which is likely to arise is the following: In 1920 the
Hawadle claimed the land which the community of Burdere occupied and which it was maintained had been granted to the
community thirty-eight years previously. The tribe held that
the grant had been only provisional and that the ground was
now required for its own use, especially since several Hawadle
families had already settled in the lands of the jamā'a. Since
the head of the jamā'a continued to ignore their requests tribesmen continued to move into the community's lands without
admission to the Order. The shaikh was then moved to protest
to the Italian Administration claiming that the disputed lands
had been obtained not from the Hawadle but from an adjacent
tribe, the Baddi Addo. The case was solved by the government's forcing those Hawadle who had illegally joined the community to withdraw after the harvest of their crops. Sufism
triumphed and the community's rights were upheld against those
of the tribe. The position of jamā'as has further been strength-
ened by the administration's policy of appointing qādis from
the ranks of Ṣūfī brethren (wadaad) (Cerulli, 1923, pp. 28-9,
32-4). But government policy does not always seem to have

been consistently on the side of the Orders and it has doubtless frequently turned disputes between tribes and religious Orders to its own advantage.(27)

We have noted how the differences in ecology between the northern terrain occupied by the nomads and the southern occupied by semi-nomadic and sedentary cultivators govern the territorial disposition of jamā'as. There is naturally a much higher proportion of permanent Ṣūfī settlements in the south than in the north, and consequently a higher proportion of autonomous communities freed from tribal allegiance. In the south jamā'as occupy an interstitial position in the social struc- ture parallel to their territorial distribution. It is hardly sur- prising then that the communities are generally more closely entwined in the lineage structure of the northern nomads than in what remains of that of the southern cultivators. The eco- logical differences between the north and south of Somaliland are reflected in the retention of the lineage organization among the nomads and the necessity for communities to maintain tribal affiliations in the north, while in the south where the lineage structure is in active disintegration communities tend to exist as independent settlements.

Genealogical assimilation
We have seen how Quraysh is the symbol of divine grace and how the genealogies of Ṣūfī shaikhs and khalifas vaunt con- nexion with the Prophet's lineage. We have also seen how in its client status, and thus at some point in the history of every jamā'a, the community is identified with its head and with his genealogy. It is the incorporation of such genealogies, I believe, which leads ultimately to the inclusive ascription of the Somali nation to the Qurayshitic lineage of the Prophet. The Orders as they today exist in Somaliland do not date from before the fifteenth century (the time of the introduction of the Qadiriya) but it is unlikely that they could have assumed their present constitution and strength without some earlier proto-tariqa organization (cf. the development of Sufism in Morocco: Drague, 1951, pp. 9-117)). It appears probable, therefore, that the Qurayshitic pattern of Somali genealogies has developed in step with the formal emergence of the Orders in Somaliland. As emphasized earlier, tariqas are not alone responsible for the introduction of Qurayshitic genealogies. Many of the immigrant Arabs who established chiefly dynasties among the Somali and who naturally brought their Arabian genealogies with them were doubtless not all Ṣūfīs. Some of them may indeed, have been the true descendants of Quraysh. Nevertheless, it is significant that the Somali celebrate as the authors of their faith and ven- erate as they do Ṣūfī saints, figures such as Shaikhs Isħaaq and Daarood, who if not themselves historical personages are certainly the types of such. Sociologically it is apparent that the claim of descent from Quraysh is the necessary outcome of the application of the Somali lineage principle to the part played

by Islam generally, and Sufism in particular, in the social
structure. This consistency is made possible by the parallel
functions of Ṣūfī and Somali genealogies. That the nomads
have stronger traditions of descent from Quraysh is to be
expected, since, unlike the southern cultivators (Sab) whose
arable lands facilitate the formation of autonomous independent
Ṣūfī communities, the jamā'as of the northern nomads are seldom self-contained and are generally identified with the tribal
structure. The same is genealogically true, as we have seen.
The closer genealogical assimilation among the nomadic population seems to explain why tribal families of the 'Soomaali'
group such as the Isḥaaq and Daarood, as opposed to those of
the 'Sab', are referred to genealogically as though they represented vast Ṣūfī communities. Such an interpretation is consistent with the role of Sufism among the Somali.

The concluding sections of this essay (Part II) will examine
the religious assumptions which underlie this process of assimilation.

PART II

III CUSHITIC RELIGION

In the first part of this paper we followed the development of
the Ṣūfī ṭarīqa organization in Somaliland after the introduction
of Islam and examined the functions exercised by Ṣūfī communities in the social structure. We interpreted the closer social
and genealogical assimilation of jamā'as among the nomadic tribes
in terms of lack of arable land available for the foundation of
independent settlements. It was argued that the genealogical
idiom in which social relations are normally described, especially amongst the nomads, is extended to the jamā'as by virtue
of their identification with the Arabian genealogies of their
shaikhs. The incorporation of such Ṣūfī genealogies was held to
explain how the Somali lineage system is in its furthest extension extrapolated by the Qurayshitic lineage of the Prophet.
Ṣūfī and Somali tribal genealogies, it was suggested, have
parallel religious functions which make such assimilation possible. In the light of these similarities of religious function,
and, in order to provide a theological framework for the discussion of syncretism which concludes this essay, it will be necessary to make some attempt to compare pre-Islamic and Islamic
Somali theology. This should reveal the factors which underlie
the rise of Sufism in Somaliland.

The present account of Cushitic religion in Somaliland is
limited mainly to the Hawiye tribes of southern Somalia. Cushitic
features of Hawiye belief and practice have been recorded in
some detail by Cerulli; information on the northern Somali is

scanty and much less satisfactory. Religion only will be considered and pre-Islamic customs such as the levirate, sororate,
circumcision and infibulation, etc., which are not specifically
religious and do not in themselves elucidate religious concepts
will be ignored. As has been emphasized, Islam is interpreted
through the medium of the earlier Cushitic substratum which
is being continuously modified and progressively Islamized. In
the present context it is not necessary to go into the racial
history of Somaliland(28) in any detail beyond recalling that,
even prior to the twelfth century,(29) the Somali had begun
their southern expansion at the expense of their Galla (Cushitic)
predecessors. As the Galla withdrew before the advancing
Somali, they took much of their common Cushitic culture with
them, while the Somali increasingly adopted Islam. Islam had,
as we have seen, made its appearance in the coastal centres
shortly after the Hejira. However, there are still today a few
tribes which preserve much of their Cushitic culture unmodified
by Muslim influence. The Hawiye retain sufficient of their old
religion to indicate its general characteristics.

Zār and Waaq
The Supreme Being of Cushitic religion is a Sky God who is
regarded as Father of the universe. The entire world of nature,
including man and his possessions, is ultimately God's. The
root-name for the Sky God may be *Zār*, since, according to
Cerulli (1923, p. 2) *Zār* occurs in this context with only slight
modifications in most Cushitic languages and is the form used
among the pagan Agao whose religion has been taken as the
archetype of Cushitic religion (cf. Ullendorff, 1955, pp. 63-4).
Since, however, comparative study of the Cushitic languages
is in its infancy this theory is uncertain. Among the northern
Somali *Eebbe* (Father) is a common name for God - now Allah -
and among the Hawiye of the south the word used is *Waaq* (cf.
Galla, *Waaqa*(30)). *Waaq* in northern Somaliland occurs in
certain obscure expletives but is not generally used to designate
God. *Zār* itself appears to occur in the form *Saar*, which, as we
shall see, connotes a spirit-refraction accreted to Islam as a
malignant jinn. *Eebbe* and *Waaq* are now, of course, applied to
Allah and these Cushitic names and their derivatives are still
found as personal and place-names.
    God's exalted position is indicated in the songs addressed to
Him. 'Children are Yours, women Yours, cattle Yours.' 'If You
are pleased with our fine horses, take them. If our slaves
please You, take them, and if our wives find favour in Your
sight take them also.' God is apprehended as He watches over
creation in the sun's light, just as man is aware of his surroundings through the gift of sight. Prayers run; 'Watch us God,
You who have eyes, know and we shall know, for after You
have known we know'.(31) 'Knowledge is Yours, sight is Yours,
watch us with good eyes. Make us see well. Sight is Yours.'
The semantic relation is eyes, seeing, sun, and light. God's

eternal constancy is compared to the central-pole of the hut.
'May the central-pole be as of iron.' Without support man's
house collapses, but God, 'the same without the central-pole',
is full of wonder and power. Somali still sing 'This Sky, the
same unchanging, without the central-pole according to the
Divine Will' (Cerulli, 1923). The Sky God's belt is the rainbow,
and the rains are in his keeping as a gift for man; certain
individuals have power over the rains through their relation to
God.

   Saar in Somali describes a state of possession by a spirit also
called saar. The extreme symptoms are frenzy, fits, or madness,
and the spirit itself is, in the Islamic setting, described as a
kind of jinn whose malignant powers cause certain types of
sickness. Among the eastern tribes of northern Somaliland
'invisible' wadaad (see above) act similarly to saar but have
less serious effects and are merely responsible for some minor
forms of illness. Saar can be expelled by persons who have
acquired mastery over the spirits through having themselves
been previously possessed. In northern Somaliland such 'doctors' (alaqa) are generally women, for visitation is here con-
fined almost exclusively to this sex, especially to the wealthy.
Rich women who believe that a saar is troubling them have
recourse to an alaqa: poor women cannot afford to be afflicted
by saar because treatment is costly. Such an illogical situation
leads sceptical Somalis to abandon their belief in saar. This is
not the place nor is there at present sufficient material on the
social contexts in which saar are active, to enter into a sociological discussion of the subject. It seems possible, however,
that we are concerned with a form of the witchcraft which is
associated with wealth and polygamy elsewhere and which
serves as a vehicle for jealousy and as a buttress of social
status. Saar are expelled in the 'dance of the saar' which is
apparently fairly extensively practised in Somalia although
violently opposed by Muslim wadaad. In northern Somaliland,
where official opposition is such that many devout Muslims deny
its existence,(32) the dance is sometimes still performed by
women. It seems that the dance acts as a form of exorcism of
the malevolent jinn causing possession, and perhaps less frequently as a means of attaining possession. In Somalia, the
opening movement is called or-goys and consists of those
assembled beginning to sing and to raise their arms rhythmically towards the sky. Soon someone falls in a faint and his
companions 'beat the saar', forming a circle round him and
breaking into 'the song of the saar', sung at first slowly and
then with increasing tempo. Drumming, castanet-playing, and
handclapping swell the singing. Slowly the fallen dancer revives,
and moving his limbs in rhythm, seizes a knife or lighted brand
which he thrusts between his teeth and dances into the semi-
circle formed by the others. The tempo increases until the
dancer again succumbs and falls panting to the ground. After
a little he rises completely restored and the saar is said to

have left him.(33) The dance is widely distributed among the
Cushitic peoples of north-east Africa and often the possessed
dancer acts as an oracle(34) (see Leiris, 1934). Beyond the
Cushitic areas, it occurs as far away as Egypt (Kahle, 1912),
the Anglo-Egyptian Sudan (Trimingham, 1949, pp. 174-7), and
even the Ḥijāz (Hurgronje, 1888-9, II, pp. 124-8). The explanation seems to be that the saar (Zār) dance has spread far
beyond the bounds of Cushitic culture with the export of slaves
from Ethiopia where it has its Cushitic origin (Cerulli, 1933,
II, p. 35).

Other religious concepts
The realm of the Sky God includes a multitude of subsidiary
spirits; the spirits of the bush, certain animals, some snakes,
scorpions, termites, and other insects frequently credited by
Somali with malignant powers. In certain situations tribes are
described as linked to trees and animals which are addressed
by maternal kinship names, but the connexion does not appear
to be totemic. Spirit-refractions are said to have their seats in
those possessed, and, among the Cushitic Agao of Gondar in
Ethiopia the spirit-ridden subject is referred to as the spirit's
'horse'. A similar spirit is encountered and overcome in the
crossing the threshold ceremony (*kalaqaad*) which marks a male
child's first expedition outside his mother's hut. The baby is
carried over the threshold by his mother's brother (Cerulli,
1919, p. 23). Although generally obscured by and syncreted
in Islam, divining and various forms of sympathetic magic are
still practised. Ordeals and oath-taking by swearing on stones
are used to establish testimony. Charms and amulets, especially
as prophylactics, enjoy wide popularity. Their efficacy, now,
of course, depends upon association with the Holy Qur'an. In
this context it is perhaps not irrelevant to mention the fire-
kindling ceremony of *dabshid* which is widely observed and
marks the commencement of the solar year.(35) The festival is
condoned in some parts of Somalia by representing it as a
Muslim expiatory rite; in one district it is known as the 'feast
of beating'.

In southern Somaliland death is regarded as a transformation.
In the grave the corpse lies clothed and provided with a supply
of food. The dead are remembered in periodical ceremonies
('sweeping the tomb') at which cattle are slaughtered and food
distributed amongst the poor, slaves and servants, and the
aged. Gifts of food and clothes are sometimes offered, often in
response to dreams. 'I dreamt that my father showed me his
torn clothes. Here are some clothes, let him take them.' Or
again, 'I have given my dead mother an ox, now my father is
thin and hungry and wants something to fatten him. Here is
another ox, let him come and take it'. Old men are constantly
preoccupied in amassing their *wáh la-i-gú dúgo* (what is buried
with me) and, according to Cerulli, on occasion set aside as
much as three-quarters of their inheritance for the performance

of 'sweeping the tomb' ceremonies after their death. Sacrifice
(*Waaq da^Cil, Rabbibari*) plays, as we have seen, an important
part in the life of the Somali. From the structural point of
view its crucial form is the annual celebration held at the tombs
of the founding ancestors of lineages. The assimilation within
Islam of this, the most vital aspect of sacrifice in relation to
the lineage system, will be discussed below.

To recapitulate: a brief description has been given of the
Cushitic world of power manifest in an apparently incoherent
and rather vague hierarchy of refractions of the Sky God
(Waaq). This world presided over by God comprises the phenomena which we call 'natural'; the sun, moon, and stars, the
winds, rainbow, rains, and the rest, as well as the more
contiguous parts of nature, the hills, trees, and water, which
make up man's immediate surroundings. Certain configurations
of these phenomena are fraught with power, available sometimes
to ritual experts only, sometimes to whoever chances to cross
their path. One of the tribal religious expert's (wadaad) special
skills is his knowledge of the skies and power to interpret the
movements of the heavenly bodies (Cerulli, 1929, 1931). But
power appears too in the interaction of the more remote phenomena of the skies with man's immediate environment. At Lugh-
Ferrandi in Somalia, for example, the moon is believed to set
in a clump of tamarind bushes and whoever is touched by a
falling leaf as the moon disappears will die (Ferrandi, 1903,
p. 300). Many similar examples could be cited. Apart from
individual, chance, and private, rather than collective, relations with the world of power, such as those indicated and,
for example, in the saar dance, the influence of God appears
at a higher structural level and correspondingly higher potential in tribal sacrifice. We have already noticed how the religious
nature of chieftaincy is established in sacrifice and how a
chief may have powers of rainmaking. The chief was seen to
have a special relation with God. From his sanctity follows his
power to bless and curse his people and the force of the fire
within him which makes his glance 'the burning eye' (*il kulul*).

IV SUFISM AND SYNCRETISM

Sufism and the Shari'a
Muslim mystical theosophy may be regarded as embodying the
vital and flexible spirit of Islam. Like all mysticism Sufism
concentrates on the personal relationship between the believer
and God, and must be regarded by those who consider that the
core of religion is to be found in an 'I-Thou' relationship as
the mainspring of Islam. The Shari'a - the law of the Islamic
community - originated in a theocracy which had transcended
the bonds of tribalism, and has in its subsequent elaboration
always referred (in theory at least) to a religious state. That
part of the Shari'a which relates only to purely ritual or

religious observance applies equally well to tribe or state
because it deals with the relations of the believer to God, but
the sectors of the Sharī'a which elaborate a corpus of private
and public law based upon the concept of citizenship are not
applicable, save with major limitations, to a stateless tribal
society.(36) The ecological dichotomy reflected in the divergence between nomadism and sedentary cultivation in Somaliland,
which as we have seen, is ultimately responsible for the two
different types of jamā'a organization - dependence and identification in the case of the nomads, independence from tribal
allegiance and less close assimilation in the case of the cultivators - operates in the same sense here. In the urban centres
of the coast and in the arable lands of the south where the
lineage principle has largely disintegrated, the purely legal
as opposed to purely religious - to make a separation which in
traditional Islam is largely artificial - ordinances of the Sharī'a
naturally have wider jurisdiction.(37) But amongst the nomadic
Somali the application of the Sharī'a(38) tends to be restricted
to intra-tribal affairs and certain matters of personal status.
Its relevance outside this narrow field is, of course, recognized
by the tribesmen but is not always upheld in practice. Even
within the tribe, the jurisdiction of the Sharī'a is limited by the
force of tribal custom (ħeer, tastuur) - not an unusual situation in the Muslim world. It is true that the recognition given
to the Sharī'a in the British and Italian judicial systems provides
an extended mechanism for the regulation of external tribal
relations. Thus the Sharī'a is one of the sources of the law in
the settlement of tribal disputes although the case may not be
heard in a qādi's court. There are, however, many wadaad
issuing from the ṭariqas who practice as qādis outside the
governmental judicial structure. The scope of their application
of the Sharī'a, although supported by strong religious sanctions, is limited by the power of the tribal chiefs. This state of
affairs represents the traditional social order before the advent
of the Pax Britannica or the Pax Italiana. Despite these differences in the jurisdiction allowed to the Sharī'a, there is little
difference between the nomads and cultivators in the importance
attached to the fundamental principles of Islam. Except for a
few tribes who have remained relatively sheltered from Muslim
influence, the five 'Pillars of the Faith' - the profession of the
Faith; prayers; fasting, somewhat irregularly observed perhaps;
almsgiving; and pilgrimage - seem to be universally practised.
Competent witnesses have generally been struck by the devout-
ness of the Somali tribesman.

There is, of course, no opposition between Sufism as a movement and the schools of Muslim law, but the material reviewed
in this essay suggests that Ṣūfī theosophy - as opposed to the
Sharī'a - is in its basic principles particularly suited to Somali
society. These principles have been firmly assimilated while
what in the Sharī'a is inapplicable to a tribal society has been
largely ignored. The further penetration of Islam and the

Shari'a is opposed and retarded by the barrier of tribal custom,
part but not all of which relates directly to the lineage organization whose interaction with Islam we have been considering.
On the other hand, various customs, which appear to have no
necessary connexion with the lineage system nor to be essential
to nomadism, persist and resist the full application of the
Shari'a. On the whole, however, Somali society has interpreted
Islamic institutions in the light of its own tribal structure and
has produced the Ṣūfī organization which I have outlined. But
it would be wrong to argue that because Somali tribalism is
opposed to the application of the Shari'a the only possible response is Sufism. The difference between the theory and
application of the Shari'a has always been considerable, in
state as well as tribe. The suitability of Sufism to the conditions of Somali society is much more important than the imprac-
ticality of part of the Shari'a. We turn now to consider the
adoption of Sufism in terms of the assimilation of Sufi theosophy
to Somali pre-Islamic belief.

The nature of God and his world
Although clearly delineated with greater precision, the absolute
supremacy of Allah (indicated in the believer's submission
(Islam) to Him) closely resembles the omnipotence of the Sky
God. As in the cult of Waaq, men are God's creatures subject
to His Will and must live in constant fear of Him and praise Him
always. Similarly to Waaq, Allah stands at the centre of His
universe as its Supreme Power and Creator. The Muslim doctrine
of determinism finds its crude parallel in the attitude of submission and resignation in the face of Waaq. But Muslim fatalism
is more rigidly determined and more elaborately worked out,
since man's actions are predetermined and set down in the
tablet which is before God, similar to that Divine Archetype
from which the Qur'an was delivered to the Prophet. The same
tendency towards a greater systematization in Islam finds
expression in the much more clearly defined position of Allah
in the awarding of right and punishment of evil. Waaq upholds
right but there is little indication that He does much more.
Muslim eschatology accordingly strikes a new note. Death was
a transformation but not to an exact equivalent of the anth-
ropomorphic Muslim paradise. Formerly the spirits of the dead
were to a certain extent localized about the sites of their tombs.
We shall examine below the way in which this affects the reverence paid by Somali to the tombs of Muslim saints. Fundamentally, however, man's relation to Waaq closely mirrors his
relation to Allah and it is hardly surprising that Somali should
now apply the names of the former Cushitic Sky God to Allah
and call Him Eebbe and Waaq.
  The fact that Islam is a 'revealed religion' appears at first
sight to constitute a fundamental difference between the two
religions. But whereas there is apparently nothing in the cult
of Waaq comparable to the tradition of revelation of Allah to the

earlier prophets and finally to Muhammad as the 'Seal', Sūfī
theology has concentrated on those texts and traditions(39)
referring to the immanence of God in the world and has interpreted these as justifying a continued revelation and more
immediate knowledge of Allah. In Sufism, emphasis has veered
from the position of the Sunna towards an interpretation of the
Prophet's role as that of logos, and the approach to Allah has
been correspondingly widened. The approach to God, first
through the Prophet, and then through Ṣūfī shaikhs and saints,
finds its parallel in the association of sacrifice to Waaq with
lineage ancestors.

Comparison of the pre-Islamic Somali spirit-world with Muslim
angelology and demonology reveals again the much higher degree
of systematization in the latter. In Muslim theology, angels,
pre-eminent amongst whom is Gabriel, generally figure as Divine
Messengers created by God to serve and worship Him. They
are charged with recording man's actions in this life, receiving
his soul in heaven, and acting as his counsel on the day of
judgment. On the other hand, jinn are those rebellious spirits
created similarly to man, but of fire in place of earth, and committed to Solomon's keeping, who seek to lead man astray and
to subvert the teachings of the prophets. It is as jinn that the
majority of pre-Islamic spirits previously associated with Waaq
are assimilated in Islam. This is illustrated in the following tale
current among the Gasar Gudda tribe of Somalia.

> Solomon, son of David, on whom be peace, commanded all
> men, all the animals, the wind, spirits, and demons, the
> entire kingdom of the Great King. One day the jinn were
> at work as usual, and Solomon, leaning against a tree,
> seemed to be watching them although he gave no sign of
> repose. Solomon was dead, but remained supported by the
> tree while the jinn unaware of what had happened went on
> with their work. At last the termites succeeded in eating
> their way through Solomon's support precipitating him
> heavily on to the ground. The jinn quickly ran to the spot
> and saw that the son of David was dead. They began to
> rejoice for now they could stop working since their master
> was dead. They hastened to the termites and made a pact
> with them, saying, 'You make your nest of earth and we
> will bring the water for its strengthening'. From this time
> forth jinn and termites are in alliance (Ferrandi, 1903,
> p. 309).

Here within Islam the spirits attendant upon the mysterious
construction of termite mounds are associated with jinn in
Solomon's keeping. The relation 'spirits-termites' is given
Muslim sanction in Solomon's authority over jinn. Similarly the
source of the efficacy of divination, ordeals, charms, and
prophylactic amulets has been transferred from Waaq to Allah
when beneficent and to jinn when mischievous or evil. Now

the favourite amulet is the Ṣūfī rosary (tusbaħ) whose 99 beads remind the believer of the innumerable praise-names of Allah and help him to perform his prayer-tasks. Perhaps equally popular as amulets are small leather pouches armed with inscriptions from the Qur'an. Thus phenomena which formerly owed their power to some connexion with Waaq now originate in Allah, the ultimate source of all power.(40) Saar spirits are described by Somali as a kind of jinn. The whole spirit hierarchy of Waaq is being progressively Islamized. This is a process which naturally also applies to God's attributes. Among the Gasar Gudda, again, the rainbow, from being the Sky God's belt, has become the path good souls take to heaven, although it is also contended by some to be the smoke made by rain falling upon termite hills. Rain-drops are believed to turn into angels (an understandable evaluation); thunder (uri) is the voice of angels (malaika) or the noise of their combat in striving to stop rain. Lightning (birk) darts forth from the armpits of melek Mikail, the archangel Michael.(41) Michael (Sura, II) appears thus to be taken as a symbol of war. These are a few examples indicative of the way in which the Muslim spirit hierarchy is understood in terms of Cushitic cosmology.

The sab in Islam

The traditions which surround the outcast artisan peoples of Somaliland provide illuminating material for the study of the interaction of pre-Islamic and Muslim religion. The sab: Yibir, Tumaal, Midgaan, etc., leather-workers, saddlers, smiths, and 'sweepers', who act as hunters and mercenaries, and perform other menial tasks for Somalis, are shrouded in an aura of magic and witchcraft. Their position lies between that of freedom and slavery and they may perhaps be described most appropriately as bondsmen. They lack almost all those rights common to freeborn Somali (Lewis, 1955, pp. 51-5). They have no political rights vis-à-vis Somalis, they own no tribal lands, and in no place do they constitute an independent territorial group. In all their relations with freeborn Somalis they act through the noble Somali family to which they are attached as servants. They are separated from freemen by the usual barriers to commensalism. Sab are also supposed to speak amongst themselves special dialects which are hardly intelligible to freeborn Somali. Because of their habit of eating portions of meat (head, tripe, and feet) which noble Somali scorn and class with pork as unclean in a religious sense, they are branded as being in a perpetual state of ritual impurity (nijaas). For the same reason they are often referred to as 'corpse-eaters' (bakhti'une). Of this despised class the Yibir are especially interesting. They enjoy a high reputation for magic and sorcery and wander through the country blessing newly born children and newly wedded couples. They receive in return small gifts which are recognized to be due to them by right and could only be refused at the risk of incurring grave misfortune. These presents made to Yibir are represented by Somali as part of the compensation owing to them in perpetuity for the murder of their ancestor Muḥammad Ḥanīf by Shaikh Aw Barkhadle.(42) Shaikh Aw Barkhadle is associated with Shaikh Isḥaaq, founder of the Isḥaaq tribal family, as one of those who brought Islam to Somaliland from Arabia. In fact, according to tradition, he was summoned to Somaliland to deal with the pagan magician Muḥammad Ḥanīf. The Yibir ancestor was tricked into entering a mound which Aw Barkhadle's superior powers caused to collapse imprisoning the unfortunate magician inside. Thus in this context was the pre-eminence of Islam established. Associated with the mysterious disappearance of their ancestor is the belief that no one has ever seen a dead Yibir.(43) These traditions describing the origin of the customary gifts to Yibir are to a certain extent inconsistent with present practice inasmuch as normally an unattached Yibir is not covered by blood-compensation. But it is significant that what is feared and what is revered should be attributed to a common origin in which pagan sorcery is overcome by Muslim baraka.

Saar rites and dhikr

To return to the saar dance. It is evident that this ceremony has inherent susceptibility to syncretism in the services (*dhikr*) of the Ṣūfi ṭarīqas. Especially is this true of the most popular forms of the dhikr, where trance states in which 'fading' or 'death' of self, believed to result in mystical union with God, are induced by direct stimulation. The dhikr held by the Aḥmadiya at their annual pilgrimage to the tomb of Shaikh ^cAli Maye Durogba have been described as follows. 'Thousands come to the tomb from all parts of Somalia. The festival lasts fifteen days and culminates in a great dhikr on the last night when the pilgrims form an immense circle and, to the accompaniment of singing, recite their formulae in raucous saw-like voices rhythmically swaying their bodies. This continues until daybreak. Once they have got well worked-up, large numbers fall foaming to the ground in induced epileptic convulsions' (Barile, 1935). This is neither an informed nor a sympathetic description but it serves to indicate how closely the ṭarīqa dhikr resembles the saar dance and suggests a syncretism which is well established in Egypt and elsewhere.(44) The similarities between the attainment of spirit possession (or the release from possession) and absorption in Allah which are the objects of the dance and the dhikr respectively have already been pointed out.

The assimilation of baraka

In the foregoing various aspects of the conversion of spirit-refractions of Waaq to Muslim equivalents have been discussed. These are variations upon the general principle of the translation of Cushitic power into Muslim baraka.(45) From the functional standpoint the most fundamental application of this exchange is that underlying the absorption of Ṣūfi genealogies

which leads ultimately, as I have suggested, to the inclusive
ascription of the Somali people to the Qurayshitic lineage of
the Prophet. For it is this equivalence which permits Muslim
saints to be venerated and communed with in sacrifice and
prayer at the sites of former pre-Islamic shrines. Shrines
which were formerly venerated for their Cushitic power are
now venerated for their Muslim baraka. These are the places
which famous Somali Muslim saints are believed to have visited
in their peregrinations or at which they are believed to have
appeared to believers in dreams. Tombs are scattered all over
Somaliland and more of them are places of manifestation or
visitation than the actual burial grounds of the saints whose
baraka is sought in pilgrimage to them. Thus as in all Muslim
countries, old shrines continue to command respect although
the source of their power has been transferred to Islam. The
veneration of saints' tombs has, however, a more specific
significance since it is through sacrifice to eponymous ancestors
at such local shrines that tribal relations were maintained with
Waaq at all levels of the social structure. Moreover, the emphasis placed on genealogies and the importance attached to eponymous ancestors, celebrated at their tombs, have promoted and
continue to promote the adoption of Ṣūfī genealogies and the
transfiguration of the founders of ṭarīqas and jamā'as into
eponymous tribal founders. Thus within Islam the ancestors
of clans and clan segments are represented as saints or shaikhs,
while the whole system is validated in the attribution of Somali
origins to immigrant Arabians, in the case of tribal families,
to figures such as Isḥaaq and Daarood. This process, in turn,
is facilitated by the continuous immigration of Arabs which
provides the historical component in Somali traditions of descent
from Arabia.

This short discussion of Cushitic religion and its Islamization
has been included to provide a framework for the study of
Somali and Ṣūfī institutions which forms the substance of this
paper. The apparent similarity of the concepts of Cushitic
power, immanent in Somali genealogies, and baraka, immanent
in Ṣūfī genealogies, which attach to the institutions of sacrifice
to founding tribal ancestors and to saint worship respectively,
underlies the transfiguration of tribal founders into Islamic
saints. The organization of both cults depends upon a lineage
system in which religious power of a similar nature inheres. It
has seemed appropriate to investigate the nature of the power
inherent in Somali genealogies (independent of Ṣūfī accretion)
by viewing it in the general setting of the pre-Islamic hierarchy
of Cushitic power. The spirit-refractions of Waaq could hardly
be supposed to bear no relation to the religious functions of
Somali genealogies and the significance of these genealogies is,
as we have seen, elucidated by considering their functions in
Cushitic religion. The persistance of pre-Islamic beliefs and
customs is a commonplace in Islamic countries. In particular,
the syncretism of pre-Islamic 'animistic' cults is frequently

described in the literature on Islam. The assimilation of such cults to Muslim baraka is well attested. There is therefore nothing new in the general scope of this essay. But it has been my object to try to trace in detail the mechanism of this assimilation in relation to Sufism on the one hand, and, on the other, to the lineage organization which is the basic principle of Somali social organization. I have suggested, and I believe this could be substantiated by reference to many other parts of Muslim Africa and to Arabia, that Sufism although in origin a product of the sophisticated and highly civilized centres of the Muslim world, is eminently suitable to tribal society. Especially is this true of certain features of its religious organization. In tribal societies where stress is placed upon the power of lineage ancestors to mediate between man and God, Sufism provides an interpretation of Islam which, while preserving the supreme absoluteness of Allah, mitigates the uniqueness of the Prophet in favour of more accessible and more immediate intercessors.

NOTES

1 In the transcription of Somali words I have wherever possible used the orthography of B.W. Andrzejewski as adopted by C.R.V. Bell in his work 'The Somali Language' (Longman), 1953. In this orthography vowel length is represented by doubling vowel letters, i.e. long 'a' is written 'aa', etc. In some cases, however, I have had to adhere to the spellings given by my Italian authorities. Somali place-names, such as Mogadishu, are 'anglicized' from the Italian. Arabic words are transliterated according to common usage.

   This paper is based on library research and not on my subsequent (post-1955) fieldwork in Somalia. I wish to acknowledge the help in the preparation of this this paper which I have received from many scholars and to express my gratitude in particular to Ali Garaad Jama and Musa Haaji Isma'il Galaal of the British Somaliland Protectorate, to Mr A.M. Abū Zaid, Mr B.W. Andrzejewski, Dr P.T.W. Baxter, Professor E.E. Evans-Pritchard, Sir H.A.R. Gibb, Dr G. Mathew, and Professor R.B. Sergeant.

2 The same conclusion is reached by Drague in his masterly 'Esquisse d'Histoire Religieuse du Maroc', p. 8.

3 The authorities upon whose work this classification rests are cited in the Cushitic bibliography at the end of Part II of this paper.

4 By 'Ṣūfī genealogies' are meant, as indicated above, the personal genealogies of the shaikhs who are the founders and heads of the Somali Ṣūfī Dervish Orders.

5 It is important to distinguish the 'Sab' from the 'outcast' client peoples of Somaliland who have no independent tribal

organization and do not own lands. These artisans and craftsmen have a clearly defined subject status and are written *sab*
(see Lewis, 1955, pp. 51-5). It is unclear whether *sab* and
Sab are linguistically identical or whether there are any
ethnic connexions between the two peoples.

6 This division is, as Professor R.B. Serjeant has suggested
to me, reminiscent of that between the northern and southern Arabs who trace descent from ᶜAdnān and Qaḥṭān
respectively.

7 Correctly as above indicated 'Soomaali'.

8 Clients are called *magan* in the northern dialects; in the
south ᶜ*arifa,* and among the Digil, *sheegad.*

9 The extent of exogamy appears to vary from tribe to tribe,
partly no doubt dependent upon size, and it is at present
impossible to generalize definitively.

10 Contrast the classical definition of Ibn Khaldūn, 'Prolegomènes', trs. de Slane, I, p. 382.

11 The generic word for any form of offering to God and for
sacrifice in its widest sense is amongst the northern Somali
Rabbibari, which Andrzejewski translates 'beseeching God';
among the Hawiye of Somalia *Waaq da*ᶜ*il* 'offering to the
Sky God' is used according to Cerulli (1923).

12 Professor Serjeant's study of south Arabian MSS, has shown
conclusively that the 'two great centres of diffusion of trade
and the faith' were Zeila and Mogadishu (personal communication)

13 Professor R.B. Serjeant, personal communication.

14 An account of his life is found in al-Shillī's '*al-Mashra*ᶜ *al-
Rawi*' (A.H. 1319, printed in the ᶜAmīriyah Press), II,
pp. 34-41.

15 *Wadaad* is the Somali equivalent of the 'marabout' or 'mullah',
sometimes described as 'hedge priest', found in all Muslim
countries. His functions are manifold since as well as
expounding the Qur'an and *hadīth* as a theologian, he
assumes too all the functions of itinerant qāḍī. The origin
of the word *wadaad* is uncertain, it may equally be an
Arabic borrowing or of Cushitic derivation.

16 See Lewis (1955) p. 154; Anderson (1954) pp. 44 ff.

17 On the subject of a suitable script for Somali see:
King, J.S., Somali as a Written Language, 'Indian Anti-
quary', August and October, 1887; Maino, M., L'alfabeto
Osmania in Somalia, 'RSE', 10, 1951; Galaal, M.H.I.,
Arabic Script for Somali, 'Islamic Quarterly', I, 2, 1954,
pp. 114-18; Maino, M., 'La Lingua Somala Strumento
d'Insegnamente Professionale', 1953; Andrzejewski, B.W.,
Some Problems of Somali Orthography, 'Somaliland Journal'
(Hargeisa), I, 1, 1954, pp. 34-47.

18 See Cerulli (1923) pp. 12, 22, who describes the shaikhs
as one of the most important proseytizers of the Qadiriya
in the hinterland of Somalia, although, as indicated above,
the Order had already at the beginning of the nineteenth
century assumed some prominence in the interior with the

foundation of the community of Bardera on the Juba river. 'Awês' is a Somalization of 'Uwais' and the shaikh's full name is Uwais ibn Muḥammed al-Barāwī.

19 See above, and Cerulli (1923), p. 22.

20 The ħaaji's full name is Sh. ^CAbd Allāh ibn Yūsif al-Qalan-qūlī al-Qutbī al-Qādīrī ash-Shāfi ^Cil-Ash^Carī. The work was published in Cairo in A.H. 1338 (1918-19) and printed by Mustafà al-Bābī al-Halabī in two volumes. It constitutes a most valuable collection of the lives of the Somali Qadiriya shaikhs.

21 See below, p. 144.

22 Cf. Gibb (1947) p. 55.

23 See Lewis (1955) p. 17.

24 The Saraman tribal cluster comprises the Lisan Horsi, Lisan Bari, the Rer Dumal, Garuale, Luwai, Hadama, Jiron, and the Maalim-wena (see Lewis (1955) p. 35).

25 For this important Rahanwiin tribe see Lewis (1955) pp. 36-9, 40, 121, etc.

26 Cerulli (1927) pp. 404-6. See also Moreno, M.M., Il dialetto degli Ašrāf di Mogadiscio, 'RSE', 12, 1953, pp. 107-39.

27 According to Cerulli (1923, p. 29) the policy of the Italian Administration was to admit the leaders of *jamā'as* as religious leaders but to allow them no political authority. The development of *jamā'as* in the fertile riverine area was actively discouraged and the foundation of new settlements constrained as far as possible. In the arable lands thus protected from the further encroachment of *jamā'as* the government saw the possible realization of their aim to establish the economic independence of the colony in extensive agricultural development.

28 For a tentative account see Lewis (1955) pp. 45-8.

29 See Huntingford (1955) p. 19.

30 For an excellent account of the religion of the Galla of Ethiopia see Huntingford (1955) pp. 74-87.

31 Cf. Qur'an, *Sura* II, 30.

32 In fact in 1955 the British Somaliland Protectorate Advisory Council unanimously agreed that legislation should be introduced to make the practice of saar rites illegal. 'War Somali Sidihi', no. 60, 23 April 1955.

33 Among the Cushitic Agao of Gondar in northern Ethiopia, the refractions of the Sky God (Zār) which possess people are called zār, are associated especially but not exclusively with women, are inherited in the family, and have genealogies corresponding to their territorial distribution (Leiris, 1934a, pp. 134, 126).

34 The Afar (Danakil) of southern Eritrea and of Ethiopia have a similar ceremony in which the possessed dancer is called *jenile* (jinn?). See Licata (1885) p. 267; Thesiger (1935) p. 8.

35 See Lewis (1955) p. 62.

36 It would be misleading to overemphasize the significance of

this distinction, since, except in the earliest centuries of Islam there has always been a wide divergence between the theory and practice of the Shari'a in all Muslim countries.

37 This is reflected, perhaps fortuitously, in the extent to which the qādi's competence in the administration of the Shari'a has been recognized by the Governments of British and Italian Somaliland. In Somalia qādis have a limited jurisdiction in criminal proceedings, while in British Somaliland criminal cases are expressly excluded from their jurisdiction. See Lewis (1955) p. 124; Anderson (1954) pp. 43 ff. For the Arabs, cf. Montagne (1947) p. 96.

38 According to Cucinotta, 1921a, p. 34, the important sources of Shari'a in Somalia are: al-Nawawi's 'Minhaj at-Talibin'; the works of Ismaᶜil Muqri (Brockelmann, 'GAL', II, p. 190; 'Suppt.', II, p. 254), and of Abū Ishāq ash-Shirāzi (O. Löfgren (ed.), 'Arabische Texte zur ... Aden', Uppsala, 1950, pp. 20, 55, 94 ff). Subsidiary sources are: Ibn al-Qāsim al-Ghazzi's 'Fath al-Gharib'; Abū Yahyā Zakariyā' al-Ansāri's 'Fath al-Wahhāb' (Brockelmann, 'GAL', I, pp. 395-6), and Muhammad ash-Shirbini's 'al-Iqnā' fi hall al Fath' (Brockelmann, 'GAL', Suppt., II, pp. 441 ff). See also M. Maino's interesting article, La valutazione del danno alla persona nella dottrina giurdica musulmana, 'Meridiano Somalo', November 1951.

39 For a readily accessible compilation of hadiths used by Sūfis as a basis for their ascetic and theosophical interpretation of theology see Arberry (1950) pp. 24-30.

40 Cf. the fate of the pre-Islamic Gods and spirits in Arabia, Koran, Sura XXXVII. For general indications of the universality of such syncretisms in Islam, see Gibb (1947) pp. 23 ff; Milliot (1949) p. 643.

41 Ferrandi (1903) pp. 298 ff.

42 Cerulli, 'RAL', ser. 6, IV, 1931, 67, has suggested that Saint Aw Barkhadle ('Au Bakhardi'), whose tomb at the site named after the shaikhs is a favourite place of pilgrimage of the Habr Awal tribe, may be identified with Yūsuf Barkatla, ancestor of 'Umar Walashma', founder of the Ifāt dynasty. For the position of the tomb see Drake-Brockman (1912) pp. 217 ff.

43 The Yibir ancestor bears, in point of name and circumstance, some superficial resemblance to the Shiᶜite 'hidden' Imām Muhammad ibn al-Hanafiya.

44 See Massignon, 'Enc. Is.', IV, 668.

45 Among the Christian and Muslim Agao of Gondar this syncretism leads to the coexistence of Zār Shaikh Muhammad (Muslim); Leiris (1934a) pp. 126-9.

BIBLIOGRAPHY

Abbreviations
'AAE' 'Archivo per l'Antropologia e la Etnologia' (Florence)
'AAI' 'Annali di Africa Italiana' (Rome)
'BSAI' 'Bolletino della Società Africana d'Italia'
'BSOAS' 'Bulletin of the School of Oriental and African Studies'
  (London)
'Enc. Is.' 'Encyclopaedia of Islam'
'GJ' 'Geographical Journal'
'JEANHS' 'Journal of the East African Natural History Society'
'JRAI' 'Journal of the Royal Anthropological Institute'
'JSA' 'Journal de la Société des Africanistes'
'RAL' 'Rendiconti del Reale Accademia dei Lincei' (Rome)
'REI' 'Revue des Etudes Islamiques'
'RC' 'Rivista Coloniale' (Rome)
'RETP' 'Revue d'Ethnographie et de Traditions Populaires'
'RSE' 'Rassegna di Studi Etiopici' (Rome)
'RSO' 'Rivista degli Studi Orientali' (Rome)
'S.d. Ph.-Hist. Kl. d. K. Akad. d. Wiss.'
  'Sitzungsberichte der Philosophisch-Historischen Klasse der
  Kaiserlichen Akademie der Wissenschaften' (Vienna)
'Z.f.Eing.Spr.' 'Zeitschrift fur Eingeborenen Sprachen' (Berlin)

*Cushitic**
Battara, P. (1934), Le osservazioni antropometrichi eseguite
  dal Prof. A. Mochi in Eritrea, AAE, 66, 1934, pp. 5-172.
Bruna, R. (1907), Monografia sulle popolazioni delle Acchele-
  Guzai, 'Relazione sulla Colonia Eritrea. Camera dei Deputati'
  (Rome), 32, pp. 657-732.
Bryan, M.A. (1947), 'The Distribution of the Semitic and
  Cushitic Languages of Africa', London, OUP for the Inter-
  national African Institute.
Cerulli, E. (1922), 'The folk-literature of the Galla of southern
  Abyssinia' (Harvard African Studies, III). Cambridge, Mass.
Cerulli, E. (1933), 'Etiopia Occidentale'. Rome, 2 vols.
Chambard, R. (1925), Notes sur quelques croyances religieuses
  des Galla, 'RETP', pp. 125-35.
Chiodi, V. (1937), Gruppi sanguigni in relazione alla razza;
  loro possible applicazione alla risoluzione dei problemi
  etnoantropologici riguardanti l'Africa Orientale Italiana, 'AEE',
  67, pp. 160-72.
Cipriani, L. (1940), 'Abitazioni indigene dell'Africa Orientale
  Italiana'. Naples.
Conti Rossini, C. (1903-4), Al-Ragali, 'Boll. Soc. Ital. di
  Espl. Geog'.
Conti Rossini, C. (1913), Schizzo del dialetto Saho dell'Alta
  Assaorta in Eritrea, 'RAL', 22, 5, pp. 151-246.

*No works on the Beja are included here. For a full bibliography of
the Somali, Afar (Danakil), and Saho see Lewis (1955) pp.177-94.

Conti Rossini, C. (1914), Studi su popolazioni dell'Ethiopia:
    Gli Irob e le loro tradizioni, 'RSO', 3, pp. 849-900.
Conti Rossini, C. Note sugli Agau, 'Giornale Soc. Asiatica
    Italiana' (Florence), pp. 17-18.
Conti Rossini, C. (1937), 'Risultati Scientifici di un Viaggio
    nella Colonia Eritrea', Florence.
Huntingford, G.W.B. (1955), 'The Galla of Ethiopia: the
    Kingdoms of Kafa and Janjero'. (Ethnographic Survey of
    Africa, North-Eastern Africa, Part II.) London, International
    African Institute.
Jahn, A. (1909-10), Lautlehre der Saho-Sprache in Nordabes-
    sinien, 'Jahresbericht der K.K. Staats Realschule' (Vienna),
    23, pp. 1-38.
Leiris, M. (1934a), Le culte des Zars à Gondar, 'Aethiopia',
    4, pp. 96-136.
Leiris, M. (1934b), 'L'Afrique fantôme', Paris.
Lewis, I.M. (1955), 'Peoples of the Horn of Africa: Somali,
    Afar and Saho'. (Ethnographic Survey of Africa, North-
    Eastern Africa, Part I.) London, International African
    Institute.
Licata, G.B. (1885), 'Assab e i Danachili', Milan.
Lucas, M. (1935), Renseignements ethnographiques et linguis-
    tiques sur les Danakils de Tadjourah, 'JSA', 5, pp. 182-202.
Nadel, S.F. (1943), 'Races and Tribes of Eritrea', Asmara,
    Eritrea, British Military Administration.
Odorizzi, D. (1907), La Dankalia italiana del Nord, 'Relazione
    sulla Colonia Eritrea, Camera dei Deputati' (Rome), 32,
    pp. 1915-63.
Paulitschke, P. (1880), 'Beiträge zur Ethnographie und
    Anthropologie der Somal, Galla, und Harar', Leipzig.
Pollera, A. (1935), 'Le Popolazioni Indigene dell'Eritrea',
    Bologna.
Reinisch, L. (1886-7), Die Afar Sprache, 'S.d.Ph.-Hist.Kl.d.
    K.Akad.d.Wiss'. (Vienna), 111, 1886, pp. 5 ff; 113, 1886,
    pp. 795-917; 114, 1887, pp. 89-169.
Reinisch, L. (1889-90), 'Die Saho-Sprache', Vienna, 2 vols.
Schmidt, W. (1940), 'Der Ursprung der Gottesidee', Bd. VII,
    Münster i. W.
Seligman, C.G. (1939), 'Races of Africa'. First revised edn,
    London, Thornton Butterworth.
Sergi, G. (1897), 'Africa, Antropologia della stirpe Camitica',
    Turin.
Thesiger, W. (1935), The Awash River and the Aussa Sultanate,
    'GJ', 85, pp. 1-23.
Trimingham, J.S. (1952), 'Islam in Ethiopia', London, OUP.
Ullendorff, E. (1955), 'The Semitic Languages of Ethiopia',
    London.
Venieri, L. (1935), Sulla etnografia dei Saho, 'AAE', 65,
    pp. 5-59.
Vernau, R. (1909), 'Anthropologie et Ethnographie'. (Mission
    Duchesne Fournet en Ethiopie, Part II.) Paris.

General

Barnes, J.A. (1954), 'Politics in a Changing Society. A Political History of the Fort Jameson Ngoni', London, OUP for the Rhodes-Livingstone Institute. (See esp. pp. 47-63 for a sophisticated discussion of lineage systems.)

Evans-Pritchard, E.E. (1940), 'The Nuer: A Description of the Modes of Livelihood and Political Institutions of a Nilotic People', Oxford, Clarendon Press.

Evans-Pritchard, E.E. (1954), The meaning of sacrifice among the Nuer, 'JRAI', 84, pp. 21-33.

Forde, D. (ed.) (1954), 'African Worlds: Studies in the Cosmological Ideas and Social Values of African People', London, OUP for the International African Institute.

Fortes, M., and Evans-Pritchard, E.E. (eds) (1940), 'African Political Systems', London, OUP for the International Institute of African Languages and Cultures.

Gaster, Th. H. (1954), Myth and Story, 'Numen', I, pp. 184-213.

Leeuw, G. Van Der (1933), 'Phänomenologie der Religion', Tübingen. (Translated by J.E. Turner as 'Religion in essence and manifestation', London, 1938.)

Nadel, S.F. (1954), 'Nupe Religion', London.

Smith, Sir W. Robertson (1889), 'Lectures on the religion of the Semites', Edinburgh.

Islam

Ammar, H. (1954), 'Growing up in an Egyptian Village', London, Routledge & Kegan Paul.

Anderson, J.N.D. (1951), Homicide in Islamic law, 'BSOAS', XIII, 4, pp. 811-28.

Anderson, J.N.D. (1954), 'Islamic Law in Africa'. (Colonial Research Publications, no. 16.) London, HMSO, for the Colonial Office.

Arberry, A.J. (1950), 'Sufism: An Account of the Mystics of Islam', London, Allen & Unwin.

Arberry, A.J. (1953), 'The Holy Koran: An Introduction with Selections', London, Allen & Unwin.

Bernard, A., and Milliot, L. (1933), Les qânoûns kabyles dans l'ouvrage de Hanoteau et Letourneux, 'REI', VII, pp. 1-44.

Caspani, E., and Cagnacci, E. (1951), 'Afghanistan, Crocevia dell'Asia', Milan.

Cerulli, E. Article Zār in 'Enc.Is.', IV, p. 1217.

Daualibi, M. (1941), 'La Jurisprudence dans le Droit Islamique', Paris.

Drague, G. (1951), 'Esquisse d'Histoire Religieuse du Maroc'. (Cahiers de l'Afrique et l'Asie, II.) Paris.

Evans-Pritchard, E.E. (1949), 'The Sanusi of Cyrenaica', Oxford, Clarendon Press.

Fakhry, Majid (1954), The theocratic idea of the Islamic state in recent controversies, 'International Affairs', XXX, pp. 450-62.

Feilberg, C.G. (1944), 'La Tente Noire', Copenhagen.

Fyzee, A.A. (1949), 'Outlines of Muhammadan Law', London, OUP.

Gibb, Sir H.A.R. (1947), 'Modern Trends in Islam', Chicago.

Gibb, Sir H.A.R. (1953), 'Mohammedanism', London, OUP.

Gibb, Sir H.A.R., and Bowen, H. (1950), 'Islamic Society and the West', vol. I, London, OUP for Roy. Inst. Internat. Affairs.

Goldziher, I. Article Fiḳh, 'Enc. Is.', II, pp. 101-5.

Hurgronje, C. Snouck (1888-9), 'Mekka', Haag, 1888-9, 2 vols and atlas.

Ibn Khaldūn (1863-8), Muqaddima (trs. de Slane as) 'Les Prolegomènes d'Ibn Khaldoun', Paris.

Jaussen, A. (1908), 'Coutumes des Arabes au Pays de Moab', Paris.

Kahle, P. (1912), Zār-Beschwörungen in Egypten, 'Der Islam', III, pp. 1-41, 189-90.

Lammens, H. (1944), 'L'Islam', Beyrouth.

Lewis, B. (1950), 'The Arabs in History', London.

Massignon, L. (1922), 'Essai sur les origines de Lexique technique de la Mystique musulmane', Paris.

Massignon, L. Article Ṭarika, 'Enc. Is.', pp. 667-72.

Massignon, L. Article Taṣawwuf, 'Enc. Is.', pp. 681-5.

Massignon, L. (1947), L'Umma et ses synonymes: notion de 'Communauté sociale' en Islam, 'REI', (14,) années 1941-6, (pub.) pp. 151-7.

Milliot, L. (1949), La conception de l'état et de l'ordre légal dans l'Islam, 'Acad. de Droit International, Recueil des Cours', II, pp. 596-686.

Milliot, L. (1953), 'Introduction a l'étude du droit Musulman', Paris, Recueil Sirey.

Montagne, R. (1947), 'La civilisation du désert', Paris.

Moreno, M.M. (1935), 'La Dottrina dell' Islam', Bologna.

Nallino, C.A. (1940), 'Raccolta di Scritti Editi e Inediti', vol. II, 'L'Islam: Dogmatica-Sufismo-Confraternite', Rome, Istituto per l'Oriente.

Nallino, C.A. (1942), 'Raccolta di Scritti Editi e Inediti', vol. IV, 'Diritto Musulmano, Diritti Orientali Christiani', Rome, Istituto per l'Oriente.

Peters, E. (1951), The Bedouin of Cyrenaica, MS. thesis, Oxford D.Phil.

Rachid, A. (1937), L'Islam et le droit des gens, 'Acad. de Droit International, Recueil des Cours', II, pp. 371-506.

Rodwell, J.M. (tr.) (1909), 'The Koran, translated from the Arabic', London, Dent and Sons.

Santillana, D. (1926-38), 'Istituzioni di Diritto Musulmano Malichita', Rome, 2 vols.

Schacht, J. (1950), 'The origins of Muhammadan Jurisprudence', Oxford, Clarendon Press.

Schacht, J. Article Shari'a, 'Enc. Is.', IV, pp. 320-4.

Trimingham, J.S. (1949), 'Islam in the Sudan', London, OUP.

Wustenfeld, F. (1852-3), 'Genealogische Tabellen der

arabischen Stamme und Familien mit historischen und geographischen Bemerkungen in einem alphabetischen Register', Göttingen.

Somali

Barile, P. (1935), 'Colonizzazione Fascista nella Somalia Meridionale', Rome.
Bell, C.R.V. (1953), 'The Somali Language', London, Longmans.
Bottego, V. (1895), 'Viaggi di Scoperta nel Cuore dell'Africa: il Giuba Esplorato', Rome.
Burton, Sir R.F. (1894), 'First Footsteps in East Africa', Memorial edn., London, 2 vols.
Cerulli, E. (1918), Testi di diritto consuetudinario del Somali Marrēhân, 'RSO', 7, pp. 861-76.
Cerulli, E. (1919), II diritto consuetudinario della Somalia Italiana Settentrionale, 'BSAI', 38, pp. 93 ff. (Reprint)
Cerulli, E. (1923), Note sul movimento Musulmano nella Somalia, 'RSO', 10, pp. 1-36.
Cerulli, E. (1924), Un gruppo Mahri nella Somalia Italiana, 'RSO', 11, pp. 25-6.
Cerulli, E. (1926), Le popolazioni della Somalia nella tradizioni storica locale, 'RAL', ser. 6, II, pp. 150-72.
Cerulli, E. (1927), Nuovi documenti arabi per la storia della Somalia, 'RAL', ser. 6, III, pp. 392-410.
Cerulli, E. (1929), Le stazioni lunari nelle nozioni astronomiche dei Somali e dei Danakil, 'RSO', 12.
Cerulli, E. (1931), Tradizioni storiche e monumenti della Migiurtina, 'AAI', 4, pp. 1-2.
Cerulli, E. (1931b), Nuovi appunti sull nozioni astronomiche dei Somali, 'RSO', 13, pp. 2-9.
Cerulli, E. (1936), 'Studi Etiopici. I. La Lingua e la Storia di Harar', Rome, Istituto per l'Oriente.
Cerulli, E. Article Somaliland, 'Enc. Is.', IV, pp. 483-8.
Colucci, M. (1924), Principi di Diritto Consuetudinario della Somalia Italiana Meridionale', Florence.
Corni, G. (ed.) (1937-8), 'La Somalia Italiana', Milan, 2 vols.
Cucinotta, E. (1921a), Delitto, pena, e giustizia presso i Somali del Benadir, 'RC', 16, pp.15-41.
Cucinotta, E. (1921b), Proprieta, ed il sistema contrattuale nel 'Destur' Somalo, 'RC', 16, pp. 243-64.
Cucinotta, E. (1921c), La constituzione sociale Somala, 'RC', 16, pp. 442-56, 493-502.
Deschamps, H. (ed.) (1948), 'L'Union Française, Côte des Somalis-Réunion-Inde', Paris, Berger Levrault, pp. 1-85.
Drake-Brockman, R.E. (1912), 'British Somaliland', London.
Drysdale, J.G.S. (1955), Some aspects of Somali rural society to-day, 'Somaliland Journal' (Hargeisa), I, 2.
Ferrand, G. (1903), 'Les Comalis: Matériaux d'études sur les pays Musulmanes', Paris.
Ferrandi, U. (1903), 'Lugh. Seconda Spedizione Bottego', Rome.

Guillain, C. (1856), 'Documents sur l'histoire, la géographie, et le commerce de l'Afrique Orientale', Paris, A. Bertrand, 3 vols.

Hunt, J.A. (1951), 'A General Survey of the Somaliland Protectorate, 1944-50', London, Crown Agents for the Colonies.

La Rue, A. De. (1937), 'La Somalie Française', Paris.

Laurence, M. (1954), 'A Tree for Poverty: Somali Poetry and Prose', Nairobi, Eagle Press.

Lewis, I.M. (1953), The Social Organisation of the Somali, MS. thesis, Oxford B. Litt.

Lewis, I.M. (1955), 'Peoples of the Horn of Africa: Somali, Afar (Danakil) and Saho'. (Ethnographic Survey of Africa. North-Eastern Africa, Part I.) London, International African Institute.

Mohammed, Ali, Shaikh (1954), The origin of the Isaaq peoples, 'Somaliland Journal' (Hargeisa), I, 1, pp. 22-6.

Moreno, M.M. (1952), Problemi culturali della Somalia, 'Affrica', VII, 9, pp. 235-50.

Palermo, G.M. DA. (1915), 'Dizionario Somalo-Italiano e Italiano-Somalo', Asmara.

Puccioni, N. (1931-6), 'Antropologia ed Etnologia delle Genti della Somalia', Bologna, 2 vols.

Puccioni, N. (1937), 'Le Popolazioni Indigene della Somalia Italiana'. (Manuali Coloniali.) Bologna.

Reinisch, L. (1900-3), 'Die Somali-Sprache', Vienna, 3 vols.

Robecchi-Bricchetti, L. (1889), 'Somalia e Benadir', Milan.

Stefanini, G. (1924), 'La Somalia, Noti e Impressioni di Viaggio', Florence.

Taschdjian, E. (1938), Stammenorganisation und Eheverbote der Somalis, 'Anthropos', 33, 1/2, pp. 114-7.

Tiling, M. Von. (1924-5), Jabarti Texte, 'Z.F.Eing.Spr.', 15, 1924/5, pp. 50-64, 139-58.

Trimingham, J.S. (1952), 'Islam in Ethiopia', London, OUP.

Wright, A.C.A. (1943), The interaction of various systems of law and custom in British Somaliland and their relation with social life, 'JEANHS', 17, 1-2, pp. 66-102.

Zoli, C. (ed.) (1927), 'Notizie sul Territorio di Riva Destra del Giuba, Oltre-Giuba', Rome.

6 ALLIANCE AND DESCENT IN THE MIDDLE EAST AND THE 'PROBLEM' OF PATRILATERAL PARALLEL COUSIN MARRIAGE (1)

Donald P. Cole

I

The social structure of traditional Middle Eastern communities has almost always been described as organized according to the principles of descent. Alliance has usually been overlooked and, in some cases because of the existence of preferential patrilateral parallel cousin marriage, even denied. Descent has been considered so important in Middle Eastern social structure that some scholars have seen it as the basic principle under- lying the organization not only of small-scale local or tribal communities but of the total complex society, in spite of the existence since ancient times of such things as cities, states, and empires. According to Murphy and Kasdan, for example, 'ideally, all Arabs, whether nomadic or sedentary, form a super- lineage, the member units of which trace common ancestry to the prophet Abraham' (1959:21). They further state that 'genealogies are almost the only means given within the formal social structure for ordering larger amalgamations' (1959:23). According to Patai, 'descent, which in Middle Eastern culture means patrilineal descent, is the only factor through which ego can relate to individuals or groups outside his own small world represented by his UDG [unilineal descent group] (1965:347-8).

The aim of this article is to demonstrate that alliance is, none- theless, an important structural feature of Middle Eastern society. It occurs regularly as a result of marriages between members of units of varying sizes - patrilocal households of two to three generations depth, minimal lineages, maximal lineages, clans, and tribes - and between different strata of the society. Just as the boundaries of Middle Eastern unilineal descent groups are easily collapsed to allow fission and fusion according to the principles of segmentary descent, marriage does not always occur between groups of the same type. Yet in spite of a great deal of variation in the types of groups linked, alliance through marriage is an important principle of Middle Eastern social struc- ture and, contrary to Patai and Murphy and Kasdan, alliance, along with descent, is one means by which a person relates to individuals and groups outside his own small world.

This article also takes issue with the notion that Middle Eastern society is organized exclusively according to the principles of kinship (under which rubrics I would include both descent and alliance). The 'larger Arab society' that Murphy and Kasdan refer to (1959:23) is by no means organized accord-

ing to the principles of descent, as they claim. Nor does the
endogamous unilineal descent group exhibit any of the degree
of self-sufficiency that Patai attributes to it, even among highly
traditional and isolated bedouin tribes. According to Patai,

> the endogamous UDG . . . is genetically self-sufficient. This
> means, first of all that there is no necessity for it to maintain
> any social relations with outgroups, since it replenishes and
> augments its human contingent by in-breeding. It also pro-
> vides itself with sustenance by the common effort of its
> membership, and it guarantees its own safety by the numbers
> of its adult males. On the simplest level, the endogamous UDG
> can actually sustain itself in complete isolation from all outside
> society, in a total bio-social autarchy (1965:346).

I question, however, whether this bio-social autarchy exists
anywhere in the Middle East, even as an ideal. As I will show
in this paper, not even the most remote bedouin of the Rub[c]
al-Khali, or Empty Quarter, are self-sufficient economically but
rely on the specialized services of other groups with whom they
do not share descent but with some of whom they occasionally
marry and with all of whom they share a language, a religion,
and a general cultural identity. The economic, social, and
cultural worlds within which even the most isolated groups
operate thus definitely include groups of people from outside
their own maximal descent groups. Interaction between units
of the larger society is based not on shared descent but mainly
on the exchange of specialized goods and services and sometimes
as a result of marriages.

Much of the confusion in studies of Middle Eastern social
structure is especially evident in the attempts by anthropologists
to explain the significance of the practice of patrilateral parallel
cousin marriage and endogamy in general in the Middle East.
During the last two decades, a lively debate has occurred among
anthropologists interested in explaining the phenomenon of
father's brother's daughter marriage in the Middle East. One
of the most recent contributions to this debate (Khuri 1970) has
conveniently summarized and critically examined the explanations
offered for father's brother's daughter (hereinafter referred to
as FBD) marriage, along with presenting a new explanation for
its occurrence.

I do not propose to examine the pros and cons of the various
explanations put forth. In my opinion, each explanation contains
some elements of truth, and FBD marriage quite possibly does
all of the things people say it does: it keeps property intact
and the bloodline pure (the usual native Middle Easterner's
explanation and Baer 1964; Granquist 1931; Peters 1963;
Rosenfeld 1957); it strengthens the bonds between a man and
his paternal nephews, since the latter become his sons-in-law
as well (Barclay 1964; Barth 1954; Peters 1963); it facilitates
the ecologically adaptive process of fission and fusion among the

bedouin by not building up extensive affinal ties (Murphy and Kasdan 1959; 1967); and it contributes to harmonious family relationships, since family kinship relations already exist between the people involved (Khuri 1970). But even if we think up all the possible functions FBD marriage can or does have among those who practise it, we will still be no closer to understanding the significance of this Middle Eastern practice of close endoga-mous marriage.

The 'problem' of FBD marriage, as it has been conceived of in most of the anthropological literature, is at best misleading and confusing. This is because it is suggested, usually implicitly, that FBD marriage characterizes the marriage system as a whole, even when it is recognized that people do not always marry either a real or classificatory FBD, even when this is demogra-phically possible. At the same time, marriage practices are examined in isolation and are seldom seen as an integral part of the total kinship system, which itself is related to the complex social structure of Middle Eastern societies.

We are not dealing with a marriage practice in a tribal society organized exclusively according to the principles of unilineal descent - assuming, of course, that such societies actually exist anywhere except in the minds of some anthropologists. In the case of the Middle East and in spite of most of the literature on the area, we are confronted with a number of different marriage practices, one of which is verbally preferred, in groups in which unilineal descent is only one, though often an extremely important, principle of social organization. As I shall attempt to show by focusing on the Āl Murrah bedouin, Middle Eastern kinship systems cannot be understood by treating either marriage practices or descent as isolated phenomena. Both are inter-related, and the kinship system itself must be seen in relation to the complex, pluralistic nature of Middle Eastern society.

Since Murphy and Kasdan's seminal article on the structure of parallel cousin marriage (1959), much of the interest in this type of marriage system has revolved around the question of how it affects alliance theory. If, as Lévi-Strauss and others have cogently argued, prescriptive marriage rules are mainly ways of integrating unilineal descent groups, how does FBD marriage, which apparently does not create alliances between unilineal descent groups, affect this theory? Murphy and Kasdan explicitly argue that 'parallel cousin marriage has the opposite effect of cross-cousin marriage' (1959:23) and deny that it results in the creation of alliances.

The contrary is true, however. Alliance *is* achieved and symbolized in the Middle East, as in most other societies, through marriage, including FBD marriage. That Murphy and Kasdan and others have not seen this is because they have not heeded Leach's admonition 'to distinguish between the notion of local line (indicating a local descent group) and descent line (indicating a set of kinship categories)' (1961:57). If we follow this advice and look at local descent groups, we see that FBD marriage, at least among the bedouin, occurs between two such groups. Residence is patrilocal and brothers live together, but by the time their children are ready to marry (i.e. when the children have become second generation), the original household is divided and brothers establish new and independent households and thus create new local descent groups, each with its own herd of animals, the major property they possess. Marriages, including FBD marriage, result in the bride moving from her father's household to that of her husband's father and the consequent creation of special affinal ties between the two groups. FBD marriage is thus seen as not basically different from other marriage systems: it 'is a systematically organized affair between two social groups . . . the core [of which] is composed of the adult *males* of a kin group all resident in one place' (Leach 1961: 56; Leach's italics).

As I have already suggested, much confusion in the anthropological literature on the Middle East results from the failure to see the kinship system of the area as only one aspect or feature of the total social structure. Marriages occur not just because of the dynamics of the kinship system or the existence of preferential rules but are often related to the political and economic structure of the society as well. In this regard, I take inspiration partly from Lévi-Strauss's article, The Bear and the Barber(1963), in which he argued that the same principles of exchange underlie the social structure of two contrastingly different societies, the Australian aborigines and India. Among the Australian aborigines, integration is achieved mainly through marriage (i.e. through the exchange of women between exogamous totemic groups) whereas among the Indians, integration is achieved mainly through the exchange of specialized goods and services produced or performed by members of endogamous castes.

I cannot fully explore in this article the implications of viewing the Middle East as a pluralistic stratified society, but it is necessary to point out that even the so-called tribal groups in the area are fundamentally integrated into a more complex culture and society in which they all together make up a single category in contrast with other social categories. As Barth has very well argued,

In much of the Middle East, 'plural' societies are found, characterized by clear lines of internal segmentation, often based on ethnic criteria; such societies have a structure characterized by the summation of statuses in an involute system, in which a high degree of status differentiation is associated with a limited set of permitted status combinations. Such systems depend for their persistence on very clear criteria for status ascription. In societies other than those of extreme patriliny, this prerequisite implies a pattern of endogamy within the stratified groups, a feature often emphasized in the definition of caste (1960:145).

Whether Middle Eastern society should be discussed in terms
of caste is debatable. Leach (1960) prefers to restrict the usage
of caste as a descriptive term to the Indian sub-continent. Barth,
however, obviously shows (1960) that essentially the same
principles of social organization that underly the classical caste
societies of India are operative in at least some Middle Eastern
societies, although without the support of an ideological system
such as that provided by Hinduism. At any rate, we are not
dealing with tribal societies that are 'self-contained, politically,
economically, and culturally . . . islands unto themselves'
(Gellner 1969:2). Even the dissident tribes in the Middle East
that are (or were) politically independent 'are not culturally
independent. They are embedded in the wider civilization of the
Muslim world. In large measure they share the religion, concepts, symbols of the whole of the Muslim world' (Gellner 1969:2).
It is thus essential to conceive of Middle Eastern societies as
pluralistic, in which highly endogamous groups, sometimes distinguished by ethnic, linguistic, and/or religious criteria, are
also associated with special occupations: the mosaic, as described by Coon, in which 'the peoples of the Middle East are
organized into a complicated social system based on an ethnic
division of labor' (1958:3). Although I cannot fully explore the
pluralistic nature of Middle Eastern society in this paper, I
argue that the endogamous nature of Middle Eastern marriage
practices can only be understood as an aspect of the pluralistic
structure of Middle Eastern society. This is true even in the
case of a tribe which enjoys a high degree of territorial isolation
and which only rarely participates in exchange transactions
with other elements in the wider society.

II

The Āl Murrah, who number about 15,000 people, are one of the
most traditional and, in many ways, least changed of Saudi
Arabia's major bedouin tribes. They inhabit most of the 200,000
square mile Rub' al-Khali, or Empty Quarter, of south eastern
Arabia and extend northwards as far as Kuwait and the area of
the Iraqi-Saudi Arabian border. Although some are changing to
herding sheep and goats, most of the Āl Murrah are classic
examples of the traditional camel herding nomads of Arabia.
They express strong feelings of tribal identity and proudly
think of themselves as herders and as warriors. Although they
provide much of their own subsistence through the nomadic
herding of milk camels, they depend on market purchases for a
number of items that are basic to their diets (especially dates
and rice, as well as coffee, cardamom, tea, and sugar) and to
their pastoral activities (leather buckets, ropes, etc.). They
almost never exchange any of their own pastoral products with
outsiders nor do they regularly sell anything in markets. The
money used in market purchases comes mainly from membership

in the Saudi Arabian National Guard or as pensions in recognition of their past military service to the Saudi Arabian nation-state.(2)

Although they spend most of their days in isolated activities in a vast desert and are primarily concerned with their own internal affairs, they are very much aware of, affected by, and depend on the outside world, of which they readily recognize they are a part. They are proud to recognize that they are Saudis and say that they are not only Āl Faisal, People of Faisal. They contrast themselves with other Saudis who are not herders and warriors but proclaim their similarity to other Sharif, noble, bedouin tribespeople. Although herding has lost much of its relative importance in the changing economy of Saudi Arabia, the military activities of all the Sharif bedouin tribes continue to be extremely important, and their membership in the National Guard, to which they have exclusive entrance, symbolizes the major way in which the Āl Murrah and other bedouin are incorporated into the structure of the modern Saudi Arabian nation-state (cf. Cole 1973:123-7).

III

Patrilineal descent and the dual opposition of descent groups are major organizing principles in Āl Murrah society. When explaining the organization of their tribal structure to an outsider - inquiring anthropologist or any other tribesman - the Āl Murrah either begin with their founding ancestor, Murrah, or they begin with EGO. If they begin with their ancestor, they say that Murrah had two sons, ᶜAli and Shabib, both of whom had two sons. One of Shabib's sons had two sons, one of whom had two sons, one of whom also had two sons. If they begin with EGO, they say that we in our descent group, A, unite with group B as the sons of C. As the sons of C, we join with group D as the sons of E, joining with F, etc. until all the Āl Murrah are included. In this same fashion, more distantly related tribes are brought into association with the Āl Murrah. Figure 6.1 shows the genealogical relationships of the most inclusive, or maximal, descent groups of the Āl Murrah.

The names written in capital letters in Figure 6.1 are the names of actual descent groups which the Āl Murrah refers to as *gabila,* usually glossed as tribe. The names written in lower case letters represent genealogical links and are brought into use to show the relationship between different groups or to express temporary solidarity with another descent group, as when people from the Fuhaidah and the Jabir descent groups meet and call themselves by the name of Sa'id, their most immediate common ancestor.

Although the Āl Murrah refer to these descent groups by the Arabic term *gabila,* usually glossed into English as tribe and refer to the unit of the totality of the Āl Murrah as *gabilat*

al-Murrah, Murrah tribes, we should not think of the Āl Murrah
as a confederation of tribes. If we think of tribe as a maximal
descent unit which has at least some significant degree of
political, social, and cultural autonomy, then the Āl Murrah as a
whole are associated with a territorial unit known as *dirat Āl
Murrah,* Āl Murrah territories, and have a paramount shaikh who
speaks for all of them, although he tends to be more closely
associated with some clans than with others. In the bygone days
of raids, the Āl Murrah did not raid each other, since they
thought of their tents and herds as those of one people. The
Āl Murrah are associated with their own dialect of Arabic, have
their own pattern of greetings, and closely approach 100 per
cent endogamy.

Figure 6.1   *Patrilineal relationships of Āl Murrah clans (the
names in capitals refer to actual descent groups; the other names
express genealogical links.)*

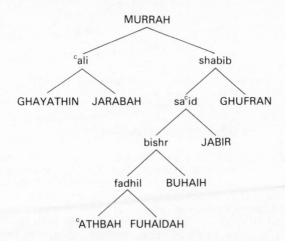

The clans are important units of reference and are sometimes
associated with territorial units and specialized activities. The
date palm oasis of Jabrin, for example, is associated primarily
with the Āl Jabir clan, which owns most of the trees there and
settles there during the summer date harvest. The Āl ᶜAthbah
are closely associated with two small oases in the same way. The
Āl Fuhaidah are thought of as eschewing any kind of sedentarization and as being mainly interested in involvement in supra-
tribal politics, especially since all of the paramount shaikhs of
the Āl Murrah during this century have come from this clan.
Each clan is an important unit of visitation, especially in urban
environments, and as a result the clan is playing an increasingly
important role in determining the foci of urban migration.
   Neither the clan nor the tribe plays any major role in organizing pastoral activities, except that access to Āl Murrah territories

accrues only to members of the Āl Murrah on a permanent basis.
The yearly cycle of herding and the pattern of summer camping
at permanent sources of water are carried out within the general
context of a unit of kinsmen the Āl Murrah call *fakhdh,* thigh.
This is a unit of five to seven generations' depth, which we may
call lineage. There is a tendency for these units to be paired
off, as in the case of clans, but seldom is this absolutely
achieved. Thus the Āl Fuhaidah divide themselves into lineages
as diagrammed in Figure 6.2. The names written in capitals are
lineages.

Figure 6.2   *Patrilineal relationships of Āl Fuhaidah maximal
lineages (the names in capitals refer to actual descent groups;
the other names express genealogical links)*

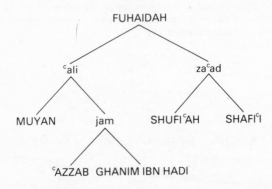

The internal relationships of the lineages within the clan is of
little importance to the Āl Murrah. Usually they are simply named
without stating the relationships between them, and in most
instances the exact relationships are unknown except to some
old men, although everyone knows that some lineages are closer
to some than to others. This contrasts sharply with the strict
duality of the clans which is easily recited, always in the same
order, by all adults and most youths.

Between the level of the lineage and the household, the Āl
Murrah recognize a grouping of about three generations remove
from the heads of households. This unit, *al garaba,* the near
ones, or minimal lineage, provides a general surname used in
identifying individuals to other members of the Āl Murrah. Both
the minimal and maximal lineages are units the members of which
tend to cling together during the course of migrations on the
way to and while in fall, winter, and spring pastures. Every
summer camp at a source of water is predominantly made up of a
majority of people from the same lineage. Aside from the fact
that the ownership of most wells is vested in the lineage, no
lineage-wide decisions are made concerning the pastoral activities
of the group as a whole. Each household is an autonomous herding unit which is responsible for the management of its own herd

and, thereby, its own subsistence. The lineage is, however, the
unit in which blood debts are shared equally.

The Āl Murrah recognize that descent is an important factor
in the organization of their social life. They also are aware that
it does not necessarily refer to historical fact but that it is a
kind of framework that reflects, in a more or less general way,
how groups relate to each other and is a guideline for behaviour
in certain instances. There is, for example, a version of their
history recorded by some Arab genealogists and often mentioned
by sedentary Saudi Arabians that claims that the Āl Murrah are
descended from ᶜAdnan, the mythical founder of the so-called
adopted, or northern, Arabs from whom the Prophet
Muhammad is descended. The Āl Murrah themselves claim to be
descended from Yam and then from Qahtan, the mythical founder
of the southern Arabs, although they are aware of the other
version of their descent. As many of them pointed out to me, the
only version that has any reality is the one that relates them to
Yam and Qahtan, because this reflects the way in which they
interact with a number of other tribes, while the version which
would tie them in with the descendants of ᶜAdnan has no importance in their present-day relationships. As one of them said,
'Whom you drink coffee with and not what the historians say is
what is important.'

Patrilineal descent, then, is a model the Āl Murrah use in
organizing the groups in their society and is the way in which
they trace relationships within the tribe. Their genealogies,
however, are not absolutely patrilineal. The names of women
appear as the founders of two clans and a number of minimal
lineages. Both the Āl ᶜAthbah and the Āl Fuhaidah take their
names from women from other clans who married two sons of
Fadhil, both of whose names have been deleted from the
genealogy. Both of these cases represent marriages with women
of powerful clans, and the use of their names in the genealogy
is clearly an expression of alliance.

Women are also responsible for certain lineages being considered of less than equal status within the tribal structure.
This occurs in at least two cases in which the founder of the
lineage is accused of having married a woman of non-tribal status,
probably a slave woman. The rest of the tribe refuse to give any
of their women in marriage to the men of these tainted lineages.
This indicates that both positive and negative alliances occur and
shows that while hypergamy contributes to upward mobility or
at least in maintaining one's high-born status, hypogamy always
results in lowering of status both within the tribe and within the
larger society.

In spite of their patrilineal ideology, full membership in the
tribe, both for groups and individuals, depends on full bilateral
descent from people of tribal status. At the same time, the actions
of a group are an important factor in their inclusion within the
tribe as full and equal members, as is evidenced in a contemporary controversy about the status of the above-mentioned tainted

lineages: many younger Āl Murrah males feel that the discrimination against these groups is unfair because, they say, whatever they were in the past, they are now upstanding and brave
tribesmen and should therefore be accorded equal status.

IV

Patrilineal descent has been so stressed in studies of Middle
Eastern kinship systems that the importance of both affinal and
matrilateral relations have generally been ignored. This partly
reflects the ideology of many Middle Eastern males who habitually
describe their relationships within their own kin groups exclusively in terms of patrilineal descent. This is also related to the
traditional males' notions about women in general that lead to
their separation and seclusion and include an avoidance of
mentioning their names of referring to them in public or to
strangers. Most traditional males are thus loath to talk about
relationships that are established through females, either as a
result of marriage or of motherhood.

The concentration on descent and neglect of marriage also
reflects the predominating influence in Middle Eastern anthropology of Evans-Pritchard's work on the Nuer and the Sanusi
(Evans-Pritchard 1940; 1949), in which he so brilliantly described the mechanics of segmentary descent systems. When FBD
marriage is added as typical of the marriage system of Middle
Eastern societies, it is not surprising that the importance of
marriage in structuring kinship relations has been ignored and
even denied by some anthropologists. Murphy and Kasdan, for
example, argue that FBD marriage does not result in the creation
of alliances (1959). Khuri forthrightly states that 'FBD marriage
does not establish new affinal relationships at all' (1970:616).

In spite of Middle Eastern males' strong patrilineal ideology and
the denial or neglect of the importance of marriage ties in
Middle Eastern societies by a number of anthropologists, females
are, nonetheless, extremely important in structuring these
societies. The de facto power and influence of women from
'behind the veil', recently explored by Nelson (1973), is only
mentioned in passing in order to concentrate on the structural
relationships that are brought into being through marriage.
Although Āl Murrah men do not mention the names of women or
refer to them in public, they are well aware that who one's wife
is and who one's mother is have important repercussions in
almost every field of activity and that affinal ties sometimes
override considerations of descent.

In considering the importance of either affinal or matrilateral
relationships vis-à-vis those based on patrilineal descent, we
should first look at the total range of marriages that are contracted. Just because traditional Middle Easterners express a
preference for marrying an FBD does not mean that FBD marriage
automatically characterizes the marriage system as a whole,

although some have assumed that it does.

Based on the marriages contracted by the members of one lineage of thirty-five households of camel nomads and three households of a minimal lineage of shaikhly status, the following set of rules can be stated for Āl Murrah marriages:

I   A man marries an FBD if he has one that is available.
II   If no real FBD is available, then
   A. He marries a classificatory FBD from within his own minimal lineage.
   B. He marries a classificatory FBD from within his own maximal lineage.
   C. He marries a real or classificatory cross cousin from outside his own maximal lineage.
   D. He marries a woman of full tribal status from within either the Āl Murrah or any other Sharif bedouin tribe.
III If a man is of shaikhly status, he makes at least one, almost always the first, marriage according to rules I and II. In addition, he marries
   A. A woman from another shaikhly family of the Āl Murrah.
   B. A woman from a shaikhly family of another tribe.
IV   A woman of shaikhly status may be given in marriage to a man of royal status.

These include all accepted marriage practices and, according to the Āl Murrah I worked with, account for all marriages that have been contracted by the Āl Murrah at present.

The picture that emerges from this set of rules is of a marriage system that is by no means exclusively characterized by FBD marriage, although it is the preferred form and is first choice. Other kinds of marriages are regular parts of the system, and the fact that they occur negates any notion that affinal ties are of no importance in these kinship systems. It is thus of little wonder that when Āl Murrah males visit members of minimal lineages other than their own, they are always keen to find out who is married to whom. The patrilineal relationships of the males are easily discerned by knowing the minimal lineage name of an individual. Although it is improper for a stranger to ask about affinal relations, any questioning a Marri does in this regard is not considered indiscreet, since, as a Marri, he is not an outsider, and such questioning is interpreted as a sincere effort on the part of a distant kinsman to understand the totality of one's social relationships. If marriage did not result in the creation of any special relationships between groups, it would seem that the men would be content simply to know the patrilineal relationships of the people involved.

Although it is sometimes stated that FBD marriages do not result in significant exchange of bridewealth, this is not the case among the Āl Murrah. All marriages, whether of parallel cousins or cross cousins or across tribal boundaries, involve the same kinds of transactions and the same movements: a *ru'ag*, a woven tent divider, usually made by the groom's mother, is presented to the bride; a cash payment, sometimes partially nullified when sister exchanges occur, is given by the family of the groom to the family of the bride; a dowry of household items is brought by the bride to her new residence. In all cases, the girl moves from the household of her father to that of her husband, which is usually in his father's household, unless the husband has already established his own household. Thus marriage of whatever type results in the transfer of goods between households and the movement of women from their natal households to that in which their husband lives.

The use of terms such as lineage, clan, and even tribe is misleading when describing bedouin and other Middle Eastern societies. Murphy and Kasdan quite correctly call attention to the 'quality of loose authority in Arab kin groups [which] does not correspond with Fortes's (1953:32) statement on unilineal, corporate groups in Africa: "As a corporate group, a lineage exhibits a structure of authority . . ." Arab kin groups have only a limited corporate nature in this sense. Internally exercised jural authority is not normative at any level' (Murphy and Kasdan 1959:61).

The basic corporate units in Āl Murrah society are patrilocal households. Herds, the major source of wealth and livelihood, are correlated with households in such a way that a one-to-one relationship always exists between them. Each household is responsible for managing its own herd, on which it depends for its basic subsistence. The division of herds and the division of households always occur at the same time. There is no sharing of herding activities between households.

Although each household, with its herd, is an independent and autonomous unit in Āl Murrah society, the pattern of migration and the composition of camps is related to considerations of both descent and affinity. Descent is the major consideration that affects summer camps, since the ownership of the sources of water that determine the location of these camps is almost always vested in a descent group such as the lineage, although any individual household is free to camp somewhere else and most summer camps include a few households from lineages other than the one which claims the well. During the fall, winter, and spring, members of the same lineages tend to graze their camels within the same general areas, but marriage relationships are the major factor that influence the uniting of households in joint camps of two to four units for extended periods during these seasons. While close agnates do unite in these camps, no special effort is made to get together unless marriage ties exist. This is especially true for households related through cross cousin marriage or through marriage with some one from outside one's own lineage, but it is also a reason given for the union of households related through FBD marriage.

The importance of affinal and matrilateral relationships can be

shown through the use of kin terms. While terms that have consanguineal connotations continue to be used when referring to or
addressing any individual of a man's wife's or mother's kindred,
a general term, *nasib*, is used both as referent and occasionally
as a term of address to any male member of the wife's kindred,
even between close agnates, and the term *khal* is extended to
include not only mother's brother but all members of one's
mother's descent group of both ascending and descending
generations. In both cases, of course, the farther removed a
wife or mother is through patrilineal descent, the greater the
kin group she is associated with and the more individuals who
are lumped under the terms *nasib* and *khal*. The Āl Murrah use
these terms denoting in-law and mother's brother equally
whether they refer to close or distant agnates, which is symbolic
of their recognition of affinity and matrilaterality, even among
close agnates.

The oft-repeated Arab proverb, 'Myself against my brother;
my brother and I against my cousin; my cousin, my brother and
I against the outsider', stresses the importance of descent in
situations of conflict. Blood guilt and the responsibility for the
extraction of blood revenge or money is shared equally by all
members of the lineage. Case studies of conflicts among the Āl
Murrah (Cole 1971:49-52; 108-10) confirm the importance of
descent in determining last resort courses of action, but they
also point to the importance of affinal and matrilateral ties in the
peaceful settlement of conflicts. Affinal and matrilateral relatives
often play critically important roles as intermediaries or go-
betweens in settling disputes both between agnates and with
outsiders. The support of a mother's brother or of a father-in-
law is often more of a decisive factor in settling a dispute than
the support of a father's brother. That this is so points to the
intertwining of the ties of descent and of affinity and matrilaterality, for to continue to oppose a group, even a single
household, actively supported by its affines and/or matrilateral
kindred is to risk conflict with the agnatic relations of these
folk as well.

There is thus no doubt that relationships established through
marriage and as a result of motherhood are important factors in
Āl Murrah social organization, in spite of the fact that they,
like most Western writers on bedouin societies, usually describe
their social organization exclusively in terms of patrilineal descent and the segmentary opposition of descent groups. This, of
course, is not at all surprising and is only worthy of remark
because so many writers on the Middle East have ignored and
even denied the importance of affinity and matrilaterality in the
societies of this area.

If all marriages were FBD marriages, the importance of affinity
and matrilaterality would be lessened since one's affines and
matrilateral relatives would be almost the same as one's close
agnates. But since marriages between members of different
minimal lineages and between cross cousins occur regularly, the

importance of these ties is greatly increased. While the majority
of marriages are with FBD, the existence of even one non-FBD
marriage is enough to establish affinal and consequently matrilateral ties of no little importance. The degree to which this
occurs is suggested by the fact that the minimal lineage, composed of ten households, with which I worked most closely, has
affinal relationships with three minimal lineages from within
their own lineage and with two from other clans. All six minimal
lineages of the lineage that provided the basis for the marriage
rules of the Āl Murrah have similar ties with other minimal
lineages. In each instance, all members of the minimal lineages
of both parties to a marriage stand in affinal relationships to
each other and all are lumped under one kinship term, *nasib*,
becoming *khal* in the second generation.

V

There is a further aspect of Āl Murrah social structure that
must be taken into consideration before the dynamics of their
kinship system can be fully understood. The Āl Murrah express
this indirectly when they describe the salient features of their
marriage practices. Contrary to what I had been led to believe
from most descriptions of bedouin marriage practices, they did
not think of parallel cousin marriage as being particularly
significant or worthy of special comment. What they stress in
their description is that they marry only women who are of
Sharif, noble, tribal status. There are practical reasons for
marrying close relatives most of the time, but any marriage
between people from any of the Sharif tribes of Arabia is *halal*,
righteous, and fully accepted. Only when the marriage is
between Sharif tribal people are the offspring granted full
membership in their father's descent groups. It is true that men
may, and sometimes do, establish relationships with women who
are of lower status, usually of ex-slave status. These relations
are never fully approved of and the offspring of such unions do
not have full tribal status, although they are protected and
defended as members of the tribe. No man, even a boy's
father's brother, will give his daughter in marriage to a son of
such a union.

By their approval of marriages only between people of Sharif
tribal status and their concomitant rejection of marriage with
people of lower status, the Āl Murrah express their identity with
a certain category of people in Arabian society that cuts across
tribal boundaries. They contrast themselves with other Arabs
according to a number of overlapping binary classifications.
These include contrasts between *al-badiya*, the nomads, and
al-hadhara, the sedentaries; *al-gaba'il*, the tribals, and *al-mush
gaba'il*, the non-tribals; and *al-Ashraf*, the nobles, and *al-mush
Ashraf*, the ignobles. Except for two or three tainted lineages,
already referred to, the Āl Murrah consider themselves and are

considered to be noble tribal nomads. The tainted lineages do
not qualify as noble, which reflects not only their reputed
descent from a union between a Marri male and a slave woman
but also the fact that in the past they did not fight and were
mainly sheep herders or herded the camels of other Āl Murrah.
The paucity of marriages between nomads and sedentaries is not
'mainly because they dislike the food of the towns, above all,
green vegetables' (Smith 1903:76), but because the noble tribal
nomads seldom consider sedentary people to be of noble tribal
backgrounds. When they are, there are no barriers to marriage.

Although hypogamy is strongly discouraged and results in an
overall lowering of status, it should be remembered that hypergamy, especially involving women of shaikhly status, is highly
approved of. The importance of alliances resulting from
marriages between women of shaikhly families from the tribes
and men of the Āl Sa^cud and the other royal families of Arabia
cannot be underestimated. King ^cAbd al-Aziz Ibn Sa^cud, the
founder of modern Saudi Arabia, and his brothers and sons
married women from almost all of these families, and especially
from among their enemies. They thereby guaranteed their
support at the same time that the tribes gained powerful patrons
and were able to reaffirm their purity and aristocratic status.
In contrast to marriages with women of lower than Sharif tribal
status, which result in the offspring taking the lower status of
the mother's group, the offspring of hypergamous marriages
are of royal status.

That the Āl Murrah do not identify themselves simply as Āl
Murrah but conceive of themselves as members of a category of
people defined in contrast to other categories is symbolic of
their basic integration or enmeshment in a complex, pluralistic
society. I have already mentioned how they and other Arabian
bedouin think of themselves as specialists in herding and in warfare. These specializations provide the basis for their economic
subsistence, and while camel herding has ceased to be of much
economic importance in oil-rich Arabia, the specialized activities
of the Sharif tribes as warriors stand as the backbone of both
the founding and the maintenance of the Saudi Arabian nation-
state and are highly influential in the states of the Arabian Gulf.
As specialists, they rely on other specialists for many services
which they are incapable of providing for themselves. It is
this pattern of specialization whereby the bedouin provided
pastoral products and military services in exchange for agricultural products and the services of religious and political
authorities that explains the integration of traditional Arabia.

Following classical descriptions of Arab society, Murphy and
Kasdan state that 'genealogies are almost the only means given
within the formal social structure for the ordering of larger
amalgamations' (1959:23) and they further claim that 'ideally, all
Arabs, whether nomadic or sedentary, form a super lineage, the
member units of which trace common ancestry to the prophet
Abraham' (1959:21). Almost none of the Āl Murrah know anything

about their descent from Abraham, and while descent *is* a means
of uniting tribes in supra-tribal confederations, the integration
of Arabian society cannot be fully explained in terms of descent.
Division of the society into tribal groupings is only one dimension. There are also ranked categories that are as much a part
of the formal social structure as genealogies. Although ranking
is contrary to Muslim theology, which considers all Muslims to
be equal, the Āl Murrah recognize that people in Arabia are
divided into a number of different categories, each one of which
tends to be occupationally specialized, highly endogamous, and
ranked.

VI

In this paper, descent, marriage, and an ethnic-based division
of labour are seen as the underlying principles of social organization of at least one Middle Eastern community, the Āl Murrah
bedouin. Murphy and Kasdan were quite correct in showing that
authority is spread equally throughout the structure of bedouin
societies and that their kin groups have only a very limited
corporate nature. Patrilineal descent and the segmentary
opposition of descent groups are shown to be important principles
of social organization among the Āl Murrah bedouin, but the integration of a larger society is shown to be based not on descent,
as according to classical descriptions of Arab society, but on an
ethnic-based division of labour.

As in Indian caste systems, integration on a society-wide
basis is achieved mainly through the exchange of goods and
services between endogamous groups. But, as both Coon and
Barth point out, the ethnic-based division of labour in the
Middle East never approaches the extreme of that typical of
India. Occupations only tend to be passed on hereditarily; some
individuals do change their occupation and move into other
groups, but the ethnic divisions remain.

Within each ethnic division, and especially among tribal groups,
descent is a major organizing principle. Since marriages only
rarely occur across ethnic boundaries and are usually contracted
between close relatives, marriage alliances are not regular means
of integration in the wider society. Affinal ties, however, are
often extremely important in tying groups together within an
ethnic category. FBD marriage is seen as only one of a number
of forms of endogamous marriage within an ethnic category, all
of which result in the building up of extensive and important
affinal relations. Marriages between father's brother's children
do not differ markedly from those between units further removed
genealogically, except that the number of affines is likely to be
greater in non-FBD marriages. It is thus misleading to concentrate on explaining FBD marriage in isolation. Descent, marriage,
and plurality are all important aspects of social organization in
the Middle East and must be considered as interrelated phenomena.

NOTES

1 This paper is based on eighteen months of field research in 1968-70 among the Āl Murrah bedouin in Saudi Arabia. This research was financially supported by a predoctoral research grant from the National Institute of Mental Health and by the Ministry of Agriculture and Water of Saudi Arabia (cf. Cole 1975). Earlier versions of this paper were presented as part of the Middle East Colloquia Series at the University of California, Berkeley, and to the Social Anthropology Faculty Discussion Group at Berkeley during the spring of 1974. Aside from comments made during these presentations, the author would like to express his special appreciation to Professors Burton Benedict, Elizabeth Colson, Nelson Graburn, and Laura Nader for their detailed comments on this paper. The interpretations expressed herein are, of course, the author's responsibility.

2 Military protection of others is a traditional speciality of the bedouin. According to the Āl Murrah, they policed the major weekly market in the town of Najran before the days of centralized government, about 200 years ago according to them. They also protected peasant villages from raids and extortion by other bedouin in return for tribute in the form of agricultural products. Bujra describes a similar pattern in South Arabia prior to forced pacification under the British in the 1940s (Bujra 1971).

BIBLIOGRAPHY

Baer, Gabriel (1964) 'Population and Society in the Arab East', New York: Praeger.

Barclay, Harold (1964) 'Buuri al Lamaab', Ithaca: Cornell University Press.

Barth, Fredrik (1954) Father's Brother's Daughter Marriage in Kurdistan, 'Southwestern Journal of Anthropology', 10:164-71.

— (1960) The System of Social Stratification in Swat, North Pakistan, in Edmund Leach (ed.), 'Aspects of Caste', Cambridge Papers in Social Anthropology no. 2, Cambridge University Press.

Bujra, Abdalla S. (1971) 'The Politics of Stratification: A Study of Political Change in a South Arabian Town', London: Oxford University Press.

Cole, Donald P. (1971) The Social and Economic Structure of the Āl Murrah: A Saudi Arabian Bedouin Tribe, University of California, Berkeley: unpublished PhD dissertation.

Cole, Donald P. (1973) The Enmeshment of Nomads in Sa'udi Arabian Society: The Case of the Āl Murrah, in Cynthia Nelson (ed.), 'The Desert and the Sown: Nomads in the Wider Society', Berkeley: University of California, Institute of International Studies, Research Series no. 21.

Cole, Donald P. (1975) 'Nomads of the Nomads: The Āl Murrah
  Bedouin of the Empty Quarter', Chicago: Aldine-Atherton.
Coon, Carleton, S. (1958) 'Caravan: The Story of the Middle
  East', New York: Holt, Rinehart & Winston.
Evans-Pritchard, E.E. (1940) 'The Nuer: A Description of the
  Modes of Livelihood and Political Institutions of a Nilotic
  People', London; Oxford University Press.
Evans-Pritchard, E.E. (1949) 'The Sanusi of Cyrenaica',
  London: Oxford University Press.
Fortes, Meyer (1953) The Structure of Unilineal Descent Groups,
  'American Anthropologist', vol. 55.
Gellner, Ernest (1969) 'Saints of the Atlas', London: Weidenfeld
  & Nicolson.
Granquist, Hilma (1931) 'Marriage Conditions in a Palestinian
  Village', Helsinki: Societas Scientarum Fennica.
Khuri, Fuad (1970) Parallel Cousin Marriage Reconsidered: A
  Middle Eastern Practice that Nullifies the Effects of Marriage
  on the Intensity of Family Relations, 'Man', n.s. 5:597-618.
Leach, Edmund (1960) Introduction: What Should We Mean By
  Caste?, in Edmund Leach (ed.), 'Aspects of Caste', Cambridge
  Papers in Social Anthropology no. 2, Cambridge University
  Press.
Leach, Edmund (1961) The Structural Implications of Matrilateral
  Cross-Cousin Marriage, in Edmund Leach (ed.), 'Rethinking
  Anthropology', London: Athlone.
Levi-Strauss, Claude (1963) The Bear and the Barber, 'Journal
  of the Royal Anthropological Institute', 93:1-11.
Murphy, Robert and Leonard Kasdan (1959) The Structure of
  Parallel Cousin Marriage, 'American Anthropologist', 61:17-29.
Murphy, Robert and Leonard Kasdan (1967) Agnation and
  Endogamy: Some Further Considerations, 'Southwestern Journal
  of Anthropology', 21: 325-50.
Nelson, Cynthia (1973) Women and Power in Nomadic Societies in
  the Middle East, in Cynthia Nelson (ed.), 'The Desert and
  the Sown: Nomads in the Wider Society', Berkeley: Institute
  of International Studies, University of California, Research
  Series no. 21.
Patai, Raphael (1965) The Structure of Endogamous Unilineal
  Descent Groups, 'Southwestern Journal of Anthropology', 21:
  325-50.
Peters, Emrys (1963) Aspects of Rank and Status among Muslims
  in a Lebanese Village, in J. Pitt-Rivers (ed.), 'Mediterranean
  Countrymen', Leiden: Mouton.
Rosenfeld, Henry (1957) An Analysis of Marriage and Marriage
  Statistics for a Muslim and Christian Arab Village, 'Inter-
  national Archeology and Ethnography', 68:32-62.
Smith, W. Robertson (1903) 'Kinship and Marriage in Early
  Arabia', Boston: Beacon Press.

7 THE PAUCITY OF RITUAL AMONG MIDDLE EASTERN PASTORALISTS

Emrys Peters

In the literature on pastoralists in the Middle East some
admirably detailed accounts are given of a wide range of their
activities, but descriptions of their rituals are conspicuously
lacking. Information on the jinn and the evil eye - superstitions
that are given unaccountable precedence - abounds, and it is
often deployed to substitute for religion and ritual. Apart from
scattered bits and pieces of this sort, nowhere in the literature
is there any systematic treatment of ritual, a lacuna made more
obtrusively obvious by the several excellent analyses of Muslim
religious orders.(2) In an article on the bedouin family, I wrote:
'The equalitarianism of the desert denudes the Bedouin of ritual
riches'.(3) At the time that was written I held the view that the
elaboration of rituals which characterise the lives of peoples in
Africa, India, Australia and Oceania is quite alien to the Arab
pastoralists of Cyrenaica, and that what ritual appears among
them is distributed disconnectedly, on a small scale, throughout
social life. The view that rituals are inconsequential among
bedouin is implicit in the dearth of information in earlier works,
such as those of Burckhardt (1831), Musil (1928), Murray (1935),
and Dickson (1949), and in the more recent writings of Cunnison
(1966), Marx (1967), Asad (1970), Cole (1975), Irons (1975),
and Behnke (1980). Although Cole devotes a chapter to religion,
his treatment of it is so perfunctory as to be of little value. The
other authors might well justify their omission on the grounds
that an analysis of ritual is irrelevant to their subject matter,
consisting, as it does, largely of political problems. This is
hardly acceptable since ritual permeates so many social institutions, political institutions particularly, that to detach it is to
exclude an important part of these institutions. Or it might be
argued that it occurs in such dribs and drabs as not to merit
much attention. Barth is explicit about the matter: 'The Basseri
show a poverty of ritual activities quite striking in the field
situation', and he continues: 'What is more the different elements
of ritual do not seem closely connected or integrated in a wider
system of meanings; they give the impression of occurring without reference to each other, or to important features of the
social structure.'(4) Unlike many others, Barth sees ritual
paucity as a problem. Why there should be this poverty is a
question Barth and I sought to answer, and although we arrived
at different views we both assumed that there exists in societies,
those of Middle East pastoralists included, a need for ritual,
and that the elaboration of ritual should match, or at least be

consistent with, the social structure. At the end of his quest
Barth is able to fulfil this kind of need; I will argue that if a
need exists at all it is not a need of a structural kind.

Mary Douglas urges the need for the anthropologist to grasp
the 'fact' that 'there are secular tribal cultures', lest, 'when he
comes across an irreligious tribe', he should 'squeeze his information harder to make it yield. . . . Or he dredges for at least
something to put in a final chapter on religion'. Omnisciently
asserting that Barth was 'driven to write a special appendix to
clear himself of the possible charges of insensibility to religious
behaviour', Douglas proceeds to give Barth a patronising pat
on the back, thus: 'Good marks to Barth for so frankly recording his own surprise and professional frustration.' Without
considering Barth's proposition, Douglas dismisses it out of
hand, suggesting instead 'that a society which does not need to
make explicit its representation of itself to itself is a special
type of society'.(5) Confident that the Basseri are virtually
devoid of ritual, Douglas chooses to ascribe secularism to them.
Barth at least sees a problem in the absence of ritual; if
Douglas is right in saying the Basseri tribe is a secular society,
why should this be, what makes it 'a special type of society'?
These are precisely the questions Barth attempts to answer.

It is important to bear in mind that Barth postulates - indeed,
stipulates - a need for the structure of society to be sustained
by a matching structure of ritual, because his will to find it and
the direction his search takes are both conditioned by this. For,
in effect, he says that the absence of ritual as it is generally
known is striking, but, since there is a need for it, it must
exist, and to locate it a redefinition of ritual is necessary. Ritual
as it is generally known Barth speaks of as 'a sort of "common
sense" view'.(6) Adopting the latter temporarily he lists what he
considers would pass as rituals in a conventional sense. The
cursory descriptions of such acts are put into three categories,
relating to (1) the annual cycle (2) the life crises, and (3) a
miscellany of acts which cannot be placed in either of the other
two categories: a categorisation which could be applied to any
people, and hence, unsubtle; but it must be added that these
rituals are primarily included as a compilation of acts which he
observed, relating to rituals when taking a common sense view.
Rather than attempt anything more, with this kind of data,
than a crude categorisation, he then turns to the possibility of
'greater sophistication in the definition of ritual' which 'might
lead to an expansion of the field of inquiry'.(7) That is to say,
Barth now proposes to redefine ritual in such a manner that acts
which on a common sense view had fallen outside his purview,
can be incorporated, and thus supply ritual where, hitherto,
he thought it to be absent. This more sophisticated definition of
ritual which Barth uses stems from the general ideas on ritual
in one of Leach's earlier writings, and to understand Barth
better a brief digression is necessary to see what Leach has to
say.

'Ritual', Leach asserts, 'serves to express the individual's
status as a social person in the structural system in which he finds
himself for the time being'.(8) This 'aphorism', as Leach calls it,
expresses his general view of what ritual does, but not what it
is. In arriving at the latter, he begins by discussing the
Durkheimian dichotomy between the sacred and the profane as
separable realms of social activity. It is to this assumption that
Leach takes exception. Very few social actions, he argues, are
purely technical (profane) acts with an elementary definable
function as an end. Most actions are accompanied by 'technically
superfluous frills and decorations',(9) which are symbolically
charged, and which it is the business of social anthropologists
to interpret. Durkheim's dichotomy excludes a large part of this,
since the sacred embodies only those acts in which specifically
religious symbols are used - but Leach would describe as ritual
any non-technical actions 'whether or not they involve directly
any conceptualisation of the supernatural or the metaphysical'.(10)
For this reason he rejects the Durkheimian dichotomy as untenable, as does Barth ('Though Durkheim's dichotomy of sacred
and profane is untenable . . .'(11).) Instead Leach prefers to
think of all actions as falling somewhere along a continuum, at
one end of which profane, entirely functional, purely technical
acts are to be placed, and at the other, entirely sacred, technically non-functional acts. In between these two poles falls
the bulk of social actions. The recognition of these two poles
implies, of course, that the Durkheimian dichotomy is valid in
distinguishing certain actions, but the utility of his view Leach
sees as offering the liberty for dispensing with the necessity of
taking actions as wholes, to be placed in one of two types;
rather, the attention is to be directed to this or that aspect of
an action, the choice being determined by the problem, so that
any action can come to be endowed with a number of aspects
and, therefore, fall into several positions along the continuum.
The view that most actions are bundles of aspects is uncontro-
versial, but it still remains an obligation to identify these
aspects, to set apart what is technical from what is not. The
rule-of-thumb Leach offers for this purpose is that technique
is to be recognised by its measurable material consequences;
ritual is communication in the sense that it 'says' something
about the individuals involved in the action'.(12) Leach is confident that he knows, in general terms, what this communication
is about: ritual action is a symbolic statement about the social
order.(13) For this reason, a close consistency between the
structure of ritual and social structure always exists, so close
that 'ritual makes explicit the social structure'.(14) This
thoroughgoing Durkheimian view is repeated at almost every
point in the book which touches on ritual,(15) and in his basic
assumption that there is an ever present structural need for
ritual Leach is again in harmony with Durkheim, and for that
matter with Barth, Evans-Pritchard, Fortes, Middleton, Tapper,
Turner, to name only a few at random.(16) Individuals need to

be reminded, in symbol, of the underlying order which is supposed to govern their lives, 'if anarchy is to be avoided'.(17)
Ritual is a prophylactic against anarchy - or, perhaps, a kind
of talisman. Without ritual society would disintegrate. What
power to ascribe to ritual! Why should this function be reserved
for ritual rather than some mundane forms of control? Perhaps
the question is a non sequitur, since ritual, residing only in the
frills and decorations of technical acts, is, for Leach, itself
mundane.

Barth subscribes to Leach's redefinition of ritual both in the
general statement of his views and the sort of facts he analyses.
On two points, however, he differs. According to Leach, all
symbolic aspects of acts are ritual. Barth finds difficulty in
accepting this, as well he might after the somewhat cursory
examination he makes of the actions included in the three categories to which reference was made earlier. He departs from
Leach to the extent of admitting that rituals are not merely
symbolic, but that they are 'especially pregnant with meaning'
and are set apart from other acts because they are 'more
important'; so that ritual now becomes 'the symbolic aspects of
acts in contexts vested with particular value'.(18) In seeking
ritual, attention has to be directed at contexts since it is these
that give it its importance, and endow it with pregnancy of
meaning - although, it must be noted, that the importance is
unrelated to anything save to other undefined acts, that the
pregnancy of meaning is an evaluation of rituals, not a guide for
their identification, and that contexts of particular value are
to be assessed in relation to a predetermined notion of what the
value of ritual ought to be. In his analysis, Barth makes it
clear that his qualms over accepting the outcome of Leach's
views have led him to make a number of qualifications which,
taken together, mean that, culminatively, rituals must compre-
hend society in its entirety. In this, Barth is close to Leach
again, except that for Leach all frills and decorations have
something to say about the society, the social order, and its
structural arrangements; Barth is hankering after the core of
society, the entire structure and meaning of which is discernible
if one only has the sophistication to alight on a context especially
pregnant with meaning - a not uncommon view, held, for
example, by Gluckman,(19) and, less explicitly, by Evans-
Pritchard.(20)

The second point of departure from Leach's view is equally
important. In the first place, Barth limits the range of acts
Leach regards as rituals by the significance to be attributed to
the context in which they occur. In the second, he extends the
field of ritual by including acts Leach would reject as technique.
Whereas Leach wishes to distinguish between technique and
superfluous frills which contain the symbolic communications,
Barth considers the form of an act to be inconsequential. Ritual,
for Leach, resides in those aspects of an action that are unnecessary on grounds of technical expediency. For Barth

'technical imperatives' (whatever 'imperatives' might mean here)
are of equivalent importance to frills and decorations: 'there is
no reason why . . . technical imperatives may not *also* be vested
with central and crucial meaning in a symbolic system or context'.(21) This leaves the field of ritual virtually undefined,
since any act of any kind may or may not be ritual, depending
on an appraisal of its context; with the consequence that
bewildered readers are left to fend subjectively for themselves.

The data and the argument Barth presents to enable him,
using these notions of ritual, to make good the apparent ritual
deficiency that would otherwise characterise Basseri life, are
now summarised. This summary need only be brief since the
evidence and the argument together extend to only a few pages.
He begins with the affirmation that if sets of acts or aspects of
acts, which bear meaning in contexts vested with particular
value, are sought, 'it becomes overwhelmingly clear that the
whole basic system of activities involved in the economic adaptation of the Basseri, of camping and herding and travelling, are
pregnant with such meanings . . . and the context of the great
migration in which they take place is vested with extreme
value'.(22) His analysis starts with the small camps of the
Basseri, and he has this to say about them: 'The camp itself
with its semi-circles of fires, alone in an empty landscape, and
constantly re-pitched in new localities in changing circumstances,
serves as a clear expression of the social unity of the group
which inhabits it, and of the mechanisms whereby that group is
maintained.'(23) The camp shows nothing of the kind. All it
shows, as such, is that a number of people (including 'several
men . . . of Qashqai extraction' in at least one camp)(24) have
arrived at some kind of modus vivendi; otherwise, presumably,
they would not be together. What does the semi-circle of camps
contribute to the pregnancy of meaning in the camps? The empty
landscape gives an impression of a sparsely populated area, but
not of social unity, or of the mechanisms that maintain it. In any
event, both are such vague 'meanings' that they can plausibly
be applied to people who live in groups anywhere, and in this
context they mean little more than togetherness. An analysis
of the composition of the camp in terms of its age and sex distribution, related to productive needs and the means to support
those too young or too old to work, might reveal many features
of the camp, and these might account for the way in which
people are residentially disposed, making it a sociologically
meaningful unit. In another part of the book, Barth does offer
a brief analysis of the kinship composition of camps, and has
something to say about the herding arrangements that are undertaken.(25) Yet a rigorous analysis of the relations suggested
yields only a definition of a socio-geographical grouping, not of
a ritual community. It is possible to define a socio-geographical
grouping for any gathering of people, by plotting the concentration of various kinds of relations - for example, economic co-
operation, clustering of agnates or cognates, marriage linkages,

and so on - and drawing a boundary at those points where the
relationships are weakest. Possibly, material constraints operate
to keep these within a definable location, and act to inhibit the
free mobility of people from one group to another. If ritual constraint is absent, men are held to their group for expedient
reasons, and for the same reasons they can opt out of it: rules
are devised, among some peoples, to meet such contingencies.
But if desertion is mystically controlled, if a man has a right to
die in a particular place among certain people, and if such rights
are derived from membership of a group using resources sanctioned as its property by an oath given at a saint's tomb, these
added ritual constraints turn a socio-geographical unit into a
religious community.

In Cyrenaica the top of a tent is made of raw sheep's wool,
with a strip on either side of the central seam made of goat hair,
and the outer edges made of camel hair. Wool has *baraka* (divine
blessing) in it; baraka has a protective force about it which
makes the tent a sanctuary and surrounds it with *haram* (a
holiness which prohibits a range of actions), even to the very
ends of its ropes. Inside hangs a *hijab* (amulet), consisting of
an inscription from the Qur'an written by a holy man on a piece
of paper, with a pen made of a twig (a modern pen or pencil
was considered inefficacious), using the natural oil fried out of
wool as ink, the paper folded into a little square package, sealed
with the seal of Solomon (of identical design to the star of David),
and sewn into a leather satchel. When a new tent is erected,
women use henna to draw simple designs on the interior of the
tent top on both sides of the central seam. After a new tent has
been pitched, whether for a newly married couple, or as a
replacement for an old one, or by someone joining a camp, a
sacrifice must be offered. Indeed, when the tent of a newcomer
is pitched in a camp, each head of a tent kills an animal 'for the
new tent', in succession, usually over several weeks. Many of
the conversational sayings allude to the tent, almost invariably
spoken in religious language, and most bedouin sentiments contain a reference, at least, to it. The kind of tent referred to
here is not a mere abode. A tent of a military or camping type is
called a *khaima*; and that used by a widow, or aged woman whose
husband has left her for a younger wife, which is pitched near
her son's, and used only as a domicile at night, is called an
'ashsha. For a *bait* must have within its household a promise
of a future, whether this be in a married couple, a married
couple and their children, or an assortment of relatives one of
whom is an unmarried young woman or an able-bodied man; a
future, moreover, which is in the hands of God. Hence the
many sayings associating the tent with children, to be heard
when women weave tent tops, when a new tent is pitched, and
at a wedding, itself spoken of as 'making a tent', 'pitching a
tent', or 'spreading out a tent'. It is all these aspects which
turn a tent into a tabernacle, and endow it with a ritual significance having nothing to do with the frills and decorations of

technique, but having a great deal to do with a people's corpus
of religious beliefs.

Cyrenaican camps in winter and spring are small, composed of
some five to ten tents at most. Whether in their summer or winter
locations, it is a characteristic of the camps that their tents are
separated by unequal distances. Some might be as much as
twenty yards apart, and unconnected through their ropes.
Others are very close, and their ropes cross. There is more to
this than mere proximity. Since the haram of a tent extends to
the ends of its ropes, tents with crossed ropes are of one haram.
Thus, a man and his sons are more than likely to have their
tents aligned in this way, and these arrangements persist until
the sons have grown sons of their own, or the father has died
and his property has been divided, when they separate to form
a similar cluster. A fugitive, or a maternal relative of another
corporate group, or a temporary resident, like myself, cross
their tent ropes with an appropriate tent in the camp. The men
of joined tents are likely to eat together, and the women to work
together. Their animal wealth remains joint wealth while they live
like this - 'they are of one cooking pot'. Bound by joint ownership and constituting a joint family, the motive impelling them
to behave in this way is religious, and such living is held to be
religiously virtuous for a period in a family's development. While
there is this specially close relationship between these people,
the others of the camp are also drawn together closely. Almost
entirely agnates, they are not necessarily the closest agnates,
for people are free to change camps within the corporate group
of which they are a part - and they occasionally make such
moves. They are, however, linked through women, as are non-
agnates in the camps. An analysis of these small camps shows
characteristic patterns of age and sex composition, to provide
the labour force for herding and tending the animals attached
to them and raising a crop, and to make provision for those
precluded from manual labour by age or status. But the composition of a camp is only partly to be understood as an economic
unit for herding and crop growing. It is also a ritual community
of selected people, who give recognition of their distinctive
relationship in the eating of sacrificial meals together, always.
Whenever a man sacrifices an animal from his own flock or herd
- and the sacrifice must be of an animal from one's own *rizq*
(wealth) - all adult males gather in his tent to partake of the
meal, as a matter of course. On the occasion of a circumcision,
men, women, and children of the camp gather in the tent where
the rite is being performed. At a funeral, it is the agnates of
the camp who are obliged to provide the sacrificial animals,
whatever offerings other agnates or other people might bring.
A man might be negligent of his herding responsibilities, or a
woman of her domestic tasks, but neglect of one's ritual obligations is tantamount to expulsion; it is a *fitna* (sin) which, if it
is to be dealt with at all, can only be prehended by ritual (to
borrow Fortes's mode of expression).(26)

Small camps cluster around a well in summer to form a larger camp, although they remain easily discernible in the cluster. The men of this camp share water resources, grow a crop in the same area and arrange for it to be guarded in the same large grain store, laid out in individual mounds heaped on the ground. Details of herding, watering animals, harvesting and transporting grain to the store can be shown to have the mark of expediency about them, derived from the common sense of experience. There is no common sense reason for prohibiting easy entry into the group or exit from it. Neither, however, are undertaken lightly. Both require the consent of the group as a collectivity; for this is the one body, the corporate group, which, in its material sense, owns the natural resources of a particular piece of territory, controls the use to which these are put, and defends these against any threat of assault. There is no reason for concluding an incorporation ceremony with a sacrificial meal, but, for the bedouin, entry into a corporate group is not a mere contract in words witnessed by all; the new member must be included in the ritual community, otherwise much of the behaviour required of him would appear as unnecessary frills. At the incorporation ceremony, the presence of a holy man among the witnesses is also essential, his baraka giving his witness a precedence above all other and of a quite different kind. The oneness of this group is manifested best, perhaps, on three occasions. First, on the morning of the Great Feast, or the Feast of the Flesh as the bedouin more commonly refer to it, each head of a tent sacrifices an animal, and all the men of the group pray together, either in the form of a crescent or in ranks. During the following two days, men visit corporate groups round about them where they have connections, not as individuals but as representatives of their group. Second, all people able to do so go together on a pilgrimage ('a move', in their idiom) to a saints' tomb, the head of each tent taking an animal for slaughter, to be cooked by the women; the meat is brought in large wooden bowls into an open space, where the numerous bowls are placed so as to form a huge circle, no man eating from the bowl of meat to which he has contributed nor from the same bowl as his nearest agnates. Except in the context of bedouin beliefs there is little common sense in these actions, nor are the bedouin compelled to behave in this way by mundane considerations. Third, all agnates are required to attend funerals, and bring an appropriate gift. If anyone arrives late in the week of mourning, when it would have been possible to be there on the first day, and brings an inappropriate gift – sugar and tea, say, in lieu of an animal – it is generally accepted that this behaviour is an indication of splitting away from the corporate group. That is to say, secession does not occur until a ritual bond is severed. But perhaps the most dramatic demonstration of the ritual unity of the corporate group is given when a man kills a fellow agnate of his own corporate group, intentionally. His only immediate course of action is to

flee, for his own safety. The widespread fear, at this time, is
that 'the owner of the blood' (the nearest agnate of the victim)
might, while 'his blood is boiling' exact vengeance precipitately,
and thus incur the loss of two agnates. The offender is likely
to remain alienated from his camp for years, the duration of his
exile depending on the circumstances of the killing. When the
information he gathers suggests that his return would be
acceptable, he re-enters his camp, conventionally by stealth,
crossing his tent ropes with those of the camp's shaikh, and
he hastens, as soon as decorum permits, to perform a sacrifice.
A homicide within a corporate group is an act which gives
anguish to its members, even to speak of it. It leaves them non-
plussed. There are no arrangements for dealing with violence of
this sort, nor should they be necessary for people of a community
of religious oneness, for to kill within this range is 'to betray
God'. Yet, 'later on' the offender is permitted to return to full
membership and residence with his people, a reconciliation
which must be effected – and can only be achieved – through a
sacrifice. This done, the offender and 'the owner of the blood'
sit, together with all their fellowmen in the camp, around 'the
one bowl' to partake of the sacrificial meal, and become again
al-'asabiya al-wahid (the one solidarity), the idiom the bedouin
use to designate the unity of the corporate group, expressing
a sense of communitas developed to its highest pitch, super-
seding all economic and jural bonds. At the time of the killing,
when the offender, a member of the group, had no recourse
other than to become a fugitive, secular means of dealing with
the problem had been seen to have failed, a failure which
doubled the loss of members to the group. Ritual, the executive
arm of their religious beliefs (to adopt Fortesian idiom again),(27)
is the only remedy for solving the problem.

The insertion of these references to Cyrenaican bedouin here
is intended as an indication of the kind of data I would seek if
the tent, the small camp, and the large camp, one encapsulated
by the other, distinctively different but also one, were to have
any 'meanings' other than as expedient collections of males and
females; and also what would be required to accept the claim of
'clear expression of social unity'.(28) Mere territorial disposition
of camps, people performing activities concertedly, are not in
themselves symbolic of unity, certainly not one of the variety of
forms of ritual unity.

The camp is only one form of gathering which Barth cites to
demonstrate how acts of any kind are potentially pregnant with
meaning. Much more important is the caravan into which small
camps form when seasonal movements are undertaken. The facts
he gives about these caravans are simple, and somewhat superficial. The camps form processions, which, because the route
takes them through valleys and across passes, is unavoidable
anyway. The number of tents is very large – over 1,000(29) –
and the occupants of these form scores of smaller caravans when
they are on the move.(30) These caravans pass through sedent-

ary communities, and are watched by sullen and hostile spectators.(31) With these few facts, the three meanings Barth
derives from the caravan on its journey can be examined.

First, the daily processions and the nightly camps 'repeat the
facts of group allegiance and divisions'.(32) Why repeat these
twice daily for months? Is group allegiance so fragile and the
divisions so uncertain that they have to be 'ritually' represented
so excessively frequently? The nature of this allegiance is not
easy to fathom from the data offered. 'Each tent is occupied by
an independent household, typically consisting of an elementary
family; and these households are the basic units of Basseri
society.'(33) Further, the 'independence and self-sufficiency of
the nomad household, whereby it can survive in economic relation
with an external market but in complete isolation from all fellow
nomads [sic!], is a very striking and fundamental feature of
Basseri organisation'.(34) Lest this repetition leaves the reader
unconvinced, it is again stated that 'the autonomy, both economic
and political of individual Basseri tents has already been repeatedly emphasised; it is a fundamental feature of Basseri organisation'.(35) Obviously, a herding unit founded on the elementary
family can only be transitory, at best. Also, since it is such a
small unit it is vulnerable to a variety of contingencies: the
hazards of birth and death, childlessness, imbalance between the
sexes, and so on.(36) In another part of the book referring to
camps, the comment is made that: 'The camp is very unwilling
to admit new members even as hired shepherds.'(37) Yet when
the elementary family is unable to provide the labour force for
herding, the son of a brother or close agnate may be adopted,
households may co-operate for herding (most of them do), and
shepherds are hired. Astonishingly, this leads Barth to conclude
that these 'devices serve to maintain the isolated, individual
household as a viable unit by supplementing its labour pool from
outside sources'.(38) Since recruitment of labour is such a
regular and urgent necessity the stress Barth gives to the
independence, autonomy, isolation of the household, both
economically and politically, cannot be right.

Camps are of two kinds. In winter they are composed of 2-5
tents, and at all other times of the year 10-40 tents (also given
as '30-60 tents, or 200-400 individuals').(39) According to Barth
they 'are in a very real sense the primary communities of Basseri
society. . . . The members of a camp make up a very clearly
bounded social group; their relations to each other as continuing
neighbours are relatively constant, while all other contacts are
passing, ephemeral, and governed by chance.'(40) This dis-
creteness is again stressed and amplified in a reference to 'the
social isolation in which each camp lives',(41) a statement which
Baxter regards as 'startlingly bizarre to anyone who has lived
among East African pastoralists'(42) - and, I must add immediately, to anyone who has lived among North African bedouin
as well. Moreover it is an odd statement to make for the Basseri
when other facts relating to camps are taken into account. First,

camps are composed of bilaterally related people, which provide them, naturally, with external connections.(43) Nearness of kinship, however, is irrelevant to the composition of the herding units of which the larger camp comprises, for it is the unity of the camp, expressed in its leader, to which, Barth considers, precedent must be given.(44) While this view might be accept- able, the diagrams showing the kinship connections between small camp members,(45) incomplete though it is, makes it very clear that these connections are so dense that they must be a significant force in camp formation, and the most significant elements in the position of the leader. It does not follow that because there is such an abundance of kinship connections of a bewildering variety of types, that kinship can be relegated to a peripheral role. Barth feels able to do this because types of kinship do not discriminate between people;(46) but he also notes that the relationship with the mother's brother, and with affines, appears in behavioural patterns.(47)

Second, movement in and out of camps is not restricted by rules, and, over a period, their composition can wholly change. Third, it is not surprising that camps are heterogeneous with regard both to the *oulads* (an *oulad* is an internally unstructured aggregate of persons, forming a subdivision of a *tira*, one of the twelve divisions of the Basseri) and even to the tribes repre- sented in them.(48) Fourth, a single disagreement about the movement of camps leads to fission, an almost recurring threat it would seem, since, because the Basseri strike and re-pitch their camps on a hundred and twenty days in a year,(49) agreement on such matters must be reached very frequently. Barth attaches much importance to these recurring decisions that every day re-test the cohesion of the group,(50) although else- where he contradicts this in saying that 'those at the head [of the caravan] lead the way, they must decide which path to take, while those behind can have no part in that decision'.(51) It is reasonably safe to deduce that, where cohesion has to be re- tested daily, there is inherent instability. Fifth, the Basseri necessarily come into contact with other tribes, particularly with the Turkish Qashqai and Arab tribes. Finally, the migration of the Basseri tribe along its *il rah* (tribal road, or migratory route) is carefully controlled and co-ordinated,(52) and for this to be done successfully, wide scale co-operation between camps is to be presumed.

In his endeavour to give a sense of unity, or group allegiance, to camps (which, as will be seen presently, culminates in an aggregation of significances in the annual migration), Barth proceeds by building it from the household, until it enlarges to envelop a camp of some three hundred people disposed in about fifty tents. The independence, autonomy, even isolation of both units is stressed, presumably to establish their ritual integrity, then to bring them together in the caravan as an 'aggregation',(53) itself to be endowed with a ritual unity or allegiance by virtue of mere aggregation. The household and the camps have been dis-

cussed in detail to refute Barth's views about them. With regard
to the social divisions which camping allegedly restates daily,
'the relative location of tents in a camp is not such as to give
any clear impression of its internal structure',(54) and in what
is said of the caravans, save for the remark that 'members of
the same herding unit tend to travel together'(55) (although,
because of the different speed at which people go about packing
and loading, some families finish before others and move off,
thereby dispersing the camps for part of the time, at least),
there is little material to indicate the divisions in the caravan.
The meanings of group allegiance and divisions, supposedly
almost pictographically represented in the activities of camping
and movement, cannot, therefore, be accepted.

The second meaning Barth derives from the great migration
is that 'the sullen hostility of unfamiliar spectators wherever
the caravan road goes through a village marks the caravan off
as a group totally different from the sedentary communities'.(56)
One cannot forbear from asking whether this kind of simplistic
meaning is what is to be expected from the adoption of 'greater
sophistication in the definition of ritual'.(57) The meaning is
nothing more than an observation of journalistic superficiality,
and, like most such observations, it is misleadingly erroneous:
facts given elsewhere in the book leave no doubt about this.

After the abdication of Reza Shah in 1941, the majority of
the Basseri remained settled, and the nomad population is still
on the decline.(58) This is largely due to 'a high rate of sedentarisation',(59) and when Basseri settle they do not all concentrate in one place: 'Settled, landowning Basseri are found
scattered over a very large area'.(60) The process of settling
is continuous, with the result that numbers of people from each
camp are 'sloughed off in each generation',(61) particularly
the smaller sibling groups, some of which are pushed into settlement in their entirety. Also, there are occasions, such as a
change of government representative, rapid growth of population
followed by a serious loss of animals, or other calamities, when
a 'major fraction of the population' is obliged to settle.(62)

For these reasons, perhaps, Barth is constrained to comment
on the absence 'of an extreme ethnic contrast – the language,
religion, and major aspects of custom are shared',(63) as,
indeed, they must be, since a very large number of the farmers
with whom comparison is made here are Basseri themselves.
Apart from these relatives, the nomadic Basseri have dealings
with people other than Basseri both as a tribe or corporate
sections of it, and as individuals.(64) Economic relations between
settled and nomadic people are not mediated by the Colonel in
administrative charge of them (but, when, in other circumstances,
he functions as mediator, this is cited as an instance of the tribe
acting corporately – a curious use of the concept), but are
separate and individual, creating such a multiplicity of individual
dyadic ties between settled and nomadic people that they become
enmeshed wherever 'the tribe is related to sedentary communities

along its migration route'.(65) From settled people, the nomads buy agricultural and industrial products, for which they pay by selling animals and their products. Purchases of this sort are negotiated between partners, who enjoy a stable relationship sufficiently strong to permit debts to be left over many months. Here it must be stressed that this trading is not with a market, remote from the migration route, but with villagers on that route. 'Every nomad has stable relations with a number of such trading partners in villages scattered along the migration route of his section.'(66)

Many nomads own agricultural land, and have opened bank accounts.(67) Successful herdsmen transfer some of their capital wealth in animals into land, acquiring plots of different sizes 'along their whole route of migration', while remaining nomads and renting their lands,(68) thus acquiring the status of landlords, a status that is highly desired, giving the nomad an entrée into the local elite of village and district, and for the wealthier into the provincial or national elite. Landownership provides the nomad with an income with which to buy agricultural products, the main items in his diet; it offers good capital growth; it is a security against disaster befalling his herds; and to ensure that his investment retains its value the nomad, vested with 'great powers over his tenant', controls and supervises him in the work he does as well as in other matters.(69) 'A number of Basseri in every generation pass through this development, progressing to become sedentary landlords in villages in or near the Basseri migration channel, frequently camping in tents in the gardens of their houses half the year, and with a continuing emotional interest in and identification with nomad life and ways.'(70) Unsuccessful herdsmen do not remain nomads either. Without animals, a man sinks into debt with his trading partners and has no other recourse but to seek to make a living in a settled community: Barth calls this process sedentarisation by impoverishment.(71) The movement, however, is not a one-way affair. When national political conditions are reasonably stable the drift into villages quickens, but when they are disturbed 'even whole sedentary communities' take to nomadic life(72) – although where all these people obtain animals is not specified. It is much more likely that these movements from and into nomadism are caused by the retirement from the rigours of pastoralism of the successful and the failures, and the opportunists among settled people chancing their luck at animal rearing. induced to do so by the attraction of the wealth they know can be made from it. Many tribesmen, Barth records, are of tenant parentage, and large numbers of nomads are able to trace their origin to sedentary ancestors, two generations ago.(73) Whatever the exact cause of this two-way movement in the past, the effect is that people of the pastures and the sown have become inextricably intertwined.

The regularity of nomads settling (in the past as well as the present), the enduring trading partnerships between pastoralists

and villagers (so vital to both), the landownership of nomads
and their relations with their tenants, the ex-nomads in villages
and erstwhile settled people among the nomads, must, surely,
engender an intimacy of relationships, which are so deeply
rooted in ties of kinship and marriage, debt relationships,
partnerships, institutionalised friendships, and the like, that
the nomads are indistinguishable from settled people, the
majority of whom appear to be Basseri anyway. And how all this
contrasts with the relationships between camps which are rarely
mobilised as corporate units in opposition - 'the prevailing fear
and suspicion keeps groups at a reasonable distance from each
other'!(74) Conceptualising the people who are pastoralists at a
given moment as 'totally different' from people who happen to be
living a settled life at a given moment is to make a fiction of
what is in fact a symbiosis between two sectors of one economy,
and of a people who are socially, culturally and religiously of
one breed.

The third interpretation of the symbolism Barth claims the
great migration contains is that which brings together all Basseri
nomads as one society. By taking the caravan as a whole, with
its mass of tents at night-time and its scores of small caravans
by day, he sees it as serving to 'dramatise the community of
membership in tribe and confederacy, and their segmental
structure'.(75) Unfortunately the information given about the
tribe and its sections is insufficient and the analysis is so unclear
that it is difficult to fathom the community of membership of any
Basseri groupings. Like Tapper,(76) I find the analysis of the
camp, and particularly its relation to the oulad, to be unsatisfactory. Emphasis is given to bilaterality as a feature of camps,
but this kind of kinship appears in local groups among the Nuer
without inhibiting the development of a segmentary lineage
system, and although it has been argued that the bedouin of
Cyrenaica do not conform to lineage theory in their behaviour,
the variety of types of kinship to be found in camps is not held
to account for this: indeed, most non-urban communities are
likely to contain a range of types of kinship.(77) It is the consequence of the bilateral relations in the Basseri camps that are
serious, because, according to Barth, in matters of rights and
duties there is no distinction between patrilineal kin and
others.(78) Camps are the local residential groups which constitute the oulad (which is translated to mean family, but which,
derived from the Arabic root w-l-d, surely means sons, children
or progeny(79)), and this is based on patrilineal descent.
Members of an oulad share inherited pasture rights,(80) as they ·
do their rights to the migratory route and travel schedule.(81)
Therefore, these rights must be vested in agnates in camps,
despite the fact a man is free to attach himself to any group
within an oulad. Several suggestions can be made to account for
this confusion. Many, if not most, matrilateral and affinal kinsmen are agnates as well, since 30 per cent of the marriages are
between close cousins, and about another third are between

members of the different camps of an oulad.(82) In daily life,
granting the density of kinship suggested by these figures, it
is not to be expected that agnatic rights will occupy the attention
of people to whom they are common, particularly when they are
on the move and preoccupied with individually owned animals.
Further, there is no information on the conditions obtaining,
with regard to rights, in those areas which the Basseri occupy
in summer and winter. Finally, Barth spent most of the short
period he was among the Basseri in the camp of their chief (ex-
chief to be more precise),(83) and this might have been peculiar
in many ways, bearing in mind the unbelievable autocratic powers
Barth accords to chiefs.(84)

The composition of Basseri local groups has a comparative
interest beyond the scope of this discussion. For present purposes it is the ritualisation of the 'community of membership'
which is at issue. Unity of some kind ties a camp together if it
is only the vague unity of undifferentiated kinship, and if its
inhabitants are recruited from kinspeople by its leader – a practice reminiscent of the way in which local communities are
recruited by 'bulls' among the Nuer. This is unity enough to
anticipate its ritualisation in one form or another, but the
inevitable inclusion of camps in the great migration – even though
the members of camps tend to travel together – is, possibly, no
more than temporary companionship, expediency, or a necessity
imposed by the topography: it is always prudent to draw the
distinction between acting in unison and acting in unity. In one
passage there is clear evidence of a camp unity other than the
contrived ritual sort with which Barth endows them. In a section
on 'common sense' rituals, it is said that within the tenets of
Islam the Basseri are free 'to develop and elaborate their
ceremonies and customs as an autonomous folk system.'(85) One
of these ceremonies or customs relates to pilgrimages to a locally
renowned saint's tomb. Most camp groups, as they pass near
it, make a detour to spend a day of celebrations at it, everyone
dressed in their best clothes, several persons from each tent.
Somewhat surprisingly – since this is the only reference to it –
each tent sacrifices an animal, although it is common practice for
tents to combine for a single sacrifice: to save animals, Barth
opines, without pausing to ask why all tents are not clustered,
or why one sacrifice does not suffice for the whole camp, or why
some tents should squander animals on single sacrifices. Perhaps
the answers to these simple questions would wreak havoc with
his insistent view that bilaterality leaves the kindred of the camp
undifferentiated in their rights and duties. More surprisingly,
Barth does not attempt to tease any symbolic meanings out of the
pilgrimage or the acts of sacrifice. Instead, he concludes the
woefully incomplete account thus: 'Throughout, there is a general
lack of ceremonial, and a gay and carefree feeling of a festive
picnic prevails.'(86) In short the affair is not to be taken
seriously; the serious requires solemnity – such a puritanical
posture! Long ago, in a short introduction to a book on the

religious festivities of saints' days, Evans-Pritchard comments
that 'The gay and secular side to religious ceremonies is an
essential part of all popular religious festivals. . . . There must
be plenty to eat and drink and the meats must be of a kind that
are not daily eaten. . . . The secular festivities bring people
together and make the occasion a memorable one in their lives.
A man remembers what he has enjoyed. The religious rites
provide the festivities with a purpose and a centre round which
they move.'(87) The gay and secular side of religious festivities
is an integral part of them, and often makes explicit what is left
unsaid in ritual. Were we given details of the sacrifices, and
who were the people who combined to give a sacrifice and
followed it with a commensal meal, an abundance of ritual riches
and symbolic meanings would become apparent.

Community of membership, it is said, is made symbolically
evident in the great migration not only in camps but in tribes
and their 'segmental structure'. In the absence of evidence, in
the chapter on ritual, indicating the nature of community – save
that very many people, belonging to very many groups, pass,
with their animals, through an area at the same time – it is
reasonable to suppose that it appears elsewhere in the book.
What has first to be sought is their 'segmental structure', a
peculiar use of 'segmental' for 'segmentary' since, although both
are identical in meaning, in anthropology 'segmentary' is the
common usage, unless a nuance of meaning, not natural to the
words themselves, is intended. Although the Basseri speak of a
camp as if it were a single patrilineage, which again forms a
segment of a larger lineage in a merging series, culminating in an
ancestral apex,(88) the camps themselves are unsegmented (89);
they never constitute patrilineal descent segments of a larger
oulad,(90) they are not homologous with the oulad,(91) the
genealogies do not fit the social organisation;(92) in short this
is not a segmentary lineage system.(93) Between the camp and
the oulad, the processes by which they emerge and are maintained are fundamentally different, and to press the point Barth
adds that this break 'is not merely an artifact [a use which
perverts the meaning of the word] of the mode of description'.(94)
There is this break because, above the level of the oulad, the
processes 'emanate from the central chief of the Basseri tribe,
and have their source in part outside the Basseri tribes'.(95)
The Basseri chiefdom – a more appropriate designation, perhaps,
than tribe – is divided into twelve *tira* (units), which in turn
are divided into an irregular number of oulads. Each of these
units has the same type of estate (as Barth calls it – a better
choice of word than property) differing only in that the tira
subsumes all the estates of the oulads and the chiefdom subsumes
all the estates of the tiras. These estates consist of rights in
grazing areas, and in the migratory route and schedule.(96)
But although each superior section encloses its structurally
inferior section, sections do not fuse – fissure – in an ordered
manner; they are not in balanced opposition, as in a segmentary

system. Instead, they function through leadership, the headman in the case of the oulads, and the chief of the Basseri for the chiefdom and the tiras, presumably, since the latter have neither chiefs nor headmen. The relations of camps to their oulad head-men, and of headmen to chiefs, are as disparate units at both levels of authority, not as fused segments. Perhaps it is for this reason that Barth has chosen 'segmental' in preference to 'segmentary' to convey the idea of separate strands gathered in the hands of headmen and chiefs respectively. Confusion arises because, in the discussion of tribes and their section, considerable attention is devoted to issues of descent, the role of agnation, the genealogical structure, the process of segmen-tation, and the like, when in fact it is the chief who subdivides an oulad 'when it has grown too large' (for what? - administra-tive convenience?). Conceptually this is the wrong mould in which to set the facts. Many of the issues referred to above have an importance in their place, no doubt, but the basis of the social organisation in this area is as a territory in a state which governs through its appointed bureaucrats, whether they be familiar faces or an army Colonel. The power of the chief is overwhelming. The headmen are his channels of communication, not a separate echelon in a chain of command.(97) 'Oulads serve as the administrative tools of the chief: through the headmen of oulads he regulates and allots pastures.'(98) The chief is the sole representative of the tribe in its relations with the Iranian government, and he is expected to make decisions for the tribe in this and other fields. Once made, his decision is final: 'any definite statement is a decision, whether expressed as an aside in a conversation, or while washing his hands or taking a meal'.(99) When Barth was among the Basseri, the chief was no longer in office. Consequently, the full details given of the chief's powers, his role in the tribe, and his relations with other chiefs and government functionaries are the reflections of an ex-chief on conditions as they were when he was in office - hearsay evidence from an individual's perception of a past form of social organisation, but not to be taken seriously as a record of conditions as they actually existed. Barth accepts the chief's account of the past because the reconstruction of the system based on it (and written as if it is contemporary) 'is meaningful because that system, and not the present one (par-ticularly not in its officially sanctioned form), belongs as an integral part with the other persisting features of Basseri organisation which I describe'.(100) Barth resided in the chief's camp. Most of his data is derived from that source. His descrip-tion of Basseri social organisation, therefore, inevitably corrobor-ates the chief's account: they are one and the same reconstruc-tion. If there is any accuracy in the chief's account - and if the powers of the army Colonel, who governed the Basseri during Barth's time with them, were similar to those attributed by Barth to the chief - the picture that emerges is one of a very harsh administration, represented among the Basseri by a tyrant with

almost unbridled powers. This being so the dramatisation of the
'community of membership' in the tribe and its segments in the
great migration is a mirage.

There is nothing in the facts about the procession of caravans
in the great migration to suggest a tiered social organisation.
People move with their animals in parallel lines; we are not told
whether there is any significance in being to the fore or in the
rear; apparently there are mounted leaders in the caravan, but
precisely where they travel in the caravan, how they relate to
each other, and where the general direction of the caravan comes
from cannot be inferred from the description. What Barth saw
was a lot of camps and the animals moving en masse to summer
pastures: no hint even of an inauguration ceremony. If, in the
description, there appears to be so little of interest, why then
should Barth ascribe such ritual import to the caravan? The clue
is to be found in the meanings he attaches to the acts of migration, which, he claims, are of the same logical order as ritual
idioms of religious ceremonies. There is no logic in what is an
assertion of comparability; perhaps he is making an assumption
or stating a belief. But 'They [the acts of migration] can only
be compared with these [religious ceremonies] if the context in
which they are placed is of correspondingly predominant
value.'(101) What is this predominant value? It cannot refer to
the rituals of the life crises, of the sacrifices at the saint's
day festival, or, scraping the bottom of the 'common sense
ritual' barrel, beliefs in the evil eye; all these have already
been dismissed as unconnected, unrelated to important features
of the social structure, and it is after dealing with all these in
ten pages that Barth adds: 'I feel that the above attempt at an
exhaustive [sic] description of the ceremonies and the explicit
ritual practices of the Basseri reveals a ritual life of unusual
poverty.'(102) Religious ceremonies often loom large in the lives
of people in most countries about which anthropologists write,
and, to the extent that they sometimes gather large sections or
whole populations in congregations, they are thought to say
something big, because the span of the activities is so wide;
they also give the impression of tying together so many strands
of social relationships. This needs to be underscored because
the paucity of rituals which engages Barth's attention is the
paucity of big rituals.

Camping and travelling, involving thousands of people – and
animals – puts the migration on a par with religious ceremonies:
but does it have the same sort of value as them? Barth says it
does. It has this value for three reasons.(103) First, time and
space are interpreted with reference to migration – and, one can
add with the confidence of certainty, to other activities as well;
the phenomenon of relating these two concepts to social activities
has passed into general acceptance since Evans-Pritchard wrote
about the connection in his first major work on the Nuer. There
is nothing very remarkable about its appearance among the
Basseri relating it to the migrations or any other activities.

Second, when the administration collapsed in 1941 and the Basseri were left free to move again, they resumed their migration. When nomads were forced to settle in the 1930s, it is highly probable that provisions for assimilating them were inadequate, and that when the ban on movement was lifted some of the Basseri - but by no means all of them - took to pastoralism, more as a Hobson's choice than out of some instinctive drive to wander. Overall, the nomad population is on the decline, in any case.(104) As Baxter so rightly points out, 'sedentarization is not necessarily aberrant, nor regrettable, though in their own folk ideologies most pastoralists hold it to be so'.(105) So too with Cyrenaican bedouin: many of those I knew as lean and lithe men in the camps in 1949, men who had never been in a town and scorned the mode of living they had heard of there, had, by the mid-1960s, left the semi-desert to grow fat and waddle about in villages; the suggestion that they might return to their former way of life struck them as drollery. The Basseri are not in any way exceptional. A brief life history that Barth gives is instructive in this connection. It is about a man who began his career as a herdsman with a few sheep. He prospered and saved enough to buy a piece of land. During the period of enforced settlement he built a house, but instead of living in it he bribed the police to allow him to continue herding. Later he sold his land in order to buy a larger and better plot. In this he built a house where he now lives in comfort with his wife and children, while his remaining animals are herded by relatives.(106) This man went out of his way to remain a herdsman at a time when nomads were being pressed to settle, and yet he chose to settle when the Basseri were left free to roam. Clearly, in taking both decisions he gave precedence to his material interests, not to some special value he attached to nomadism per se.

The tendency for nomads to settle if it profits them operates in most pastoral areas. Baxter, basing his judgment on his experience among East African pastoralists, and a survey of the literature on that area and the Sudan, is of the opinion that ' "Itchy feet" may come to afflict some of those reared in pastoral camps, but I would suggest that nevertheless, if a sedentary life could be achieved without detriment to their stock, then most pastoralists would settle cheerfully, even eagerly'.(107) On the basis of my experience in Libya, I wholly concur with this view. In 1948, when Libya was still governed by a foreign power, the bedouin showed no sign of wishing to settle. Two years later the administration became increasingly Libyan, in preparation for independence in 1951. Some bedouin chose to settle then: there was insufficient wealth in the country at the time to absorb large numbers of settlers. By 1964, eight years after the discovery of oil and with budget surpluses accumulating on a scale undreamt of a few years earlier, the bedouin were leaving the semi-desert in droves. In that year, I lived on an olive plantation in Tripolitania, where previously the farms had all been owned by Italians. By this time roughly three-quarters of the farms had

been bought by Libyans, mainly ex-bedouin. The cost of one of
the smaller of these farms at that time was £10,000, a sum well
beyond the means of most bedouin. Encouraged by government
loans, readily available if the prospective buyer of a farm could
find half the cost, the bedouin soon began forming partnerships
to raise the money. Each partner sold some or all of his animals,
and gained a share in the farm appropriate to the contribution
he made from the sale of his animals. A few families of the
partnership took up permanent residence on the farm; the rest
remained in the semi-desert tending the animals left over after
the sales, those of their settled partners included. In summer,
at harvest time, many of the pastoral partners moved to the
farm, pitching their tents around the house while one or two
shepherds and their families stayed to water the animals and to
wander with them as they ranged widely in search of clumps of
the more succulent plants that are able to withstand the rigours
of the summer drought. Similar arrangements were adopted in
Cyrenaica. On a visit to Libya in 1969 most of the bedouin I
knew from earlier years were living in villages, but they still
kept flocks of sheep and herds of camels in the areas where they
had previously lived, tended now by only a few men and their
families - the very men who were reputed to be good shepherds
and herdsmen in 1948. That is to say, all but the professional
herdsmen left to live a settled life. (108) There was no question
of them severing the pastoral link altogether, nor did the
Tripolitanian olive farmers. Indeed, in some parts of Tripolitania
areas that were considered unsuitable for the mixed crop cum
pastoral economy are now used for camel herding, even though
the small herding camps have to be very mobile, so sparse are
the pastures. Over the years, the market value of sheep and
camels had soared and to have cut the pastoral connection completely would have been folly. Cultivation and pastoralism have
become fused into one economy in Libya. This, it seems to me, is
very similar to what has been happening among the Basseri.

   The third value Barth bestows on the migration is that the
nomadic Basseri are emotionally committed to it. Acknowledging
that this emotionalism might be nothing more than a subjective
experience, he attempts to measure the 'notable tension, excitement, or emotional involvement', (109) by conducting what might
be called a time and motion study. Out of this he produces a
graph showing times of awakening, packing, and departure of
the chief's camp in the caravan over ninety days of the migration.
These he records on the assumption that rising tensions would
be expressed in earlier times for these activities. As he reads
his graph, it confirms his assumption. As I read it, the most
conspicuous feature is that the duration of daily migration
decreases after the thirty-eighth day. On one or two of the
remaining fifty-two days people rose early, but otherwise rising
times were much the same as they were in the first part of the
journey. Were his reading correct, one would still be left won-
dering why it should be assumed that early rising is indicative

of heightened tensions. There are many more plausible explanations. The camp in which he took records was the chief's camp,
and it might well have been customary procedure for the people
of this camp to arrive at the destination ahead of the others. Or
it might have been that as the end of the journey became nearer,
people were prompted to hurry along a little; unfortunately, the
distances travelled each day are not given, and without this
information early rising could be viewed as purely fortuitous.
There is a third possible explanation. In Cyrenaica in spring-
time the bedouin delight in drinking camel milk. For long
stretches, the bedouin are chronically constipated. Camel milk -
apart from the pleasure it gives them to drink it - acts as a
purge (*burg*, as they put it). They are moved by it in more ways
than one - a little fact of fieldwork that tells much more of their
daily habits than any amount of graphwork.

   At best, the attempt to demonstrate objectively the emotional
involvement of the Basseri in the migration is inconclusive. But
what would this have established? Is emotional involvement to be
equated with ritual, or even construed to be one of its necessary
components? Tapper thinks that Barth's demonstration is per-
suasive, the analysis illuminating, but he suggests that the
migration ritual presents the authentic characteristics of
liminality. (110) The source of this inspiration is Turner's work
on pilgrimages. (111) Turner, in turn, borrowed the term
'liminality' from Van Gennep. The latter used it to refer to a
transitional phase in a rite de passage, in which social status
is undefined. (112) Turner, in his use of the term, follows Van
Gennep's meaning closely: 'During the intervening liminal period,
the state of the ritual subject (the "passenger" or "liminar")
becomes ambiguous, neither here nor there, betwixt and between
all fixed points of classification.' (113) Both Barth and Tapper
conceive the regularly recurring annual event of the migration
as a rite de passage because of the movement of people from one
place to another. (114) A rite de passage is not a right of way,
whatever jollifications or other displays of emotion might accompany the exercise of that right. What may be called liminality is
made explicitly clear among Cyrenaican bedouin when a stranger
enters a camp. He is received courteously, and for about fifteen
minutes he exchanges conventional greetings with his host. He
is not required to reveal his identity, or to enter into conversation with his host. He simply sits or reclines in his host's tent,
mute for most of about a two-hour period, while the meat of an
animal which has been sacrificed is likely to be made ready for
eating. All men of the camp now gather in the host's tent to eat
the meat, which is done in complete silence, except that the host
urges his guest to 'Eat, eat!' Shortly after the meal has been
finished, the tea things are placed in front of one of the men and
conversation begins, slowly at first but soon to become most
animated. Host, guest and the other men present, in a veritable
torrent of conversation, recall events connecting them, seek a
relationship, however tenuous, with the guest, and demands can

now be made on the guest, the thought of which would not have
been entertained only a few hours earlier. The bedouin are prone
to volunteer, at this stage, that 'we are now equals'. They also
make it unambiguously clear that the change in the relationship
has been brought about by a sacrifice. There is nothing in either
Barth's or Tapper's descriptions of the migrations they saw to
suggest a change in social status comparable to that achieved
by a sacrifice.

At the end of the migration the women in the caravan burst
triumphantly (presumably) into song, although what they sang
is not divulged. The end of the journey for the Basseri is also
the triumphant end of Barth's quest for ritual: 'I suggest, therefore, that the poverty which seemed to characterise Basseri
ritual life is an artifact [a second unfortunate use of the word]
of the descriptive categories I have employed.'(115) The riches,
which a more sophisticated definition of ritual is likely to yield,
are contained in the statement that the value placed on migration makes it 'the central rite of nomadic society'.(116) Moreover,
the realisation of this transforms the general description of
Basseri life 'an external and objective description of the economic
and social arrangements within a tribe to a description of central
features of that tribe, the meanings and values which make up
their life'.(117) It is important to bear in mind what Barth is
doing here: he is giving completeness to his model of Basseri
society. This, it seems to me, is the crux of the matter; the
model is given priority over the data. It is a curious fact of
Iranian fieldwork that so many of the research reports are conspicuously lacking in basic data but replete with models - Rubel,
Salzman, and Spooner are three examples that come to mind
immediately.(118) Barth is no exception. Apart from the completeness given to his model by the central rite of nomadic
society, there are at least three other references to the need for
the facts to fit the model. First, the account given by the
deposed chief of his former powers is accepted without a trace
of scepticism because it: 'belongs as an integral part with the
other persisting features of Basseri organisation which I
describe'.(119) Second, although he shows an awareness that
the population data and the few figures are inadequate for
establishing the neat balance between the nomadic and the rural
population,(120) Barth accepts the figures because: 'all the
data fit the general schema which I have outlined'.(121) Third,
the rituals that Barth observed by taking a common sense view
of ritual are abandoned because he is unable to 'integrate' them
into his description.(122) This insistence that all the parts
should fit tightly produces a neat model, albeit of incredible
simplicity, but one that is full of fallacy; and, like most models,
it affords little understanding of the pattern of people's lives.
It needs to be said, however, that Barth was among the Basseri
for only three months, during the peculiar circumstances of the
migration, and in the chief's camp at that. For these reasons, a
harvest of data is not to be expected, and what could be reaped

in as short a period as this is likely to give an unbalanced impression of the migration and the structure of Basseri society.

In his work on highland Burma, to which reference was made earlier, Leach is concerned not only with ritual but also with the merit of thinking in terms of a society. He fundamentally disagrees with the general use of this concept, because he finds he is unable to draw a boundary around a particular group of people occupying a defined territory. The criteria he uses in his attempts to do this produce a number of boundaries that are not coincident, so that 'any particular individual can be thought of as having a status position in several different social systems at one and the same time'.(123) Since the status of a person changes, since an awareness of other attainable statuses leads some individuals to pursue purposively a change in their condition while others involuntarily lose theirs, Leach recognises a state of flux in people's relations, and it is the analysis of this that aids the better understanding of the process of social change. Elsewhere, I have argued that an acceptance of the elaborate Cyrenaican genealogy, culminating in a single ancestress, is not to be taken as a model of the social structure of a society. It is a very useful way to conceive the disposition of groups of people in territories arranged in an ascending order of ecological differentiation. Among the camel herders of the semi-desert, these groups are corporate, but vary conspicuously in the number of members, and in the ecological resources of their territories; and their political power varies from that represented by the insignificant shaikh to that of the shaikh who exercises sway over his own large corporate group and others as well. This distribution of power reflects the heavy dependence of some groups on others, and the marked dominance of a few over those around them. It is misleading to view these corporate groups as homologous parts of a segmentary lineage system; it is even more erroneous to think of them fissuring and fusing as the context of relationships alter. At any moment a pattern of relationships is discernible for any particular corporate group and, as in highland Burma, individuals strive to alter their condition, so too do the bedouin re-configure their relationships over a period of years. Since this striving is continuous, the process of change from this pattern to that is also continuous. Administratively demarcated boundaries and the limits set by the genealogical framework coincide, except on the boundary with Egypt,(124) and this coincidence adds substance to the idea of a self-contained social structure. On the edges of these boundaries, however, relationships do not cease, although in these areas they obtain between people who are disparate in many important respects. Therefore, to reduce bedouin relationships to the a so-called lineage model, enclosing them within a structure of a society, is an encumbrance to the understanding of the patterns by which the lives of the bedouin are guided. Salzman thinks otherwise. Acknowledging that the application of lineage theory is fraught with difficulties, and admitting that it does not seem to work most of the time, he nevertheless opts for the view that a lineage system is a system 'in reserve' - like a skeleton in the cupboard!(125) Gellner's view is not unlike Salzman's. Following Montagne, he is of the opinion that a segmentary lineage works in practice, as it should in theory, some of the time, and the fact that it patently does not work all the time is no reason for abandoning it. Nor, indeed, would it be; but if the assertion that it does work in some contexts is to be accepted, at least an indication should be offered of the contexts in which it does and does not work, why it works in this but not in that context, so that some kind of sociological characterisation could be given to these radically differing contexts. Without any of this kind of characterisation, I stick to my earlier view that what we have done is to take over elaborate genealogies from the pastoralists who use them, clothe them in anthropological language and convert them into the social structure of a society. In short, there is no bedouin society, in the structural meaning given to the term. Unequivocally, there is no Basseri society in this sense either.

The lack of ritual among the bedouin, about which I wrote in the article cited at the beginning of this discussion, concerned the absence of ritual gatherings at which were rallied groups of a larger order than the localised corporate group. That is to say, it was anticipated that the ordering of groups in lineage fashion, reducing in stages to an apex, would be mirrored in a matching order of ritual gatherings - the elegant form of the genealogy serving as an admirable palimpsest for a bedouin version of ancestor worship. Since I have discarded the concept of the structure of a society, and its ordered arrangement of parts, the expectation becomes redundant. There can be no big rituals because bedouin groups do not congregate, either en masse or by representation, for any purpose.

The absence of one type of ritual - the large-scale politically integrative ritual - does not in itself necessarily mean ritual paucity. The details of the so-called life crises rituals alone are impressive. To be added to these are the rituals associated with the bedouin way of life: sacrifices during drought, sacrifices at the opening of wells at the onset of the watering season, rituals associated with ploughing and the handling of grain either in the stores or as flour, sacrifices when disease strikes animals, sacrifice when a lost flock is safely returned, sacrifice when a stranger comes to camp, sacrifice when a tent is added to a camp, and so on. Then there is the sacrifice of the Feast of the Flesh, or the Great Feast, when the head of each tent slaughters an animal, and the sacrifice preceding someone's departure for the pilgrimage to Makkah where an animal is also sacrificed on the morning of the Great Feast. There are also a number of rituals which correspond, in a very general manner, to Barth's category of special practices. Charming rituals are observed by women when a young man undertakes a long and hazardous journey, particularly if he goes alone. When a kinsman returns to camp

after a long absence his covenant with his people is renewed by
a sacrifice, as the covenant with his corporate group is renewed
annually at the Feast of the Flesh. Sacrifice is performed to
heal a breach in relationships, and a peace meeting after a
homicide must be accompanied by a sacrifice as an impelling
obligation. If a man, or his wife, or his child falls seriously
sick, he sacrifices at a saint's tomb if there is one in the
vicinity, or, if not, in the camp. When an individual has
successfully negotiated a threat to his life, he is likely to
sacrifice.

Impressive as this list of rituals may be, it by no means
exhausts the number or variety of rituals the bedouin practise.
On numerical grounds alone they cannot be dismissed as inconsequential; indeed it is an embarrassment, when I reflect that
twenty-three sacrifices were made in one camp in which I
resided, that I had ever thought the semi-desert to be poor in
rituals. Neither is their number the most important aspect of
bedouin rituals. The prime index of ritual, to my mind, is the
constraint a supernatural referent imposes on people - an aspect
to which Fortes, referring specifically to sacrifice, has recently
given weight: 'and there is generally if not always, an implica-
tion of mutual constraint, and indeed of actual or potential
mutual coercion in the act'. (126) Without wishing to expound on
bedouin sacrificial exegesis here, it is necessary to add the one
gloss that the bedouin view sacrifice as an act which creates a
debt between people, so that it simultaneously creates a new
relationship and projects it into the future. What is more, the
constraint in sacrifice is empirically verifiable. The case cited
earlier of the sacrifice performed when a stranger entered a
camp showed how it shifted the relationship between the host
and his guest from the level of courteous formality, the emblem
of unease if not hostility, to the level of familiarity and close
questioning - a change made possible by the liberating effect of
sacrificial blood constraining the participants to engage forth-
with in a new relationship. A second case is, perhaps, even
more telling in this respect.

In 1964, when I was resident on an olive plantation in Tripolitania, the farms of which were inhabited almost entirely by ex-
bedouin, a serious dispute arose between two contenders for
power. One of these men was the president of a local co-operative,
to which all owners of farms had contributed relatively large
sums of money, intended mainly for the purchase of a very
expensive piece of equipment for general use. The president's
rival was a member of the co-operative committee, and for this
reason he came to see some of the documents sent to the president by the Italian firm supplying the equipment. The rival was
convinced that the president had not only cheated by overstat-
ing the cost, thereby saving his own contribution, but that the
equipment had been bought in his name, thus giving him the
legal powers to charge for its use later on. As far as I could tell
the rival had a sound case, but the president brushed the

allegations aside, contending that he had misread the documents.
The rival then wrote to the Director General of co-operatives
asking him to investigate the matter. As soon as the president
heard of this, he also wrote to the Director inviting him to a
meal at his farmhouse. On the day of the visit, the president
slaughtered five sheep - a lavish sacrifice by any standards -
and invited all the members of the committee, his rival included,
to the meal. Nothing was said about the president's alleged
impropriety until tea was taken after the meal, when the president informed the Director that some difficulty had been
experienced over the legal aspects of the purchase of equipment,
but that everything would soon be put to rights. The Director
thanked the president for his assurances, praised him for the
exemplary way in which he conducted the business of the co-
operative, and waxed eloquent on the generosity of the president
in sacrificing five of his own animals, ending with a little homily
on the meaning of sacrifice in their religion. The rival, most
properly and respectfully, tendered his resignation that same
evening. The president accepted with alacrity, a thorn in his
side had been removed. Now this incident could be analysed as
primarily a political matter, the wealth and followings of both
contenders for power carefully assessed. It could be argued that
the men assembled were more impressed by the president's display of wealth, or by the surfeit of food they had consumed.
These elements were undoubtedly present, and Leach and Barth
would be justified in labelling it as a ritual occasion. That, however, is not the point, for although people had been brought
together as the result of competition between rivals, the president inflicted a humiliating and lasting defeat because of the
impelling constraints that had been put on the behaviour of his
rival by the sacrifice.

How different is the effect of sacrifice compared with the frills
and decorations which conventionally accompany tea-drinking
among bedouin. During a session of tea-drinking, which lasts an
hour or longer, numerous frills are added to the simple technique
of boiling water, mixing it with tea and sugar, and drinking it.
The proceedings begin with a brief argument about who is to
make the tea. This decided, the little tea glasses and the small
enamel teapot are placed in front of him on a tray. Embers are
brought in on a piece of metal and put near the tray. The water
is boiled in a vessel called a *kilu* - a small can distributed by the
Italians for holding the ration of a kilogram of oil during the
days of the concentration camps. All these items are standard,
and no others would serve the purpose. As soon as the tea-
maker has put the water on to boil, the assembled men fall to
conversing. They converse with conspicuous zest; not to do so
would be improper. As the water comes to the boil, the tea-
maker pours some into the small teapot, adding a handful of
tea and two or three handfuls of sugar. The conversation, meanwhile, continues unabated. After the mixture has been boiled to
a thick syrup-like brew, the tea-maker fussily washes a few

glasses, arranges them in front of him in a row, and then, from
a great height, pours some tea into the little glasses, mixes it,
and pours it back into the pot again. He then replaces the lid of
the teapot by slapping it shut with quite unnecessary vigour,
as if angry with it. Three or four such mixings usually suffice.
He then pours off a small amount of tea into a glass, again holding the pot extraordinarily high above it, tastes it, pours the
remainder back into the pot, and, without comment, returns the
pot to the smouldering embers, his every move watched with
absorbed attention by those sitting around him. Depending on
the general mood, the tea-maker performs these actions a greater
or lesser number of times, before tea is finally poured into all
the glasses and handed round. Each man brings the glass to his
mouth in a circuitous trajectory, before quaffing the tea noisily.
Three rounds of tea are offered by the camel-herding bedouin.
Each round is prepared with the same flourishes. When the
third round is complete, the men rise as if propelled and depart
abruptly. What does this plethora of frills and decorations, or
the technical acts themselves, say? Bedouin say that tea-drinking
opens the mind and liberates the tongue. It is true that I have
never known tea-drinking to be anything other than convivial,
but it does little other than provide a context, twice or three
times daily, for conviviality. Of course questions such as who
provides the tea and sugar, whether the quantities are generous
or mean, how frequently this or that person provides tea in the
camp, are indicative of a variety of things. But tea-drinking
does not alter the relationships of people. Routine is not ritual.
As I soon learned, I could not repay the hospitality of sacrificial
meals by using my supplies of sugar and tea lavishly. The power
in the blood of the lamb is, for the bedouin, worth more than
all the tea in China – at least in the effect it has on social
relationships.

To my mind, Barth and Leach wish to remove the supernatural
referent from ritual. The supernatural, for them, is unreal,
and, consequently, ideas relating to God can be reduced to more
mundane aspects of people's lives. It is the latter which are real
for Barth and Leach. For the bedouin, however, God is as real
as rain, water, crops, and their social relationships: indeed
he is involved as much in all these as are the bedouin themselves.
Every sacrifice is the making of a renewal of a covenant between
people and God, and the behaviour of these people is subject
to its constraints immediately it has been made. There is nothing
comparable in directing bedouin behaviour. Full cognisance must
be taken of what is real for the bedouin, whatever our personal
estimations.

The number of rituals the bedouin practise and the significance
attached to them have been described in relation to small groups
of people, a few hundred at most. In saying this, it is not
suggested that the significance of bedouin rituals is limited to
these sorts of groups only, creating what might be called local
cult groups. Predominant ritual value for Barth is a matter of

social scale, manifested by the aggregation of people performing
an action or represented in it: the great migration is a spec-
tacular example. What Barth and I neglected when reporting a
paucity of ritual for the Basseri and the Cyrenaican bedouin
respectively, is that scale, particularly in the religions of the
great traditions, has little to do with numbers of people or
political representation. It has to do with ideas, which are of
such span as to include vast areas, and huge aggregates of
people. Basseri and bedouin are both Muslims, who recognise
the one God. Middle East pastoralists are often described as lax
in their performance of religious duties, ignorant of the tenets
of Islam, or both.(127) Cyrenaican bedouin pray irregularly.
They all know that to make the pilgrimage to Makkah is meritorious,
but prefer to leave it until old age, since it removes the stain
of their sins, and were they to make it earlier they would have
to lead a blameless life thereafter, an impossibility for human
beings in their view; the vast majority of them leave it until it is
too late. What is true is that the bedouin are not as piously
punctilious in the more orthodox duties as are their urban or
village brethren. The rites of Islam they practise nevertheless
connect them more meaningfully with the core of Islamic beliefs
than any numbers of genuflections. For sacrifice is the core of
Islam, as it is of other religions. When the bedouin sacrifice in
their small camps, they are aware that all bedouin perform the
same rites, and are motivated by the same beliefs. They know,
further, that not only do bedouin adhere to these beliefs but
that they are common to all Muslims in Islam. In this sense there
is bigness about the sacrifices performed in the little camps.
Barth felt the need for integrative ritual to be so compelling
that he had to invent a new kind of ritual to make good its
absence, to integrate each part of the segmental structure with
tribe and confederacy into one structural system, the society
of the Basseri. I have argued that bedouin society, in a structural sense, is a fiction, but that the locally performed bedouin
sacrifice is the central rite of the Islamic society.

NOTES

1 Versions of this paper were read to seminars in London and
  Oxford. I am grateful for the comments made at both seminars.
2 See Evans-Pritchard (1949); Eickelman (1976); Gilsenan
  (1973).
3 Peters (1965), p. 125.
4 Barth (1964), p. 135.
5 Tapper (1979), pp. 37, 38. He is critical of Douglas on the
  same count.
6 Barth (1964), p. 146.
7 Barth (1964), p. 146.
8 Leach (1954), pp. 10, 11.
9 Leach (1954), p. 12.

10 Leach (1954), p. 13.
11 Barth (1964), p. 147.
12 Leach (1954), p. 12.
13 Leach (1954), p. 13.
14 Leach (1954), p. 14.
15 Leach (1954). See, for example, pp. 11, 13, 87, 103, 104, 279, 286.
16 Evans-Pritchard (1949); Fortes (1953); Middleton (1960); Tapper (1979); Turner (1957).
17 Leach (1954), p. 16.
18 Barth (1964), p. 147.
19 Gluckman (1958).
20 Evans-Pritchard (1937).
21 Barth (1964), p. 147.
22 Barth (1964), p. 147.
23 Barth (1964), p. 148. Since people are able to change camp at will, the unity is dubious, and it can hardly be said, for the same reason, that the group is maintained.
24 Barth (1964), p. 37
25 Barth (1964), pp. 25ff.
26 Fortes (1966), p. 411.
27 Fortes (1966), p. 411.
28 Barth (1964), p. 148.
29 Barth (1964), p. 148.
30 Barth (1964), pp. 42, 43.
31 Barth (1964), p. 148.
32 Barth (1964), p. 148.
33 Barth (1964), p. 11.
34 Barth (1964), p. 21.
35 Barth (1964), p. 34.
36 Barth (1964), p. 16. Only youths and boys herd animals, and this makes the household even more vulnerable, at least as far as its labour needs are concerned.
37 Barth (1964), p. 47.
38 Barth (1964), p. 21.
39 See Barth (1964), p. 25, and Barth (1959-60), p. 10.
40 Barth (1964), p. 25. This is repeated almost exactly on p. 46.
41 Barth (1964), p. 47.
42 Baxter (1975), p. 213.
43 Barth (1964), pp. 41, 36.
44 Barth (1964), pp. 26, 29.
45 Barth (1964), p. 40, and the pullout at rear of book.
46 Barth (1964), p. 39.
47 Barth (1964), p. 32.
48 Barth (1964), pp. 22, 27, 38, 40.
49 Barth (1964), p. 15.
50 Barth (1964), p. 43.
51 Barth (1964), p. 148. Also p. 43, where the statement is made that camp sites, during the migration, are chosen by 'the riders in the lead'.
52 Barth (1960), p. 348; and Barth (1959-60), p. 3.

53 Barth (1964), p. 148.
54 Barth (1964), p. 42.
55 Barth (1964), p. 43.
56 Barth (1964), p. 148.
57 Barth (1964), p. 146.
58 Barth (1964), p. 3.
59 Barth (1964), p. 65.
60 Barth (1964), p. 109.
61 Barth (1964), p. 66.
62 Barth (1964), p. 68.
63 Barth (1964), p. 78.
64 Barth (1964), p. 93.
65 Barth (1964), p. 97.
66 Barth (1964), pp. 98, 99.
67 Barth (1964), p. 20.
68 Barth (1964), p. 104.
69 Barth (1964), p. 105.
70 Barth (1964), p. 106.
71 Barth (1964), p. 108.
72 Barth (1964), p. 118.
73 Barth (1964), p. 118.
74 Barth (1964), p. 47.
75 Barth (1964), p. 148.
76 Tapper (1979), p. 260.
77 See Peters (1967) and (1980).
78 Barth (1964), p. 39.
79 Barth (1964), p. 50.
80 Barth (1964), p. 55.
81 Barth (1964), p. 54.
82 Barth (1964), p. 65. The information on marriage is unclear,
    since no indication is given either of the type or degree of
    cousin relationship. Nor is the origin of spouses given.
83 Barth (1964), p. 38.
84 Barth (1964), p. 27 and chapter 7.
85 Barth (1964), p. 136.
86 Barth (1964), p. 138. The whole account is only a half page.
87 Evans-Pritchard (1941), pp. X, XI
88 Barth (1964), p. 39.
89 Barth (1964), pp. 42, 58, 59.
90 Barth (1964), p. 59.
91 Barth (1964), p. 61.
92 Barth (1964), pp. 56, 63.
93 Barth (1964), p. 67.
94 Barth (1964), p. 49.
95 Barth (1964), p. 50.
96 Barth (1964), p. 54.
97 Barth (1964), p. 75.
98 Barth (1964), p. 62.
99 Barth (1964), p. 77.
100 Barth (1964), p. 71. Barth comments that when he arrived
    in Basseri territory, the Colonel sent him to the chief.

101 Barth (1964), p. 148.
102 Barth (1964), p. 146.
103 Barth (1964), pp. 148-52.
104 Barth (1964), p. 3.
105 Baxter (1975), p. 207.
106 Barth (1964), p. 106.
107 Baxter (1975), p. 209.
108 Baxter (1975), pp. 211, 212.
109 Barth (1964), p. 149.
110 Tapper (1979), pp. 178-83.
111 Turner (1974), chapter 5.
112 Van Gennep (1960), pp. x, 11, 20, 21.
113 Turner (1974), p. 232. This is an almost exact repetition of
    the statement about liminality in ch. 3 of Turner (1969).
114 Barth (1964). He does not actually use the phrase, but it is
    strongly implied in his description.
115 Barth (1964), pp. 152, 153.
116 Barth (1964), p. 153.
117 Barth (1964), p. 153.
118 Rubel (1969); Salzman (1971); Spooner (1971).
119 Barth (1964), p. 71.
120 Barth (1964), pp. 115 ff. I very much doubt whether the
    population was kept as neatly in trim as Barth suggests. His
    model requires that it should be so, but for this to obtain
    the drift from settled to nomadic areas must have been
    greater than his information leads one to believe. If the
    movement of people to and from settled areas was not in
    balance, the population pressure in settled areas must have
    been considerable, but nothing is said about this.
121 Barth (1964), p. 120.
122 Barth (1964), p. 135.
123 Barth (1964), p. 8.
124 One of the major branches of the Cyrenaican genealogy is
    represented by the descendants of an ancestor named 'Ali.
    They form a congeries of groups known as the Aulad 'Ali
    who inhabit the area stretching from the eastern Cyrenaican
    border, across the Western Desert, as far east as Alexandria.
125 Salzman (1975), p. 69. This view is given in an article in
    'Man', 1978, vol. 13, no. 4, which repeats, almost identically,
    the 1975 article.
126 Fortes (1980), p. XIII.
127 Tapper (1979), p. 15. He refers to these opinions, citing
    several authors, and, quite rightly, expresses his scepticism
    about them.

BIBLIOGRAPHY

Asad, T. (1970) 'The Kababish Arabs', Hurst, London.
Barth, F. (1959-60) The Land Use Patterns of Migratory Tribes
    of South Persia, in 'Norsk Geografisk Tidsskrift', vol. 17.

Barth, F. (1960) Nomadism in the Mountain and Plateau Areas of South West Asia, in 'The Problems of the Arid Zone', UNESCO.

Barth, F. (1964) 'Nomads of South Persia', Allen & Unwin, London.

Bates, D.G. (1971) The Role of the State in Peasant-Nomad Mutualism, 'Anthropological Quarterly', vol. 44, no. 3.

Baxter, P.T.W. (1975) Some Consequences of Sendentarization for Social Relationships, in 'Pastoralism in Tropical Africa', IAI, ed. T. Monod.

Behnke, R.H. (1980) 'The Herders of Cyrenaica', University of Illinois, Chicago.

Burckhardt, J.L. (1831) 'Notes on the Bedouins and Wahabys', Colburn & Bentley.

Cole, D.P. (1975) 'Nomads of the Nomads', AHM Publishing Corporation, Illinois.

Cunnison, I. (1966) 'Baggara Arabs', Clarendon Press, Oxford.

Dickson, H.R.P (1949) 'The Arab of the Desert', Allen & Unwin, London.

Douglas, M. (1973) 'Natural Symbols' 2nd edn, Barrie & Jenkins, London.

Eickelman, D.F. (1976) 'Moroccan Islam', University of Texas Press, Austin.

Evans-Pritchard, E.E. (1937) 'Witchcraft Among the Azande', Clarendon Press, Oxford.

Evans-Pritchard, E.E. (1941) Foreword to 'The Moulds of Egypt', by J.W. McPherson, N.M. Press, Cairo.

Evans-Pritchard, E.E. (1949) 'The Sanusi of Cyrenaica', Clarendon Press, Oxford.

Evans-Pritchard, E.E. (1951) 'Kinship and Marriage Among the Nuer', Clarendon Press, Oxford.

Fortes, M. (1953) The Structure of Unilineal Descent Groups, 'American Anthropologist', vol. 55.

Fortes, M. (1966) 'Religious Premisses and Logical Technique in Divinatory Ritual', Phil. Trans. Roy. Soc. of London. Series B. vol. 251, London.

Fortes, M. (1980) Anthropologists and Theologians: Common Interests and Divergent Approaches, in 'Sacrifice', ed. M.F.C. Bourdillon and M. Fortes, Academic Press, London.

Gellner, E. (1979) Problems of the Model. Paper presented at a Conference on Leadership and Development in the Arab World: American University of Beirut, Beirut.

Gellner, E. (1973) Introduction to Nomadism, in 'The Desert and the Sown', ed. C. Nelson, University of California, Berkeley.

Gilsenan, M. (1973) 'Saint and Sufi in Modern Egypt', Clarendon Press, Oxford.

Gluckman, M.G. (1958) 'Analysis of a Social Situation in Modern Zululand, Rhodes-Livingston Paper no. 28.

Irons, W. (1975) 'The Yomut Turkmen', University of Michigan, Ann Arbor.

Leach, E. (1976) 'Culture and Communication', Cambridge University Press, Cambridge.

Leach, E. (1954) 'Political Systems of Highland Burma', Bell, London.

Marx, E. (1967) 'Bedouin of the Negev', MUP, Manchester.

Middleton, J. (1960) 'Lugbara Religion', OUP, London.

Murray, G.W. (1935) 'Sons of Ishmael', Routledge, London.

Musil, A. (1928) 'The Manners and Customs of the Ruwala Bedouins', American Geographical Society, New York.

Peters, E.L. (1965) Aspects of the Family among the Bedouin of Cyrenaica, in 'Comparative Family Systems', M.F. Nimkoff, Houghton Mifflin, Boston.

Peters, E.L. (1967) Some Structural Aspects of the Feud among the Camel-herding Bedouin of Cyrenaica, 'Africa', vol. 37, no. 3.

Peters, E.L. (1980) Aspects of Bridewealth among the Bedouin of Cyrenaica, in 'The Meaning of Marriage Payments', ed. J. Comaroff, Academic Press, London.

Rubel, P.G. (1969) Herd Composition and Social Structure: On Building Models of Nomadic Pastoral Societies, 'Man', vol. 4, no. 2.

Salzman, P. (1971) Movement and Resource Extraction, 'Anthropological Quarterly', vol. 44, no. 3.

Salzman, P. (1975) Does Complementary Opposition Exist? 'American Anthropologist', vol. 80.

Spooner, B. (1971) Towards a Generative Model of Nomadism, 'Anthropological Quarterly', vol. 44, no. 3.

Tapper, R. (1979) 'Pasture and Politics', Academic Press, London.

Turner V.W. (1957) 'Schism and Continuity', MUP., Manchester.

Turner, V.W. (1969) 'The Ritual Process', Aldine, Chicago.

Turner, V.W. (1974) 'Dramas, Fields and Metaphors', Cornell University Press, London.

Van Gennep, A. (1960) 'The Rites of Passage', trans. M.B. Vizedom and G.L. Caffee, Routledge & Kegan Paul, London.

8 HONOUR GROUPS IN TRADITIONAL TURKMENIAN SOCIETY

V.N. Basilov

Veneration of the Prophet Muhammad's family is a tenet of Muslim tradition raised by the Shi^{c}a branch to the status of a religious dogma. Kinship with the Prophet and, for that reason, a special standing in society are claimed by some groups among the peoples who have adopted Islam. These are called variously by the Arabic words *sharif* (noble) in North Africa and *saiyid* ('master') (1) in the Near East. The term *sharif* is unknown in Central Asia, but the word *saiyid*, as the name for the posterity of the Prophet is, however, used there (mainly by Uzbeks and Tajiks). Yet much more widely in use in Central Asia as a name of the group claiming descent from Muhammad is the term *jodja* ('master' in Persian).

The relation between the terms *saiyid* and *hodja* is still in need of clarification. According to V.V. Bartold they are synonymous. 'The honour to be a saiyid was considered to be so high, while the hodjas were not inclined to let strangers into their privileged group through marriage, that in the nineteenth century even sovereigns had to take daughters of hodjas forcibly as their wives in order that future sovereigns should have the honour of being called a saiyid. Such is the origin of this title which was borne by many sovereigns in all the three khanates of that time – the Bokhara, Khiva and the newly-formed Kokand.'(2)

Information regarding the Bokhara emirate provided by V.V. Krestovsky differs:

The saiyids and the hodjas rank as the first two division of society in the state, a sort of the latter's aristocracy. The saiyids are descended from Khazrati-Osman and Khazrati-Ali Shiri-Khuda by the daughters of the Prophet Muhammad. The hodjas are descended from Abu Bakr Saddyk and Omar Ul-Faruk and also from the above mentioned Osman and Ali but by wives other than the daughters of Muhammad. But the saiyids and hodjas could claim the authenticity of their descent from some of the four above-mentioned persons only on the strength of written genealogical documents (*shadzhara*).(3)

The latter evidence is confirmed by other researchers (N.N. Khanykov, O.A. Sukhareva, and B.H. Karmysheva).(4) Thus, B.H. Karmysheva writes that in the southern area of Tajikistan and Uzbekistan the saiyids were considered to be the descendants of Fatimah, the daughter of Muhammad, and Ali, the fourth caliph. 'The saiyids who claimed their descent from their son

Hasan were called the Hasani while those who claimed descent
from the second son Husain - the Husaini. The hodjas were the
posterity of Muhammad's companions or some saints.'(5) I
would like to add here that in North Afghanistan there is a
group of hodjas claiming descent from Abu Bakr.(6) Still there
is an impression that the traditional difference between the
saiyids and the hodjas carried a strong element of convention
even among the Uzbeks and Tajiks. The histories of descent of
some groups of hodjas, as recorded by B.H. Karmysheva, point
to their kinship with Muhammad.(7) As for the Turkmen and the
Khazakhs, the hodjas are considered the posterity of Ali and
Fatimah, i.e. the posterity of Muhammad in female tail.(8)

The saiyids and the hodjas living in small groups among the
common people were revered by the latter. A. Borns recorded
that even Mir-Khaidar, the Bokhara emir, always dismounted
from his horse in order to greet a saiyid or a hodja.(9) The
saiyids and the hodjas - who were numerous in Central Asia -
did not all enjoy the same social standing. Not all representatives
of this society's division were members of the clergy or rich
people. Many of them were artisans or engaged in agriculture.

Groups of the hodjas and the saiyids were found among the
Turkmen, too. The hodjas were the most honoured group in
society and they were not identified with the saiyids. Apart
from them, the Turkmen honoured another four groups - the
Shikh, Ata, Magtym and Mudjevur, whose histories of descent
are connected with the first ('righteous') caliphs or prominent
Muslim saints. Among the Turkmen (and only among them) all
these groups were called *ovlyads*. The term originates from the
Arab word ولد *g* (*volad*) - 'son' in plural, and is used in its
original sense (children-posterity) in the Turkish, Uzbek and
some other languages; it has not yet lost this meaning in the
Turkmenian language. However, the Turkmen understand this
word as a term close to the word *ovliya* (övlüyä in Turkmenian)
which is the plural form of the Arab word ولی *g*, (*vali*) - 'friend',
'saint', but is used by the Turkmen and other peoples of Central
Asia as the singular form in the meaning of 'saint', 'holy place',
which explains the translation of the term *ovlyad* one comes
across in many works: 'holy' or 'sacred' tribe. Although this
translation of the Turkmenian word is almost exact, it fails to
convey the real position of the ovlyads among other Turkmenian
groups ('tribes'). It would seem more appropriate to call them
honour groups.

In Turkmenian society whose distinctive feature was the
division into 'tribes', the ovlyads were regarded as 'tribes' in
their own right. Usually they considered themselves to be of
Arab descent rather than Turkmen. This was a point of view
evidently shared by the famous historian, the Khiva Khan
Abu-l-gazi (seventeenth century). Discussing Turkmenian
tribes, he left out the ovlyads.(10) Even when the ovlyads did
not insist on their Arab descent, they preferred not to identify
themselves with the Turkmen. Echoes of this tradition still per-

sisted until recently. I, for example, met old Shikhs who claimed
their descent from the saint Ismamut-ata (the Takhta District of
the Tashauz Region) and who in reply to the question about their
nationality said: 'I am not a Turkman and not an Uzbek, I am a
Shikh!' The data about the numbers of the ovlyads are not to
be fully relied upon. According to some evidence, the Shikhs and
the saiyids of south-eastern Turkmenia numbered 400 nomad
tents at the end of the nineteenth century.(11) Other available
evidence refers to the 1920s and places the total number of
hodjas, Shikhs, Atas, Magtyms and Mudjevurs approximately
at 30,000.(12)

The ovlyads had no single territory. They usually lived among
other Turkmenian 'tribes' in small groups though there exist
whole villages inhabited predominantly by representatives of
some or other honour group. Thus, the fact of the existence of
some settlements almost wholly consisting of the hodjas and the
Magtyms (in Atek, the foothills of the Kopet-dag) was noted in
censuses taken and studies made, already in the pre-Revolution-
ary times.(13) The Shikhs lived in compact groups in Bakharden,
Kizil-Arvat and Geok-Tepe while the settlement of Bendesen
(the Kizil-Arvat District) consisted wholly of the Shikhs. The
Atas lived in compact groups in the vicinity of Kizil-Arvat, in
the Tedjen and Serakhs Districts, in Dargan-ata.

Among the Turkmen the ovylads were held in esteem which
sometimes took the form of superstitious veneration, a fact noted
in literature: 'The Turkmen considered that to have representatives of those tribes [i.e. the ovlyads] in their *auls* was agree-
able to God and the most eminent of them were given donations.'(14) Another researcher writes that it was considered
reprehensible not to have the ovlyads in the Turkmenian 'tribes',
and 'such tribes or groups were called contemptuously *ovlyadsyz-
lar*' ('without ovlyads' in a literal translation).(15) Usually, the
Turkmen's cemeteries arose around the tomb of some saint, most
often a hodja, Shikh or a representative of other groups of the
ovlyads. It was considered that a holy ovlyad gave protection
to both the living and the dead.

The Turkmen had a custom of giving a special prize to the
representatives of the ovylads at festivities where sports com-
petions (horse racing, wrestling) were held. The herald called
on an ovlyad to come forward and receive a prize and only
then was the competition started. Usually, the representatives
of the hodjas came out to receive the prize for they were held
by the Turkmen in the highest esteem. If the hodjas were not
present the prize would go to the Shikhs or representatives of
other groups of the ovlyads. In some places, there was a custom
of giving several prizes according to the number of the various
groups of the ovlyads living in the given locality. Thus the
Gerkez-Turkmen inhabiting the Middle Sumbar and between the
mountainous country called Kara yaila established sometimes four
prizes for their festivities: for the hodjas, Shikhs, Atas and
saiyids.(16) The custom was built on the fear of getting the

upper hand of the ovlyad for it was believed that in such an eventuality the winner would thereby incur a misfortune. Sh. Annaklychev describes wedding ceremonies at which 'a hodja was given three large prizes without making him take part in wrestling. . . . Sometimes, wrestlers did struggle with the hodja just out of interest but surrendered purposely'.(17)

The belief that a severe retribution awaits anyone offending an ovlyad has given rise to the tradition according to which both the person of an ovlyad and his property were inviolable. The ovlyads remained unaffected by the military raids which so complicated the life of the Turkmenian tribes. In the last century the Shikhs in the south-west of Turkmenistan could without hindrance maintain their livestock and carry on trade amid inter-tribal strife and armed pillage; thieves and robbers did not dare to touch their property.(18) The same attitude was shown in the south-west of Turkmenia to the Atas. References to the inviolability of the hodjas can also be found in written sources. In particular, in the nineteenth century, a group of armed Turkmen, subjects of the Khan of Khiva, made a foray upon the Akhal Oasis (south-west of Turkmenistan). On the outskirts of the Geok-Tepe settlement 'they came across four yourtas belonging to the hodjas but spared them'.(19) The belief that it was impossible to infringe upon the safety of the ovlyads' property with impunity was extremely strong. One can hear in various parts of Turkmenia a story about a man who came to a shepherd to enquire as to whom did the ram he had stolen the other day from the herd belong to. 'To a hodja' was the reply. It turned out that the thief had eaten the ram and had since been suffering from a severe pain. The man went to the hodja to acknowledge his guilt and to compensate him for the loss.

Many Turkmen believed that due to their descent the ovlyads were endowed with supernatural powers and could, among other things, cure the sick. The amulets with inscriptions made by some literate hodja or Shikh were considered a dependable remedy against illness, the evil eye, and spirits. One of the Russian travellers who visited the south-west areas of Turkmenia in the second half of the last century wrote: 'it was enough for a Mahtum to do as much as to spit on the sick man once to have the latter surely recovered'.(20) The Turkmen believed that the ovlyads could by their prayers help infertile women to have children. If born after such supernatural intercession, the children were usually given such names as Hodjaberdi (the hodja gave), Hodjageldi (the hodja came), Hodjanepes (the hodja's breath), etc.

The attitude shown to the same group of the ovlyads could, however, be different in various areas of Turkmenistan. The Ata group was, for example, held in highest esteem among the Yomud and Teke Turkmen in the south-west of Turkmenia while on the other hand, the population of the basins of the Tedjen and Mourgab rivers (the Tekes, the Salyrs, the Saryks) did not show any particular esteem for the Atas and did not even consider them as ovlyads. Not all Turkmen considered the Mudjevurs as ovlyads. In the western part of Turkmenia the Mudjevurs are unknown at all and on hearing that such a group of the ovlyads exist in the Tashauz Region the old men only shrug their shoulders. But whatever the local peculiarities, the general attitude to the ovlyads was one of deference because their kinship with the known Muslim saints (the first four caliphs, in particular) and the Prophet himself associated them in the minds of people with those supernatural powers which in popular belief their forefathers possessed.

The Turkmenian ovlyads, as a rule, stuck fast to the custom of not allowing their daughters to marry men from groups other than the honour ones. Still living in folk memory are romantic episodes about dare-devils attempting to steal the beauties of noble blood who had won their hearts but most often pursuers overtook the fugitives and a savage reprisal was the lot of both the youth and the girl.

As for the origin of the ovlyads, various conjectures have been made on that account in literature. The earliest of them gives full credence to the legends of the ovlyads, according to which they are Turkmenized Arabs.(21) But since this opinion is based only on legendary lineages it has been made an object of a just criticism,(22) because the ovlyads exhibit in their culture no peculiarities which may point to their ties with the Arabs. According to another conjecture, the ovlyads were one of the first heathen groups to adopt Islam,(23) but no argument has been offered in support of this opinion. A view was also advanced that the ovlyads represent the descendants of some pre-Islamic priest groups(24) but this viewpoint has also not been confirmed by any factual evidence and, after some time, its author himself recognized that a search in other directions might be more fruitful.(25)

A great deal of reliable and well-checked evidence regarding the ovlyads (in particular, about their genealogical traditions) was obtained in the course of the research done in recent years. The factual evidence that has been accumulated thus far indicates, beyond any doubt, that there is a certain connection between some of the Turkmenian honour groups and Sufism. In other words, the origins of some ovlyad groups should be sought in Sufism because in the Turkmenian context the descendants of well-known Sufis (pir, sheykh, ishan) became ovlyads while the Atas were descended from a religious community made up of descendants and murids of a Sufi sheyikh.(26) The latter point of view has not yet been criticized in Soviet literature and the available evidence seems to corroborate it. Let us cite now the data on which this hypothesis has been built.

First of all, despite the wide renown that many ishans (representatives of the Sufi clergy) who hailed from the common folk enjoyed, the popular tradition still identified ishans as such with the ovlyads. Sev was the first to note this: 'The Turkmenian ishanism exhibits a peculiar phenomenon consisting in the exist-

ence of the so-called ovlyad tribes . . . in which everybody considers himself an ishan. . . . Probably, what made the ovlyad,
i.e. holy tribes also ishanic tribes, was their Arab descent and
the concept of ishan as a saint.'(27) To consider that this statement is true in all respects would hardly be correct. Of course,
the fact that each representative of the ovlyads considered himself an ishan is open to doubt. For example, the Turkmen
belonging to other groups did not look upon the Shikhs from
Ismamutata and the hodjas from Nokhur as ishans and did not
call them so. But many Turkmen believed, indeed, that ishans
usually came from the midst of the ovlyads. A view was also
widespread that there was no difference between ishan and
hodja (opinions to this effect can be heard from old people, for
example, in the Serakhs and Tahta-Bazar Districts). Part of the
believers in the Tedjen District considers that the ishan usually
comes from the midst of the ovlyads (hodja, Magtym, Shikh),
that any hodja, even an illiterate one, is an ishan and he should
be addressed accordingly, even if he is still a boy, with the
words 'Ishan-aga'. In the Kaahka District the Turkmen from
other groups usually said 'Ishan-aga' in addressing a Magtym.
The common people use the same form of address in relation to
the Shikhs living, for example, in the Serakhs District because
the Shikhs are believed to have ishans among their ancestors.
    Further, according to genealogical legends, the hodjas, the
saiyids, and the Magtyms are the descendants of Ali (and consequently, of Muhammad), while the Shikhs - the descendants
of Abu Bakr, and the Atas - of Osman. This peculiarity of the
legends accords with Sufi ecclesiastical lineages (*silsilla*, 'chain')
which are listings of the saints, heads of the given order of
darweshes or community who handed down the teaching and the
blessing. The 'chain' of ishans was traced usually to the first
caliphs and to Ali.(28) With the vulgarization of Sufism the
spiritual ties came to be understood as physical kinship. Many
Sufi sheyikhs found the temptation to ascribe to themselves
kinship with the Prophet or the first caliphs too great to resist,
even going to the length of composing false documents.(29)
    The word hodja could acquire currency as the exact trans-
lation of the title of saiyid, but there are reasons to believe
that it came to be used as the name for honour groups in a
different way. We already pointed out above that in Central Asia
the names of the hodja and the saiyids were not considered as
synonymous everywhere. But they certainly would be if the term
hodja had appeared as the local equivalent of the term saiyid.
It is quite possible that the term hodja as the name of one of the
honour groups can be traced to the title hodja (master) used by
murids in addressing their sheyikh (*pir*)(30) and also was
appended to the names of popular Sufi saints. We would like
to add here that the word 'master' in its turkic form (törä) was
considered by the Uzbeks as the synonym for the hodja and
saiyid and was used in Tashkent as the title of prominent
ishans.(31)

Clear evidence of the connection between the ovlyad groups and the Sufi saints can be found in the former's genealogical legends existing both in the oral and written form. Thus, one of the hodja groups who lived among the Nokhurli Turkmen (the Bakharden District of the Ashkhabad Region) considered themselves to be the descendants of the Khorezm Sufi Shikh-Sherep (Sheyikh-Sheref), the fourteenth century saint who in the 'Yusup-Akhmet', the popular Turkmenian folk *destan*, is referred to as pir, ustad, and ishan.(32)

Among the Turkmen, there are several groups called Shikhs. One of them, the most numerous, while claiming its descent from Abu Bakr, considers Pakyr-shikh as their immediate ancestor. His tomb is situated in the outskirts of the Bendesen settlement in the Kysil-Arvat District. In Central Asia and the entire Muslim world the Arab word ‎شيخ‎ (sheyikh - 'old man', 'elder') also had another meaning, leader of the dervish community (*pir*, *ishan*). The Turkmen usually preserved for posterity the honourable title of their forefather (in this way, there arose within the 'tribes' certain groups called '*yuzbashi*', '*beg*', '*kazy*', etc.). Possibly, the appellation Shikh was continued to be borne by the descendants of an ishan, who, in his time, was a well-known figure (in Tashkent the descendants of the venerated Sufis were also called sheyikhs)(33). The use of the name Pakyr (from the Arab word *faqir* - 'poor man', 'in need of something') in the legends of the Bendesen Shikhs is explained by the fact that their holy forefather (who later married a daughter of the local khan) was a poor man.(34) Probably a poor man he was but not in the direct meaning of the word: in the Muslim world the term faqir was used to denote itinerant dervishes.(35)

Another group of Shikhs who do not claim descent from Abu Bakr consider Kheleway, a servant of the saint Ismamut-ata, as their ancestor. According to oral legend, Kheleway, a son of a rich Turkman and considered a dolt, once decided to drive into the ground 40 (or 360, etc.) pegs for tying horses. All thought it was just another oddity of his but after some time 40 (or 360, etc.) equestrians rode up to the *aul*. It was Ismamut-ata with his retinue. In this episode the ancestors of the Shikhs possess a trait characteristic of the stories about holy dervishes: what seems at first sight to be a sign of mental inferiority turns out to be a manifestation of holiness.

According to tradition the Magtyms descended from Ali. In their lineage which originates from Adam we find Muhammad, Ali, Husain, Zein-al-abidin and then one's attention is drawn to the factual ancestor of this group - Habib-ed-din Magsym, who settled in Gorgan (northern Iran) because 'the divine passion, love had come upon him', i.e. a mystic love of God, so characteristic of Sufi teachings. A special place is occupied in the lineage by Makhzum Agzam, the descendant of Habib-ed-din in the eighth generation. In the legends he is called the ruler in his *villaiyet* and his close ties with the local Sufis are emphasized. After he died in 1494-5, it was the Sufi clergy who arranged his

funeral. In the procession composed of the sheykhs and murids
his body lay on a white she-camel. The mausoleum over his tomb
still exists today in the valley of the Sumbar river. In the
Magtyms' oral legends Makhzum Agzam figures as their leader
and patron.(36) He remains in the memory of his descendants
under the honourable title, Makhzum Agzam - 'Great Master'
and it reminds us about the traditions of medieval Sufism.
'Makhdum' مجدوم is a title of eminent pirs, leaders of Sufi
orders or individual communities.(37) The hodjas who took over
power in Kashgaria in the seventeenth century and then for a
short period in Fergana were the descendants of a well-known
sheykh Makhdum-i A'azam who came from the Fergana settlement
Kasan, and died in 1542.(38) It is evident that the 'Makhdum-
Aazami', a Sufi order, whose followers were to be found in
Kokand and Bokhara, took its name after him.(39) In north-
eastern Turkmenia the word *makhsum* was used for the
descendants of ishans.

The Magtyms are divided into three groups. The Gylly Magtym
group represents those descendants of Makhzum Agzam who have
moved to the Akhal Oasis. A special place among them is occupied
by Issa-pir whom legend pictures as a powerful saint. The Pir
Magtym group takes its name after Pir Magtym whose lineage
reports that before he came to be venerated as a saint he 'was
in the hands of one pir'.(40) Genealogical legend associates the
Magtyms with the Sufis (ishans) who were well known at the
time.

According to the legends the Mudjevur group has Sheykh
Akhsan-baba, called Dana-ata, as their ancestor whose venerated
tomb is located in south-western Turkmenia.(41)

The ancestor of the Ata group was Gyozli-ata, a descendant
of Caliph Osman and a *murid* of the holy pir hodja Akhmed
Yassavi, who founded the Sufi order of Yassavia. The word
Gyozli means here the all-seeing. The legends relate that he
was a powerful saint while yet a *murid* of his sheykh. The
connection between the Atas and Sufism is confirmed also by
the fact that it was none other but the Atas who kept up among
the surrounding population the custom of performing zikr (the
Sufi collective devotional exercise)(42) in its 'loud' form (*djahr*).
Turkmen of any 'tribe' could participate at *zikr* but the right to
officiate at the occasion was traditionally reserved only for the
Atas (in the south-western parts of the area - also to the
Magtyms).(43)

For researchers studying Sufism by the religious philosophical
works written by the founders of various teachings the statement that there is a connection between the Turkmenian honour
groups, the ovlyads, and Sufism and that this connection has
to be traced on the basis of isolated details may, of course, seem
rather strange. The distance between the intricate conceptions
of Muslim mysticism and the traditions of the supernatural
veneration of some isolated groups is very large. Yet the ties
we are trying to establish between the Turkmenian ovlyads and

Sufism were quite real, and the very historical destinies of Sufism
in Central Asia provide a convincing explanation to that effect.

During the many centuries of its existence, Sufism did not
remain unchanged. In various periods and among various peoples,
this phenomenon took on a specific aspect and played a different
role in the religious life of the population. In Central Asia,
Sufism, whose characteristic feature is rightly considered to be
syncretism (the ability to mix elements most diverse in their
origin, including the rituals and beliefs of the ancient local
cults),(44) assimilated in the course of its spread, already in
the early Middle Ages, the traditions of pre-Islamic religions
and, particularly, shamanism. This has already been pointed
out.(45) I wish to add here that in connection with the general
economic, political and cultural decline that took place in Central
Asia during the last centuries Sufism did not remain unaffected.
Its pantheistic philosophy remained unknown not only to the
common people but even to the representatives of the Sufi clergy
- the ishans (pirs). Sufism has, on the whole, made a strong
impact upon the religious life of the Central Asian peoples but
it is in fact, mainly the outward aspects that have been really
assimilated by them. As for the content of the beliefs associated
with the personality of ishans and also with the specific Sufi
rituals, the preponderance in them belonged, in many cases, to
the local heathenish traditions reflecting the most archaic concepts. Alisher Navoi, the renowned Uzbek poet who lived in
the fifteenth century, wrote about the Sufi zikr: 'When in
pursuit of the beauty of the pari he (sheykh) performs his
trance dance, sputtering with saliva, he shows up his fanaticism.'(46) For Navoi the connection between the ritualistic practices of the Sufis and the ancient belief in the possibility of
sexual intimacy, while in the state of frenzy, between the chosen
people (usually shamans) and the *pari* spirits was all too evident.

The ability for the ishan activities was understood in the folk
practice in the concepts of shamanism. Thus, the Bokhara
residents considered that the magic powers are possessed
only by those ishans or duokhons (healing by prayers) who
have a patron spirit. After the ishan dies the spirit 'chooses'
his successor from among his descendants. According to the
Bokhara residents, the spirit 'molests' the chosen one in order
to compel him to take upon himself the 'burden' of stewardship.
If the man who considered himself to be a 'chosen' one had
mental instability he often fell ill. The inheritance of the ishan
power, social position and riches was attributed to the existence of a patron spirit in the family.(47)

The itinerant dervishes - *divana* (*dumana*, *Dubana*)m to be met
in all parts of Central Asia, reminded people of the Muslim
mystics by their life-style. Their attire, which had a ritualistic
importance, was determined by local pre-Muslim traditions. The

Kirghizian dumanas wore, for example, a dressing-gown which
was sewn from shreds of fabric, a cap made of swan skin, sometimes adorned with bells, and carried in their hands a staff
with metal pendants or bells. The dumanas were looked upon as
people possessing the faculty of fortune telling, soothsaying,
driving away evil spirits and curing the sick.(48)
  As already indicated above, in Central Asia (as also in other
regions of the 'Muslim world') Sufism did not exist in real life
as a sophisticated philosophical and religious teaching. In the
life of the common people Sufism established itself as the cult of
miracle-worker saints, of people chosen by God or 'friends of
God' - all in combination with various pre-Islamic beliefs. This
peculiarity of Central Asian Sufism also shows up in the traditions connected with the Turkmenian ovlyads.

In the veneration shown to the ovlyads one can easily discern
the survival of the cult of ancestors. The Turkmenian beliefs
retain traces of the conviction in the importance of kinship
ties between saints and those who venerate them. Some old men
still think that the closest saint for the believer is the one with
whom he has kinship ties. But since the Turkmen endowed their
saints with their own views on life, the saints, in turn, the
Turkmen believed should be more inclined to help their relatives.
These beliefs in the preferential attitude of the saints towards
their posterity goes to explain the superstitious fear of the
ovlyads. With the aid of their patronizing holy ancestors, the
ovlyads (and the posterity of ishans) are, allegedly, able to
show a miraculous force and punish offenders. This belief finds
its manifestation in the most diverse spheres of folk life. Thus
one can hear from old people a story about a man who died after
stealing a horse from a hodja because the latter called in the aid
of his ancestors in his prayers. One can also hear of a hodja
horse which always won a prize at races. Many people were
certain that the hodja called in the aid of his ancestors (*ata-
babasyni chagyryer*). Therefore, one man whose horse participated in the race held out a 10-rouble note to the hodja and
said: 'Give me a benediction (*pata*). Let your ancestors be
impartial.' Having accepted the money (i.e. a donation to his
ancestors) and having sealed the donation with his prayer,
the hodja was thus unable to resort to their aid. The above-
mentioned special prizes given to the ovlyads before the start
of horse races or wrestling constituted, in fact, also an instance
of donations for the ancestors.
  Considering that the saint might be more inclined to respond
to his own posterity, some believers used to approach the
ovlyads (or the posterity on an ishan) with a request to solicit
the benevolence of the ancestor in their favour. In such cases,
the believers said: 'Call in your ancestors, apply to them with
a request.' This custom clearly reveals the traces of the formerly
priest functions performed by the relatives of a venerated man
in old times.(49) The cult of ancestors also demands that it is

the posterity of the saint who should look after his grave and accept donations from pilgrims. Today this view is shared by only a small number of believers but in the past it was held widely. The reason why the word 'sheykh' (*shikh* - in Turkmenian) has come to mean in Central Asia 'keeper of the tomb of a saint' apart from its former meaning, and has thus become identical with the Arab word *mudjavir* lies precisely in the fact that the functions of the keeper of the tomb of a saint (most often a Sufi, a *sheykh*) were performed by his posterity who continued to bear the title of his ancestor (*sheykh*). Let us return in this connection to the way the word Shikh might have made its appearance as a name for a number of the ovlyad groups. This word could become the name of the given groups already in its new meaning just like the word *müdjevür* (in Turkmenian) has become the appellation of a special group of the ovlyads.

The belief in the importance of kinship ties with saints indulged by the Turkmen and some other Central Asian peoples was not inspired by Islam. It belonged to a number of local pre-Islamic religious traditions and reflected the structure of the society based on kinship ties. Thus, a major role in the formation of the ovlyad groups was played by the clan-tribal traditions which continued to preserve their force and it should be noted that the ovlyad groups as well as other Turkmenian 'tribes' were divided into branches and sub-branches precisely in accordance with those traditions.

Another layer of pre-Muslim religious beliefs and rituals from which the special position of the ovlyads in Turkmenian society stems is represented by the clear survivals of shamanism. Strong survivals of the shamanistic cult are exhibited by the Ata Turkmen who practised zikr (*zikir, zyakir* in Turkmenian). This ritual, in its Turkmenian form, is a graphic example of how a Sufi ritual has turned into a shamanistic act.

Among the Atas, zikr was still practised as a folk custom until the 1930s. Zikr was usually performed in order to cure the sick who were harmed by the spirits, jinns, in cases where the prayers of the mullah proved ineffective. During the zikr the felt cover of the yourta was taken off for the curious (men and women) to see what went on inside. Zikr could be started in the morning or in the evening. There were cases when zikr lasted for several days or even for a whole month, but with interruptions. The ritual was performed only by men. These were the Shikhs who ascended into a trance, readers of spiritual verse (*gazalchi* or *khapyz*) and 'people performing zikr'. All of them were, necessarily, from the Ata 'tribe'. Among the 'people performing zikr', there could be Turkmen from 'tribes' other than the Atas but the reader and the Shikh could be only from among the Atas. We are thus coming across a new meaning of the word Shikh among the Turkmen: Shikh is the main participant at zikr, an Ata in origin.

Having received a benediction from a clergyman (*akhun*, ishan), the reader begins reading from memory loudly and in a singing voice verses from Sufi poets (Diwana-i Mashrab, Khakim-ata, Dyrdu-shikh, Hodja Akhmed Yassavi, and others). There is no musical accompaniment and when one reader became tired he could be substituted by another. The reading of the verse brought the central figure of the ritual - the Shikh - to a state of excitement. He was also inspired by the cries of people performing zikr. Standing around the Shikh in a circle and strongly holding each other's arms they cried out 'Oh-Oh!' in hoarse voices and in rhythm between couplets. Their voices became louder and then died down, their actions being regulated by the *khapyz*. The Shikh fell into a frenzy. He performed motions which are conveyed by the Turkmenian word *yikylmak* - to fall. In his strange dance he beat his head against the framework of the yourta. One of the witnesses saw for himself how a corpulent Shikh deftly climbed a staff forming the dome of the yourta and through the flue to the top of the yourta without the staff even sagging. Another old man related how he saw a famous Shikh known by the name of Kebelek (butterfly). Soon after the khapyz began singing the verse and the performers of the zikr started their guttural cries, he jumped up and began, to the accompaniment of the cries, running inside the yourta on its framework 'like a fly'. His dressing gown was flapping and the whiffs of air could be felt even by those who were outside the yourta. One could hear the people saying that if the Shikh would not arise to the singing of religious verses after falling unconscious the mullahs would surely have to read the *surah* 'Yasin' from the Holy Qur'an to him.

During the zikr the Shikh beat the sick person on the face, on the back and threw him against the framework of the yourta. In this way he was driving away the spirits which had caused the disease. According to other legends, the Shikh might not even touch the sick person. For example, one story has it that near the tomb of Gyozli-ata pilgrims, the Yomud Turkmen, asked the Atas to cure a raving girl who was lying nearby, bound hand and foot. Among the Atas there was a Shikh and a khapyz. The khapyz began singing while the Shikh soon began in his frenzy to snatch at burning coal with his bare hands. Three butterflies were flying over the girl. The Shikh rubbed one part of the burning coal with the palms of his hands and one butterfly dropped dead. The Shikh rubbed the coal again and the second butterfly died. The Shikh again pressed the burning coal and the third butterfly lay motionless near his legs. The girl immediately recovered. It was believed that the Shikh saw the jinns, struggled against them, called in the aid of saints, and was victorious, driving them away for ever.

According to the stories, a Shikh falling into a trance lost all sensibility. He fell down from the top of the yourta on the ground, threw himself into the fire fanned out nearby for cooking food, poured boiling water on himself from a samovar, all without incurring any harm to his person. In short he was not like the usual man. The story about one Shikh has it that during zikr sparks flew out of his mouth and singed the beards of other performers of the ritual. During the zikr the Shikh was engaged in fortune-telling. If someone asked whether he would have children, the answer given by the Shikh would be correct. He could tell what gifts he was going to receive, and could tell who from among the performers of the zikr and the spectators had not performed the ritual ablution. He drove away such people.

While any literate person could be the reader, the Shikh was endowed with unusual abilities from above. These abilities are conveyed by the word *keramat* which means the 'force' of a saint, a miracle. While recognizing that in the old times there were saints from among the Shikhs, a majority of believers did not, however, place the Shikh and the saint on the same level. One can hear explanations that the Shikh receives his abilities from Allah and he should 'give his hand to a pir', be 'pure' in the religious meaning of this word and to observe faithfully the old traditions which are called by the general name of Turkmenchilik. According to a most widespread belief the Shikh has helping spirits at his disposal, 'comrades' (*yoldash*). Some believers are inclined to consider that it is none of their business to know which spirit aids the Shikh. The Shikh himself would not venture to tell about his comrades for he may otherwise lose his force and be killed by them. He does not even dare to say: 'I have comrades'. Nevertheless, the helping spirits are called jinn, *arvakh* (in the Turkmenian language these words are identical in meaning) or *al* (the latter exists also in the combination *al-yoldash*). Certain Atas consider that a Shikh has only one jinn or *al* in the form of a camel, bull, tiger, snake, dog, etc. But this was not a common conviction. One of the respondents, for example, thought that the spirit was a girl whom the future Shikh met somewhere in the steppe; the Shikh should pull out a hair from her head, put it in his bread and constantly have it on his person.

The spirits (or a spirit) of the Shikh tell him about the future; they also help him to drive away the jinns of a sick man by entering into the struggle against them. The spirits causing diseases and harming people are 'infidel' (*kapyr*) jinns. The Shikh's jinns are Muslims. The patient can be cured only if the Shikh's comrades are stronger than those which have caused the disease. If a Shikh should decide to struggle against the spirits which are superior in force to those of his comrades he runs the risk of being harmed, becoming a madman, or dying.

Thus the Shikh has much in common with the shaman. He goes into a trance, is aided by spirits in the form of animals and his ritual practices follow the actions of the shaman during his performance. The Turkmenian shamans also drove away the spectators who had failed to do the ablution, were soothsayers and also guessed what gifts were brought to them. This similarity, had its effect upon folk beliefs. Though the shamans

called *porhan* by the Turkmen are not to be found among the
Atas, the Turkmen from other tribes, who are neighbours of
the Atas, consider that the *porhans* are usually from the Ata
'tribe'.

The shaman and the Shikh were also united in having a
specific illness which manifested itself, when the jinn 'joined'
them. The fits of the illness continued even when the rapport
with the spirits was firmly established. From time to time, the
Shikh suffered breakdown. He spent his time at home bedridden,
and covered with blankets for he was cold. He could neither eat
nor drink. Only zikr could cure the Shikh. To the singing of
the spiritual verse and the guttural, hoarse cries of the performers of the zikr, the Shikh livened, then fell into a frenzy,
took burning coal into his hands or put the coal into his mouth,
walked barefoot on burning coal – in short he performed everything he was called to do during the ritual. After the zikr the
Shikh felt fully recovered from the illness. Thus, to take part
in zikr from time to time and sometimes to have the ritual
performed only to unburden his heart was a requirement for the
Shikh.

The man who could potentially become a Shikh showed his
abilities at festivities when the songs to the words of Navoi and
other poets were performed to the accompaniment of the *dutar*:
he could not sit quiet. He betrayed himself also during the zikr.
From the stories of old people it does not follow that the abilities
of the Shikh were inherited though there were some isolated
cases when the son became the Shikh after the death of his
father.

Sometimes the Shikhs arranged a sort of competition between
themselves to see who was the strongest – like the Siberian
shamans. It was believed that the jinns of the Shikhs began in
this case to battle each other and the Shikhs whose jinns suffered
a defeat were obliged to follow the orders of the victor.

Sometimes women also performed as Shikhs. Old men remember
a woman Shikh named Tyotyovi who died in 1937. There was a
time when she went into a trance to the singing of verses. Once
in the year 1916, she ascended into a state of strong excitement,
ran out of the yourta; the clergymen who were present at the
zikr said to her: 'Remain seated, sing verses but do not *fall*
(*yikylma*), it is awkward for a woman to have her body
exposed'. Since the women did not participate in the dervish
devotional exercise together with men, this incident can be
possibly explained in the light of the traditions of female
shamanism known in Central Asia.

Any traces of the connection between this Ata ritual with the
Sufi zikr have almost entirely disappeared. People think that
the origins of this custom of performing zikr go back to the
Prophet Zaccaria. At one time, running away from 'infidels', he
hid himself in a tree which had in response to his command split
apart and then closed. But a piece of his shirt stuck outside and
a magpie which pulled at it with a cry turned the attention of the

pursuers to the tree. The 'infidels' chopped off the top of the tree and then began sawing the trunk of the tree from the top down, and the teeth of the saw cut into the head of the Prophet. By uttering 'Oh - Oh' in their hoarse voices, the performers of the devotional exercise imitate the groans of Zaccaria and bemoan him. This legend that was connected with the ritual probably because the name of the Prophet and the word zikr sound almost alike goes to show that the Sufi interpretation of zikr has disappeared from folk beliefs. Only once did I hear an opinion that Hodja Akhme Yassavi somewhat changed this custom which had been continued since the time of Zaccaria. Many old men from the Ata 'tribe' explain the particular nature of their tradition by the fact that the Shikhs have been given to the 'tribe' by God.

Rather curious is the further destiny of the Turkmenian zikr. Brought by the Atas to the south-west of Turkmenia it began to be performed by the end of the nineteenth century, already by the Yomoud Turkmen but only as a laity youth dance; in the 1940s this dance moved eastward and is now known in the Akhal Oasis. In our days, this dance is usually accompanied by performing roundelays which are far from the religious themes but the people still remember also the spiritual verse which the dancers used to cry out.

The comparison of some couplets recorded by ethnographers with the verses by a Fergana mystic Diwana-i Mashrab leaves one in no doubt that the dance represents the Sufi devotional exercise.(50)

Yet another example of the persistence of the shamanistic cult in religious practice is provided by the folk beliefs associated with the hodjas living among the Nokhurli Turkmen (in particular, in a large settlement of Nokhur, the Bakharden District of the Ashkhabad Region). The residents from Nokhur and the surrounding settlements believed that it was a family ability of the hodjas to have at their disposal subservient spirits (jinn, *arvakh*), 'comrades'. Allegedly, those spirits could help some hodjas to foretell the future, to know what was taking place elsewhere, to command an unusual physical force and, what was most important, to cure nervous patients, the mentally deranged, infertile women and impotents. According to traditional beliefs the reasons for those ailments lie in the activities of evil, 'infidel' spirits which 'strike' the man or are with him constantly. The Muslim-jinn who are subservient to the hodjas, allegedly drive away evil spirits in the course of the struggle against them. In folk stories, both categories of the jinn are pictured as people ('troops' - *goshun* in Turkmenian). In an effort to drive away the 'infidel' spirits with the aid of his 'troop' of spirits the hodja reads prayers, calls in the aid of his ancestors, and sometimes beats the patient with a lash.

Folk beliefs contain traditional ideas regarding the very process of driving away the jinn which have caused harm to a certain man. For example, once Ovez-Hodja who lived in the second half of the last century was invited to a settlement in the

valley of the Sumbar River to cure a raving person. No sooner
had the hodjas entered the house than he saw the jinn who had
caused the ailment. The jinn said to the hodja: 'If you do not
come to heal the person I am going to strike next I shall go
away'. The hodja agreed, and the jinn warned: 'I am going to
Kara-Kala to strike the bride of a rich man.' The jinn disappeared
and the patient immediately recovered. Ovez-Hodja stayed in the
settlement for the rest of the day. He was already going to leave
when a man from Kara-Kala appeared with a request from the
local rich man to cure his daughter-in-law who had suddenly
become mad. The hodja understood it was the deed of the jinn
and declined the request. However he was compelled to agree.
Having arrived at the house of the rich man, Ovez-Hodja dismounted, and entered. He began beating the raving girl with a
lash, saying prayers and repeating: 'Who are you to come here?'
The spirit said: 'Hodja! You promised not to come but you
haven't made good your promise. Therefore, I will strike your
daughter.' The jinn disappeared while the rich man's daughter-
in-law recovered from the affliction. Ovez-Hodja took a second
horse from the rich man and immediately set out for Nokhur
where he lived. On arriving there, he saw that the jinn had
implemented his threat: the hodja's daughter was ill. The hodja
began beating the jinn with a lash again and said. 'Who are you
to come here?' Then the jinn asked for mercy: 'Ovez-Hodja, you
will not leave me alone. I will leave this place for good.' He
disappeared and the hodja's daughter recovered from her illness.

It was also believed that the hodja had to take great pains to
gain victory over the jinn of the sick man because the latter's
jinn turned out to be stronger. There were also cases when
while in difficulty one hodja asked another for assistance and
the latter sent him his own 'troop' of jinn. It once happened that
Ovez-Hodja was attacked by a madman who began getting the
upper hand. The hodja cried out: 'Uncle Mammed. Help me!' At
that time, Mammed-Hodja was in Nokhur among his countrymen.
Suddenly, he took off his sheepskin coat and lay at some distance
away from them on the ground having covered himself all over
with the coat. After some time, he stood up and approached his
surprised countrymen again. 'My Hodja, what happened?', some-
body enquired. Mammed explained: 'Now in Iran, Ovez-Hodja
is healing a raving man with prayers. The jinn of the sick man
began to win over the hodja's jinn and he sent to me two jinns
with a request to help him. I dispatched part of my own troop
to his aid. And now, after my troop joined Ovez-Hodja's the jinn
of the sick man has been vanquished.' His countrymen did not
believe him. Mammed said: 'Ovez-Hodja will return to Nokhur
tomorrow in the evening. Ask him.' The following day the residents of Nokhur instructed several people to meet Ovez-Hodja
on the road beyond the settlement. When they saw Ovez-Hodja,
those people began asking him where he had been and what he
had been doing. Allegedly Ovez confirmed what had been said
by Mammed-Hodja.

There was a widespread belief that if the hodja sustained a defeat in the struggle against the patient's jinn, he was to lose his former strength and fall ill. According to some old men, after Ovez-Hodja had to call in the Mammed-Hodja's aid, he contracted pain in the small of his back.

Of interest may be the local beliefs regarding the way a hodja acquired his helping spirits. There are three various groups of hodjas living in Nokhur. They regard themselves as descendants of Ali and Fatima but associate with various branches and various saints. It was usually one hodja in a whole group who could have jinns at his command. After the Hodja died, his 'troop' was handed down to his son or another relative.

In the stories of the 'Iranian' hodjas, the Padishah of the jinns in the image of a girl suggests that the hodja should take possession of the spirits. The earliest story about this is devoted to Myatykhan-Hodja (the middle of the eighteenth century; the date is determined on the basis of the genealogical tree). Once on the top of a high mountain Myatykhan met a girl. She suggested that they test their forces in the struggle. Myatykhan agreed and, having read a prayer, won. Then he understood that it was not a man before him but a spirit, and produced a knife. The girl said to him: 'Do not kill me. I am the padishah of the jinns. I will bring you much good.' She gave hodja an amulet on which there was a list of names of all the jinns. After Myatykhan died, the girl met Garry-Hodja on the top of the mountain who also gained a victory in the struggle. She also met Ovez-Hodja on the bank of a river but disappeared before he touched her. The transfer of power over the spirits to Ovez-Hodja took place in different conditions.

According to one of the legends, after the death of Garry-Hodja Ovez-Hodja was awoken in the darkness of night by two people who said to him: 'Our padishah invites you to Gyzyllyk (an old cemetery). Don't be afraid. Follow us.' And they went there. At the foot of the mountains Ovez-Hodja saw crowds of people who had gathered around fires. Two jinns led Ovez-Hodja over to the throne on which the padishah was seated – that very girl whom he had met near the river. The girl said: 'I have already tested you. You are able to command the spirits. Therefore, I will give you a troop of jinns which belonged to your ancestors.' Ovez-Hodja did not utter a word. The girl said: 'Tie a belt round his waist.' The two jinns took a thin rope made of a sheep (goat) intestine with many knots on it, uttered something unintelligible and tied it around him. The girl-padishah explained: 'Each knot signifies part of the troop. When in need of aid, you will have only to utter the name of the knot and to touch it.' She then conveyed to him the names. The jinn's rope was visible only to its possessor. According to other versions of the story Ovez-Hodja was also given an amulet.

In the legends about the Khiva group of hodjas the engirdling with a rope figures as the main ritual in transferring the spirits. For example, the above-mentioned Mammed-Hodja before his death

tried, all by himself, to transfer his 'troop' to his grandson
Ishan-Hodja. He led him to a desert place and ordered him to
look south. 'Do not be afraid of anything. Whatever you may
see, or whatever you may be spoken to about, do not utter a
word. If you show ability to go through this ordeal then part
of the jinn troop will be yours.' While pronouncing those words,
Mammed-Hodja tied a white belt tightly around his grandson.
Ishan-Hodja saw a troop of horsemen riding straight towards
him. When several horsemen began walking around him and
touching his belt Ishan-Hodja proved unable to bear the ordeal
and cried out 'Go away from me!'. Mammed-Hodja said: 'You
have neither the knowledge, nor a brave heart; you will not be
able to preserve the jinns', and he decided thereupon to transfer his 'troop' to his three-year-old grandson Yacoub-Hodja.
Mammed-Hodja took off his belt, tied it around the waist of his
grandson, bent down on his knees before him and began praying.
The women who were watching the ritual with uneasiness cried
out: 'The child is dying!'. Mammed-Hodja untied the belt and the
boy came to his senses. Mammed said: 'You cried in vain. If he
had lain (with the belt on) a little longer I could have provided
him with more troops.' According to another version of the
legend Mammed-Hodja did not pay any attention to the weeping
and crying of women and continued his prayers. Yacoub died
three times and came back to life again. Then Mammed-Hodja
said to those present: 'After my death, my place will be taken by
him.'

Though clothed in a Muslim garb, the beliefs contain some
features pointing to their shamanistic origin. The possession
of helping spirits, inheriting the spirits, the ability to tell
fortunes, to find lost things, and to cure lunatics – all these
features are typical of the Turkmenian *porhan*. The legends
about the initiation of Yacoub-Hodja find their parallel in the
folk beliefs of the peoples in Siberia according to which, in
becoming a shaman, a man dies and then rises from the dead.
The very ritual of curing the sick as practised by the hodjas
has some features in common with shamanistic performance.
Thus, both the hodja and the shaman tell what colour of wool
the animal to be sacrificed for propitiating the spirits and
obtaining the cure should be.

From the point of view of the Nokhurli Turkmen the difference
between the shaman and the hodja having spirits in his possession
is negligible. This can be easily understood if we take into
account the fact that the last shaman in Nokhur named Allahverdi
was descended from a hodja (from the group of the 'Ekme' -
Hodjas). Why is it then that hodjas possessing the jinns are
called *porhan* in some but not in other cases? Old people from
Nokhur are unable to provide any clear answer. Some elders
reduce the matter to literacy: if the hodja who meets a 'troop'
should be illiterate he becomes a shaman. But others disagree.

Evidently the hodjas themselves equated their activities and
shamanistic practices. The following witness account goes to

confirm this. A shaman from another village was invited to
Nokhur to cure infertility in the beautiful wife of one of the
local residents. At the height of the shaman performance Nazar-
Hodja (the son of Ovez-Hodja) entered the house. He stood and
said nothing but all those present noticed that the excitement of
the shaman diminished. One of the Nokhurli upbraided Nazar-
Hodja for this and said: 'Why do you interfere? What have you
come for?' The hodja beside himself with anger jumped to the
middle of the room and caught something in the air with his
hand (what he caught was the jinns of the shaman). He said to
the porhan: 'You have no right to carry on your rituals where
we are now!' The performance of the shaman was, of course,
discontinued. In this story the hodja felt insulted that the
driving away of the jinns had been entrusted to someone else.
In other words, one shaman was offended only because the
invitation was extended not to him but to another shaman. This
story also points to the identity of the functions performed by
the shaman and by the hodja, with the jinns at his command. In
fact, the only detail that places them apart consists in the way
they are performed. The hodja heals by prayer, the shaman -
by specific rituals. It does not follow from the story that, compared to the shaman, the hodja with his troop should necessarily
be superior in force. To the question 'Who is stronger - the
hodja or the *porhan*?' - some believers replied, 'The stronger is
the one whose "troop" is larger'.(51)

Such beliefs associated with the hodjas are not specifically
Turkmenian. Among other peoples of Central Asia there were
cases when some representatives of the hodjas were endowed
with shamanistic functions. For example, in the Uzbek settlement
Karamurt (the Sairam District, the Chimkent Region of the
Kazakh SSR) in the 1930s one Abbaskhan, a representative of
the local group of the hodjas, showed unexpected shamanistic
abilities. In his youth he was a pupil of a mullah and wished to
become a reader of the Holy Qur'an but could not remember the
words because of his poor memory. He was passionately fond of
riding on horseback. His nimble and fast horse was famed far
and wide and some people were even convinced that the horse
possessed invisible wings. When, fearing for the life of his son,
Abbaskhan's father sold the horse, Abbaskhan fell seriously ill.
He was constantly raving, pronouncing some lines from spiritual
verses and accompanying his declaration with gestures. Once he
spent a night near the tomb of a saint and saw spirits in his
dream. The latter instructed him to hold during the reading a
rattle made from the deer horn. This was made by the local
smith and Abbaskhan was thus given the nickname 'Shakildak-
ishan' (rattle-ishan).

Abbaskhan spent little time at home. Usually, he walked
around the surrounding villages and loudly sang spiritual verses
for which he received donations from believers. Like the calandar
dervishes of the Nakshbandia order he attached to his belt a
special vessel 'kashkul' for collection of alms. Abbaskhan's con-

stant occupation was reading spiritual verses and it was taken
by the people as a manifestation of his contact with spirits.
Once he was asked as to why he kept his eyes closed and
his head bowed low when reading the verses. 'When I am
reading the verses the spirits – *devs, paris,* jinns – are hover-
ing over my head', replied Abbaskhan, 'Once I already looked
at them and have become insane'. His rattle was considered a
ritual object. When Abbaskhan swung it people would say, 'He
is calling in the troop (of his jinns).'

Abbaskhan also undertook to cure the sick. His ritual of curing
was simple. He applied his rattle three times to the forehead of
the sick person, said a prayer and then pronounced: 'God help
you, go, you will recover.' He was also famous as a skillful
fortune-teller. Since, in the opinion of believers, he was assisted
in curing and fortune-telling by spirits he was regarded as a
kind of shaman and was also called Abbaskhan-bakshi (*bakshi*
is shaman in Uzbek). Thus, Abbaskhan manifested the features
of both the itinerant dervish and the shaman.(52)

In summing up the foregoing, I wish to point out that the customs
associated with the honour groups among the Turkmen contain
strong pre-Muslim elements. The general Muslim tradition of
venerating the Prophet's descendants is united with the ancient
local traditions traced to the cult of ancestors, which was
brought into being by the tribal-clan structure of society.
Especially strong are the survivals of shamanism. There are
a number of facts which provide a sufficient basis for a hypothesis that the emergence of some groups of the ovlyads was
associated with local Sufism in its declining, vulgarized, and
common folk forms. The evidence cited in this paper confirms
the scientific view that the local peculiarities of Islam in some
parts of the 'Muslim World' owe their existence to those beliefs
and rituals which are an echo of earlier cults.

NOTES

1 See 'Enzyklopaedie des Islam', B. IV, Leiden and Leipzig,
  1934, S. 81, 349–54; H.A.R. Gibb and J.H. Kramers, 'Shorter
  Encyclopaedia of Islam', Leiden and London, 1961, pp. 489,
  529–33.
2 V.V. Bartold, 'Historia kulturnoi zhizni Turkestana' (A
  History of the Cultural Life in Turkestan), Collected Works,
  v. II, part I, Moscow, 1976, p. 276.
3 V.V. Krestovsky, 'V Gostiah u emira Bokharskogo' (Visiting
  the Bokhara Emir), Collected Works, v. VII, St -Petersburg,
  1905, p. 63.
4 N. Khanykov, 'Opissanye Bokharskogo Khanstva' (A description of the Bokhara Khanate), St -Petersburg, 1843, p. 94;
  O.A. Sukhareva, 'Islam v Uzbekistane' (Islam in Uzbekistan),
  Tashkent, 1962, p. 66; B.H. Karmysheva, 'Ocherki etnicheskoi

istorii yuzhnikh rayonov Tajikistana i Uzbekistana' (Essays
on the history of southern areas of Tajikistan and Uzbekistan),
Moscow, 1976, pp. 148-53.

5 Karmysheva, op. cit., p. 148.

6 L. Dupree, Aq Kupruk = A Town in North Afghanistan,
'American Universities Field Staff', South Asia series, vol. X,
N 9, New York, 1966, pp. 4-6.

7 Karmysheva, op. cit., p. 151.

8 Here and further in the text, if there is no reference to
literature, it means that the author makes use of his own
field materials.

9 A. Borns, 'Puteshestviye v Bukharu' (A trip to Bokhara),
part II, Moscow, 1948, p. 440.

10 See A.N. Kononov, 'Rodoslovnaya turkmen, sochineniye Abu-
l-gazi, khana Khivinskogo' (The genealogy of Turkmen, a
treatise of Abu-l-gazi, the khan of Khiva), Moscow-Leningrad,
1958.

11 F.I. Mihailov, 'Tuzemtsi Zakaspiiskoi oblasti i ikh zhizn'
(The aborigines of the Trans-Caspian region and their life),
Ashkhabad, 1900, p. 38.

12 G.I. Karpov, Turkmenia i turkmeni (Turkmenia and the
Turkmen), 'Turkmenovedeniye' (The Turkmen Studies)
magazine, no. 10-11. 1929, p. 40.

13 See, for example: Zapiska g.-sh. polkovnika Kuzmina-Karaeva
o vvedeniyi russkogo upravlenia v Ateke v 1885 g. (The
memorandum on the introduction of Russian administration in
Atek in the year 1885, submitted by Colonel Kuzmin-Karaev),
in 'Sbornik geographicheskih, topographicheskih i statisti-
cheskih materialov po Azii' (Collection of geographical, topo-
graphical and statistical materials for Asia), issue XXI,
St Petersburg, 1886, pp. 154-5.

14 G.I. Karpov, 'Plemennoi i rodovoi sostav turkmen' (The
tribal and clan composition of the Turkmen), Poltoratsk
(Ashkhabad), 1925, p. 5.

15 K. Ataev, 'Nekotoriye danniye po etnographii turkmen-
shikhov' (Some ethnographic data on the Turkmen-shikhs).
The transactions of the Institute of History, Archaeology
and Ethnography of the Academy of Sciences of the Turkmen
SSR, v. VII, Ashkhabad, 1963, pp. 72-3.

16 S.M. Demidov, 'Turkmenskiye ovlyadi' (The Turkmenian
ovlyads), Ashkhabad, 1976, pp. 20-1.

17 Sh. Annaklychev, 'Byt rabochikh-nephtyannikov Nebit-Daga
i Kum-Daga' (The mode of living of oil workers in the Nebit-
Dag and the Kum-Dag) /istoriko-etnographicheskii ocherk/
(essay), Ashkhabad, 1961, p. 137.

18 Ataev, op. cit., p. 79; K. Bode, 'Ocherki Turkmenskoi
zemli i yugo-vostochnogo priberezhya Kaspiiskogo morya'
(Essays on the Turkmenian land and the south-eastern
littoral zone of the Caspian Sea), St -Petersburg, 1856, p. 66.

19 'Materiali po istorii turkmen i Turkmenii' (Materials on the
history of the Turkmen and Turkmenia), v. 2, Moscow-

Leningrad, 1938, p. 410.
20 P.P. Ogorodnikov, 'Na puti v Persiyu i prikaspiiskiye
provintsii eyo' (On the way to Persia and its near-Caspian
provinces), St -Petersburg, 1878, p. 170.
21 A. Bogolyubov, 'Kovroviye izdelia Srednei Azii' (The carpets
of Central Asia), issue I, St -Petersburg, 1883, p. 5;
N.V. Brullova-Shaskolskaya, Plemennoi i rodovoi sostav
turkmen (The tribal and clan composition of the Turkmen),
in 'Narodnoe khozyaistvo srednei Azii' (The National Economy
of Central Asia), Tashkent, 1927, no. 4, p. 88; K. Iomudsky,
Bitoviye osobennosti turkmen Turkmenskoi SSR, a ravno
kavkazskikh i zarubezhnikh turkmen, ikh plemennoye i
rodovoye deleniye (The mode of living peculiarities among the
Turkmen in the Turkmenian SSR and also among the Caucasian
Turkmen and the Turkmen abroad, and their tribal and Clan
composition) 'Izvestia of Sredazkomstaris', issue no. 3,
Tashkent, 1928, pp. 193, 195; G.I. Karpov, see note 14, p. 5;
G.I. Karpov, see note 12, no. 10-11, 1929, p. 39; D.M.
Ovezov, Turkmeni murchali (The murchali Turkmen), 'Trudi
Yuzhno-Turkmenistanskoi Kompleksnoi archeologicheskoi
ekspeditsii' (The Transactions of South-Turkmenistan Complex
Archaeological Expedition), v. IX, Ashkhabad, 1959, p. 269.
22 See S.M. Demidov, 'K voprosu o religioznom syncretisme u
turkmen XIX - nachala XX veka (On the Question of the
Religious Syncretism among the Turkmen in the 19th - the
beginning of the 20th Century), A report at the VII International Congress of Anthropological and Ethnographical
Sciences, Moscow, 1964, p. 7; G.E. Markov, 'Ocherk istorii
formirovaniya severnikh turkmen' (Essays on the history of
the formation of the Northern Turkmen), Moscow, 1961, pp.
94-5.
23 K. Ataev, see note 15, pp. 77-8.
24 S.M. Demidov, see note 22, p. 8.
25 S.M. Demidov, see note 16, p. 12.
26 In more detail, see V.N. Basilov, 'Kult svyatikh v Islame'
(The Cult of the Saints in Islam), Moscow, 1970, pp. 113-14;
also by the same author, O proiskhozhdenii turkmen=ata
/prostonarodniye formi sredneasiatskogo sufisma/ (On the
Origins of the Ata-Turkmen - the folk forms of the Central
Asian Sufism), in 'Domusulmanskiye verovaniya i obryadi v
Srednei Azii' (The pre-Moslem Beliefs in the Central Asia),
Moscow, 1975; S.M. Demidov, 'Magtymi' (istoriko-
etnographicheski etud) (The Magtyms - a historico-ethno-
graphical essay), in ibid. Also by Demidov, see note 25; and
'Sufizm v Turkmenii' (Sufism in Turkmenia), Ashkhabad,
1978, pp. 125-9, 150-3.
27 Sev. Zametiki o turkmenskom dukhovenstve (Notes on the
Turkmenian Clergy), 'Turkmenovedeniye' (The Turkmenian
Studies) magazine, 1928, no. 3-4, p. 14; also N.V. Brullova-
Shaskolskaya, see note 21, p. 88.
28 I. Goldziher, 'Lektsii ob Islame' (Lectures on Islam), Pg.

1912, p. 146; T.P. Hughes, 'A Dictionary of Islam', London, 1895, p. 117.

29 V.V. Bartold, see note 2, p. 276; V.I. Vyatkin, Sheikhi Djubari (The Djubari Sheikhs), in the collection 'V.V. Bartoldu' (To V.V. Bartold), Tashkent, 1927, p. 3.

30 See E.E. Bertels, Nur al-ulum, in 'Sufizm and sufiskaya literatura' (The Sufism and the Sufi Literature), Moscow, 1965, pp. 265, 275 and other.

31 N.G. Mallitsky, Sistema naimenovaniya u korennogo naseleniya goroda Tashkenta (The System of Names as Used by the Aboriginal Population of the Tashkent City), 'Izvestia Sredazkomstaris', issue 3, Tashkent, 1928, p. 246.

32 G.A. Magrupi, 'Usup-Ahmet', Ashgabat, 1943, pp. 62, 65, 72 (in Turkmenian).

33 N.G. Mallitsky, see note 31, pp. 245-6.

34 K. Ataev, see note 15, p. 76.

35 T.P. Hughes, see note 28, pp. 115-23.

36 In more detail, see S.M. Demidov, 'The Magtyms' (see note 26).

37 P. Pozdnev, 'Darvishi v musulmanskom mire' (The Dervishes in the Moslem World), Orenburg, 1886, p. 130.

38 V.V. Bartold, see note 2, p. 276; see also 'Materiali po istorii turkmen i Turkmenii' (Materials on the History of Turkmenia), v. II, Moscow-Leningrad, 1938, p. 208.

39 A. Vamberi, 'Ocherki Srednei Azii' (Essays on the Central Asia), Moscow, 1868, p. 180.

40 S.M. Demidov, 'The Magtyms' (see note 26), pp. 173-8.

41 In more detail, see S.M. Demidov, see note 16, pp. 159-66.

42 About zikhr, see T.P. Hughes, note 28, p. 703.

43 In more detail, see V.N. Basilov, 'O proiskhozhdenii Turkmen-ata' (On the origins of the ata-Turkmen).

44 O.A. Sukhareva, see note 4, p. 44.

45 M.F. Köprülüzade, 'Influence du chamanisme turco-mongol sur les ordres mystiques musulmans', Istanbul, 1929; S.P. Tolstov, Religiya narodov Srednei Azii (The Religion of the Peoples of the Central Asia) in 'Religiozniye verovaniya narodov SSSR' (The Religious Beliefs of the Peoples of the USSR), v. I, Moscow-Leningrad, 1931, pp. 259-60; Yu. V. Knorozov. Mazar Shamun-nabi, 'Sovietskaya Etnographia', 1949, no. 2; O.A. Sukhareva, O nekotorikh elementakh sufisma, geneticheski svyazannikh s shamanstvom (About Certain Elements of Sufism Connected Genetically with Shamanism), in 'Materiali vtorogo soveshchaniya arkheologov i etnographov Srednei Azii' (The Materials of the Second Conference of Archaeologists and Ethnographers of the Central Asia), Moscow-Leningrad, 1959.

46 O.A. Sukhareva (see note 4), p. 49.

47 See note 4, pp. 49-50.

48 In more detail, see T.D. Bayalieva, 'Doislamskiye verovaniya i ikh perezhitki u kirghizov' (Pre-Islam Beliefs and their Survivals among the Kirghizes), Frunze, 1972, pp. 120-1.

49 V.N. Basilov, Nekotoriye perezhitki kulta predkov u turkmen (Some Survivals of the Cult of Forefathers among the Turkmen), 'Sovietskaya Etnographia', 1968, no. 5.
50 In more detail, see V.N. Basilov, note 43; S.M. Demidov, note 25, pp. 140-50.
51 In more detail, see V.N. Basilov, note 26, pp. 92-118.
52 Use is made here of the field materials of K. Taizhanov and H. Ismailov (the Academy of Sciences of the Uzbek SSR).

9 HOLIER THAN THOU: ISLAM IN THREE TRIBAL SOCIETIES

Richard Tapper

SOME PROBLEMS IN THE SOCIOLOGY OF ISLAM

Classic problems in the sociology of Islam (or of any world religion) are how to deal descriptively with the wide variations in religious belief and practice, and how to explain these variations by relating them to differences in culture and social organization. In this paper I attempt to establish a simple descriptive framework and to use it in a comparison of three tribal societies which are unrelated but similar in their environments, in their pastoral nomadic system of production, and in being non-Arab Muslims. I begin by suggesting four major descriptive categories, based on the kinds of categories commonly found in the literature.

Descriptions of particular Muslim peoples, by observers of various persuasions, sooner or later assess their subjects in terms of four scales or dimensions. First, how orthodox or orthoprax they are in their knowledge of and adherence to prescribed Islamic duties and legal provisions - we can summarize this in the term 'orthodoxy'. Second, how far are they pre-occupied with religious (especially eschatological) ideas as reasons for their behaviour - this can be termed the scale of 'religiosity' or 'piety'. Third, what kind of communal religious rituals do they practise, in particular how far ecstatic and emotional behaviour is involved in formal religious rites - this I shall call the 'mosque' dimension. Fourth, what is the role of informal or peripheral religion, especially pilgrimage to shrines, spirit possession, beliefs and practices associated with evil eye - such 'shrine' religion generally involves personal approaches to the problem of misfortune. The four terms are of course far from ideal summations of the four categories, and the categories are neither clearly discrete nor necessarily related to each other; they will be of use primarily for heuristic and descriptive purposes.

In some respects it is possible to arrive at evaluations of a particular people in a more or less objective, statistical fashion. For example, the extent to which they do conform to prescribed duties of fasting, prayer, alms-giving, pilgrimage to Makkah (Mecca); their familiarity with and adherence to the laws of inheritance, marriage and the family; their observance of regular Islamic festivals and ritual occasions such as the ^CIds, communal Friday prayer for Sunnis, Muharram ceremonies for Shi^Cis; pilgrimages to other shrines, and the occurrence of

ecstatic behaviour - all this can be counted and compared from
society to society. In other respects, however, quantification
may be impossible or misleading, and differing subjective assessments may be anticipated from three sources: the observer, the
actors, and their neighbours. In the case of orthodoxy and piety,
for example, evaluations by the latter two sources are sociologically more interesting than any 'objective' assessment by an
outside observer. Moreover, such assessments in the literature
are often accompanied by explanations, for example for a given
people's general unorthodoxy or lack of interest in religion,
which are quite simplistic and sociologically inadequate.

Theories that have been and could be offered as to why
religious institutions vary throughout the Muslim world are of
four main kinds. Perhaps the most popular is syncretism - the
idea that religion in any one place represents an accommodation
between Great Tradition Islam and earlier pre-Islamic culture and
religion. This kind of theory is sometimes held to 'explain'
differences between, for example, Arabs and non-Arabs, or
between adherents of Sunni and Shi^{c}a sects. At the risk of
oversimplifying his argument, I would suggest that Geertz's
comparison of Islam in Morocco and Indonesia (1968) is a highly
sophisticated elaboration of the syncretism theory; at anything
less than such a broad holistic level, this kind of theory cannot,
any more than can any other 'survivalist' theory, account for
local variations.

A second kind of explanation of religious variation has to do
with cultural geography. It is sometimes argued simply that the
main determinant of orthodoxy is the factor of literacy and access
to the Great Tradition of the Qur'an, its teachers and officials.
This theory cannot explain why some people have access to the
sources of religion and do not make use of them, while others
achieve access in spite of great difficulties. A more common
argument of this kind is based on ecology. Thus, special religious
attitudes are held to follow from living in the desert, away from
other men and in contact only with God (cf. Cole 1975:113,126f).
Further, pastoral nomadism, as opposed to a settled agricultural
or urban existence, is often seen as economically precarious and
therefore as bringing its practitioners into a special close
dependence on God. In a similar vein are Spooner's proposal
that nomadism be treated as a 'trait of cultural ecology' characterized by a 'lack of interest in fixed property and fixed resources',
and his suggestion that nomads' dependence on an 'unimproved
natural environment . . . generates a characteristic nomadic
ideology in all nomadic populations' (1973:3-4). But a contradiction emerges here between those who argue that nomads communicate directly with God, and those who hold that since many
nomads are illiterate and have no access to the Book, they will
seek mediation through shrines, saints and related semi-orthodox
institutions. Gellner has resolved this contradiction, specifically
in the Maghribi context, using Ibn Khaldun's notion of the
'tribal circulation of elites': the natural tribal religion of the

desert is hierarchical, calling for mediation, but it is much more
liable to be energized by a preacher of an ideology of 'direct
communication' than is the urban population from which the
preacher comes. 'No people are as quick as the Bedouin to
accept religious truth and right guidance' (Ibn Khaldun 1967:
120; cf. Gellner 1969). Modern examples include the spread of
the Sanusi order in Cyrenaica (Evans-Pritchard 1949) and the
Wahhabis in Arabia (Dickson 1949:56; Cole 1975:116f). De
Planhol (1959 and 1968) makes a good case for such a geogra-
phical-ecological approach to religion, but again it cannot deal
with differences within one ecological type, e.g. among different
groups of pastoral nomads.

A third kind of theory may be characterized as structural-
functionalist, in the traditions of Durkheim and Weber but again
derived in this case from Ibn Khaldun. Such a theory holds that
tribal organization, featuring egalitarianism, lack of division of
labour, social cohesion and solidarity, will be represented by
religious forms different from those found in urban, stratified
society. It produces the same kinds of correlations as previous
theories, but fails in itself to distinguish sufficiently between
different kinds of tribal or urban organization. It can be elaborated, however, to account for such variations within the type:
for example, for present purposes, tribally organized societies.
It is commonplace that Middle Eastern tribal societies do vary
widely in both principles of organization and the forms they
exhibit: features like the importance of descent ideology, political
contract, clientship or confederation, the kinds of production
system and the composition of local groups, vary widely as
between the Berbers, North African and Arabian bedouin,
Kababish and Baggara Arabs, Somalis, Kurds, Pathans. Are
these political and economic variations related to variations in
religious organization, or in attitudes to Islamic institutions?
One approach is that of Douglas, in her formulation of a matrix
typology of societies according to whether 'grid' or 'group'
are strong: 'the most important determinant of ritualism is the
experience of closed social groups' (1973:33). Where the boundaries of social groups are perceived as clearly drawn, and where
social roles are rigidly defined, then there is likely to be considerably more symbolic elaboration - society representing itself
- than in a society where membership of social groups is more
fluid and unstructured and individuals perform their roles in a
personal manner with a degree of flexibility in response to
changing demands of situation. The problem with this type of
approach is that it is hard to identify the elements which differ-
entiate the experiences of 'grid' and 'group', and the ecological
or other determinants of such experiences; moreover, with
Douglas at least, it is not clear what is meant by 'ritual', which
in places is equated with controlled as opposed to spontaneous,
with sober as opposed to ecstatic, with magic as opposed to
communion, with symbolism as opposed to emotion. However,
theories of this kind are essential to the understanding of vari-

ations in form of ritual, however this may be defined.

But a fourth kind of theory is needed to account for certain important variations in religious beliefs and institutions. This concerns the extent to which religion, particularly claims to Islamic orthodoxy and piety, is used politically. This may apply at two levels: within a political community, as an ideology for differentiation on a class basis, that is as part of the previous kind of theory; or externally, on the boundaries between two neighbouring or rival political and religious communities. Thus, school or sect differences may or may not be important criteria for ethnic identity; for example, the Sunni-Shi^{c}a distinction is less important for political affiliation among Kurds than among Turks. Moreover, on boundaries between ethnic groups following the same school of Islam, religious factors may or may not be of political importance. The concern of this paper is less to explain these variations than to examine their role in determining religious behaviour within communities. A preliminary hypothesis might be based on the premise that within Islam the only legitimate claim to superiority by descent is holy descent from Muhammad and his associates, so that where a given group uses descent claims in confrontations with its neighbours it also will claim religious superiority (cf. bedouin, Somali, Pashtun), and may well attempt to validate this with adherence to what it sees and can demonstrate as orthodox practices.

If we want to compare Muslim communities with reference to their religious belief and practice, any sociological hypothesis must take account of several different kinds of factors: a hypothesis based only on ideas of syncretism, or on ecological or cultural variables alone, will be inadequate; it must account for variations in principles and forms of social organization in the communities themselves, and for variations in ethnic boundary relations.

We can now return to a particular category of Islamic societies - tribally organized nomads - and assess the considerations relevant to a comparison between them. The first consideration is the common assumption of the religious deviance of nomads.

RELIGION AMONG THE NOMADS

In the ethnography of Middle Eastern societies, settled or nomadic, tribal or peasant, perhaps the most neglected area of life is the whole realm of religion, ritual, symbolism and ideology, particularly at the level of the local community. Many ethnographers of nomads, for example Cunnison (1966) Asad (1970), Bates (1973), Ahmad (1974), Irons (1975), Glatzer (1977), pursuing their main interest in economics, kinship, social structure and politics - are content to record that their subjects are Muslims and to note ways in which their customs differ from Islamic prescriptions. A familiar theme in this literature is the antipathy between nomads and peasants, and its cultural expression among nomads in a distinctive ideology in which movement, tents, animals and other items take on symbolic values and organizational importance, to the extent that settlement implies a radical transformation of society, typically detribalization. Now this indeed applies to many nomadic peoples, including the Basseri and the Shahsevan – to be described in more detail below (see also the analysis of Haaland 1969). But it must be realized that such ritual evaluations are by no means universal among nomads, nor can one so simply derive a characteristic nomadic ideology from the ecological adaptation as Spooner (1973: 3-4) seems to suggest. Among some nomadic populations of the Middle East movement, tent-dwelling and stock-rearing are not imbued with central meanings at all, and the supposed nomadic ideology of independence, etc. (Goldschmidt 1971) turns out to be characteristic of tribally organized people, settled or nomadic, pastoralist or cultivators. In these cases, nomadism is an economic rather than an ecological, cultural or political adaptation, and there is no clear 'ideological polarization' that might inhibit settlement.

Nomad-peasant antipathy is usually found in regions where pastoral nomadism is pursued by a single tribal group forming a significant minority within the social environment and in competition with the settled majority for pastures and power (cf. Bates 1973:22). An exception, though its circumstances seem to prove the rule, is the case of the Saçi Kara Yörük, a very small nomadic group in a complex ethnic environment in south-eastern Anatolia, who do not, according to Bates, regard nomadism as central to their identity, although they are the only pastoral nomads in the area. More important for them is their tribal identity, which they all feel 'would not be lost with settlement' (1973:23). Many Yörük have in fact settled, but only in the last twenty years, in large groups of families and among neighbours of very different ethnic and cultural backgrounds. It is not surprising then if 'there is no social discontinuity separating nomadic from sedentary households' (1973:27) of Yörük, whose values allow for settlement.

Otherwise uncommitted nomads fall into two main categories. Some are members of large, politically dominant ethnic groups, often with unified genealogies justifying this dominance: examples include the Durrani (Ferdinand 1969:128, 147; personal information, see below), some Arabs (Cole 1975: 155f), northern Somali (Lewis 1961: 90f), and Fulani (cf. Monod 1975: 141-7). Others belong to minority groups living in remote desert or mountain areas, where they predominate numerically if not politically – probable examples (the evidence is unclear) include Kurds and Lurs of western Iran, and the Baluch of southeastern Iran and western Pakistan (cf. Salzman 1975). Exceptions here, again proving the rule, are the Yomut Turkmen of northeastern Iran, who value their nomadism highly; they were long able to dominate their marginal territory, but only by remaining nomadic, whether their economic base was pastoralism or cultivation (Irons 1975).

A central criterion in the 'ideological polarization' in the Middle East, whether between nomadic and settled or tribal and peasant people, is religion. Settled/peasant people, strongly influenced by the urban centres from which Islamic orthodoxy emanates, consider the nomads/tribesmen to be poor Muslims who, ignorant or careless of their religion, fail to observe the proper ritual duties (cf. Gulick 1976: 169; Digard 1978: 506). Gellner has recently called for an examination of such stereotypes, which have long been current also in the literature on the Middle East: are the nomads really lax in religious belief and performance, or 'conspicuously devoid of religious ritual', and if so, why? (1973: 8).

Various recent ethnographies have borne out the stereotype, describing nomads as admitting to either laxity in the performance of prescribed duties, or ignorance of Islamic precepts, or both, for example, the Cyrenaican bedouin under the Turks (Evans-Pritchard 1949: 62), the Marri Baluch of Pakistan (Pehrson 1966: 106), the Basseri (Barth 1961: 135), the Bakhtiyari (Brooks, private communication) and other Lurs in Iran (Black-Michaud, private communication). But, as Evans-Pritchard (1949: 63) emphasizes, laxity in ritual should not be taken to imply irreligiosity, and the same nomads are often described as 'sincere and proud Muslims', claiming the validity of their own approach to God as opposed to that of the state-favoured orthodoxy. All these groups, it should be noted, on the one hand subscribe to the religion of the state which claims sovereignty over them, while on the other hand maintaining some degree of political autonomy from the state by means of their tribal organization if not their nomadism. It may then be concluded that they are using a religious attitude of dissension symbolically for political purposes.

Indeed, the stereotype of the impious nomad, like that of the nomad implacably hostile to settled life, has no general validity. Nomads other than those following the Sanusi and Wahhabi movements are reported to claim and practise orthodox forms of Islam, for example the northern Somali (Lewis 1961:26) and the Durrani of northern Afghanistan (see below). Of the Somali (Lewis 1961), Cyrenaican bedouin (Evans-Pritchard 1949: 63) and Durrani it is reported that tribal custom is confused with Islamic precept and practice. These are the same peoples who form a major category of 'uncommitted' nomads, large, politically dominant ethnic groups, claiming special religious descent. In the Durrani case at least, the tribal ideology is inextricably linked with the notion of religious orthodoxy, the whole complex far outweighing any notion of identity as nomads.

Another nomadic people reported as good and pious Muslims are the Yomut Turkmen (Irons 1975: 8). The fact that they are a Sunni minority within Shi^{c}ite Iran may explain how they reconcile (in terms of the model proposed here) their political use of nomadism and their claims to orthodoxy. The same probably applies to other Sunni nomads in Iran, such as the Baluch (Salzman 1975).

Thus current generalizations about nomad religion and ideology are not empirically sustainable. Among Islamic nomads at least, there are wide variations in degree of 'orthodoxy', as well as in the extent to which component elements of nomadism are ideologically or ritually valued. What of the convention of nomads as lacking in symbolism and ritual performance? As Barth notes when writing of the Marri Baluch, 'Islam provides some very basic and moving idioms for the expression of corporate unity, especially in the collective prayers facing Mecca, in the Friday meeting, and in the communal fast' (Pehrson 1966: 106). In his analysis of Basseri social structure Barth was struck by the poverty, disconnection and apparent irrelevance of their ritual activities (1961: 135) and, in a purple passage which has received some notoriety in studies of both ritual and nomadism, was led to re-examine the concept of ritual and to propose the tribal migration as 'the central rite of nomadic society'. Douglas applauds Barth's frankness in reporting his frustration with Basseri ritual poverty, but holds that his anxiety to explain it away was misdirected. He assumes, she says, that 'tribal society must have a straight Durkheimian religious expression' (1973: 38), and as it is her thesis that this is not so she dismisses without due consideration his demonstration that Basseri society does indeed express itself in ritual behaviour. Basseri secularity, she implies, should be accepted and attributed to a particular form of social experience, though she does not pursue this far in the Basseri case. She would have had more luck with the Marri, for when Barth examined Pehrson's and his own material on their ritual and religion he again found 'no correspondences between secular social groupings and what might be described as cult groups', but this time he was content to attribute the deficiency to the 'non-corporate basis of Marri social life' (Pehrson 1966: 106).

Whatever the validity of Barth's claims for the Basseri migration (cf. R. Tapper 1979: 176-82), the kind of analysis out of which it arises, of the way in which a nomadic society represents itself symbolically, has been surprisingly undeveloped in other studies of nomads. Indeed, however controversial, Barth's account of religion, ritual symbolism and ideology, and his attempt to analyse their sociological relevance, have remained almost unique in the literature on nomads, at least in the Middle East. Apart from Barth's frustrated attempts with the Basseri and the Marri, and my own recent efforts for the Shahsevan (R. Tapper 1979), I know of only two other studies of Middle Eastern nomads which consider how far religion, either as a system of symbols or as a system of ritual practices, is involved at the local level in political and social relations between individuals and groups. Peters gives an intriguing if incomplete account of how the move from particularism to universalism in Cyrenaican bedouin society is shown in the changing significance of certain communal ritual activities at the level of local groups (1976). Of the Al-Murrah bedouin, Cole writes that

there is no need for big celebrations that bring all the members
of a big social group together. Independence of action rather
than social solidarity is the first demand of the ecological setting in which they live (1975: 135).

This, however, is unconvincing, as the accounts of communal
prayer (pp. 117-18) and the feasting associated with Ramadan
(p. 130) indicate that camps and lineages among the Al-Murrah
are religious congregations as well as residential and social
groups.

RELIGION AND ETHNICITY IN THREE ISLAMIC TRIBAL SOCIETIES

The rest of this paper is a limited comparison between three
Islamic tribal societies: the Shahsevan of northwestern Iran,
Turki-speaking Shi^cites; the Basseri of southwest Iran,
Persian-speaking Shi^cites; and the Durrani of north-central
Afghanistan, Pashtu-speaking Sunnites. Relevant material on
Shahsevan and Basseri is drawn from published sources
(R. Tapper 1979; Barth 1961), while the ethnography of the
Durrani is still largely unpublished (but see N. Tapper 1979;
Glatzer 1977). The description will be kept to a minimum
account of social structure, the tribal and ethnic boundary
parameters, and the major features of religious and ritual
organization. First, let us return to the descriptive categories
suggested earlier: 'orthodoxy', 'religiosity', 'mosque' and
'shrine'. It should be noted that for evaluation along the first
two dimensions, orthodoxy and religiosity, the significant data
are cognitive, i.e. each group's self-evaluation by comparison
with their neighbours. With the other two scales, mosque and
shrine, we can assess the three tribal peoples of our example
by comparison with each other. On the basis of the comparison,
I shall suggest first, that the differential self-evaluations of
piety and orthodoxy, in which Durrani occupy one extreme,
Basseri the other, with the Shahsevan in between, are related
to the kind of ethnic boundaries which they maintain; second,
that such self-evaluations at least in part determine the
character of religious behaviour at the local level; and third,
that the role of communal ecstatic ritual in the mosque context
is related in a fairly simple Durkheimian way to the social
organization of local groups, and that its importance is probably
inversely related to the degree of involvement in shrine religion.

Shahsevan
About 40,000 Shahsevan nomads form a small minority of the
population of northeastern Azarbayjan, Iran. A rather larger
number of Shahsevan tribesmen are recently settled, but the
majority population of the region are agricultural peasants and
townsmen with no tribal affiliations, known to each other and

to the Shahsevan as 'Tat'.

Shahsevan nomads recognize individual ownership not only of animals but also of grazing rights, which are disposable and inheritable. This has implications for the formation, size and composition of households and camps, which are basically groups of closely related agnates. Nomadic social structure may be summarized as a series of groups with more or less well-defined boundaries, relations of conflict and co-operation between them, and a series of personal networks cutting across the boundaries of all the groups. The household, occupying a single tent, is clearly defined, patriarchal, autonomous and exogamous. Households co-operate for herding purposes in winter and summer camps, which have agnatic bases and jointly held pasture estates. For the 100-mile spring and autumn migrations, camps join to form a migratory community of some thiry households, which was once also an individual winter and summer camp, but is now typically a coincidence of tribal section and maximal lineage, under the leadership of an Elder. There is quite a wide range of wealth, the Elder and one or two others in a community owning several hundred head of sheep and appropriate pasture rights, while several members, with no pasture rights at all and barely a dozen animals, subsist by selling their labour. Different camp leaders and the community Elder form a hierarchy of authority.

The community is also a ritual congregation, gathering exclusively for the major Shi^{c}ite Islamic festivals. It is also united symbolically through the ideology of common descent, shared honour, and joint control of marriages, all focused in the Elder. It is a closed group, and internal disputes are not admitted to outsiders; yet conflicts, arising from the pasture tenure system and the recent history of estate and camp fragmentation, lead to relations of latent hostility between component camps of a community.

Above the level of the local community, descent plays little part in Shahsevan political organization. Different communities, though united into tribes, are not systematically allied to each other through descent or marriage ties. Members of different communities, however, and members of the same community, are linked in personal networks through ties of affinity and friendship, summed up in institutionalized reciprocal feasting obligations.

A tribe is an explicitly political and territorial group, headed by a chief, and based on transactional but hierarchical relations between the chief and the Elders of the component communities (tribal sections) - yet tribes show considerable continuity and cultural identity, largely through their territorial definition and a strong tendency to endogamy. The different tribes, of diverse origins but largely shared language and culture, group into a loose confederation.

If we follow Fortes (1953: 35-6) and also Douglas in so far as she maintains that 'the most important determinant of ritualism is the experience of closed social groups' (1973: 33), then we may anticipate that the sharply defined structure outlined above will have a clearly expressed ritual dimension. That is, we can anticipate that groups and networks will be defined and con-solidated in Durkheimian fashion through shared emotional experiences and through competition and spatial contraposition in ritual contexts. At the same time, leaders of groups and persons in the networks may consciously or unconsciously use the ritual to their own political, if not economic, advantage, while conflict in the social structure, and hostilities between groups and individuals, may find in certain ritual contexts either expression or temporary relief or both.

All Shahsevan public ritual behaviour, whatever its political function, marks stages in three different dimensions of time and space: formal Islam, the individual life-cycle, and the nomadic herding year. These dimensions form a framework in which the most general underlying symbolic structure is an opposition between the other-worldly concerns of the formal religion and the political and economic concerns of society. The Islamic year and its events are opposed to the herding year and its events, while the ceremonies of the individual life-cycle bridge this opposition.

Islam defines a yearly cycle of twelve lunar months and a weekly cycle of seven days, a social world oriented to Mecca and a spiritual world oriented to paradise. Days and weeks are marked by regular ritual purification and prayer; the year by various festivals, especially in a five-month period which includes fasting and alms-giving in Ramadan, sacrifice and pilgrimage in Dhu' l-Hijja, and mourning and sexual abstinence in Muharram. The life-cycle is marked for all adults by marriage and funeral, for men by circumcision and sometimes by the pilgrimage to Makkah, all of which involve elaborate feasts and ceremonies which define the social position of individuals and establish the membership of groups and networks. The solar year of four seasons determines the nomadic herding and migratory cycle, in which the main events, which are strongly ritualized and take the form of a rite de passage, are associated with the new year and the spring migration. An analysis of all these rituals (R. Tapper 1979: 153-83) shows that all social entities of significance - groups, networks, authority roles - are, as anticipated, both physically defined and characterized by ritual activities of various kinds in all three spatial-temporal dimen-sions. In particular, the hostilities within the community are expressed in the ritual of the migration, which is as much a ritual of rebellion as a ritual of collective solidarity; while the solidarity of the community is particularly ritualized by the enthusiasm with which Shahsevan observe the ceremonies of Ramadan and Muharram.

Shahsevan public ritual life is certainly unusual in its rich-ness for a Muslim nomadic society. In so far as Islam is con-cerned, Shahsevan religious belief and practice are located mainly within the context of communal and emotionally intense

experience of certain orthodox rituals, and they are little
interested in 'peripheral' phenomena. They consider themselves
to be good Muslims, though lax in many respects compared to
their Tat neighbours. Few of them pray regularly; they have no
mosques and there are very few mullahs to be found resident in
nomad camps. However, on occasions of communal religious
significance, during the period from Ramadan to Muharram and
at funeral wakes, they become highly enthusiastic and bring in
mullahs from settled society. Indeed, for Ramadan and Muharram
the nomad communities assemble in tents specially set apart by
the Elders as mosques. During the ceremonies of Muharram,
when Shi^{c}ites commemorate the death of Imam Husain, the nomads
work themselves into frenzies of grief, often attaining near-
trance states. Women, who are secluded from men in daily life,
are not excluded in religious matters: they participate physically
and emotionally, if separately, in funerals and during Ramadan
and Muharram.

Apart from these communal ceremonies, many Shahsevan maintain scepticism, if not if religious premises, at least of the religion
taught them by visiting mullahs. They question the orthodox
cosmology, the prohibitions on music, dancing and card-playing,
and the mullahs' ambivalent attitudes to misfortune and to
politics and secular power. Generally they have a pragmatic
attitude to illness and misfortune. There is no involvement in
Sufi orders - though a historical note should be added here.
The Shahsevan tribes are said to have been brought together
and given their name ('lovers of the Shah') around 1600, as
fanatical adherents of the Safavid order, whose leaders had set
up a new Shi^{c}ite dynasty in Iran. This ideology of direct
religious devotion to the Safavid dynasty remained with them
for a long time, giving legitimacy to claims of superiority over
other groups in the country. The Safavids have now long gone,
and with their more recent history of tribal independence and
rebellion the Shahsevan espouse the typical nomad ideal of
freedom from town-based constraints, especially those of orthodox religion. Yet their name and their legendary origins still
encourage them to claim a certain religious superiority over
those who do not share them, for example the Tats of the region.

Those nomad men who can afford it have the ultimate aim of
pilgrimage to Makkah and the Shi^{c}ite shrines at Karbala. Also
important, and more often achieved, is the pilgrimage to Imam
Rida's shrine at Mashhad. Most camp leaders and other leading
men and women in a community are Mashhadis; one person in
every two communities is a Hajji - not usually the Elder himself,
as the status of Hajji is felt to be above the sordid and petty
political dealings in which Elders have to dirty their hands;
Hajjis are called in to mediate in disputes. Apart from these
pilgrimages, the nomads, men or women, rarely visit the numerous
local shrines for intercessionary appeals, and ridicule Tats for
so doing. Many nomads believe in a limited variety of spirits
which can cause harm, particularly among women and in associa-

tion with childbirth, and appropriate herbal and magical pre-
cautions and remedies are sought and applied on occasion. But
in no case did I record the occurrence of possession fits or
exorcism among the nomads - here again they tend to ridicule
Tats for addiction to such 'superstitions'.

Northeast Azarbayjan is well defined by geographical and
administrative frontiers, which separate it from similar regions
to the west and south and from the Soviet Union on the north
and east. Shahsevan have no contacts across the Soviet frontier,
and few with tribal nomad and settled groups in neighbouring
regions of Iran. Within the region, tent-dwelling pastoral nomads
are by definition Shahsevan; settlement leads sooner or later,
nowadays, to detribalization and loss of Shahsevan identity.
Many Tats are of Shahsevan origins, though they may not
recall or emphasize this, while Shahsevan camps include many
groups and individuals of known Tat origins. Tribal names
become village names and vice versa. There are regular exchanges
between Shahsevan and Tat, individually and in the market.
Traders and craftsmen visit camp regularly; nomads visit towns
to shop; wealthy nomads own village lands; wealthy Tats send
flocks to graze with nomads. Beyond these formal economic
exchanges, there is some social interaction in feasting contexts,
and some judicious marriage alliances, but generally Tat and
Shahsevan are socially distinct.

Shahsevan conceive themselves as nomadic tented tribesmen,
distinct from settled village farmers. Otherwise Tat and
Shahsevan are both Turki-speaking and Shi^{c}ite, and to the
observer there are only the smallest differences in language,
religious belief and practice, oral literature and life-cycle
ceremonies; in many cases differences are smaller than those
found between Shahsevan tribes. Yet claims and counter-claims
are made: Shahsevan claim among other things to observe
stricter moral standards and to achieve a more direct and
religious approach to God, while Tats claim to be more orthodox
and law-abiding. These religious claims are stereotypes, in no
sense criteria for membership of the respective categories, which
depend simply on the more basic settled-nomad distinction.

In sum, the Shahsevan, possibly for historical reasons, conceive themselves as more religious than others, but as nomads
they disdain orthodoxy, which they impute as a deficiency to
their settled neighbours. This supposed difference in religious
attitudes, now of little significance, may have played a more
important role in former, less peaceful times, when nomad and
settled were in greater competition for the region's resources.
Their typical nomadic dissidence is accompanied by a complex
ritual life, in which mosque religion is of central importance.
A series of well-defined social boundaries and structured
authority patterns is closely mirrored in ritual forms. Their
pastoral adaptation produces conflict within the local community,
while major communal rituals, both mosque-centred and migratory, are observed with emotional intensity and can be inter-

preted variously as rituals of rebellion or solidarity. This
communal emotional experience is complemented by a lack of
interest in magico-religious phenomena such as shrines or spirits.

Basseri
The ritual life of the Basseri and the ways in which it is related
to social structure contrast with the Shahsevan. Basseri nomads
reckon their ancestry several generations further than the
Shahsevan, solely it seems in order to claim rights to grazing
areas, which are held in common by an *oulad*, a lineage of
roughly 90 families, and controlled and allocated to this group
by the chief of the Basseri. Above the level of the oulad, the
Basseri tribe (some 15,000 members), and the confederation
of which it forms a part, are organized on principles similar to
the Shahsevan: political allegiance of different groups to a
powerful chief, with little or no notion of common descent.

The oulad subdivides into two or more migratory camps –
these are the primary nomadic communities and indeed they are
the equivalent of the Shahsevan communities. Each such camp-
community comprises several herding units, composed of well-
defined and autonomous households. But unlike among the
Shahsevan, all these herding units and camps are ephemeral
and unstructured: their component households are not
necessarily agnates, but bilateral kin and affines, and they
are free to move and join other groups within the oulad at any
time. Quarrels are solved simply by such movement, and the
communities are not threatened by structural conflicts such as
those of the Shahsevan. There is little wealth differentiation
among the nomads; headmen of camps have comparatively little
authority, and all nomads are held equal before the chief.

The Basseri seemed to Barth to have a 'ritual life of unusual
poverty' (1961: 146); they 'are generally uninterested in
religion as preached by Persian mullahs, and indifferent to
metaphysical problems' (p. 135), while Ramadan and Muharram
'are observed and celebrated by few' (p. 137). Barth was led
to identify the nomadic spring migration as 'the central rite of
nomadic society' (p. 153), in which the important social groups
(herding unit, camp, tribe and confederacy), their structure
and the processes by which they form, are dramatically
expressed. In particular, the migration is a rite of collective
solidarity for the camp community, whose unit is based on consensus rather than enforced co-operation, as in the Shahsevan
case. Basseri ritual life then is not so poor. Moreover, in contrast again with the Shahsevan, they appear to be somewhat
richer in terms of their interest in shrines (pp. 137-8) and the
variety and extent of their beliefs and practices concerning
evil eye and other supernatural influences (pp. 138-45).

Unlike Shahsevan, Basseri have no history of religious
fanaticism, and they apparently make no claims to special forms
of piety or religiosity. They interact with a large number of
other nomadic tribal groups, not to mention the local settled

peasantry – Barth talks of the province of Fars as one of 'great
ethnic complexity and admixture' in which 'tribal units are best
defined by political rather than ethnic or geographical criteria'
(p. 1). Religion or religious claims appear to play no part in
inter-tribal relations. As regards their laxity and lack of
orthodoxy in matters of Islam, Basseri like Shahsevan may be
making statements about their relation to settled, mullah-
dominated society. Basseri too are tribesmen with a pastoral
nomad economy, in contrast with a settled peasantry. As nomads,
they too appear to be proud of their laxity and freedom in
matters of religion (pp. 135f) – they value their independence of
settled authorities, both political and religious.

Durrani

The Durrani case is somewhat more complex in terms of both
ethnic environment and religious organization. Pashtuns (Pathans)
make up over half the population of Afghanistan. A single
genealogy unites the three major tribal groups, one of which,
the Durrani of the west and south, provided the rulers of the
country from 1747 to 1978, and constituted an interest group to
which economic and political privileges (tax concessions, freedom from conscription) accrued by virtue of descent. Although
legislation now (i.e. by 1972, the end of my fieldwork) provides
for the equality of all Afghan nationals, Durrani domination still
pervades all branches of political and administrative life. If only
for this reason, the poorest nomad or peasant who can claim
Durrani identity is able to maintain, at least in the eyes of
fellow-Durrani, a position of social superiority to members of all
other ethnic groups except Sayyids.

In the Saripul region of north-central Afghanistan, Durranis
comprise an ethnic minority of some 15,000 in a population of
150,000. When they first arrived in the region as pastoral nomads
around the turn of the century, they prospered: there was
vacant pasturage and rich agricultural land for all who wanted
it. This situation has changed radically in recent decades.
Flocks, pastures and farmland can no longer be expanded, while
the local population has increased rapidly, intensifying competition over the now limited resources.

The Saripul region is one of considerable ethnic and linguistic
diversity. Unlike the two cases from Iran, here the nomad/settled
distinction does not define ethnic boundaries. Different Durrani
groups, for example, are pastoral nomad, settled cultivator, or
a mixture of both. Many Durrani are among the poorest people
in the region, but they can claim some political advantage
through their tribal association with the rulers, as well as with
the local Khans. The region is dominated by one powerful
Durrani Khan family, whose ancestor led the migration from the
southwest and was granted many privileges from the throne
which enabled the Khans to gain control of vast areas of productive farmland and tenants, several years' tenure of the local
governorship, and later the parliamentary seat. The role and

behaviour of the Khans as landowners and oppressive barons
over the non-Pashtuns is much opposed by their fellow-
tribesmen, who nonetheless find their services as patrons and
mediators with the state indispensable if expensive.

Pastoral nomadism in the region is practised mainly by
Pashtuns, including Durrani and others, but members of all
such groups retain their ethnic and tribal identities when
settled. Durrani are in continual competition for resources,
both farmland and pasture, with a variety of other ethnic
groups. They use a variety of criteria for defining their own
identity, stressing different ones on different boundaries.

To be a Durrani in northern Afghanistan, one must speak
Pashtu and practise Sunni Islam, but more important one must
be able to trace pure patrilineal descent within a recognized
Durrani tribe and thereby through fixed genealogies to the
Pashtun ancestor Qais ^{C}Abd al-Rashid, a companion of the
Prophet; and one must never give women in marriage to men of
other ethnic groups, though one may in practice take wives
from them.

Durrani perceive three main ethnic categories in their environment: Farsiwan, Uzbek and Hazara. They call themselves
Pashtun or Afghan, often denying this label to Ghiljai and
other Pashtun tribes from the east, but always to several groups
who came with them from the southwest, call themselves Pashtun,
speak Pashtu and follow Durrani custom, yet are regarded by
Durrani as 'fakes'; they belong to no recognized tribe, are said
(by Durrani) to give daughters even to Shi^{C}ites, and are sus-
pected of practising Shi^{C}ism and of speaking Persian (hence
Farsiwan or Parsiwan - 'Persian-speaking') in the privacy of
their homes. It is such Farsiwans who are in the most direct
competition with Durrani for farmland and pasture.

All non-Pashtu-speaking Sunnis are often termed 'Uzbek'
by Durrani. This category in fact includes not only the Turki-
speaking Uzbeks but Persian-speaking Tajik, Aymak and Arab,
who together form the indigenous majority of peasants and
townsmen, subject to the economic and political ascendance of
the Pashtun Khans, against whom they have frequently risen in
the past. Durrani here stress their own superior religious
descent, and claim that Durrani custom is nearer to Islamic
orthopraxy than that of the 'Uzbeks'. They deride as 'Uzbek
nonsense' such 'non-Islamic' practices as seclusion of women.
Uzbeks, of course, stress their own version of piety and
orthodoxy, valuing seclusion, literacy and purity, and maintaining that the Pashtuns have changed little since they arrived in
the area as ignorant savages, hardly less polluting in their
nomad camps than infidel foreigners or Shi^{C}ite Hazaras.

All Shi^{C}ites are called Hazaras, especially the Persian-speaking
tribesmen of supposed Mongol origins whom the Durrani
encounter in their high summer pastures as well as in several
important immigrant village colonies near Saripul. This third
ethnic frontier is not so important politically to the Durranis as

it once was. Given the main barrier of religion, with the ban on
inter-marriage, individual ties across the frontier are sometimes
close, taking the form of economic exchanges, friendship and
social relations of many kinds.

Durrani consider themselves equals, members of an endogamous group within which (and outside the degrees of kinship
forbidden by Islam) there is complete freedom to marry. They
insist that subdivisions of the ethnic group - tribes, lineages,
subtribes - are not relevant for marriage purposes. Although
descent is formally relevant only at the level of the ethnic
group, where it determines marriage choice and political
allegiance, it is still a fundamental principle of social organization which in effect underlies concepts of social grouping.
Descent determines membership of a Durrani tribe and of various
tribal divisions, none of which are corporate in character. One
or more local descent groups form the core of a subtribe: subtribes are collections of two or three camps or villages, perhaps
100 to 150 families, and though based on an ideology of common
descent are essentially political groups with some territorial
unity and potential for joint action. Apart from their name,
most often that of a recognized Durrani tribal division, symbols
to unify the subtribe are few and unimportant: notions of joint
responsibility in matters of honour are not worked out systematically in the ideology and certainly not in practice; there are
neither common property nor common rituals; not even residence
is necessary for effective membership of a subtribe. Generally,
organization and co-operation at the local level are unstructured
by segmentary opposition or any other single principle, but
instead by a combination of agnation, cognation, alliance,
friendship, forming shifting clusters around wealthy and
ambitious men.

In sum, all residential groups such as camps, villages and the
subtribe are heterogeneous, fluid in composition and only vaguely
bounded or structured. The vital boundary for Durrani is
membership of the ethnic group; within this boundary only the
household is particularly clearly defined or corporate. As with
the Shahsevan and Basseri, Durrani households are ideally
independent and self-sufficient, but in the absence of any
single organizing principle, the dominant theme of social relations
at the local level is of household heads in constant competition
with close kin and neighbours for control of both productive and
reproductive resources.

So also, leadership roles within a subtribe are quite unstructured compared with Shahsevan, while wealth differentials are
at least as great, and certainly greater than among Basseri
nomad communities. Each village or winter camp has an official
headman, who if he happens to be particularly wealthy may
acquire personal followers and the status of Khan. But community decisions are made by councils of Elders and Hajjis,
representing all households of the group, and autocratic,
domineering behaviour is heartily resisted, unless those domin-

ated are already economically subordinate as tenants, clients or employees. The people should decide.

Durrani are Sunnis. They see their customs and beliefs concerning all areas of social life as forming a single complex, sanctioned by Islam, by the Qur'an as expounded to them by those qualified to do so. They believe themselves superior in this respect to all other ethnic groups except Sayyids.

Durrani cosmology and specifically religious beliefs do indeed approximate orthodoxy compared to those of the Shahsevan and Basseri - though not perhaps the Uzbeks. Allah, the only and supreme God, is omnipotent and yet widely regarded as directing only the forces of good, while the forces of evil, represented by devils and jinns, are independent of his immediate, though not his ultimate concern; his ways are unknowable; discussion of the 'problem of evil' is discouraged, as is the problem of reconciling notions of the efficacy of prayer and the inescapable predestination of each man's fate.

Again, compared with Shahsevan and Basseri, Durrani may be judged remarkably conscientious in observing the formal duties of Islam: prayer, fasting, alms, pilgrimage. Every Durrani settlement has at least one mosque, built by common effort and expense, with a resident mullah who leads prayers and other rituals there, performs general Islamic offices, and conducts classes for boys of wealthier families. Collective prayer sessions, including the Friday prayer, are not obligatory nor generally attended, but senior men usually gather in the mosque to perform the last two daily prayers. Even nomad camps commonly have a small place nearby marked out with stones for a mosque, and many have a resident mullah from a leading family.

During the two major ^cIds, at the end of Ramadan and at the Feast of Sacrifice, all men of the community gather at the mosque, greet each other, smooth over quarrels, and spend much of the day in prayer and celebration. Neither on such occasions, however, nor at other large ceremonial gatherings such as weddings or funerals, are the congregations exclusive or likely to be the same on any two occasions, and visitors and strangers are welcome.

Durrani Islam is a religion of moderation, piety and sobriety. At formal religious gatherings, at funerals or prayers at the mosque, extreme emotion or ecstasy are never displayed. Nomadic migrations have very little emotional or ritual content; few people go unless they have to for economic reasons. Durrani (in this region at least) do not appear to value nomadism and tent life as such, though they continue to class themselves as pastoralists in preference to farmers. The migrations lack organization and planning, and camp composition on the trek varies from day to day.

Durrani Islam is also a religion of the powerful and successful, which culminates for them in the performance of the ultimate duty, pilgrimage to Makkah, which frequently marks the retire-

ment from competition of an active leader from competition.
Women, though in other respects comparatively unsegregated
from men, have no part in mosque-centred rituals and must
pray at home.

The differential status of the sexes and of the successful
and unsuccessful within each are more manifest in a series of
religious activities to do with Sufism, saints, shrines and
spirits which, though important in Durrani life, have a somewhat ambiguous connection with the Islam of the mosque and
the mullah. Almost all active participants in these are men or
women who appear to sense their own weakness or failure in
terms of the major cultural expectations: production in the
case of men, reproduction for women. But this 'shrine
religion' too is controlled by prominent religious and secular
leaders.

Scattered around the country are lodges of various Sufi
orders, where spiritual leaders (Aghas) may receive their
disciples, though they usually tour the country during spring
and summer to visit the latter. Most Durrani in Saripul are
Qadiri, but acknowledge different Aghas as their leaders.
When an Agha arrives in a community his male disciples gather
to receive instruction and to take part in performances of the
dhikr, involving ritual repetition of God's name, controlled
breathing and subsequent controlled trance, though occasionally
uncontrolled fits. One in three men - almost always from poor
families - have participated in such rites at some time.

Men with claims to secular power in the community, or to any
degree of religious piety and learning, take an ambivalent
attitude to such Sufi activities. They never take an active
part, but they do not discourage others from doing so, declar-
ing the performances to be beneficial and proper means of
communication with God. Aghas are respected by all, and have
the power to curse if their authority is flouted. Local and
sometimes distant (but renowned) Aghas are called on for
magical purposes, for exorcism, and to resolve disputes and
make peace between blood enemies. Sufi activities are almost
exclusive to males: among Durrani, women's Sufi leaders are
extremely rare, though women may be disciples of a male
Agha if he exorcises a spirit possessing them.

Possession affects the lives of many women directly or
indirectly. One in three married women are said to have been
afflicted at some time, all of them suffering from some combination of complaints, never just one alone: barrenness, lack of
sons, death of young children, physical complaints stemming
from childbirth complications, illness, poverty, difficulties
with husband or with co-wife. Possession can be interpreted
as a response to a condition of failure in the reproductive role
of wife and mother. It is diagnosed in certain cases of illness,
insanity and fits, and possibly after the death of the victim or
her children. Spirits are amoral and usually antisocial. Treatment always takes the form of attempts at exorcism, by both

Aghas and more orthodox functionaries. The condition is often alleviated by such attempts, whether or not they are successful. They establish a relation of spiritual discipleship, as well as bringing attention and consideration on the part of the victim's family. There are no possession cults.

Only very few men, usually ill and from poor and divided families, were diagnosed as suffering possession. Men who felt themselves powerless and disadvantaged more often found both excitement and consolation in Sufi rituals. The only other men to have had contact with spirits were some community leaders who claimed to have survived encounters with particularly malevolent spirits because, though terrified, they steadfastly resisted and outwitted the spirit, or destroyed it by prayer. Such tales are retold by people normally somewhat sceptical in these matters, and are regarded as authentic proof of the existence and power of spirits; clearly they also demonstrate both the power of prayer and the power of leaders who normally confine their religious activities strictly within the confines of orthodox Islamic practice.

Possession cases are also taken to shrines. The best known and most attended of these are the graves of famous Aghas, martyrs or other holy men. Pilgrims to local shrines are almost always women, who go in the hope of alleviating problems ranging from possession to physical ailments and marital difficulties.

Compared with the Shahsevan at least, Durrani society is intensely competitive and individualistic. The weakest households cannot survive except in relations of dependence, in which they acknowledge failure to achieve the cultural expectation of productive and reproductive self-sufficiency. Islam itself provides an alternative ideology, of egalitarianism, which confronts the realities of inequality, but the practice of orthodox Islam is dominated by the successful and the privileged. Men and women who fail seek consolation through personal experience in ambivalent religious activities, men in Sufi ritual, women in pilgrimages, spirit possession and exorcism.

Durrani social organization is competitive, unequal, and unstructured. Islamic, mosque-centred rituals, rather than demarcating social groups and patterns of authority, manage both to declare the theory of equality and to stress the reality of inequality. Durrani conceptions of their historical identity, and of their relation to other ethnic groups with whom they are in constant political and economic competition, lead prominent and successful Durrani to an orthodox and unemotional observance of Islamic ritual. Unsuccessful Durrani, by contrast, pursue ecstatic experiences associated with Sufism, shrines and spirit possession.

The central concern of this essay has been to show how external relations between ethnic or tribal groups, particularly where they involve competition for resources, are likely to be expressed in claims of religious superiority, whether in terms of religiosity or of orthodoxy, and how far these claims determine the character of religious belief and behaviour within the ethnic group. Thus the role of ecstatic ritual in mosque or shrine religion is related partly to ethnic and historical self-conceptions and partly to social organization. Durrani claims to orthodoxy and piety in comparison with their competitors inhibit the expression of ecstasy in mosque contexts, though allowing it to social 'misfits' in shrine contexts. Shahsevan emotional involvement in mosque rituals is less related to their self-conception as pious Muslims than to the complexities of social relations within the congregation. Basseri, who claim neither orthodoxy nor piety, ignore the religion of the mosque and focus their religious interest on shrine activities. Both Basseri and Shahsevan, finally, in defining themselves as tribal nomads and as independent and comparatively unorthodox in matters of religion, experience the nomadic migrations as forms of ritual, though in different ways that are related again to differences in their social organization, particularly the structure of nomadic communities.

NOTE

Earlier versions of this paper, originally inspired by an unpublished paper by Jacob Black-Michaud, were presented at anthropology seminars since 1972 in London, Sussex and Belfast. I am grateful to Dr Black-Michaud for allowing me to read his paper, to members of those seminars for comments on mine, and particularly to Nancy Tapper for her suggestions over the years since the paper was first constructed. Its faults remain my responsibility.
    Fieldwork in Afghanistan was conducted in 1971 and 1972 on Study Leave from the School of Oriental and African Studies, on Social Science Research Council Project no. HR 1141/1.

BIBLIOGRAPHY

Ahmad, Abd-al Ghaffar Muhammad (1974), 'Shykhs and Followers. Political Struggle in the Rufa[c] a al-hoi Nazirate in the Sudan, Khartoum University Press.
Asad, Talal (1970), 'The Kababish Arabs. Power, Authority and Consent in a Nomadic Tribe', Hurst, London.
Barth, Fredrik (1961), 'Nomads of South Persia: the Basseri Tribe of the Khamseh Confederacy', Universitetsvorlaget, Oslo; Allen & Unwin, London.
Bates, Daniel (1973), 'Nomads and Farmers: a Study of the Yörük of Southeastern Turkey', Anthrop. Papers, Museum of Anthropology, no. 52, University of Michigan, Ann Arbor.
Cole, Donald (1975), 'Nomads of the Nomads. The Al Murrah Bedouin of the Empty Quarter', Aldine, Chicago.

Cunnison, Ian (1966), 'Baggara Arabs. Power and the Lineage in a Sudanese Nomad Tribe', Clarendon, Oxford.

Dickson, H.R.P. (1949), 'The Arab of the Desert', Allen & Unwin, London.

Digard, Jean-Pierre (1978), Perspectives anthropologiques sur l'islam, 'R. franc. sociol.', XIX, 497-523.

Douglas, Mary (1973), 'Natural Symbols. Explorations in Cosmology', Penguin, Harmondsworth.

Evans-Pritchard, E.E. (1949), 'The Sanusi of Cyrenaica', Clarendon, Oxford.

Ferdinand, Klaus (1969), Nomadism in Afghanistan. With an Appendix on Milk Products, in L. Foldes (ed.), 'Viehwirtschaft und Hirtenkultur. Ethnographische Studien', Akademiai Kiado, Budapest.

Fortes, Meyer (1953), The Structure of Unilineal Descent Groups, 'Amer. Anthr.', LV, 17-41.

Geertz, Clifford (1968), 'Islam Observed: Religious Development in Morocco and Indonesia', University of Chicago, Chicago.

Gellner, Ernest (1969), 'Saints of the Atlas', Weidenfeld & Nicolson, London.

Gellner, Ernest (1973), Introduction: Approaches to Nomadism, in C. Nelson (ed.), 'The Desert and the Sown. Nomads in the Wider Society', Institute of International Studies, Research Series no. 21, University of California, Berkeley.

Glatzer, Bernt (1977), 'Nomaden von Gharjistan', Südasien-Institut, Universität Heidelberg, Beiträge zur Sudasienforchung, 22. Steiner, Wiesbaden.

Goldschmidt, Walter (1971), Independence as an Element in Pastoral Social Systems, 'Anth. Qurtly', XLIV, 132-42.

Gulick, John (1976). 'The Middle East: an Anthropological Perspective', Goodyear, Pacific Palisades.

Haaland, Gunnar (1969), Economic Determinants in Ethnic Processes, in F. Barth (ed.), 'Ethnic Groups and Boundaries', Allen & Unwin, London.

Ibn Khaldun (1967), 'The Muqaddimah', trans F. Rosenthal, ed. N. Dawood, Routledge, London.

Irons, William (1975), 'The Yomut Turkmen: a Study of Social Organization among a Central Asian Turkic-speaking Population', Anthrop. Papers, Museum of Anthropology, no. 58, University of Michigan, Ann Arbor.

Lewis, Ioan (1961), 'A Pastoral Democracy', Oxford University Press, London.

Monod, Théodore (1975), Introduction, in 'Pastoralism in Tropical Africa', Oxford University Press, London.

Pehrson, Robert (1966), 'The Social Organization of the Marri Baluch', F. Barth comp., Aldine, Chicago.

Peters, Emrys (1976), From Particularism to Universalism in the religion of the Cyrenaica Bedouin, 'Bull. Br. Soc. Middle East Stud.', III, 5-14.

de Planhol, Xavier (1959), 'The World of Islam', Cornell University Press.

de Planhol, Xavier (1968), 'Les fondements géographiques de l'histoire de l'islam', Flammarion, Paris.

Salzman, Philip (1975), Islam and Authority in Tribal Iran. A Comparative Comment, 'The Moslem World', LXV, 186-95.

Spooner, Brian (1973), 'The Cultural Ecology of Pastoral Nomads', Module in Anthropology no. 45, Addision-Wesley, Reading (Mass.).

Tapper, Nancy (1979), Marriage and Social Organization among Durrani Pashtuns in Northern Afghanistan, unpublished Ph.D. thesis, University of London.

Tapper, Richard (1979), 'Pasture and Politics. Economics Conflict and Ritual among Shahsevan Nomads of North-western Iran', Academic Press, London.

10 TRIBAL WARFARE IN AFGHANISTAN AND PAKISTAN: A REFLECTION OF THE SEGMENTARY LINEAGE SYSTEM

Louis Dupree

'Revenge is the best way to get even.' (Archie Bunker)(1)

To label any type of warfare 'positive' may seem strange in an age of weapons so sophisticated that personkind worries about self-annihilation. MAD refers not only to a satirical comicbook, but Mutually Assured Destruction. Volumes have been written since the Second World War to prove that the human species is not biologically computerized to fight, theorizing that the blame lies in culture (learned behavior). Human endeavors, according to this hypothesis, can be directed toward completely peaceful goals through judicious manipulation of cultures.(2)

Others maintain that personkind's basically aggressive nature precludes any such induced cultural changes.(3) The new socio-biologists advocate the supremacy of the genes: Any species, as groups and as individuals within groups, responds to the natural and social environments as a result of predetermined, genetically structured, biological and behaviorial traits which have evolved to maximize group survival potential.(4)

Wars, be they tribal feuds or world holocausts, must be justified by those who fight them. Blaming wars on man's assumed aggressive, atavistic instincts satisfies few. Neither do thematic variations on territorial integrity, property rights, or group honor. Possibly, elements of all the above factors (plus others) may contribute at different points in time and space to cause conflicts between individuals and groups.(5)

Whatever the reasons, the track record is clear. Throughout history and deep into prehistory, the evidence shouts of wars and rumors of wars. Some of our first decipherable written records (about 5,000 years ago) record Middle Eastern wars of conquest, complete with lists of tribute rendered by the conquered.(6)

Students of warfare often overlook the relationship between leisure time to fighting in the annual cycle of preindustrial peoples, even after contact with - and often dominance by - technologically superior imperialists. Warfare still plays a major seasonal role in some preindustrial societies, either in its pursuit or institutionalized avoidance, in itself a variety of conflict.(7)

During the annual economic cycle (agriculture, herding, gardening, hunting, gathering, or combinations of these), kin-oriented groups of varying sizes (depending on local ecology at any given period) work together to survive. In Afghanistan and Pakistan, in spite of massive expenditure on development (not unique in the Third World), agriculture and herding are still primarily subsistence oriented.

From early spring through early fall, the economic cycle dominates, and the intensity of the agricultural and herding activities force people to work cooperatively. Hard work helps suppress any tensions that arise. A period of relative leisure drifts in with late fall and lasts until the spring planting or migration with the herds. During the slack months, agricultural tools, mud huts and walls, tents and nomadic gear require only so much time to repair; folktales and folksongs can be told and sung only so many times before boredom sets in. No movies, professional sports, friendly neighborhood bars, or television exist to offer diversions, particularly in the zones of relative inaccessibility.(8) Even the ubiquitous transistor radios cannot contain off-season boredom and tensions. Long periods of inactivity and intimate contact bring latent (culturally induced, as we shall see) aggressions to the surface.

The formalized segmentary lineages in rural Afghanistan and Pakistan (strongest in the areas along the Durand Line of 1893) have developed a sensitive network of interlocking, reciprocal rights and obligations, not only between the kin-units, but between patrons and clients. Figure 10.1 illustrates an idealized Pushtun kin-tribal structure. The segmentary system functions with various levels of intensity depending on the situation at any given time. Different types of external and internal stress trigger off different responses. For example, when the British invaded Afghanistan four times in the nineteenth century (1839, 1842, 1878, 1879), the important political (i.e. military) responses came from the tribes, some opposing the British, some supporting.

Before the Second Anglo-Afghan War (1878-80), the sedentary Pushtun of south-central Afghanistan lived in clan villages or clan communities. Probably no pure single clan villages ever existed because *hamsaya* (clients or retainers), used as farm or casual labour, were other Pushtun who, for one reason or another, had been cast out from their local kin-unit. Outcast members of non-Pushtun ethnic groups also sought asylum with strong Pushtun khans.

Pre-1880 tribal and subtribal loyalties (see Figure 10.1) were largely territorial, and these loyalties are still important in areas of the original Pushtun homeland, the mountains along the Durand Line. The more important social and economic interactions took place at the clan community level. Lineage and clan (broken down in the late nineteenth century to become sub-lineages, with no commonality of residence) leadership governed the actions of the villagers.

When no external invasions (i.e. Persian, Moghul, British, Russian) threatened, the blood feud continued unabated among smaller kin-units, usually sublineage and below, because, in spite of the residual rights and obligations functioning at the lineage level and above, tensions can and do build up between individuals, families, and sublineages.(9) In south-central Afghanistan, most villages consist of several sublineages.

Figure 10.1 Simplified kin-tribal structure in Afghanistan

Approximate English equivalent	Pashto/Dari* terms	Kin-political units (one example)
Nation-state	Heywad (P); Watan (D)	Afghanistan (geographic entity)
Confederation	Wolus (P); Mellat (D)	Pushtun: Afghanistan in the cultural sense; or an individual ethnic group
Tribe	Qaum (DP); Qabila (D); Tabar (P)	Durrani: ethnic group in the political (often territorial) sense
Subtribe	Also Qaum, Qabila, Tabar; Khater, mainly Tajik	Zirak
Section	Suffix -zai, usually	Barakzai
Lineage	Suffix -zai, also P'sha (P)	Mohammadzai
Sublineage (sib) (former clan)	Khel (DP)	Yahya Khel
Extended family (with residential unity)	Khanawada (D); Plarghaney (P);** Nikaghaney (P)***	
Extended family (no residential unity - minimal reciprocal rights and obligations)	Kahol (P); Kurani (D)	Musahiban
Nuclear family	Famil; hastavi (DP); aulad (DP); dastaken (refers to group eating on same cloth): sandali (refers to group which gets warmth from same charcoal stove)	Ghazi

* Terms used by Dari speakers are often Arabic. In addition, the same terms often have different meanings in different areas.
** Term used if ego's father or uncle the head.
*** Term used if ego's grandfather is head.

In-group tensions usually relate to the inheritance of property and sex. Islamic law and local customs carefully delineate inheritance patterns, but wily brothers and uncles sometimes out-snooker less wily brothers and nephews. In many cases, inheritance rights of women (guaranteed in Islam) are either ignored or altered beyond recognition. Fights occur, and families break up to form new nuclear kin-units, which often results in self-perpetuating blood feuds.

When the village becomes two, it only favors enemies.(10)

Competition for mates can precipitate a crisis within a group. Afghan and Pakistani rural society is basically patriarchal, patrilineal, and patrilocal. Many matri-aspects survive, however, for marriage usually takes place within the village or a nearby village. In addition, preferred marriage is with father's brother's daughter, or as close to that kin status as possible, so male cousins are potential or actual rivals for daughters of paternal uncles. In reality, however, the ideal conditions often cannot be met, and marriages with mother's brother's daughters and even mother's or father's sister's daughters occur frequently. The competition for mates is further intensified because the adult male to female ratio is about 116 to 100.(11)

Families usually arrange marriages without consulting the principals, who ideally accept without complaint. Absence of open protest, however, does not imply the absence of subsurface emotional tensions in either or both of the potential mates.

Language sometimes reveals unarticulated (or downplayed) conflicts in a society. The term for cousin in Pashto is *turbur* the word for the worst kind of hatred is *turburghanay* which could be literally translated 'cousin-hatred'. But the non-literate, rural Pushtun deny this interpretation. They say: 'Turbur is turbur and turburghanay is turburghanay. They are separate words. How can they relate? How could I hate my cousin? I would fight to the death with him. I would never leave his body behind in a fight. I would give him my last crust of bread.'

The overwhelming majority of Afghans and Pakistanis cannot read and write, so showing them that the written *turbur* is a prefix and -*ghanay* a suffix, which, when combined create a compound word, fails to impress. Several Pashto proverbs, hint at 'cousin-hatred'.

A cousin's tooth breaks on another cousin's tooth.
Keep a cousin poor - and use him.

Traditionally, out-group Afghan and Pakistani (particularly among the Pushtun and Baluch) feuds involve *zan* (women), *zar* (literally gold, symbolizing portable property), and *zamin* (land, and other immovable property, including water rights). The Pushtun live by local versions of the Pushtunwali (or Pukhtunwali), the 'way of the Pushtun.' the 'code of the hills.' For one version, see the Appendix.

Nang,(12) the generic term for honor, sums up the whole. Several proverbs dealing with honor and shame give a clearer picture of the concept than a thousand words:

Die for the honor of family or friend.
I sacrifice my wealth for my head, but my head for my honor.
May my friend be shameless, and may I be shameless before him.
Look to a man's deeds, not whether he is short or tall.
The sweetest fellowship is that of the sword.
A dog surrounded turns tail, a man fights.
The brave man has no faults, and the true coward no shame.
Do not take a path that your father and mother would not follow.
Fear and shame are father and son.

Feuds may last for several generations, and current participants may have forgotten the original cause. At times, feuds lie dormant for years and then explode with unpredictable violence. The tribesmen of Afghanistan can be described as having a short fuse and a long feud.

Tribesmen fight to perpetuate their own groups and not to destroy or annihilate the enemy. They expend much more energy running up and down hills or riding horses and camels across deserts and plains than in fighting. Firefights can help drain off the sexually oriented, culturally induced, in-group aggressions. Men are killed, but the deaths seem almost incidental to the act of fighting. Enough are killed, however, to keep everyone's adrenalin up, and contesting groups remain emotionally tuned for the next round.

Blood must always be about equally spilled and property equally destroyed or taken, because if one side gains materially at the expense of the other, the seasonal feud might extend into the agricultural cycle contrary to the interests of both sides.

Tribal warfare, therefore, channels potential in-group violence over property rights and mate-preference toward out-group elements, usually neighboring tribes or subtribes within a tribe. This seasonal process of externalising internal aggression simply means shooting the hell out of strangers rather than one's kinsmen.

Tactics and weapons also limit casualties. Combatants favor surprise attacks just before dawn, hit and run and off with the loot.

> For a man, either a swift blow, or a swift flight.
> (Sir Jack Falstaff would be pleased! - L.D.)

Weapons ranged from matchlocks, flintlocks (with eighteenth to nineteenth century Tower firing mechanisms) and percussion cap rifles to high-powered weapons from Europe and the United States. Reasonable facsimiles of modern weapons are manufac-

tured in home industries at Darra (near Kohat) in Pakistan.
Protected by the separate laws that govern the six Federally
Administered Tribal Agencies (FATAs)(13), artisans produce
by hand (recently, some electrically powered machinery was
introduced) everything from Sten and Bren guns to Colt .45 cal.
automatics and Beretta 9mm (M1934) pistols, complete with
manufacturers' marks. The favorite weapon is still the old
reliable, bolt action British Lee-Enfield .303 rifle, 1908 model
(modified). Many tribesmen still use the breech-loading,
single-shot Martini-Henry rifle (1887 model).

Cottage industry weapons usually cannot be operated rapid
fire, for two reasons: the rifling in the barrel tends to warp,
and bolts sometimes fit improperly. But give the artisan a bolt
(stolen from the Pakistan army or the Frontier Corps) and he
will build a superb weapon around the bolt.(14)

Knives and daggers of all sizes and shapes are favorite
weapons for hand-to-hand fighting, avoided whenever possible,
however. Swords, once primary weapons, are seldom used today.

Let us now examine two examples of tribal warfare.

LUMBER RUSTLING IN PAKTYA

Paktya Province in eastern Afghanistan is one of the country's
few extensively wooded areas. Lumbering in winter brings in
sizeable extra, non-agricultural incomes to those groups lucky
enough to own forest stands. Both the Afghan and Pakistani
governments periodically attempt to exercise some control over
both the cutting and sale of the trees. For example, the Republic
of Afghanistan (1973-8) offered to pay top prices for the lumber
usually smuggled to Pakistan. The part-time lumbermen of
Paktya simply sold the government second-class lumber at first-
class prices, and continued to smuggle the best quality into
Pakistan, primarily through Parachinar to Thal. On both sides
of the Durand Line, a little baksheesh goes a long way - and
so does the lumber.

The Mangal and Jadran (sometimes spelled Zadran), two neighboring tribes engaged in the off-agricultural season lumber
trade, are traditional blood enemies.(15) Since the Second World
War, the Mangal-Jadran feud has been relatively quiet, but
occasionally explodes, usually affecting one or two local sections.

I spent part of the winter of 1962 in Paktya. One evening,
while collecting kinship terms in a Mangal village, someone in
the hut said, 'Be quiet!' We all listened as the clear, crisp sound
of axes felling a tree echoed. The headman picked up his Lee-
Enfield .303 and walked out, followed by the others. Thus
recommenced a feud which had been dormant for almost a decade.
The neighboring Jadran needed more mature trees to fill orders
from Pakistan, across the Durand Line.

Within a month, nine men out of a total 103 adult males in the
Mangal village lay dead. Almost an equal number (eight) of

Jadran had been killed, or so I learned later when I visited the Jadran area.

The folktales concerning 'the great lumber fight' reveal some basic elements in the concepts of local tribal warfare. When the Mangal tell the story, the Mangal 'win'; when the Jadran tell the story, the Jadran 'win.' And that is how it should be. In tribal warfare, *both* sides must 'win', which accounts for the insistence on an approximate equality of blood spilled and property looted.(16)

LIVESTOCK RUSTLING IN KUNAR

Figure 10.2 Idealized map showing raiding patterns (Kunar: 1963-4 raids = circled numbers)

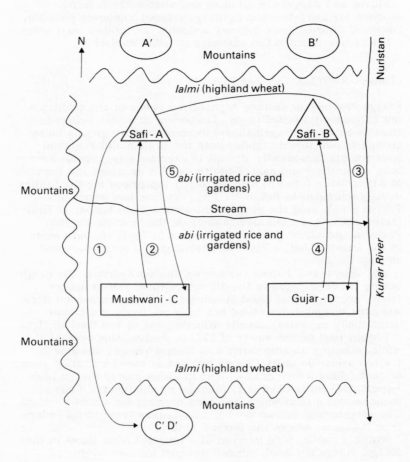

The Kunar River in Afghanistan flows along the edge of
Nuristan,(17) past a number of ethnolinguistic groups:
Nuristani, Mushwani Pushtun, Safi Pushtun, Gujar. The
Nuristani, in particular, fight over the diminishing grasslands.
The annual livestock raids, however, are more complicated than
the lumber rustling in Paktya.

Figure 10.2 illustrates the raiding patterns along a tributary
of the Kunar from late summer 1963 to early spring 1964.

The stream which flows west to east from the mountains into
the Kunar separates two Safi villages (A and B) from a Mushwani
Pushtun village (C) and its Gujar client village (D). The Gujar
(traditionally herdsmen) now own land and are primarily cultivators, a recent development (within the past thirty years).
They own livestock, mainly sheep and goats, but also some
cattle, the pattern for all groups in the region. The Gujar also
serve as herdsmen for the Mushwani, who include the Gujar
in their political sphere. The Gujar support the Mushwani in
return for protection.

The Safi summer pasturelands are labelled A' and B';
Mushwani, C'; Gujar, D'. The Mushwani and Gujar pasturages
overlap, and livestock sport distinctive painted designs and
clipped ears for ownership identification. Most shepherds,
however, know their flocks by sight. Only a small percentage
of the villagers in each group go to the mountains, a trip of
only a few hours, with the flocks. Young wives often accompany
their husbands, but seldom do the elderly move to the *yilaq*
(summer pasturages). The villages to which all move for the
winter are called *qishlaq*.

In the spring and summer, most people in all four villages
remain behind to farm, either in the lower irrigated area (*abi*),
or in the highland, unirrigated area (*lalmi*), adjacent to the
mountains. The lalmi is dependent on rainfall and snow melt.

During the late summer, crops (mainly wheat) in the lalmi
area are reaped, threshed, and winnowed. Several families move
to the lalmi, to watch over the threshed wheat, and assist in
the work.

Raid 1
In late summer 1963, while the wheat was being threshed and
winnowed, about a dozen young Safi from village A planned a
raid on the Mushwani yilaq (C'). Normally, raids begin after
the threshing floors are cleared, but the village A Safi smarted
because the Mushwani had struck early the year before. The
Safi warriors infiltrated at night and struck at first light, and
made off with a number of cattle, sheep, and goats. In the
brief firefight (about fifteen shots per side in 2-3 minutes),
one Gujar shepherd was killed by an explosive bullet.

The raiders made it safely back to village A. (Distance between
village A and village B is no more than 10 kilometers.)

Raids 2 and 3

The Mushwani waited until late October to retaliate. On a moon-less night, about twenty crossed the stream and struck straight at Safi village A. Little resistance met the dawn attack, and the Mushwani wondered why. The raiders killed three old men who put up a token resistance while the women and children fled. The Mushwani scooped up what portable loot they could carry, including rifles, ammunition, jewelry, metal bowls and jars, tins of vegetable oil, tea and sugar. They recovered most of their stolen livestock, and added a few Safi sheep and goats.

An almost full 5-gallon tin of gasoline, used for Petromax lanterns, encouraged the Mushwani to burn seven huts, normally not done, for this complicates the revenge requirements. Not only an eye for an eye, and a tooth for a tooth – but a house for a house. Although the houses are primarily sun-dried bricks and pressed mud, much lumber is used for roof beams, door frames and supports, and twigs and thatch interlace the roof beams. Fire may cause the roof to come tumbling down, but the walls usually stand, for they will be hardened by the fire.

> Although my house has been burned down, my house walls are stronger. (Interpreted: Out of evil comes good.)

Meanwhile, across the valley, the missing Safi males from village A had joined a group from village B to attack the Gujar village (D). Therefore, Raid 3 overlapped Raid 2. The Mushwani had waited so long to retaliate for the first raid that the Safi decided to strike again.

The Safi dawn attack forced the Gujar to flee to the hills. One old man in the village fired on the raiders, wounding one, and the other Safi, about twenty-five in number, hacked the old man to death with knives.

Smoke rising in the northwest startled the Safi warriors, so they immediately returned to their respective villages (A and B), laden with whatever household goods and commodities they could carry.

Raid 4

Safi village A now had to rebuild seven burned huts – and plot revenge. The Mushwani and their client (*hamsaya*) Gujar quickly planned a raid on Safi village B. The forty-man war party included about equal numbers of Mushwani and Gujar. The warriors hit village B in mid-December. The usual dawn attack proved successful, and the raiders returned laden with house-hold goods and a sizeable herd of sheep and goats. But one Mushwani and one Gujar had been killed, and several others wounded as the party slowly carried the corpses back to their respective villages for burial.

As time for spring planting approached, the score card stood as follows:

Safi	Mushwani-Gujar
3 killed.	4 killed.
Several wounded.	Several wounded.
Livestock stolen about equal, but Mushwani had slight advantage.	------------------
Household goods lifted about equal.	------------------
7 houses burned down.	No houses burned down.

Therefore, approximate equality in death and destruction existed in all categories but 'burned houses.'

·Raid 5

Several times during the lulls, the women from the four villages met informally by the stream. They exchanged information about the results of the raids: numbers of livestock lost, casualties, etc. A late-February moot by some women resulted in the fifth raid, during which the Mushwani moved in with their Gujar clients, leaving village C open. A small Safi raiding party entered village C unopposed and, having brought along their own kerosene, burned six empty houses. A seventh failed to ignite, as the kerosene gave out.

After Raid 5, both sides piled stones on a traditional mountain peak to the west, the equivalent of burying the hatchet - until the next fall.(18)

Not all annual feuds end as peacefully as the one described above, and seldom are houses destroyed. (Incidentally, a family of six can rebuild a mud hut in a week or two. The problem is to replace the lumber for the roof, doors, etc.; the Mushwani had removed these to the Gujar village, but the Safi had been caught with their roofs up.)

But, as is traditional, both sides 'won', or, in the words of the proverb: 'Neither was the ass mauled, nor the stick broken.'

WOMEN IN CONFLICT: ENEMIES AND LOVERS

When you're wounded and left on Afghanistan's plains,
An' the women come out to cut up what remains,
Jest roll to your rifle and blow out your brains -
An' go to your Gawd like a soldier.
                    (The Young British Soldier, from 'Barrack
                    Room Ballads,' by Rudyard Kipling)

Pathan [Pushtun-L.D.] women will come out and hack off the genitals. Then they will cram them in their [the dead English soldiers'-L.D.] mouths, the lips of which will be sewn over them.
                    ('By Command of the Viceroy,' by Duncan
                    MacNeill, New York, 1975, p. 29)

The ferocity of women toward prisoners taken in warfare has
been reported from the Plains Indians of North America all
across Asia.(19) Some women have been glorified in legend and
real combat. The probably mythical Amazons of the Classical
World had real-life counterparts among the partisan women of
the Second World War, and the French Foreign Legion fought
several tough battles against the 'Amazon regiments' of the king
of Madagascar (1892-4).(20)

Afghan history and folklore laud several women-warriors. The
Pushtun heroine, Malalay, used her veil as a standard, and
encouraged the fighting men at the Battle of Maiwand (27 July
1880) by shouting the following couplet (*landay*):(21)

Young love, if you do not fall at Maiwand;
By God! Someone is saving you as a token of shame!

The Afghans decisively defeated the British at Maiwand.
More often, however, women send their husbands and sons off
to fight with songs that encourage them (in the spirit of old
Sparta) to come home with their shields or on them:

If you don't wield a sword, what else will you do!
You, who have suckled at the breast of an Afghan mother!(22)

My beloved returned from battle a coward.
I regret the kisses I gave him last night!(23)

Without women like these in most societies, peace might have
a better chance, or, as James Garner said in the role of naval
Lt. Charles E. Madison in the movie 'The Americanization of
Emily': 'Wars are perpetuated by widows weeping over graves.'(24)

But it is probably culture and not 'human nature' that determines such attitudes.

More importantly, in the tribal societies of Afghanistan and
Pakistan, women are the ultimate repositories of *nang*, the
term that embodies the totality of a group's honor.(25)

Play jests, but not with a married woman.
When a man feels no shame about his own sister,
     what scruples will he feel about another man's?

The traditional penalty for adultery is death by stoning for
both participants. Contrary to popular belief, however, probably
more sexual hanky-panky exists in the villages of Afghanistan
and Pakistan than in Western suburbia. In arranging assig-
nations, women are usually the aggressors, for this is one way
they can strike back at the men, who consider them inferior.(26)

Someone said to the woman, 'Your lover is dead.'
     She asked, 'Which one?'

She said, 'What have you done by leaving me?
     I, who have curls lying on my face,
     shall take a better lover.'

Villagers and nomads don't just talk about it; they do it.

> A love meeting, though just for a moment's duration,
>   is sweeter than the grapes of Kohistan -
>   or the melons of Kandahar.

The group does not want to purge itself of two important
economically functioning and biologically productive individuals,
so, in most cases, a conspiracy of silence covers the lovers.
Only when both parties become flagrantly open about the affair
will the wronged spouses and close kinsmen resort to the ultimate stoning - a rarity.(27)

Occasionally, tribesmen steal women during feuds, or women
voluntarily leave with lovers for another group. The affront to
nang is much more serious than internal adultery, and much
blood has been shed over such insults to group honor. In
addition, wives and daughters of *maldar* (wealthy nomads) wear
coins of various denominations and ages (some going back to
the Indo-Bactrian dynasties, 2,000 years old), sewn or
embroidered into their clothing. These women are virtually
walking banks, so women-stealing is as much for fiscal as
sexual reasons.

To end a feud over woman-rustling, honor must be satisfied.
Either, the group that has gained a woman must agree to send
one in exchange to the deprived husband or father, or, amounts
of money and property, mutually agreed upon in a *jirga* (village
council) must be paid.

Women, therefore, help launch and perpetuate feuds (just as
Helen of Troy launched a thousand ships) by encouraging their
men to fight, and involving other men to fight for their charms.
Being the embodiment of the group's nang has its drawbacks -
and its compensations. Inferiority (as defined by the male) and
superiority (as perceived by the female) combine in a charming
- and deadly - mass of contradictions.(28)

PREINDUSTRIAL WARFARE AND POPULATION CONTROL (29)

Marvin Harris (quoting Joseph Birdsell) recently pointed out
that females are more important than males in limiting, maintaining, or increasing populations - if cultural patterns do not
interfere.

> Undoubtedly, one able-bodied male could keep ten women
> continuously pregnant. . . . This would produce the same
> number of births as if the group consisted of ten men and
> ten women. But if we can imagine a local group of ten men
> and only one woman, the birth rate would necessarily be ten
> percent of the former example. *The number of women deter-
> mines the rate of fertility.*(30)

Pastoral nomads recognized this fact quite early in the
domestication of animals. Also, modern herdsmen prefer to sell

or eat rams and billy goats rather than ewes and nannies. Many groups castrate or otherwise render young male animals infertile to increase herd wealth, leaving only a few destined for stud-dom.

Cultural factors can limit male access to females as efficiently as an actual physical shortage of females. Two factors (one cultural, one physical) in rural Afghanistan and Pakistan encourage the perpetuation of this inaccessibility, thus creating a sizeable pool of frustrated bachelors. The effect of transferring bachelordom's frustrations to the political scene (especially in the cities) remains a subject for study.

The two factors mentioned above are (1) widows of slain warriors often do not remarry, and, therefore, have no further offspring, or, if they become pregnant, prefer to abort;(31) (2) female infanticide, mainly through neglect. These (and other) factors, such as rural-urban migrations, have helped keep the rural population relatively stable until recently. Tribal warfare has been an integral part of the process. To quote Harris:

> Bands and villages were exceptional in their use of warfare to achieve very low rates of population growth. They achieved this not primarily through male combat deaths – which, as we have seen, are always easily compensated for by calling upon the remarkable reproductive reserves of the human female – but by another means that was intimately cojoined with and dependent upon the practice of warfare yet was not part of the actual fighting. I refer to female infanticide. Warfare in band and village societies made the practice of female infanticide sex-specific. It encouraged the rearing of sons, whose masculinity was glorified in preparation for combat, and the devaluation of daughters, who did not fight. This in turn led to the limitations of female children by neglect, abuse and outright killing.(32)

A great affection exists between fathers and daughters in Afghan and Pakistani tribal society. Do fathers feel an unconscious guilt for those who died and therefore compensate with excessive tender, loving care?

Sons are preferred for several reasons: (1) if a man has ten sons and three are killed in a feud, he has seven left, a source of political power; (2) the more sons, the more land the family can farm, either as actual owners, or in various owner-tenant combinations; (3) surplus sons can be set up in bazaar shops, and increase the family's economic power; (4) or, temporarily, work on development projects; (5) many families want to send sons to school to train to become government bureaucrats or military officers, giving the family influence in and protection from official interference. A son also guarantees a man's masculinity (the macho syndrome), and a woman who gives birth to a son at last achieves adult status.

Male combat deaths *do* affect population control if the culture denies males access to surviving fertile females. Let us return to the Paktya lumber war for examples. All but one of the nine Mangal fatalities had been married. Of the eight widows, only one remarried, and she became an *ambok* (second wife) of an elder brother of her slain husband. The other widows were all young enough to remarry, but two refused to become second wives and moved in with married brothers. Brother-sister ties are often more intense than any other relationships in a nuclear family. Another widow could not remarry because her 12-year-old son considered himself the man of the family - and was backed by his paternal uncles. The remaining four returned to work in their parental households. Young bachelors preferred not to accept damaged or second-hand goods. I do not know if any of the widows subsequently remarried, but adult males predicted they would not be able to find mates, in spite of the high male to female ratio.

In conclusion, let me emphasize that the ideal personality type is the warrior-poet, a man brave in battle and eloquent at the village or tribal council.(33)

TRIBAL WARFARE AND FAMILY FEUDS INTRUDE ON THE URBAN SCENE

Post Second World War development programs brought many Afghans to Kabul and other urban centers to take advantage of new economic opportunities. Some were transients who worked in the off-agricultural season and returned to their villages in the spring.(34) Others, particularly those working as servants for the expanding foreign community, remained for several years before returning home with their savings to buy land, set up shops, pay off debts, and acquire brides.

These temporary rural to urban migrations (combined with warfare, female infanticide, and the other processes discussed in this report) have enabled the villages with which I am familiar to maintain a relatively stable population, practically zero growth.

But, as a result, the urban populations have exploded drastically with the expected disruptions and dislocations of peoples and values. Although the workers became urban-based, most remained rural-oriented, which exacerbated extra-family feuds and intra-family conflicts. For example, a young Tajik from the Panjsher Valley north of Kabul came to the capital to work as a servant in foreigners' households. Before leaving his village, he was betrothed to a 13-year-old cousin (Fa Bro Da), but several years lapsed before he earned enough to pay the proper 'bride price.'(35)

Once or twice a year, he returned home to visit his family, and assure himself that all was well. He earned enough in five years to consummate the marriage. Elated, he brought the money to his village, only to find that another cousin (Fa Sis So) had made the bride's father (an uncle to both cousins) an offer he couldn't refuse: double the original, agreed-on 'bride price.'

The frustrated cousin and his brothers waited in ambush for the sexual usurper, and beat him senseless with wooden clubs. The assailants returned to their jobs in Kabul. The brothers of the beaten cousin cornered the father of the frustrated cousin and fractured his skull. Kinsmen brought the old man to a hospital in Kabul, and he survived.

Meanwhile, two armed bands, representing the factions involved, descended on Kabul. They stationed themselves outside the compound of the foreigner for whom the frustrated cousin worked. No shots were fired, but fist fights broke out and the police had to intervene. Several on both sides were arrested.

Police authorities encouraged the combatants to settle their differences outside the law courts. All concerned agreed to hold a *majlis* (council). Since blood spilled was about equal (and no one killed), they decided to call off the fighting. The uncle consented (under pressure from all involved) to give the frustrated cousin a younger daughter at the original 'bride price.'

Often, the two principal antagonists (the competing male cousins) had tea together in the respective foreigners' houses where they worked. The feud had ended amicably.

Modern technology brought modern elements into local feuds. The lorry and the bus followed the new and improved roads into rural Afghanistan and Pakistan. Some Afghans with urban jobs invested part of their savings on lorries and buses. As newcomers attempted to muscle into already functioning transportation networks, fights broke out. Officially, the government preferred to remain aloof unless the disputes violently sloughed over into the urban scene. Unofficially, transportation competitors bribed officials to remain neutral until the antagonists reached compromises - or one group drove the others out, or bought them off.

Some Westerners (and Western-educated Afghans and Pakistanis) have half-facetiously suggested the introduction of spectator blood sports (like soccer, football-European style) on a large scale to help channel off-season aggressions into activities less deadly than the feud. However, compared to some pre- and post-game clashes between fans and the law in Europe and elsewhere, tribal warfare might appear to be more functional, and, occasionally, less bloody.

Also, and seriously, the problem of meaningful regional autonomy must be settled in both Afghanistan and Pakistan before anything as mild as county cricket can be introduced.

Sports and games reflect cultures. (36) Buzkashi, played on horseback in the plains of northern Afghanistan, gives the *chapandaz* (master players) and spectators (who sometimes fight over goals scored, because much betting takes place) the opportunity to express violent opinions. In addition, local power elites can, like the owners of baseball teams and race horses, compete for the thrill of purchasing a team of superior horses and chapandaz. Inter-group violence at several levels may have been partly channelled into this competition. (37)

In societies where extra-curricula activities are at a premium during the slack economic season, the entertainment aspect of tribal warfare cannot be discounted. Even the women on opposing sides sometimes meet to compare casualties, i.e. scorecards.

How does the *badal* (blood feud) affect the urban educated middle class, many of whom are first generation literates? Let us examine two examples which occurred within the past five years. Both men had been educated abroad; one in the USSR, the other in a British-oriented Pakistani university. One had a brother killed; the other a son. Both prided themselves on their Western outlook and attitudes and assured me they would never get involved in a local, 'backward,' family feud. But, goes the Pashto proverb: 'When a son and brother have been murdered, who will restrain his hand?'

Both men took off their Western clothes, went to their villages dressed in loose-flowing *pyron-tombon* (pyjama-type clothing), armed with recently purchased pistols. One asked if I could get him an M-16. The feuds continue.

Blood money, the amount determined by a *jirga* or *majlis* (village councils) or such famous traditional arbiters as the Ahmadzai Ghilzai Pushtun, can be accepted. Many feuds still smoulder in Afghanistan and Pakistan, however, over *zan* and *zamin*. Both governments continue their efforts to have all cases of violent death, no matter what the cause, pass through the established legal system.

In conclusion, the positive aspects of tribal warfare (where it survives) can be summarized as follows:

1 The externalization of a group's internal aggressiveness (whatever the cause) helps limit in-group violence.
2 Both sides involved 'win,' and, theoretically, a moderate exchange of property and bloodshed results.
3 The entertainment aspect is present.
4 Population control mechanisms work through a combination of female infanticide (mainly through neglect), male deaths associated with partial denial of access to fertile females.

But 'progress' cannot be stopped, and annually more roads creep into the zones of relative inaccessibility, seldom peacefully. Much of the affected area is included in what Amir Abdur Rahman (1880-1901) referred to as Yaghistan, 'The Land of Insolence,' but he did not mean the frustrated negative insolence of urbanized, dehumanized persons in industrialized societies, but the insolence of harsh freedoms set in a backdrop of rough mountains and deserts, the insolence of equality felt and practiced (with an occasional pinch of superiority on all sides), the insolence of bravery past and bravery anticipated.

Law and order, with its attendant graft and corruption, follows the roads, and government officials, police, gendarmes and other paramilitary personnel become involved in local disputes. Some sincerely try to function as honest brokers in conflict situations; others prefer to be bought off by the most affluent among the participants. Ultimately, national politics intrude on the rural scene, often ignoring the true local and regional problems.(38)

As part of the rural sector moves (at least, temporarily) to the urban scene, and the urban scene (mainly, the government) moves to the rural, the days of positive tribal warfare become numbered as midnight-to-dawn arrests replace the early-morning ambush.(40)

Lucas a non lucendo!

APPENDIX   'PASHTUNWALI'(39)

To avenge blood.

To fight to the death for a person who has taken refuge with me no matter what his lineage. (Example: If a man, rich or poor, kills a man of another lineage, he can force anyone outside the slain man's lineage to help him simply by killing a sheep in front of that individual's tent.)

To defend to the last any property entrusted to me.

To be hospitable and provide for the safety of the person and property of guests.

To refrain from killing a woman, a Hindu, a minstrel, or a boy not yet circumcised.

To pardon an offense on the intercession of a woman of the offender's lineage, a Sayyid or a mullah. (An exception is made in the case of murder; only blood-money can erase this crime.)

To punish all adulterers with death.

To refrain from killing a man who has entered a mosque or the shrine of a holy man so long as he remains within its precincts; also to spare a man in battle who begs for quarter.

(L. Dupree, 'Afghanistan,' Princeton, 1980, pp. 126-7.)

NOTES

1   Quoted on title page of 'The Turquoise Lament,' by John D. MacDonald, 1973.
2   Marvin Harris, 'Cannibals and Kings,' New York, 1978, p. 60 and bibliography. I would like to contribute two new social 'laws': Dupree Law Number I: Personkind, regardless of race, creed, color, or sex, is rotten to the core. Given a weapon (not necessarily a gun - an automobile or legal system will do nicely) and the opportunity, he or she will prove it. Dupree Law Number II: When given a technological choice, person-

kind will select the path which is more beneficial in the short
run, and more destructive in the long run. (Harris tends to
support the latter; deny the first.)

3 Robert Ardrey, 'The Territorial Imperative,' New York, 1971;
   and his leading critic for balance, Ashley Montague, 'The
   Nature of Human Aggression,' New York, 1976.
4 E.O. Wilson, 'Sociobiology: The New Synthesis,' Harvard,
   1976.
5 Robert Harrison, 'Warfare,' Minneapolis, 1973; Morton Fried,
   M. Harris, R. Murphy (eds), 'War: The Anthropology of
   Conflict and Aggression,' Garden City, New York, 1968; M.A.
   Nettleship, R.D. Givens, and A. Nettleship (eds), 'War,
   Its Causes and Correlates,' Chicago, 1975. Specific references
   to Afghanistan in J. Anderson and R. Strand (eds), Ethnic
   Processes and Intergroup Relations in Contemporary Afghani-
   stan, 'Occasional Paper No. 15, Afghanistan Council of the
   Asia Society,' New York, 1978.
6 M. Webb, The Flag Follows Trade, in 'Ancient Civilization and
   Trade,' J. Sabloff and C.C. Lamberg-Karlovsky (eds),
   University of New Mexico Press, 1975.
7 L. Dupree, Afghan and British Military Tactics in the First
   Anglo-Afghan War (1838-1842), 'The Army Quarterly and
   Defence Journal,' United Kingdom, 107(2): 214-21, 1977. I
   cannot resist quoting E.B. White, 'The Once and Future
   King,' Dell Printing, 1964: 'Look at the Norman myths about
   legendary figures like the Angevin kings. From William the
   Conqueror to Henry the Third, they indulged in warfare
   seasonally. The season came round, and off they went in
   splendid armour which reduced the risk of injury to a fox-
   hunter's minimum. Look at the decisive battle of Brenneville
   in which a field of 900 knights took part, and only three were
   killed' (p. 235).
8 Although both Pakistan and Afghanistan have television
   (introduced with Japanese assistance), few sets exist outside
   urban centers.
9 L. Dupree and L. Albert, 'Afghanistan in the 1970s,' New York
   and London, 1974, Chapter 1. C. Lindholm, The Segmentary
   Lineage System: Its Applicability to Pakistan's Political Structure, in 'Pakistan's Western Borderlands', Ainslee Embree
   (ed.), New Delhi, 1977, pp. 41-6, discusses the problem
   from the local to the national level.
10 Pashto proverbs will be used to illustrate several points discussed in the text.
11 'National Demographic and Family Guidance Survey of the
   Settled Population of Afghanistan. Vol. I: Demography and
   Knowledge, Attitudes and Practices of Family Guidance,'
   sponsored by the Government of Afghanistan and USAID
   contract to State University of New York (Buffalo).
12 Akbar S. Ahmed, 'Social and Economic Change in the Tribal
   Areas,' Oxford (Karachi), 1977, pp. 20-2, 39; L. Dupree,
   Ajmal Khattak: Revolutionary Pushtun Poet, 'AUFS Fieldstaff
   Reports,' South Asia Series XX(9), 1976. For comparative

material, see D.M. Hart, 'The Aith Waryagar of the Moroccan Rif,' University of Arizona Press, 1976.

13 Akbar S. Ahmed, op. cit., note 12 (above). FATAs area: Bajaur, Mohmand, Khyber, Orakzai, Kurram, North Waziristan, South Waziristan - plus several Frontier Regions near Peshawar, Kohat, Bannu, and Dera Ismail Khan.

14 Robert Wilkinson-Latham and Angus McBride, 'North-West Frontier, 1937-47,' London, 1977.

15 See Ethnic Map in L. Dupree, Anthropology in Afghanistan, 'AUFS Fieldstaff Reports,' South Asia Series XX(5), 1976, p. 5. Other paired Pushtun feuds include: Afridi-Shinwari, Waziri-Shinwari, Orakzai-Durrani, Ghilzai-Durrani, Khattak-Yusufzai.

16 In a recent personal communication with Ashraf Ghani, he indicated that his research shows that major victories and defeats did occur when larger tribal units were involved. However, that is another story (nation-building) and outside the scope of this chapter.

17 For references, see L. Dupree, Anthropology in Afghanistan, cited in note 15 (above).

18 W. Divale, F. Chamberis, D. Gangloff, War, Peace and Marital Residence in Pre-industrial Societies, 'Journal of Conflict Resolution' 20(1): 57-78, 1976. The two cases (Paktya and Kunar) discussed in this chapter partly support the findings of Divale et al., that is, patrilineal groups normally fight neighboring groups with similar ethnolinguistic patterns. The Baluch (living in southwest Afghanistan, southeast Iran, and western Pakistan) prove an exception to the rule. They do fight neighboring Baluch (as well as Brahui and Pushtun, who speak different languages), but, in the eighteenth and nineteenth centuries, they undertook raids deep into Central Asia. They always returned to their home territories in Baluchistan after the raids. Probably, the Baluch 'external warfare' (Divale's term) related to their seminomadic way of life, but again contrary to Divale's findings, they were not seeking new pasturelands, but slaves and loot. They always returned to their homes in Baluchistan after the raids. Pax Britannica ended the raids in the late nineteenth century.

   Other exceptions: Nuristanis not only fight among themselves, but with neighboring Dardic speakers and Gujar, mainly over control of pasturelands. For a discussion of settlement patterns, see L. Dupree, Settlement and Migration Patterns in Afghanistan, 'Modern Asian Studies' 9(3): 385-400, 1975.

19 Possibly, torture and mutilation increase in intensity with the distance of the prisoner of war from his home country - or tribal base.

20 J. Wellard, 'The French Foreign Legion,' Boston and Toronto, 1974, pp. 59-64.

21 Personal communication, S. Sphoon. Also see A.R. Benawa, Landay, 'Paṣto' 1(1): 29-32, 1977, for a discussion of *landay* as a folk art form.

22 A.R. Benawa, 'Landay,' Kabul: Educational Press, 1958, p. 36.

23 Ibid., p. 42.
24 Quoted in R. Harrison, 'Warfare,' Minneapolis, 1973, p. 56.
25 See note 12.
26 Allah, in His Infinite Wisdom, created two sexes. Therefore,
   regardless of inferiority or superiority, He guaranteed conflict. Possibly, one root to the problem goes back to a simple
   biological fact which has bugged men for millennia: A woman
   always knows that she is the mother of her children, but a
   husband often wonders if he is the father. In preindustrial
   societies where close relatives are potential mates, biological
   parenthood is not as important as sociological parenthood,
   for the child will have some of its more intense rights and
   obligations with its mother's brother. This fuzzy biological
   father syndrome may be at least partly responsible for the
   development of the males' sexist complex, so ably articulated
   by M. Harris (see note 2, and Why Men Dominate Women,
   'New York Times Magazine,' 13 November 1977, pp. 46,
   115–23). Even in the developed world, men must realize that
   any woman, looking vaguely hominid, can enter any bar and
   emerge a short time later with a conquest. Men, on the other
   hand, can spend months attempting the same feat. The
   superiority of women in this instance cannot be denied.
27 The studies of Chaudri Mohammad Ali ('And then the Pathan
   Murders,' Peshawar, 1966) and Justice Shamsher Bahadur
   ('Some Murder Cases I Have Judged,' Lahore, 1978) reveal
   the prominence of adultery-connected murder cases in
   Pakistani law courts. For example, Justice Bahadur discussed
   twenty-two cases: three involved theft, and one each,
   property rights, a local political struggle, water rights,
   a gambling debt, a drunken brawl. The other fourteen
   involved either the murder of a husband by a lover at the
   instigation of the wife (six), or the murder of an unfaithful
   wife or lover (eight). For other examples of adultery related
   murder, see Col. (Rtd.) Eric (Buster) Goodwin, 'Life Among
   the Pathans (Khattaks),' 1969, 1975 (2nd edn), available for
   £1 from 56 Addison Avenue, London W11; J.W. Spain, 'The
   Way of the Pathans,' London, 1962; S.S. Thorburn, 'Bannu:
   Our Afghan Frontier,' London, 1876 (several proverbs
   quoted in this report are from Thorburn). A final typical
   Victorian quote from Algernon Durand, 'The Making of a
   Frontier,' London, c. 1900, referring to Gilgit and Baltistan:
   'Among the peoples murders are very rare, and are almost
   invariably the result of a slip on the part of a lady' (p. 207).
28 A study on this topic by Professor Rasool Amin of Kabul
   University is in press.
29 L. Dupree, Population Dynamics in Afghanistan (LD-7-'70)
   'AUFS Reports,' South Asia Series XIV (7), 1970.
30 M. Harris, 'Cannibals and Kings,' New York, 1977, p. 39.
   Quoted from Joseph Birdsell, 'Human Evolution,' Chicago,
   1972, pp. 357–8.
31 See note 11 (above): Abortion is discussed in detail.
32 Harris, op. cit., 1977, p. 40.
33 L. Dupree, Functions of Folklore in Afghan Society, 'Asian

Affairs,' 66(1): 51-61, 1979. For other discussions, see C.H. Wang, Towards Defining a Chinese Heroism, 'Journal of the American Oriental Society' 95(1): 25-35, 1975; D.N. Lorenzen, Warrior Ascetics in Indian History, 'Journal of the American Oriental Society,' 98(1): 61-75, 1978.

34 See Dupree reference in note 18 (above). Consult bibliography for additional sources.

35 The 'bride price' is essentially an economic exchange in Afghanistan and Pakistan. The family loses a valuable economic member if the bride leaves the vicinity of her extended kingroup, and the bride price helps compensate for the loss. In addition, the girl's dowry of household goods equals (or exceeds) the bride price. If the bride and groom live in the same or neighboring villages, neither the bride price nor the dowry travels far. If the newlyweds are close kin (the ideal), the exchange of mates and goods is socially and politically reinforcing as well. The new rural to urban migrations (even temporary) have complicated the matter by increasing competitions for brides, thereby intensifying ingroup pressures.

36 R. Lowie, in 'Indians of the Plains,' New York, 1954, calls this 'warfare as play.'

37 For descriptions of the game, see A. Balikci, Buzkashi, 'Natural History,' 87(2): 54-63, 1978; L. Dupree, Kessel's 'The Horsemen,' the Culture, the Book, the Movie, 'AUFS Fieldstaff Reports,' South Asia Series XX(6), 1978; W. Azoy, 'Buzkashi,' Pennsylvania University Press, 1982.

38 Lindholm, op. cit., see note 9 (above).

39 For other recent published works, see: A. Janata (1975) Ghairatman-Der Gute Pashtune. Exkurs über die Grundlagen des Pashtunwali, 'Afghanistan Journal,' 2: 83-97; Willi Steul (1973) 'Eigentumsprobleme innerhalb paschtunisher Gemeinschaften in Paktia/Afghanistan,' Heidelberg; Willi Steul (1980) 'Paschtunwali- ein Ehrenkodex und seine rechtliche Relevanz,' Wiesbaden.

40 This paper was written before the Soviet invasion of Afghanistan (24 December 1979). I am now writing a book about Afghan cultural reactions to the intervention. Basically, the regionally oriented vertical kinship structures, which fight one another in 'normal' times, have responded in predictable ways, just as they did when the British invaded the Afghan area in the nineteenth century. When an outside horizontal force threatens the internal vertical segmentary units, traditional rivals (such as the Mangal and Jadran) unite to drive out (or at least, resist) the invaders. Regional unity inside Afghanistan has been slowly evolving since 1980. However, given the ethnolinguistic complexity of Afghanistan, a national liberation movement will take a long time to evolve.

11 RELIGIOSITY, VALUES AND ECONOMIC CHANGE AMONG SHEIKHANZAI NOMADS

Bahram Tavakolian

The following discussion is based on field research conducted among Sheikhanzai pastoral nomads of north-west Afghanistan in the spring and summer of 1977. My objective in this research was to investigate systems of belief, ritual, and cultural values and to demonstrate their effects on patterns of economic activity and ecological adaptation. Such an investigation is novel in studies on pastoralism because of the attention devoted here to ideological aspects of adaptation and because of the apparently uncharacteristic religiosity of this population of pastoral nomads. In this discussion, after presenting a descriptive summary of aspects of Sheikhanzai society and culture, I will focus my attention on how the Islamic, Afghan, and nomadic values of the Sheikhanzai influenced their participation in the programs of the Herat Livestock Development Corporation during the period of my investigations.

SETTING

The Sheikhanzai are black-tent dwelling, sheep-and-goat herders, the majority of whom migrate between winter pastures in Gulran, in the northern portion of the province of Herat, and summer pastures near the towns of Shahrak and Chaghcharan, in the province of Ghor. They belong to the parent tribe of Pashtu-speaking Isakzai Durrani nomads who began to settle in north-western Afghanistan in the latter part of the nineteenth century at the direction of Abdur Rahman. They recognize affiliation within a segmentary lineage structure with other Isakzai; intermarriage is relatively common between these groups; and individual camp groups of Sheikhanzai are sometimes composed of members from these different lineage segments. In total there are approximately 1,000 nomadic tent-households of Sheikhanzai, and there are 500 more tent-households of Sheikhanzai who have been sedentary since the drought years of the early 1970s. They comprise a total population of 10,000 of the Isakzai's estimated 200,000 members.

SHEIKHANZAI ECONOMY AND SOCIETY

Both nomadic and sedentary Sheikhanzai are fully dependent on a livestock economy, and only scattered individuals own agricul-

tural land, which in all cases is farmed by non-Sheikhanzai.
The migrations of the nomadic camps take place according to a
pre-arranged schedule and to known and specified locations;
however, the Sheikhanzai do not own land along the migration
route, and only a few families hold official title to grazing land
in either winter or summer pasture areas. The spring migration
begins in late March, after *nowruz* or New Year, and covers
350 kilometers in a thirty-day period. The Sheikhanzai camps
move independently of their flocks in the fall, and this migration is slightly faster, taking twenty-four days in late August
and early September to complete. Although there are only these
two major population movements each year, the Sheikhanzai
also move their animals to warmer areas in late winter in preparation for spring lambing and shearing activities. In addition,
some camps are forced to move to two or three different locations
during the summer months because of annual fluctuations in the
availability of water and grass and because of land conflicts
with settled populations of Dari-speaking agriculturalists.

The nomads claim unofficial title to pasture lands, particularly
in summer pasture areas, on the basis of ancestral rights
bestowed upon them by Abdur Rahman. Their ties to winter
grazing areas are more tenuous in their view because they
shifted locations only fifteen to twenty years ago from lands
farther south. In both of their sedentary locations, Sheikhanzai
pasture rights are legally unrecorded, and land disputes with
settled village populations are common. Especially in the period
since the drought years of 1970 and 1971, during which many
Sheikhanzai and other Pashtu-speaking pastoral nomads have
not been able to carry out semi-annual migrations, much previously uncultivated land has been taken over by Taimani
villagers regardless of nomads' claims of ownership. Sometimes
nomads have worked out agreements with villagers such that
the latter group will work nomads' lands in return for a portion
of the wheat crop, but rarely do the nomads receive such compensation. It has been more common for nomads to find their
access to pasture and water blocked by new village cultivation.
If their lands are ruined by the nomads' flocks, villagers
resort to the local government to collect damage payments,
leaving the nomads feeling more cramped in pasture areas than
in the past and also feeling exploited by both villagers and
government officials.

Unlike other 'vertical nomads' in Turkey and Iran, major
population concentrations of Sheikhanzai occur during the winter
and not during the summer. Camps may be composed of as
many as fifty tents during the period from October to February,
while, during the migrations and in the summer pastures between
May and mid-August, camps are composed of as few as one tent
or as many as twelve. These camps are normally separated by
a one-hour walk from neighboring camp sites and pasture areas,
but visiting between camps is a regular activity.

The summer camp group is fundamentally a herding unit and

not primarily a kinship unit. Individual households herd their
animals together in one or more flocks of 400-600 animals, a
figure which also limits the number of households which may be
grouped together. Camp members are drawn widely from both
affinal and consanguineal groups, and some members are not
immediate relatives at all. A patrilineal ideology of common
descent is expressed when camp members refer to each other
as *kakazadeh* (or FaBrCh), but this reference is extended both
vertically, across generations, and horizontally to more distant
cousins.

Shepherds are formally hired by camp members for one-year
contracts of service to care for a single flock of 400-600 sheep
and goats. They receive one lamb (or kid) for every ten born
in the spring following their year's work. If they quit earlier,
there is no pro-rated agreement because no lambs have yet
been born. Each household owns and milks its own animals
separately although grazing them together, and the different
households contribute to the shepherd's pay, food, and other
material needs according to the number of animals they own.
The shepherd also has one or two assistants who are either
formally hired or sent out in rotation from each tent-household
at the rate of one night's work for every twenty animals owned.

Individual tents range in composition from a simple nuclear
family of three to four people to a maximum of seventeen people,
including brothers, their wives and children, unmarried sisters,
parents, and widowed aunts and uncles. The residence pattern
is ideally patrilocal, but in practice may also be avunculocal
and uxorilocal. Composition of a camp may vary from year to
year, and it may even change in the middle of a single season
in the event of conflict between households, dissatisfaction with
shepherding arrangements, or the sense that the grass for
animals might be better elsewhere. The Sheikhanzai say simply
that 'We go wherever our animals will be happy and well-fed,'
but this statement can sometimes serve as a rationalization for
other motives for separation from fathers, brothers, and other
camp members.

There are no official centralized leadership roles among the
Sheikhanzai, but certain individuals are given terms of honor
and political significance such as *sarkhel,* or headman of the
camp, and *malik* or *khan,* or big man of the lineage or territory.
The sarkhel normally owns more animals than other camp members and is headman by virtue of his chief responsibility in
joint herding and migrating arrangements. Decision-making
and leadership are very much at the local level, but the system
of segmentary lineages which cross-cuts camp divisions allows
the coordination of economic and political activities within larger
population segments. Tent-households share ancestral land
rights with other households descendant from different branches
of families with common genealogical roots. The Sheikhanzai of
Chaghcharan, for instance, share a common summer pasture
area across a number of separate lineage divisions. However,

they argue that the six Sharak lineages are not true Sheikhanzai but the descendants of a Hazara *mazdur*, or hired worker, who married a Sheikhanzai woman.

Village and nomad contacts are frequent and not always conflict-ridden. There is some exchange and purchase of animals back and forth; and, more important for the economy of both communities, there is purchase of wheat and sale of surplus wool, goat-hair tent strips, and dairy products. Animals are more commonly sold in the town bazaars, along the migration route and in summer pasture areas, and at the annual sheep market in Chaghcharan. Such sales provide the basis for cash purchases of items such as tea, candy, clothes, cooking ware, fodder, etc. throughout the year.

The part that Afghan nomads play in both the domestic and export economies of Afghanistan is considerable through their provision to the market of meat, skins, wool, karakul, *roghan* (butter oil), and *ghrut* (dehydrated whey). In drought years the price of wheat rises substantially, while animals and animal products do not increase in value as rapidly. As a consequence, nomads are threatened on two fronts in dry years:

1 The lack of rainfall results in a shortage of grass; hence the nomads' animals are less well-fed and small, less resistant to disease, and able to provide only small quantities of dairy products.
2 The value of such animals is reduced, causing cash shortages for purchases of winter fodder for animals and wheat and other items for human consumption.

The problem is self-perpetuating in that nomads attempt to make up for the lower prices available for their animals by maintaining larger flocks. Thus, grass and fodder supplies after a drought year continue to decrease, leading to further reductions in the health and value of the flocks as well as to problems of over-grazing. Normal ecological and economic processes would result in a reduction of the nomad population as they have done in Iran and Turkey, but kinship sentiment and mutual assistance activities operate among Sheikhanzai and other Isakzai nomads to maintain the nomadic population relatively constant while perhaps reducing the economic viability of the total pastoralist population.

ASPECTS OF NOMADIC IDEOLOGY:
RELIGION AND CULTURAL VALUES

Quite unlike stereotypes maintained by settled populations, and also unlike accounts of nomads in other portions of the Muslim world (Evans-Pritchard 1949; Barth 1964), the Sheikhanzai demonstrate a great respect for mullahs and for religious knowledge and participation. Regular prayer five times a day is

by no means universal, any more than it is within any other
Muslim population, but prayer is common among both young and
old, and also among some women who pray within their tents.

The Sheikhanzai belong to the Hanafi sect of Islam, but some
Sheikhanzai in Gulran and Chaghcharan are also participants
in the Nakhshahbandi order of Sufism and, as devotees of local
saints, take part in various forms of Islamic heterodoxy. Almost
every camp includes individuals who have made the hajj to Makkah,
and all who are physically able strictly observe the fast during
Ramadan. *Zakat* gifts are made directly to the poor and to
travellers, and also through the giving of sacrificial animals
to individuals in other camps who are attributed to have special
religious knowledge and abilities. Sacrifices during Eid-i-Ghorban
are mandatory, and sacrificial animals are regularly offered for
kheyrat, or blessing, to remember the dead, to ask the blessing
of Allah to make the sick well, to help the barren bear children,
and to bring rain to the pastures.

In some areas, mainly in winter quarters, nomads have
constructued underground *mesjids* protected from the cold,
some large enough to meet the official Qur'anic prescription for
forty men of the community to perform the Friday noon prayer
together. Elsewhere, some camps have separate guest tents
used for this purpose. Even where no such physical structure
exists, almost all camps in a fixed location for a period of time
– even five days – lay out stones to mark off an area for group
prayer.

Such practices are at sharp variance with the conventional
wisdom about nomad religiosity, and nomads return the compli-
ment by saying that villagers and city folk may have more substantial mesjids and more educated mullahs, but that they do not
think and act like Muslims. Although their education in orthodox
Islam comes exclusively from their own religious specialists,
the Sheikhanzai as a whole observe Qur'anic requirements and
understand the official tenets of their Hanafi faith. Their
religious beliefs and practices take on a local flavor, but they
are Islamic beliefs and practices.

The tribal flavor of Sheikhanzai piety serves as one of the
means for distinguishing their own population from 'non-Muslim'
villagers, urban merchants, and government officials. The
paying of alms is defined by the Sheikhanzai in such a manner
as to encourage the social expression of brotherhood within
kinship groups. Reciprocity within such groups and the hospitality shown to guests are viewed by the Sheikhanzai as a
means to heaven in the Final Judgment. The declaration of
faith in Allah as the true and only God, and Muhammad as his
final and definitive prophet, is also a declaration of affiliation
within the tribal nomadic group. Within the group, Qur'anic
instruction, group prayer, and the pilgrimage reinforce the
structural separation of the sexes and the division of labor.
Only men have direct contacts with non-nomads and with the
formal structures of Islam and the state.

The Sheikhanzai live close to nature, and the bounties of nature are provided by Allah. They proudly admit to a dependency on Allah for weather, grazing, fertility, growth, and protection from disease and misfortune. But they also profess the view that Allah will only help those who help themselves and not those who out of laziness or dishonesty seek gain without industry. The mobility and autonomy of the Sheikhanzai express the mode of life understood by them to be encouraged by Allah. Aside from considerations of practical necessity, such beliefs and their associated activities provide symbolic means for internal structuring of the group and for guaranteeing the certainty of Allah's benevolence.

In some areas Sufi influence has been strong enough to create extensive communities of Pirs, Aghas, Khalifas, and their followers. Such Sufi religious leaders are typically unworldly individuals who assist their followers in matters such as possession by jinn, disease, drought, infertility, missing persons, social friction, and so forth. Unlike khans, they are not asked to deal with villagers or the government in economic and legal matters. And, unlike mullahs, they do not teach; they live according to their understanding of Allah's message and communicate this to their followers through their actions. Some individuals sing passages from the Qur'an all night long; some go into trances; and they are all noted for proudly giving away all sacrificial goods they receive.

This degree of religiosity is apparently uncharacteristic of other Muslim nomads; however, I say 'apparently' in that almost no work has been done on nomadic ideology and religion. The ecological orientation in vogue in much of the anthropological research on nomads at present has contributed to this neglect at least as much as has the lack of concern for religion evidenced among or attributed to the nomads. Brian Spooner, for example, argues that:

> Pastoral nomadism is primarily a means to subsistence, and as such it involves an adaptation to a natural environment. It does not necessarily presuppose anything cultural. (1972:126)

Elsewhere he states that:

> Religious expression among nomads, even under the aegis of universalistic religions, takes the nomadic relationship between man and an omnipotent, intractable natural environment and reflects it in a stoical, unritualized relationship between man and an intractable supernatural. (1973:41)

This view echoes Mary Douglas's comment that the ritual lives of nomadic populations like the Basseri of Iran must simply be understood as examples of secular tribal cultures (1973:37) rather than as particularly subtle symbolic and belief systems.

To her, the Basseri are 'Secular in the sense of this worldly, secular in the sense of failing to transcend the meanings of everyday, secular in the sense of paying no heed to specialized religious institutions' . . . (ibid.).

Such an interpretation is not restricted to the Basseri, however, as we see in Louis Dupree's reference to Afghan religiosity in the following terms:' . . . they believe but seldom worship; they are ruggedly irreligious unless an outsider challenges their beliefs' (1973:126). As I have already demonstrated above, this generalization poorly approximates Sheikhanzai religious character. Furthermore, investigations among other Muslim nomads report similar examples of the ideological and ecological significance of a transcendent and institutionalized body of meanings and ritual (Barth 1964; Pastner and Pastner 1972; Cole 1975; Tavakolian 1976).

If we turn next to the question of cultural values(1) as they are expressed within nomadic pastoralist societies, we shall again find evidence of the importance of ideological aspects of pastoralist adaptations. The pioneering work conducted by Goldschmidt, Edgerton, and others in the Culture and Ecology in East Africa Project makes reference to such personality attributes among pastoralists as

a high degree of independence of action; a willingness to take chances; a readiness to act, and a capacity for action; self-containment and control, especially in the face of danger; bravery, fortitude, and the ability to withstand pain and hardship; arrogance, sexuality, and a realistic appraisal of the world (Goldschmidt 1965:404-5)

Goldschmidt's co-researcher, Robert Edgerton, reports that 'pastoralists freely express emotions . . . and they value cooperation, industriousness, the clan, and other kinsmen' (1971: 276). Such cultural predispositions correspond closely with the psychological orientations and attributes which Raphael Patai identifies as part of the bedouin character: hospitality, generosity, courage, honor and self respect (1973:84-96). And there is an equally great similarity between such values and those expressed within the Afghan honor code, or *Pushtunwali*.

In his work among Pathans in the North-west Frontier Province of Pakistan, Akbar Ahmed refers to the following features of the honor code:

1 The showing of hospitality to all visitors without hope of remuneration or favor (*melmastia*).
2 The taking of revenge over time or over space to avenge a wrong (*badal*).
3 The begging of forgiveness, but not in disputes over 'shame' or injury to women (*nanawatay*).
4 The upholding of the honor of the tribesman and that of the family (*nang*) (1977:39)

Dupree repeats these references for Pashtuns in Afghanistan, and he adds mention of the requisite personal characteristics of the honorable Afghan: bravery (*tureh*), chivalry (*meranah*), persistence and constancy ('*isteqamat*), steadfastness (*sabat*), righteousness (*imandari*), willingness to defend property and honor (*ghayrat*), and willingness to defend the honor of women (*namus*) (1973:126).

The dominant cultural values of the Sheikhanzai are drawn from their understanding of Islam, the Afghan honor code, and, naturally enough, from the exigencies of their nomadic pastoral way of life. In practice, these divisions are not so neatly drawn, and many reinterpretations and rationalizations abound. As Ahmed has stated for the Pathan, 'there is no conflict between his tribal code . . . and religious principles' (1976:6). Nevertheless, there are important discrepancies. Sheikhanzai nomadism is itself a contradiction of the Qur'anic emphasis on city and merchant life and the concomitants of an urban religious tradition: formal religious training, collective worship, and theocratic governance. There is also the influence of the extra-Islamic tradition in the worship of saints, the use of amulets (*ta'wiz*), and the practice of exorcism to counter black magic and to remove spirit possession by jinn.

The Afghan emphasis on blood ties and the concept of *badal* (blood revenge) contrast sharply with the Qur'anic edict that 'It belongs not to a believer to slay a believer, except it be by error' (Sura 4:94). Open conflict with non-Sheikhanzai is presently much restricted by the influence of the state, hence the concept of badal does not have much current meaning or expression. Under more traditional conditions, however, such a concept served as a basis for appropriate response to 'non-Islamic' transgressions by members of other groups. Meanwhile, hospitality toward travellers and guests is required of Muslims even in dealings with outsiders.

As I have indicated above, Sheikhanzai values concerning hospitality, generosity, rectitude, discipline, and industry are well-supported by religious beliefs and practices. To be hospitable to guests and generous with kinsmen is not only to be an Afghan, but to be a Muslim. It is by such a standard that Sunni villagers and city folk are viewed as Muslims in name only. The honorable Sheikhanzai must be self-reliant, but he must also recognize that he would be nothing without the grace of Allah and the assistance of his kin. On the issue of family ties, the Sheikhanzai say that 'A person who does not have family cannot make *ghrut* or *roghan*' (in other words, cannot survive), and 'In the name of our ancestors may Allah not leave us without brothers, and in the name of our family may we not be without sons.'

SHEIKHANZAI IDEOLOGY AS A DETERMINING INFLUENCE IN PASTORALIST ECOLOGY

The emphasis the Sheikhanzai place on reciprocity and cooperation within camp groups and segmentary lineages is not only ideological but is manifested in many areas of social, economic, and ritual behavior. For example:

1 Summer camp groups, composed of members of related segmentary lineages, camp together in groups of thirty to fifty tent-households in winter pasture areas. These related households migrate on a similar schedule and along a common route to summer pastures. They share common pastures in winters and adjacent pastures in summers.

2 It is during winters that weddings are held, commonly uniting a man with his FaBrDa, and the entire camp group and most members of the most immediate lineage groupings participate in the ceremonies. Additionally, in winter pastures, one or more Sheikhanzai individuals who are literate and learned in the Qur'an teach Arabic script and religious lessons to the young.

3 During summers, visits by relatives from other camp groups are a regular occurrence. Animals are also taken to market along with those belonging to relatives from other camps, and when animals are lost they are returned to their owners when found by relatives in other camps.

4 Conflict between camp members is resolved through kinship links; and, in instances of camp fission, tents are incorporated into new camps on the basis of kinship affiliation.

5 Normally, a single individual is identified on the basis of wisdom or wealth as the representative of affiliated camps in relations with the outside world, such as with district officials and villagers.

6 Ritual sacrifices are performed both within camps and on ceremonial occasions which bring together members of various camps. When animals are sacrificed and meat is cooked, all camp members share in the meal. Ceremonial occasions such as funerals, weddings, and feasts bring together separate but related camps frequently throughout the annual cycle.

7 Relatives provide animals, dairy products, wheat, wool, and money to those in their own camps or in other related camps who are impoverished. Camels and donkeys are loaned for transport. Even the labor of sons for shepherding and daughters for domestic chores is provided to camp members in need of such assistance.

In terms of behavioral realities, then, such social ideals as interdependence and assistance within kinship and settlement groups are widely practiced. Social solidarity is expressed through such values and behavior, and the social separation and cultural distinctiveness of the Sheikhanzai are also given support through the practice and the ideology of their nomadic pastoralism. The Sheikhanzai say that 'The life of the *maldar* (pastoralist) is difficult, but it has a "taste" (value) that other lives cannot offer through being able to see new places, being dependent on no one in the outside world and reaching the "heaven" of the *sarhad* (summer pastures)' where 'However sick and tired we are in the *watan* (winter area) and along the migration, we get well . . .'.

This emphasis on autonomy and mobility is a recurrent aspect of Sheikhanazai cultural values. The two concepts are seen as being closely linked, and, in fact, interdependent. Autonomy refers not only to the freedom to be nomadic, but also to the political and economic independence of the pastoralist which is made possible through seasonal migrations to new pasture areas. That this self-image is exaggerated, there can be no doubt since the nomad is clearly dependent on villagers and merchants for all of his grain and many of his other 'essentials' such as tea, sugar, cloth, fuel, etc. In addition the nomad must frequently pay rent for camp sites, grazing rights, and access to water. Nonetheless, the nomad sees himself as free and self-reliant, and nomadism is an expression rather than the basis for this view.

As for their pastoralism, the Sheikhanzai ridicule villagers for doing what they call the 'cow work' of agriculture. They say that 'For the Aimak (Dari-speaking villager), if there is no flood or drought one year, there will be the next year. For the maldar difficulties are only for one day.'

The Sheikhanzai also justify their avoidance of birth registration, identity papers, and military conscription by saying that 'As maldar we are doing service to the country by providing wool, meat and dairy products. If our sons are taken into military service, the people who eat our meat and use our wool should come out and help us with our animals.'

Intermarriage is avoided with village populations, and there is little in the way of direct economic symbiosis with village agriculturalists. Because of their extension of cultivation into nomad pasture areas and because of their own sedentary or transhumant forms of pastoralism, villagers are in direct competition with nomads for land, markets, and local political hegemony. Increasingly, as Bates reports for Yörük nomads in Turkey (1971), this is a battle that nomads are losing. The Sheikhanzai dislike and distrust their village neighbors and commonly buy their wheat from urban merchants instead of directly from village producers. Sheikhanzai animals are not allowed on village fields, even to clear off stubble, soften the ground, or leave deposits of manure, and the economic and political separation between the two ethnic groups is reinforced by the in-group emphasis on marriage and ethnic purity.

At this point in the discussion, we are able to offer the following general appraisal of how Sheikhanzai values affect patterns of ecology:

1 The Sheikhanzai are deeply religious and place a high

value on piety. However, this piety does not preclude and, in fact, enhances industriousness and a concern for rational economic judgments. The Sheikhanzai are realistic about practical necessities, but they define these adaptive necessities in symbolic and social as well as material terms. Hard work and success as a pastoralist demonstrates an appreciation for the bounty provided by Allah, and the material advantages attained by an individual should be shared with other Muslims.

2   The Sheikhanzai are tightly bound to the ideology and organization of segmentary lineages which cross-cut individual camp ties. They marry, assist, and cooperate with other individuals on the basis of common genealogical affiliations rather than members of other ethnic groups. They are curious about the outside world, willing to accept material improvements, but also determined to maintain traditional Afghan and Islamic standards and to uphold traditional responsibilities. They are oriented toward material success and gain, but not on a personalistic basis. Surplus wealth is reinvested in the group through the sharing of resources with kin, assistance to impoverished members, and hospitality to guests and travellers.

3   The Sheikhanzai take pride in their political autonomy, and its symbolic expression in geographic mobility, and in what they see as their economic self-reliance. Migration is appreciated for its closeness to nature, the change of scenery it brings, and the symbolic correspondence of the changes in settlement and social patterns to seasonal changes in the herds, in the land, and in climate. Autonomy represents an absence of taxes, schools, and conscription, but it is also rationalized as being necessary for the more important productive services that nomads offer to the nation.

4   Animal husbandry is valued as a basis for expandable wealth, adaptive both to meet short-term economic needs of the individual and to help correct long-term economic imbalances within the group caused by disease and natural misfortune. The Sheikhanzai look down on both settled life and agricultural work, and they have also developed a view of their own religiosity, industry, and solidarity which enhances their symbolic and socioeconomic separation from other Muslims who are villagers.

5   The key Sheikhanzai values identified above are religious piety; industry and material well-being; family and lineage solidarity, reciprocity, and generosity; hospitality; political autonomy; geographic mobility; and a pastoral economy. Such a complex of values, though similar to ones expressed among many other pastoral nomads, cannot be explained solely in terms of adaptive necessities of nomadic pastoralism. Neither are they found as an integrated whole among peoples like the Basseri who display little of the appreciation discussed here for piety and reciprocity. Nor are features of these values, especially

religiosity and family solidarity, absent among Afghan, Pathan, and other populations of Muslim villagers. The pastoralist ecology of the Sheikhanzai is shaped and perpetuated by their patterns of ideology. Sheikhanzai belief, ritual, and cultural values define and direct the nature of settlement patterns, inter-ethnic relations, political structure, and economic activity. Furthermore, Sheikhanzai ecological adaptation involves the perpetuation of their social and ideological separation from sedentary peoples in their pasture areas. As substantiation for these statements, we can next turn to Sheikhanzai reactions to an exogenous program for economic development.

SHEIKHANZAI AND THE HERAT LIVESTOCK DEVELOPMENT CORPORATION

The Herat Livestock Development Corporation is an organization founded after the near decimation of the pastoral economy in western Afghanistan during the severe drought years of 1970 and 1971. Funds for the program are derived from the World Bank, and the program is under the joint administration of the Afghan Ministry of Agriculture and a team of European economic development, livestock, and range management specialists. The HLDC has attempted to provide for the economic rationalization of pastoralism in the western provinces of Afghanistan through the development of the following institutions and services:

1   The construction and staffing of a sheep slaughterhouse in the city and province capital of Herat for the purpose of slaughtering animals to be refrigerated and marketed in Iran.

2   The organization of range-management studies and programs for controlled use of grazing areas, including programs for the reduction and control of herd size.

3   The organization of veterinary services, including examinations for disease, vaccination of animals, and sheep-dips for eradicating animal parasites.

4   The organization of economic cooperatives which would serve as the institutional basis for obtaining loans for the purchase of animals, feed, vaccine, and grazing land and for marketing the animals.

5   The stabilization of animal markets through the purchase of animals at a fixed, and higher than normal, market price.

6   The purchase of animals of controlled quality from village and nomadic pastoralists, and primarily from members of the established cooperatives, for the purpose of stocking the slaughterhouse.

7   The gradual reduction of nomadic forms of pastoralism and replacement by sedentary and transhumant pastoralism.

8   Increased control of animal marketing through scheduled rather than periodic sales, and irrespective of fluctuations in rainfall, grazing quality, and wheat and fodder prices.

9   Eventual replacement of the annual sheep market frequented

by nomads in Chaghcharan with HLDC distribution centers.

10 Eventual dependence on profit-motivated transactions in place of the traditional emphasis on kinship obligations.

11 Elimination of both animal smuggling to Iran and the dependence on cash from periodic labor migration to Iran.

At the time of my field research with the Sheikhanzai in 1977, there was practically no participation in any of these programs despite the fact that the Sheikhanzai are the primary livestock owners in the area of HLDC's operation. The Sheikhanzai are widely known by other pastoralist populations in the region as the most economically aggressive and profitable of herding groups. However, given what I have stated above, it should come as no surprise that HLDC programs are in direct conflict with Sheikhanzai values and that no livestock development of the sort envisioned by external change agents has taken place among the Sheikhanzai. We need not argue against Barth's view of nomads as calculating and materialistic individuals who are pragmatic in their adaptations to economic and environmental change. We need only understand the cultural context of Sheikhanzai conceptions of economic rationality, utility, and advantage. Economic decisions are made by Sheikhanzai in terms of this ideological framework and do not express maximizing strategies of autonomous individuals.

To be specific, I have already spoken of the emphasis on within-group reciprocity, cooperation, and autonomy. These values mitigate against the breakdown of kinship and camp ties and their replacement by artificial cooperative groups. Unless such economic cooperatives as were being planned by HLDC follow established kinship and partnership links, there is little in them to attract Sheikhanzai. Obligations to kinsmen are primary and cannot be replaced but only supplemented. Furthermore, the inculcation of values oriented toward the self-interest of the autonomous individual cannot be achieved in an environment in which Sheikhanzai or other members of cooperatives distrust and threaten their economic partners.

Second, although Sheikhanzai sell their surplus animals willingly enough, they do so only as cash purchases are necessary. Wealth is more easily transported and stored as livestock than as cash or moveable property. In addition, in the event of animal loss, it is preferable to have surplus animals on hand than to have to purchase animals from others. In sum, the Sheikhanzai had little desire to sell animals according to the schedule of HLDC, and even less interest in bringing animals to the district centers of the HLDC rather than selling them in local bazaars. In their view the labor requirement for such journeys to HLDC pick-up points outweighed the potential economic benefit of selling animals to a single purchasing agent even at a high fixed price.

The labor factor also worked against Sheikhanzai use of HLDC vaccination programs. They found it inconvenient to suffer the delay of going through vaccination centers while on migration;

and once in new pastures, they again refused to bring their animals to the HLDC technicians. Meanwhile, equally stubbornly, HLDC considered it impractical and uneconomical to take their vaccines to where the nomad camps were. As a result, most drugs, services, etc. were actually distributed to already relatively well-off villagers, further alienating the Sheikhanzai and other nomads.

The Sheikhanzai were also displeased with the loan aspects of HLDC arrangements. They considered grazing land as their ancestral right and not something which should have to be purchased or rented. Vaccines and medicine were their rightful due from the government. And the loans themselves were considered usurious and therefore contrary to Islamic beliefs.

Finally, programs for stock-reduction and increased sedentarization were not only opposed by nomad values, they were also undesirable because of nomad appraisals of the realistic, pragmatic, and utilitarian necessities of rebuilding herds decimated by the drought years and finding sufficient grass for these herds through seasonal migrations.

In sum, the Sheikhanzai have maintained traditional forms of nomadic pastoralism, supplemented by occasional animal smuggling across the Iranian border and by short periods of migrant labor both in Iran and in other areas of Afghanistan. Economic development is not contrary to Sheikhanzai objectives. Quite the contrary, they wonder why they are not its beneficiaries even to the same degree as village populations in their environment. The objectives and processes of development programs must, however, recognize the significance of Sheikhanzai values in determining their participation. In the context of the Sheikhanzai view of their ethnic identity, society, and ecology, participation in HLDC programs would be ludicrously irrational. Such programs would bring the ruination of their society, destroy their ecological balance, and force them into dominated relations with villagers and the central government. Such demands are contrary to present economic practice and to the world view which sustains Sheikhanzai patterns of adaptation.

NOTE

1 Following Goldschmidt, I define values as 'those recognized qualities that persons in the society should possess and the symbolic representations by which these desirable qualities are given overt expressions' (1959:66).

BIBLIOGRAPHY

Ahmed, Akbar S. (1976) 'Millennium and Charisma among Pathans,' London, Routledge & Kegan Paul.

Ahmed, Akbar S. (1977) 'Social and Economic Change in the Tribal Areas,' Karachi, Oxford University Press.

Barth, Fredrik (1964) 'Nomads of South Persia,' New York, Humanities.

Bates, Daniel (1971) The Role of the State in Peasant-Nomad Mutualism, 'Anthropological Quarterly,' vol. 44(3):109-31.

Cole, Donald (1975) 'Nomads of the Nomads,' Chicago, Aldine.

Douglas, Mary (1973) 'Natural Symbols,' New York, Vintage Books.

Dupree, Louis (1973) 'Afghanistan,' Princeton, Princeton University Press.

Edgerton, Robert (1971) 'The Individual in Cultural Adaptation,' Berkeley, University of California Press.

Evans-Pritchard, E.E. (1949) 'The Sanusi of Cyrenaica,' London, Oxford University Press.

Goldschmidt, Walter, (1959) 'Man's Way: A Preface to the Understanding of Human Society,' New York, Holt, Rinehart, & Winston.

Goldschmidt, Walter (1965) Theory and Strategy in the Study of Cultural Adaptability, 'American Anthropologist,' vol. 67:402-7.

Pastner, Stephen, and Carroll Mc. C. Pastner (1972), Aspects of Religion in Southern Baluchistan, 'Anthropologica,' N.A. XIV(2).

Patai, Raphael (1973) 'The Arab Mind,' New York, Charles Scribner's Sons.

Spooner, Brian (1972) The Status of Nomadism as a Cultural Phenomenon in the Middle East, 'Perspectives on Nomadism,' William Irons and Neville Dyson-Hudson (eds), Leiden, E.J. Brill.

Spooner, Brian (1973) 'The Cultural Ecology of Pastoral Nomads,' An Addison-Wesley Module in Anthropology, no. 45.

Tavakolian, Bahram (1976) The Role of Cultural Values and Religion in the Ecology of Middle Eastern Pastoralism, 'Paths to the Symbolic Self: Essays in Honor of Walter Goldschmidt,' James P. Loucky and Jeffrey R. Jones (eds), Anthropology UCLA, vol. 8, nos. 1 and 2.

12 FEUDING WITH THE SPIRIT AMONG THE ZIKRI BALUCH: THE SAINT AS CHAMPION OF THE DESPISED

Stephen L. Pastner

I

The anthropological literature on the Muslim World has often stressed the roles played by 'Saints' in popular Islam. Spiritual heirs of the Sufis - the 'wool wearing' mystics who arose in the medieval middle east - such figures as the North African Marabout and the pir of Muslim South Asia, have a variety of important functions in the wider societies of which they are a part.

One of these is the ability of saints to act as mediators in the factional, often kin-based, squabbles of the secular populace. Among Moroccan Berbers, for example, Gellner (1969), Benet (1957), and others have noted that saintly lineages, which stand outside those of other tribesmen, are in a favored position to arbitrate conflicts since they do not share obligations of collective responsibility, such as pursuit of blood-feuds, which constrain and bias laymen. In the Atlas mountains, as among Saharan bedouin (Evans-Pritchard 1949), saints' shrines are often located in areas of potential conflict, like market places, ecological transition zones, or on the territorial boundaries of lineage segments. This makes it easier for the holy men to fulfill their roles as 'spiritual wardens of the marches' (Gellner 1969, 297), their sanctity providing a buffer to the often volatile, centrifugal tendencies in the wider society.

A corollary of the capacity of holy men to reassert the unity of Islam against the pulls of secular factionalism is the part such men have played in spearheading social movements against outsiders. The Sudanese Mahdi (Holt 1958) in the 1880s rallied his supporters against the British-Egyptian government; the Sanusi religious brotherhood (Evans-Pritchard 1949) unified Cyrenaican bedouin against invading Italians on several occasions; and the Akhund of Swat (Ahmed 1976) united his turbulent Pathan followers against the British in the 1860s on India's northwest frontier. All of these religious figures stepped into the breech and assumed leadership functions when the fissile social order proved itself ineffective, thus disproving the oft-cited middle-eastern maxim: 'me against my brother; my brother and I against our cousin; and the three of us against the world.'

A third function of saints and perhaps the most important of all, is in their symbolic role as earthly reminders of God's presence. For many rural villagers, desert nomads and dwellers in teeming bazaars and souks, the legalistic debates and theological polemics of the Ulama - the 'official' clergy of the Islamic great tradition - are often remote and hard to grasp. To the devout but unlettered Muslim the saint is a ready exemplar of the reality of divine forces in the universe. By performing miracles - or having people believe he does - through use of his divine 'blessing' or power (Arabic *baraka;* Indo-Iranian *barkat*) the saint demonstrates the immediacy of Allah's exist-ence just as other latter-day Sufis, like the Pakistani Qawwali singer and the Turkish 'whirling dervish,' demonstrate by their ecstasies the delights awaiting those who embrace God.

Still another function that may be served by Sufi saints is described in this paper. Based on data gathered among the Zikris - a sect of Baluch tribesmen in western Pakistan - I suggest that saints may serve to bolster the self-esteem of their lay followers in settings where more secular avenues of status aggrandizement are closed.

II

The Baluch - an Iranian-speaking people - inhabit the deso-late eastern part of the Iranian plateau and the adjacent lower Indus Valley. Most Baluch live inside the borders of Pakistan but substantial numbers are found in Iran and Afghanistan. Nomads and farmers in the arid interior deserts, fishermen along the Arabian sea coast, the majority of Baluch are Sunni Muslims of the Hanafite school of Qur'anic interpre-tation.(1) Yet numerous Baluch (no exact figures are available but I would estimate 10-20 per cent of Pakistan's approximately 2-3 million Baluch) subscribe to a sect viewed as heretical by their Sunni tribesmates, for representatives of the sect are drawn from otherwise Sunni-majority tribes. This sect is known as Zikri for the central feature of its ritual - the *zikr* or repete-tive chants of the name of God.

Now zikr (or *dhikr*, in Arabic) is practiced by Sunni Muslims as well, particularly by members of Sufi orders who employ it, along with special breathing techniques, as a meditative aid not unlike the mantras of Hindus and Buddhists. However, it is other aspects of Zikri doctrine that have caused Sunni Baluch to regard them as *kafir* or infidels. The most basic of these is their belief in a Mahdi or messiah called Nur Pak or 'Pure Light.' Again, other Muslims sometimes express belief in an abstract concept of 'Pure Light,' a notion of divine conscious-ness which existed in the world before the time of man and which required the manifest word of God, as conveyed through the Prophet, to give it expression. But to Zikris, Nur Pak was a real figure who walked the earth before Adam and who will return at the apocalypse (*akhir zaman* or 'the last days') to restore what Zikris believe is the true Islam, which to them has been perverted by the Sunnis.

Among the most essential features of orthodox Islamic doctrine

is the belief that Muhammad was the last and greatest of the
prophets. Although Zikris revere Muhammad, they believe that
his dispensation is superseded by that of Khoda-Dad ('Gift of
God') - a vaguely defined figure reputed to have lived 'seven
generations ago,' a general idiom for 'a long time ago.' He is
said to have been born not of mortal humans and to have taught
the Baluch the way of the Zikris. Such scanty writings by
outsiders as exist on the Zikris describe the sect as having been
brought to Baluch country sometime in the late fifteenth or early
sixteenth century by an Indian Sufi - Sayyid Mahmud of
Jaunpur - or by one of his disciples (Field 1959). Although most
village-level Zikris have never heard of the Jaunpauri holy-man
I believe that he may be identified with the mysterious Khoda
Dad.

The prominence accorded to this individual by the Zikris has
set them beyond the pale of true faith in the eyes of Sunni
Baluch, although Zikris themselves obviously see matters in
quite a contrary way. Nonetheless this belief and other deviations
from Sunni norms - e.g. Zikris make a hajj or pilgrimage not to
Makkah but to a mountain in south-western Baluchistan said to
be the throne of the Mahdi - have created long-standing schisms
between Zikri and Sunni Baluch, with the former generally being
on the losing end of things.

Soon after its introduction to the Baluch, Zikriism enjoyed
considerable prestige, especially in the Makran region of what
is now southwestern Pakistan. Sardars, or chiefs, of such
ruling houses as the Buledis and Gitchkis embraced the faith
and it became something of an official religion. But by the mid
eighteenth century trouble for the Zikris began in the person of
Nasir Khan of Kalat - the head of a confederacy of Dravidian-
speaking Brahui tribes in eastern Baluchistan and an ardent
Sunni Muslim. Regarding himself as a true ghazi, or 'hero of
the faith,' he mounted a jihad, or holy war, against the infidel
- as he saw them - Zikris, destroying the sect's influence and
coincidentally adding to his domains the revenues from the rich
date-palm oases of Makran. From that point on, the Zikris have
been in political eclipse among the rest of the Baluch. Subjected
to the scorn of Sunni tribesmen of oasis settlements most Zikris
in interior Baluchistan are nowadays nomads in the more remote
areas.

By the mid nineteenth century the rise of British power in
Sind province led many Baluch, including Zikris, to migrate
eastward into the mantle of the Pax Britannica, since the English
under Sir Charles Napier and his successors were far more
tolerant in matters of religion than desert Baluch chiefs. As the
coastal trade and administrative center of Karachi grew under
British rule many Baluch - Zikris among them - abandoned
their flocks and fields and took up marine fishing. It was among
one such group that I gathered much of the material presented
here.

Although in many ways the Zikris of coastal Sind thrived as

fishermen or as middlemen in the fish trade they have never
recaptured the collective political power they once enjoyed, and
in the post-partition era see themselves once again beset by
what they regard as the bigotry and prejudice of the Sunni
Baluch amongst whom they are territorially intermingled, both
on the coast and in Karachi itself. To Zikris, Nasir Khan's
eighteenth-century campaign against them was not a holy war
but a 'great-theft' and they complain about the fanaticism of
present-day Baluch Mullahs who harangue their Sunni followers
to hold the Zikris in contempt. Sunni Baluch usually claim they
will not eat with a Zikri, while Zikris are far more ecumenical in
that many say that the main reason an item of food or an act is
haram, or impure, is if it is the result or the cause of evil
deeds. The very fact of consistent disagreement among Zikris
on matters of *halal* and *haram* (pure and impure) is itself
testimony to their Sufic orientation and the notion that such
matters are between the individual and God.

Yet, despite their differences, both Sunni and Zikri Baluch
share many essential cultural values. Both respect traditional
riwaj or custom, support kinsmen and neighbors in times of
trouble, uphold the chastity of their womenfolk and strive to
enhance personal honor or ᶜ*izzat*. For all Baluch this latter goal
really subsumes all the others. But Zikris find their quest for
honor complicated by their status as a scorned minority. One
way out of this dilemma would be to abandon their faith and
embrace Sunni Islam. After all, forced conversions, or those
based on expediency, are quite common in Islamic history.
However, although some Zikris have adopted just this course,
others who have kept the faith regard them as shameful
bargashtag, or apostates, who by their defection have lost more
honor than they have gained.

III

One way that the Zikris have tried to add to their sense of
self-esteem is through their reverence for pirs, or saints, both
living and dead. In many respects the Zikri saint cult is similar
to those found among many Muslims. Zikri sainthood, like that
elsewhere, is often a blend of achieved and ascribed characteristics. That is, personal piety and devotion are required for a
man to gain a reputation as a pir and a following of *murid* or
disciples. His *barkat*, or power, is often gained through
solitary vigils of forty days (*chillag*) in isolated deserts or
mountains - a theme harking back through Muhammad to the
prophets of the Judaeo-Christian tradition. Yet the Zikri
saints' status is ascribed to some extent as well. As in other
cases, Zikri pirs often claim *sayyid* pedigree. However, whereas
sayyids in orthodoxy are said to descend from the line of the
Prophet, to Zikris sayyids are descended from the earlier mentioned shadowy figure of Khoda-Dad who is said to have brought

the Baluch the zikr. Among the Zikris, men as devout as pirs but not of the correct lineage become *mians* instead of saints.

Once elevated to sainthood - either in his own lifetime or after a life of spiritual virtuosity has ended - a Zikri pir's barkat is regarded as a potent safeguard against the ills of the world. The earth around shrines for curing (*tik-khana*), dedicated by saints, is eaten to heal sickness; dead pirs are invoked to exorcize jinns and saints are called upon to settle disputes, to end droughts, to attract fish to long-empty nets and to ensure good crops.

Of course, all of this is quite common in other settings where Sufic traditions exist. But an interesting feature of the Zikri case is the frequency with which a particular theme recurs in a corpus of forty-eight extended case studies of pirs I collected among the Zikri fishermen of the western Sind coast. Predictably in this corpus there are the usual tales of diseases cured, lost objects found and future events foretold. However, the largest single category of cases - one-half - falls under the rubric of the competitive use of barkat, either in *chikasag* (i.e. barkat-contests with other holy men), or in conflicts with lay rivals. Significantly the antagonists in twenty out of twenty-four cases were Sunni Muslims who, needless to say, came off second-best to the Zikri heroes of the tales. This theme recurs even in some of the 'curing' and 'finding' stories, where Zikri pirs are described as being efficacious when Sunni saints had failed.

A number of cases can be cited to illustrate this theme of sectarian rivalry and Zikri triumph:

A Sindhi pir, a Sunni, jealous of the reputation of a Zikri saint, challenged him to a *chikasag* contest. The Zikri mounted his camel and rode to the banks of the Hab river (the Sind-Baluchistan border) where the Sindhi was waiting. On seeing the Zikri, the Sunni grew mute and his limbs became rigid. So forceful was this demonstration of barkat that a number of the Sindhi's Baluch murid deserted him and took the Zikri as their *murshid* or spiritual mentor.

In another story, a *karez* (subterranean irrigation aqueduct) in the Kheran region of Baluchistan dried up. The Sardar of the oasis - a Sunni of the Nausherwani tribe of Baluch - sent for numerous Sunni pirs and mullahs to restore the water flow, but all failed. Finally he sent for a Zikri pir. The Zikri called for a cow to be sacrificed. When this was done and the meat divided, the pir struck the *karez* opening with a rod and the water flowed forth. The Sardar rewarded him with a golden belt.

On yet another occasion a Sunni saint threatened to steal the barkat of a Zikri pir. To intimidate the Zikri, the Muslim threw his *tasbih* (prayer beads) to the ground and they turned into a cobra which slithered toward the Zikri. The Zikri replied by tossing his sandal toward the snake, whereupon it turned into a cat which devoured the cobra.

Such stories of sectarian rivalry can become violent as in

the case of a well known turn-of-the century Zikri pir whose
beautiful servant girl was coveted by the Jam, or ruler, of
Las Bela (a former princely state in southeast Baluchistan).
The Jam sent a troop of soldiers to abduct the girl. The out-
raged saint fired his gun in the air and so great was his barkat
that the bullet struck the Jam in his distant capital.

Events like these can be multiplied throughout my corpus of
cases. The main feature of all these stories, from a behaviorist
point of view, is the vicarious pleasure listeners derive from
their recounting even when the individual is not the murid, or
disciple, of the saint in question. Whenever a particularly potent
exercise of barkat was described by my Zikri informants, other
listeners would enthusiastically exclaim 'Wah Wah!' and 'Sha-
bash!' (bravo!) even when the point of story, to my ears at
least, seemed to have a somewhat ambiguous outcome, as in the
following:

A leader of the Baluch guerrillas, who for some years have
been waging a war of secession against Pakistan, came to a
Zikri pir for an amulet that would protect him against Pakistani
troops. The guerrilla was a Sunni, but the reputation of the
saint was such that the fighting man decided to forget sectarian
matters. The pir gave the guerrilla a turban so imbued with
barkat that it would turn the army bullets to water. One night
as the guerrilla leader slept in his camp a Pakistani commando
force attacked, blowing the guerrilla to bits. The turban, however, came through without a scratch!

IV

In their relationship with Sunni Baluch the Zikris are often
made to feel inferior and spiritually debased. Yet, ironically, in
their dealings with non-Baluch they are constrained even more
by their 'Baluchness' than by sectarian factors; for in the
multi-cultural mosaic of Pakistan, ethnicity imposes barriers of
culture and language, and the Baluch Zikri and Sunni alike are
among the more insular of the *qaums*, or ethnic groups, in the
country. Thus, receiving little in the way of respect or esteem
from the wider society (unlike qaums such as the Pathans who
may be disliked and distrusted by other ethnic groups but
who are still respected) the Zikris, as a proud folk, must
seek their self-esteem from within.

The exploits of their pirs provide the Zikris with the needed
reassurance that in God's eyes they are indeed a worthy people
whose historical treatment and present low status in the eyes
of other Muslims is the sort of martyrdom often suffered by the
just and righteous at the hands of the arrogant and powerful
who are themselves in theological error. In this context it is
significant to note that Zikris often expressed great admiration
for the country of Israel (obviously an unusual point of view in
a Muslim country like Pakistan) precisely because the Jews were

seen as another people who must struggle to uphold their faith against the same sort of foe the Zikris have contended with over the past few centuries.

It is beyond the scope of the paper to offer a comprehensive comparison between the role of Zikri pirs as described here and the functions of similar divines elsewhere in the Muslim world. However, by way of conclusion, I should like to offer a hypothesis that could be tested by other students against both existing data and future field work.

This hypothesis suggests that in settings of Islamic sectarianism or ethnic diversity, an inverse correlation may exist between the secular avenues open to individuals in their quest for status aggrandizement and the emphasis on the sectarian competition motif in their stories about the exploits of saints. That is, feuding in the realm of the spirit becomes a surrogate for secular competition, with the saint emerging as a hero whose exploits provide his followers with a vicarious sense of self-esteem.

In order to validate this hypothesis, it is by no means impossible to develop quite reasonable ways to operationalize measurements of 'status mobility,' and indeed many already exist. Likewise determining sectarian rivalry themes in stories about pirs is an equally straightforward procedure, regardless of the more subtle or symbolic elements that may also be present.

Thus it is the ultimate goal of this paper to suggest an avenue by which it can be determined to what extent the case of the Zikri Baluch pirs is representative of a pattern elsewhere in the world of Islam.

NOTE

1 Fieldwork among the Pakistani Baluch was conducted on two separate occasions in collaboration with my wife, Carroll McC. Pastner. In 1968-9 six months of research among Baluch oasis villagers and nomads in the Makran region were supported by fellowships and grants from the National Institute of Mental Health. Research among the Zikri Baluch fishermen on the Sind coast was carried out primarily during a seven-month period in 1976-7 with the support of the American Institute of Pakistan Studies. Additional summer research on the Zikris took place in 1979 and 1982 under funding from the University of Vermont and the American Institute of Pakistan Studies.

BIBLIOGRAPHY

Ahmed, A. (1976) 'Millennium and Charisma Among Pathans,' London, Routledge & Kegan Paul.

Benet, F. (1957) Explosive Markets: The Berber Highlands, in
'Trade and Market in the Early Empires' (eds K. Polanyi,
C. Arensberg and H. Pearson), New York, The Free Press.
Evans-Pritchard, E.E. (1949) 'The Sanusi of Cyrenaica,' London,
Oxford University Press.
Field, H. (1959) 'An Anthropological Reconnaissance in West
Pakistan, 1955,' Cambridge, Peabody Museum.
Gellner, E. (1969) 'Saints of the Atlas,' University of Chicago
Press.
Holt, P.M. (1958) 'The Mahdist State in the Sudan 1881-1898,'
Oxford, Clarendon, Press.
For more on the Baluch see:
Pastner, S. (1971) Ideological Aspects of Nomad Sedentary
Contact: a Case From Southern Baluchistan, 'Anthropological
Quarterly,' 44, 173-84.
Pastner S. and C.M. Pastner (1972) Agriculture, Kinship and
Politics in Southern Baluchistan, 'Man,' 7, 128-36.
Pastner S. and C.M. Pastner (1977) Adaptations to State-Level
Politics by the Southern Baluch, in 'Pakistan: The Long View'
(eds L. Ziring, R. Braibanti, and W.H. Wriggins), Durham,
Duke University Press.
Pehrson, R. (1966) 'The Social Organization of the Marri Baluch,'
New York, Wenner Gren Foundation.
Salzman, P.C. (1971) Adaptation and Political Organization in
Iranian Baluchistan, 'Ethnology,' 10 (4), 433-44.
Spooner, B. (1969) Politics, Kinship and Ecology in Southeast
Persia, 'Ethnology,' 7 (2), 139-52.
For more on Sufi saints in Pakistan see:
Lambrick, H.T. (1972) 'The Terrorist,' London, Ernest Benn
(a novel about a 1940s uprising of the Hurs, followers of the
Sindhi *Pir Pagaro*).
Mayne, P. (1956) 'Saints of Sind,' London, John Murray.
Schimmel, A. (1975) 'Mystical Dimensions of Islam' University
of North Carolina Press, Chapel Hill.

13 RELIGIOUS PRESENCE AND SYMBOLISM IN PUKHTUN SOCIETY
Akbar S. Ahmed

Among the Pukhtun tribes of Pakistan the cognitive symbols of
religion are as visible as they are seen to be important to their
members in defining orthodox forms of religion, allocating
status and measuring religiosity in society. I shall describe
how sometimes trivial symbols like growing a beard indicate
conformity with religious tradition and are interpreted as being
of social significance. The symbols in society that I shall be
describing constitute those perceived by members of society and
therefore are seen through the actor's eyes. The symbols of
religion are to be interpreted as both social and religious signposts in society; the former often overlapping with the latter.
The role of religious groups as guardians and interpreters of
Islamic mores and traditions will be discussed in the latter half
of the paper.

My arguments will be supported by data(1) gathered from
field-work conducted in 1975-6 among the Mohmand(2) tribe
in the North-West Frontier Province of Pakistan (Ahmed 1980).

The main arguments will be relevant to the sociology of
religion in Islamic societies and particularly segmentary tribal
groups. I will emphasize the sociological rather than the psychological forms of religion, i.e. the external, visible and explicit
in society rather than the internal, atavistic and implicit in the
minds of men. My explanation will thus be Weberian - 1962. A
caveat regarding symbolism borrowed from a penetrating analysis
of 'religion as a cultural system' is added:

> To undertake the study of cultural activity - activity in which
> symbolism forms the positive content - is thus not to abandon
> social analysis for a Platonic cave of shadows, to enter into a
> mentalistic world of introspective psychology or, worse,
> speculative philosophy, and wander there forever in a haze
> of 'Cognitions', 'Affections', 'Conations', and other elusive
> entities (Geertz 1973: 5).

In my paper I shall thus heed Professor Geertz: 'Cultural acts,
the construction, apprehension, and utilization of symbolic
forms, are social events like any other; they are as public as
marriage and as observable as agriculture' (ibid.).

The importance accorded to religious symbolism in society
presupposes a connected and important point that Islamic
tribes contain symbols that are universal within and common to
the Islamic world. This raises important methodological and

theoretical issues in the social sciences: Islamic tribes cannot
be studied in isolation as have, for instance, certain segmentary
tribes (Fortes and Evans-Pritchard 1970; Middleton and Tait
1970). Thus by an extension of the argument I am arguing that
methodologically and theoretically to study an Islamic society
in isolation is to remove an important dimension from it (Ahmed
1976, 1980).

The importance of the larger political framework of the
Islamic world for Islamic societies, and their interconnection
through universally accepted religious symbols, was one of the
main points I wished to make in an earlier work (Ahmed 1976)
and is a recognized social phenomenon (Coon 1952; Gellner
1969a: 2; Hart 1976: 15-16; Tavakolian 1976). In this paper I
will be concerned simply in stating how sociological roles and
normative behaviour are explained within society by reference
to what are locally understood and recognized as symbols derived
from the main body of Islamic traditions. By the sociology of
religion I will mean the location of cognitive and affective
referents that determine, at least in part, social action among
groups. The Pukhtun social world, its mores and norms, the
symbols of its society, are embedded in and often identical to
those of the wider world of Islam. Our concern with religion is
not with its theology but as a cultural system that imposes
social action that translates symbolic associations with the
supernatural into material reality.

The methodology in this paper is based on an important
assumption that 'the most obvious basis for religious behaviour
is the one which any religious actor tells us about when we ask
him – and, unlike some anthropologists, I believe him' (Spiro
1973: 112). I shall thus examine Islamic symbolism and its
relevance in society through the eyes of the actors and accept
their interpretation and apperception as a basis for analysis.

(A) RELIGIOUS SYMBOLISM

In a sociological manner that almost echoes Durkheim, 'Islam is
another name for Pukhtun society'. I wish to repeat my use of
the word sociological. The Islamic symbols are clear and easily
identified by the actors; perhaps their religious meaning in the
ecclesiastical sense may not appear relevant or even comprehen-
sible but their social significance is established by frequent
recurrence. Religious groups ensure that these symbols are
constantly activated partly to enhance their own social prestige
and permit them a certain leverage in society. I am examining
these symbols through the eyes of the actor and therefore what
may appear superficial or even trivial ones remain significant
in society. On one level I have heard in the mosque the sermon
of the mullah of Bela Mohmandan on Islamic symbolism in society.
He talked of the keeping or not keeping of beards as a measure
of religiosity, and as I did not have one it proved to be an

uncomfortable experience which would have been more so for
any local man transgressing this norm. Shamshudin, a Bela
elder, gravely confessed to me 'I am a sinner' (*ze gonangar yam*)
in 1974 as he did not cultivate a beard. Shortly afterwards he
began to make amends and now has one. Haji Hasan of Shati
Khel, who has recently returned from the *hajj* (pilgrimage) and
is basking in its glory, constantly turned beads in his hands,
and asked me one favour only in our long friendship: 'for the
love of God cut those English (*kafir*) side-burns'. When I
obliged he was as pleased as a child and commented on this
ceaselessly all the while blessing me.

On another level religious leaders have repeatedly activated
Islamic symbolism in their fight against the British. The Hajji
of Turangzai began his proclamation to the Mohmand for *jihad*
(holy war) with quotations from the Holy Qur'an, as did his son
Badshah Gul when he tried to prevent the British from con-
structing a road in the Gandab, in the Mohmand Agency, in the
early 1930s. Badshah's pamphlets argued 'Anyone who makes
friends with the British becomes the enemy of God and His
Prophet' (Home Department, Tribal Research Cell, File 220: 203).

The unity of *Pukhtunwali* (code of the Pukhtuns) and Islam
are symbolized and expressed in village social life by the
physical juxtaposition of the mosque and the *hujra* (village
guest-house). These two institutions are the focus of life in
every settlement and village. They are built simultaneously and
usually share a wall and/or courtyard. The Pukhtun accepts
religion without doubts or questions, for there is no conflict
between his Code and Islam. Indeed he sees the code as embedded in Islam, and where there is contradiction, as in the taking
of interest for loans or not allowing women their rights, he
accepts his guilt frankly. The reluctance to give property to
women may well be tied up with the importance of geographical
areas inhabited and associated with fixed sections and clans,
parts of which run the risk of alienation through the marriage
of women if they inherited property. In both cases the percentage who accepted the fact that they were indulging in
un-Islamic practice was 100 per cent of the respondents answering my Formal Questionnaires. The problem for the Pukhtun
is not one of accepting colonial law or tribal lay but one of
bringing Pukhtun custom into focus with accepted Islamic law.
Deviances from Islamic law are partly legitimized in the eyes of
society by a frank recognition of deviance and explained as
Pukhto *riwaj* (custom) as if by such an explanation the guilt
would be extenuated or even exculpated. 'Yes, there is a contradiction, we are wrong, but can a Pukhtun be anything but a
Muslim?' His attitude to the Almighty is that of a favourite.
Native exegesis rests on the assumption that the Pukhtuns were
a favoured Islamic group. The Pukhtun carries no stigma of
forcible conversion. His Islam reaches back to the origins of
the religion. Like the bedouin with whom his tribal structure
and sociological environment are so similar, he sees and feels

close affinity to God that needs no translation and interpretation:
'The Beduin could not look for God within him: he was too sure
that he was within God' (Lawrence 1962: 39). Obedience and
submission; total loyalty of his will to the infinite power of the
Almighty, that is all that is required of him and that is what he
gives willingly. He is unburdened with religious dialectics and
polemics, that, he says disparagingly, is for the religious men,
the mullahs and Mians. He is by definition a Muslim just as by
birth he obtains the inalienable right to Pukhtunness. His place
in society as a Muslim and a Pukhtun are thus secure and
defined from the moment of birth. However famous or infamous,
high or low, good or bad he cannot be ousted from this niche.

Islam, with *Pukhtunwali* and patrilineal descent, is seen as
an attribute associated with Pukhtun identity (Barth 1970).
The Pukhtun defines himself as a Muslim and as this definition
is intrinsically unequivocal it poses him no dilemmas. In any
case, the absence of larger non-Muslim groups neither threaten
his Muslimness nor prompt him to emphasize it. He may not
have come to this conclusion after philosophic debate but to him
there is no disjunction in being Muslim and being Pukhtun. This
inherent belief in his Muslimness supported by the putative
genealogical links to the Prophet through his apical ancestor,
Qais ibn ^{c}Abd al-Rashid, assure him of his special relationship
to God which, in turn, has two social consequences. First, the
Pukhtun brand of Islam is as sociologically all-pervasive as it is
tolerant. This partly explains why non-Muslim groups like
Hindus and Sikhs live in security and freedom to worship in
Tirah, an area which even non-Pukhtun Muslim groups would
find inaccessible. Second, the complete confidence in his
Muslimness constricts the role of religious groups and explains
the continuation of Pukhto custom which contains non-Islamic
elements such as the taking of usury and the denial of certain
rights to women.

Pukhtunness and Muslimness do not have to coalesce, they
are within each other, the interiority of the former is assumed
in the latter. The Pukhtun defines and assesses Islam in terms
of two fundamental sets of precepts: the first raises no problem
to him and is intrinsic to his Pukhtunness, the belief in the
foremost of the five pillars of Islam, the acceptance of the
omnipotence and monism of God expressed in the oneness of God
and the prophethood of Muhammad (*kalima*). The second has
social ramifications and may be defined as the other four pillars
of Islam:

1. Prayers (*munz*) five times a day which most Pukhtuns,
particularly after middle age, attempt to fulfil. For instance my
local field assistants, although young men ranging from 21 to
27 years, would say their prayers five times a day, often inter-
rupting a questionnaire.

2. Fasting (*rojay*) from sunrise to sunset during the month
of Ramadan. Ramadan is universally respected and during this
month almost every adult male or female fasts. To be seen eating

or smoking during Ramadan would incur serious reprimand from
the entire community and those who cannot keep the fast maintain their secret with the greatest of discretion. British officers
who served in the Tribal Areas testify that they never heard
of a man who broke the fast in the most severe climatic conditions (Pettigrew 1965: 35). The position remains unchanged
today. I was told that until a decade ago if someone did not
fast the village would blacken his face, put him on a donkey and
take him round the village. Examples of such cases were given
to me of villages near Bela. There is a general enthusiasm for
fasting among the young. For instance Ghani, the younger son
of Shamshudin, who is now 12 years old, has been keeping at
least half the fasts, about fourteen to fifteen days, since the
age of 10.

3.   Pilgrimage (hajj) to the Kaaba in Arabia once in a lifetime.
Economic conditions determine hajj but it is a major life-long
ambition of most men and women and carries a certain amount of
social prestige. The hajji, the title with which he is called after
his hajj, is expected to behave in a manner befitting his newly
acquired status.

4.   *Zakat*, $2\frac{1}{2}$ per cent of the annual fixed income to be given
to the poor. Ideally this is meant to be a personal contribution
to circulate money to the poorer of the community but as it is
left to the discretion of the individual it is difficult to assess.
Pukhtuns often talk of zakat when they house and shelter poorer
relatives. Mohmands also translate zakat as *ushar* which is a
fixed share given to mullahs or as in Bela, to the Mian, or the
poor after the crop.

Although jihad is not generally considered among the five
pillars of Islam described above, Pukhtuns attach great importance to it, for it emphasizes their martial tribal tradition and
expresses their enthusiasm for Islam. Almost every Mohmand
Malik (elder) remembers 1947 and 1948 as the years of jihad in
Kashmir, a fact they still constantly repeat in *jirgas* (assemblies/-
councils) and meetings to underline their loyalty to Pakistan
and the larger cause of Islam. Including senior Maliks like
Shahzada and Mazullah, every settlement in Shati Khel was
represented by an adult male in Kashmir. They still remember
that those were days of 'great emotion' (*der jazba*).

Personal habits are explained simply by reference to actions
of the Prophet (*sunnat*) or associated with his personal history.
Middle-aged men who keep beards in the Tribal Areas will dye
them red with henna. The explanation I consistently received
throughout the Tribal Areas, and in its most remote regions,
was that this was *sunnat*. Amirzada, the son of Shahzada,
explained why the fig is called the 'fruit of heaven' (*janati
maywa*) and used in the mosque for the beam but never burned
in the house: 'The fig lowered its branches when the Prophet
was a child and gave him milk to drink.' Near-mythical stories
involving the person of the Prophet and common to Muslim
groups in North India were repeated to me by older Pukhtun

women. For instance, the story of how the bee makes honey and the fly beats its head in a gesture of despair; the fly is said to have refused to collect the tear from the Prophet's face which the bee promptly gathered. The fly realizing its mistake now beats its head and rubs its forefeet in a gesture of eternal sorrow while the bee, being rewarded, is able to produce honey.

Personal names such as the Prophet's, Muhammad, or his agnatic descendants, Hasan and Husain, or those of his companions, ^cUmar and ^cAli are very common among male Pukhtuns just as the names of his female kin like Ruqaya, his daughter, are common among females. For instance Shamshudin's daughter is called Ruqaya.

In the month when the Prophet was dying, his wives are said to have cooked *chori* (a mixture of flour, sugar or jaggery - *gur* - and oil) to distribute to the poor and this tradition is still kept alive. Chori is cooked and distributed in Mohmand villages during this month. Daily diet and items are affected by the dietary habits of the Prophet. He was said to prefer the simplest of foods and especially onions. Perhaps making a virtue out of necessity, *mashars* (elders) would explain the simplicity of their daily diet with reference to the Prophet's life.

Elders quote the evil eye (*nazar*) stories from the life of the Prophet. Therefore, they argue, nazar has social meaning and is effective. Certain traditional measures are taken to avoid nazar. For instance a cow's skull or a black flag is placed on a new house so the nazar may shift to it and is negated. A black spot made of kohl powder is placed on a child's face to divert nazar.

A great deal of veneration and symbolism is attached to the objects associated with the two holy cities of Islam in Arabia, Makkah Sharif and Madina Sharif, that hajjis bring from the hajj and distribute in small quantities to their near and dear. 'Holy' water from the spring used by the Prophet (*abayzamzam*) is stored safely to be sprinkled ritually on the coffin; dates (*khorma*); prayer-mats and rosaries; a simple white sheet called *kappan*, for coffin, to be wrapped around the corpse; and *Makkay-Madinay khawra*) is brought as an object of veneration. *Makkay-Madinay khwra*) is brought as an object of veneration. Such Arabic objects have a symbolic value far beyond their actual value in terms of money, especially as there is a continuing mystical and emotional attachment to them and they are commonly believed to act as cures for various diseases. Hajjis I interviewed talked of feeling spiritually uplifted (*roshani*). Hajji ^cAbdullah is said to be the first hajji among the Mohmand Halimzai and Tarakzai when he performed the hajj in 1937. Since then he performed the hajj five times more. This contrasts with his arch-rivals and cousins Anmir and Shahzada who could afford to perform the hajj but refuse to do so for reasons discussed below. Recently more Shati Khel Maliks have been on the hajj. Before then Hajji Hasan, the non-Mohmand elder of Shati Khel, succinctly summed up, playing on the nuances of the Islamic framework in society, that the dominant lineages 'were simply Pukhtuns' (*Pukhtana woo*).

Locally the newly achieved status of the hajji is balanced by the status of the Pukhtun mashar. I heard Shahzada and other mashars in both areas cynical about the entire business of hajj: 'they go to smuggle watches and cloth'. They would quote a saying attributed to the Prophet – 'the hajj decides a man's course for the rest of his life: he either returns very holy or very wicked' – and agree that the hajjis they know fall into the latter category. Shahzada would pointedly refer to his rivals. It is for this reason, they argue, that they would not go for the hajj. Nonetheless, and according to both formal and informal interviews, the hajj remains the main ambition of most people including women. The general economic situation of Bela is reflected in the fact that not one person has performed the hajj from the village. Hajji Gul, the Bela barber, has been given the name as he was born on Friday.

Shamshudin's wife, as indeed other Mohmand women, would discuss their hajj plans with my wife endlessly. They were clear in their minds, and their husbands had agreed that as soon as they had enough money they would perform the hajj rather than buy land or spend it on the education of their children. Though Shahzada and other Maliks may deride hajjis, they are present at the 'seeing off' and 'receiving of' the hajjis. The receptions include a series of feasts and celebrations as participation is considered *sawab* (good deed). During this period hostilities are tacitly suspended to permit cross-factional visiting. Large Mohmand crowds gather at the railway station or airport in Peshawar with garlands, to see off and receive their kin, arriving in hired buses or cars decorated with buntings and coloured-paper otherwise used for marriages.

Pukhto names of days in the week and months in the year are said to contain Islamic symbolism: Pinzama (Tuesday), the fifth day, is dedicated to one of the greatest Sunni Saints, Hazrat Jilani of Baghdad. Shoro (Wednesday) is so called as God is said to have begun working on the world on this day. Ziarat (Thursday) and Jum^ca (Friday) are recognized as the two holy days of the week when good Muslims should attend congregational prayers in the mosque. Thursday is considered auspicious for laying the foundation of a new building or starting cultivation, just as Friday is not. Friday is meant exclusively for prayers (*da munz warz*) and designated in Pukhto as such.

Certain Pukhto months of the year are associated directly with events from early Islamic social history centring around the life of the Prophet; native local exegesis reinforces larger Islamic culture and tradition. For instance there are the months of Muharram, generally called *Asan* among the Mohmand after the two grandsons of the Prophet, Hasan and Husain, who were martyred; Rabi^c-al-Awwal in which the Prophet died and Roja, the month of Ramadan and fasting when the Holy Qur'an was revealed to the Prophet. No marriages or celebrations are held

in these months. Warokay Akhtar (small ^CId) celebrating the
end of Ramadan and the other month of Akhtar are months of
happiness (*khushali*). Lowey Akhtar (big ^CId) derives from the
incident when Abraham, the ancestor of the Prophet, almost
sacrificed his son Ismail to appease God. Every home is expected
to and does sacrifice (*qurbani*) which is then divided into three
shares: the first is given to the poor, the second to poor kin
and the third is kept for the house. Three, five or seven
people, traditionally Islamic numbers, may join to sacrifice one
cow. In the Mohmand Agency usually seven males pool together
to sacrifice a cow costing about rupees 1,000.(3) Alternatively
one sheep may be sacrificed by one man. The skin (*sarman*) of
the cow, worth about Rs. 100, is for the mullah (*de mullah shay
day*).

In his ^CId sermons the mullah talks of the unity of Islam and
honour and shame (*haya*), the general themes in Pukhto. I
attended ^CId prayers in Shati and Bela; both occasions reflected
social structure. In Bela, I sat quietly and unnoticed in one
of the back rows where I felt I would observe better. Khan
Muhammad (son of Husain), on leave from the Mohmand Rifles,
was prominent in the front row, usually reserved for mashars,
wearing his new clothes, leather-jacket, and karakuli cap. In
the mosque of Shahzada I tried to stand in the back row but was
called to the front by Shahzada to stand alongside him. He did
not wish that the hierarchy which was based on age and lineage
status be disturbed. In their selection of the ^CId day the two
areas reflected their geographical and political situations. Bela
celebrated the official government ^CId, and Shati, following
Kabul, celebrated ^CId a day earlier. Shahzada celebrated both.
The confusion invariably arises annually from different sightings
of the new moon.

Hujras and rooms in the houses have bare walls except perhaps
a calendar with the name of 'Allah' or 'Muhammad' calligraphied
in colour or one depicting Islamic rulers. A popular poster displays the late King Faisal of Arabia being assassinated, signifying
martyrdom (*shahdat*) and immortality in the next world. Symbolism
of the transitory nature of human life and the permanence of
God, a constant theme of the mullah, is physically present in
the Bela mosque. There is a wooden plank (*takhta*) hanging in
the mosque visible to all as a reminder of death in the midst
of life, for on it males and females of Bela are placed after
death as part of the funerary rites and taken to their graves.

In deference to general religious sentiments no radios or
tape-recorders are allowed to be played in Mian Mandi, the
market owned and controlled by the Mians and the main market
of the Mohmands near Shati Khel. This tradition is not restricted
to mere lip service and on various occasions while being driven
by *kashars* (young), restive of tradition, through the Mandi
I have seen them respecting the ban by promptly switching the
car radio off. As a symbol of his Islamic post-hajj stance Hajji
Hasan will not allow a radio in his house although his sons are

doing good business in transport and own three buses.

There is no question of heresy or heretics among the tribesmen, doubts such as are raised by the orthodox regarding the
Berber tribesmen in Morocco (Gellner 1969a: 22). Prayers are
a sort of social therapy. They externalize and exorcize doubts.
God is confronted directly without the aid of priests, shamans,
secret societies and ecstatic behaviour by the Pukhtun. The
mumbo-jumbo and hocus-pocus of medicine men or priests have
no place in his world. Religion is direct, monistic and personal.
Not surprisingly there are no Sufi orders in Mohmand life:
itinerant religious mendicants or temporary religious leaders,
yes, but institutionalized Sufi or extra-worldly orders, no.
There are no mystic or Sufi cults in the Tribal Areas except
among the Shi^{c}as of the Orakzai.(4) The difference in cognition
was illustrated by an interesting confrontation between
Ihsanullah, son of Shamshudin, and some other Mohmands, who
were visiting me when I was Political Agent, Orakzai Agency, in
1977, and the Orakzai Shi^{c}as when I took them to a dinner the
latter had given for me. The Shi^{c}as had promised to allow me to
witness their special rites near Hangu, in the settled Kohat
District, a privilege rarely afforded to non-Shi^{c}as and given as
a gesture of appreciation for my role in helping to solve the
long-standing Shi^{c}a-Sunni problem regarding the Shi^{c}a Mian
Ziaṛat dispute in Tirah. After dinner, the Shi^{c}as, wearing no
shoes, danced themselves into an ecstatic frenzy on an area
covered with live and burning coal which they picked from time
to time and put in their mouths. The interesting question raised
in the discussion that subsequently followed was: what was the
emic view of such ecstatic behaviour that transcended human
physical pain? The Mohmands had never seen anything like it
before and simply had no explanation for it. To them the entire
performance was sheer mumbo-jumbo and so much magic (*jado*).
The Shi^{c}as explained their transcendence over physical pain
through religious emotion and ecstasy (*jazba*). Like the Mohmand
I confess I had never witnessed anything like this before. Was
it *jado* or *jazba*?

In an illustrative conversation between Shamshudin and
Husain Khan, a Bela elder known for his materialism, on mysticism in Islam, Shamshudin often thought of the meaning of Sufism
and was attracted to the simple Sufi way of life. When I asked
them to define Sufism Husain Khan replied 'It is nothing but a
state of religious lunacy, madness (*mallangi*).' Shamshudin
then turned to me and said 'Husain Khan is only interested in
making money' to which Husain Khan replied 'God will give me
money. This is God's work (*da de Allah kar day*)'. Husain then
explained that the Muslims of today had forgotten God but that
the people of old were saints (*zbarg*) and martyrs (*shahid*).
'Today', he said, 'money counts'. Shamshudin did not answer;
perhaps he had no reply.

In more complex social systems mysticism may be an acceptable alternative to orthodox Islam but in the Mohmand areas it is

seen as surrogate for it and therefore consciously rejected.
Hence the explanation of the Mohmand to Shi^ca ecstatic trance as
mere 'magic'. Just as the Pukhtun is politically iconoclastic he
cannot be religiously hagiolatrous. Both conditions are defined
by his social code and descent structure. It is significant that
Islam is alive within tribal society not through the memory of
teachings of great scholars or saints or their shrines but is part
of everyday tribal lore and common descent memory; this partly
explains the lack of hagiolatry or anthropolatory among Mohmand
tribes unlike other Islamic societies (Ahmad 1964; Evans-
Pritchard 1973; Gellner 1969 a and b; Gilsenan 1973; Trimingham
1973). The Islam of the Mohmands is puritanical, not syncretic
or eclectic.

Sociologically it may be relevant to point out that Islam is
over-emphasized by non-Mohmand groups perhaps to even
out or obliterate the elitism of the Pukhtun; similarly junior
lineages place heavy emphasis on Islam to perform a similar
levelling operation against the elitism of the senior lineages.
The maximum number of hajjis are often among junior lineages.
Hajji Hasan, and Hajji ^cUmar, an elder of a junior lineage, would
constantly use 'if God wills' (*insha' llah*) or 'by the Grace of
God' (*masha' llah*) in their sentences. Hajji ^cUmar would speak
of the Mians with a reverence unimaginable among the senior
lineage: 'they are pure, they stand for prayers and godliness'.
Hajji Hasan repeatedly quoted the Prophet's maxim, 'to respect
a hajji means you respect me'. He would start sentences with a
self-conscious 'I cannot speak lies (*darogh nasham waylay*)'.

There is no correlation between economic development and
lack of religiosity, as is apparent by a superficial visit to the
Tribal Areas. Although the older generation, like Hajji Hasan
and Shamshudin, may talk of the young as being less religious
than themselves the fact is that almost the first investment that
the younger Pukhtuns, earning money specially from the Gulf
States, make is in a new cement mosque.

Perhaps the social bonds of religion within an extra-tribal
framework may best be explained by two personal examples.
On my tour of the Mullah Khel area, Badaon, as Political
Agent of the Orakzai, there was considerable tension. I was the
first political officer ever to have come as far as Badaon,
virtually overlooking the Afridi border of Tirah (and the most
anaccessible part of the Tribal Area), and to spend a night in the
local *hujra*. It was no coincidence that this tension, which my
junior officers felt so keenly, evaporated after I joined my
Mullah Khel hosts at prayer in their mosque by the *hurja*. In
another example, I was in an informal meeting in the evening
with the Governor of the Province, when he asked some Mohmand
Maliks to join us just as the call to prayer (*azan*) was heard.
To the Mohmand the equality in the prayer formation symbolized
the sociological importance of a common religious system between
those representing encapsulating systems and those in the
process of encapsulation. Earlier, when he was Inspector-

General Frontier Corps, the Governor deliberately selected
'Islamic' days, such as Fridays, for special occasions like the
raising of the Mohmand Rifles or the crossing of the Nahakki
Pass.

Right is clean in Islam just as left is unclean and a certain
amount of symbolism attaches to right and left and higher and
lower in society; food is eaten with the right hand while the
left hand is used for blowing the nose or washing after defeca-
tion. The child is first suckled with the right breast. When a
child is born the *azan*, the call to prayer, is said in his right
ear. In prayer the right hand covers the left hand in the
orthodox position. Charity is given with the right hand and in
death the face of the corpse points to the Kaaba to the right
side. Indeed, an angel recording the good deeds of the individual sits on his right shoulder while another one sits on the
left shoulder to record his evil deeds.

Right and left symbolism also finds translation in high and
low symbolism. Mohmands believe high, *porta*, is good and low,
khkata, is bad. God is said to reside high above in heaven
while hell is somewhere beneath the earth. The human head is
said to have been made by God himself and contains the Holy
Qur'an, while the angels are said to have made the remaining
lower parts of man. Worldly success such as in agnatic rivalry
is summed up as 'emerged on top', *'porta show'*, and failure
as 'went under', *'khkata show'*.

The respect of hajjis and their rather self-conscious post-
hajj role, the unceasing sermons of the Mians and mullahs, the
physical and focal presence of the mosque, the regularity of
prayers by the mashars and the sound of the *azan* add up to
an Islamic social if not religious milieu. Islamic symbols pervade
ordinary life and its tenets and universalistic customs regulate
it to a remarkable degree.

The history of conversion to Islam by the Prophet himself
of Qais, the Pukhtun apical ancestor, and of patrlineal descent
from him place religion as a defining factor in the Pukhtun model
along with *Pukhtunwali* (Ahmed 1980). The Mohmands must be
understood within a phyletic context - that of Pukhtunness -
and a religious context - that of being Muslim. Every Mohmand
carries a blueprint in his mind of five concentric circles that
emanate from ego and place him and define him in his universe:
the tribal sub-section (Kado Khel in Bela Mohmandan); the clan
(Tarakzai); the tribe (Mohmand); the ethnic group (Pukhtun);
and the religion (Islam). From a sociological point of view the
latent function of *Pukhtunwali* appears to be to integrate and
perpetuate the ideal-type Pukhtun society while its manifest
function has been to successfully provide diacritica from other
social systems (Merton 1968).

Having discussed religious symbolism I now describe the
religious groups in society and the role they play in activating,
disseminating and interpreting such symbolism.

(B) SAINTLY MODEL: SAYYIDS, MIANS AND MULLAHS

Although marginal to traditional Pukhtun activity such as agnatic rivalry, religious groups are integral parts of society and are involved in the entire range of rites de passage. They view themselves as essential social appendices to the clan they are attached to. In certain cases they have created fictitious lineage links to their patron clans. Such links are fictitious within society but for purposes of outsiders, defined in geographical or tribal phyletic terms, they imply a tacit admission of filiation by society including the patron clan. Technically neither feature on the tribal charter, a fact that excludes them from certain attendant privileges given by government such as rations, *khassadars* (tribal levies), etc. and duties, such as those of the *khassadars* or being liable to pay collective fines for arrant Pukhtun members of the lineage.

(i) Mians

The Prophet's saying that 'there are no genealogies in Islam' has theological and social implications. It implies the equality of believers before the omnipotence of God and that of man in relation to man in society. Qur'anic verses repeat the equality of man. However, the political sociology of Islam indicates the unique importance of descent in legitimizing or succeeding in political activity.(5) The descendants of the Prophet, the Sayyids, provide the basis for social stratification in Islamic society and are generally considered a superior group.(6) Ideally there is no social division within a Muslim community but a hierarchy is conceptualized and partly explained, as indeed is social mobility, through economic differentiation. A common Pakistani proverb states: 'Last year I was a *jolaha* (weaver), this year I am a Shaikh (disciple of the Prophet) and next year if the prices rise I will be a Sayyid.' The saying is reflected in societies with forms of stratification (Béteille 1977: 143) and embodies the concept of upward mobility and 'Sanskritization' (Srinivas 1966).

There are no Sayyids among the Mohmand. Nonetheless Mohmand religious groups generally assume the name, and with it the status, of the next senior ranked group in the idealized Islamic hierarchy. For instance, the ignorance among Mohmands in differentiating a Sayyid from a Mian presumes two facts: a general ignorance of fine and fundamental religious matters and the limited importance attached to religious status. Apart from some mashars like Shahzada and Shamshudin few people in Shati and Bela could distinguish a Sayyid from a Mian. Mians therefore get away by describing themselves as Sayyids and unless pressed for a specific definition, when he is uncertain, the tribesman describes them thus. A member of the religious group is generally defined by the Pukhtun as 'a Mian or mullah man' (*Mian mullah saray*). It is as much a definition of a role as it is the delineating of status groups and social boundaries

of action. Religious groups may also be called *stanadar* and
respected for a negative reason.

The curses (*khayray*) of the *stanadar* are said to be effective.
Mohmands often explain the fall of the Ranra lineage and the
rise of their cousins the Musa lineage in Shati by the cursing of
the former when they incurred the displeasure of the Mians
almost a hundred years ago. So while Pukhtuns may not show
Mians undue deference they will also not molest or insult them.
Although there are no Sayyids in Bela Mohmandan the Mian
of Bela calls himself and is called a Sayyid. For this reason I
am wary of accepting Sayyid category among the Mohmand as
most Mians prefer to be called *badshah* (king), a title given to
Sayyids among Pukhtuns. Over the generations the descendants
of Mians have assumed Sayyid status. The 'saint' defined as
a gloss for Sayyids, Mians and Mullahs (Bailey 1972; Barth 1972)
can lead to a misreading of Pukhtun social structure and political
life (Ahmed 1976).

The role and position of the religious groups among Pukhtun
society clearly raise interesting questions. The Mian is aware
that he is of superior social status to a member of the occu-
pational group (*qasabgar*). In private he would even argue that
as he bears the torch of faith and because of his putative
genealogical links with the Prophet (as a Sayyid) he is the
equal, if not the superior, of the Pukhtun. Mian Jalil would
say''we think we are socially higher, they think they are
higher'.

The Mians, a community of about a hundred people in the
Gandab, are the main religious group among the Mohmand and
live in three small hamlets which have split from the main Mian
village of Mian Kassai. Segmentary fissures and agnatic
jealousy are not a monopoly of the Pukhtuns. The present
respected social position of the Mians is largely a consequence
of their ownership and organization of the only and most central
market among the Mohmand, Mian Mandi. They are a self-
contained social unit and do not keep *hamsayas* (tenants) or
qasabgars. There are some recent examples, beginning in the
1960s, of Mians giving to and taking daughters from Pukhtuns,
the latter being from junior lineages. Previously Mians were an
entirely endogamous group often going to Afghanistan to their
kin in Laghman to arrange marriages. Mians are generally
educated in the Holy Qur'an and Islamic learning. Compared to
Mohmand elders they appear softer, plumper, darker and
physically better groomed.

The senior Mian of Kassai, universally called Mian Kassai,
has had five wives and innumerable descendants. His eldest
son, Mian Abdul Hakim, has nineteen sons, and traces his
descent, three generations removed, to Arabia. It is significant
that in the Formal Questionnaires the Mians traced their
descent to Arabia and not, as do almost all Pukhtuns, to Kabul.
Mian Jalil, a cousin of Mian Hakim, is a fine example of Mian
virtues. He explained ideal Mian role behaviour among Pukhtun

society. The Mian is soft-spoken, does not lose his temper, never quarrels, never takes sides in Pukhtun factions and under no condition does he carry a gun. The primary characteristic of the Mian is his pacificism; he is an almost ideal prototype Christian figure. The Mian normally dresses in white, the colour of peace, and comports himself with deliberate dignity. He is acutely aware of the predicament imposed on him by his position in society. If he deviates from the expected ideal by repeated quarrelsome behaviour or is seen to be drinking and debauching or manipulating people for political power, his neutrality and status are compromised and the respect and privileges withdrawn. For all their putative social influence the Mians remain uncomfortable in Pukhtun areas and whenever they accompanied me to Shati Khel they did so most reluctantly and with a dozen excuses. They repeated that they had no business to be there and did not wish to run the risk of being insulted. The Mian provides the ideal-type model of correct social behaviour, moral propriety and studied disinterest in political matters.

The Mian cannot compete in an arena and game into which he is not allowed by the rules or participants of that game. In spite of their social airs the Mians do not receive any of the privileges of the Pukhtuns in the Tribal Areas such as allowances, *lungis* (individual allowances), *muajibs* (sectional allowances), rations etc. which has always been a sore point with them. The local sub-section or section would resent the thought of including even the handful of eminent Mians among *lungi*-holders or *muajib*-takers. If the Mians are given political allowances this is done secretly and the clan is assured that in no way are their interests diverted or diminished. Fourteen Mians who belong to Gandab are on the Mohmand Agency electoral list (pp. 46-7) of a total of about 6,000 voters. The inclusion of the Mians is a deviance in the Tribal Areas for usually they are not included on such voting lists as they do not share Pukhtun rights or duties. For instance, Akhundzada Sa^cid, son of the legendary Akhundzada Mahmud involved in the Miss Ellis kidnapping case of 1923, could not stand for elections in 1977 in the Orakzai Agency because his name was not on the electoral list being categorized as an Akhundzada, an eminent religious leader. This was in spite of the fact that he was the recipient of various secret government favours originating from the role of his father in the recovery of the girl.

In anthropological literature the social role of the Mian might be structurally likened to the *agurram* among the Berbers (Gellner 1969a). This would be a mistake. The role of the *igurramen* and the Mians are conceptually and empirically different. The Mians do not supervise the election of the Pukhtun chiefs nor do they provide leadership against outside aggression and nor can they claim to perform miracles (ibid.: 78). The single attribute the Mian and the *igurramen* share is pacifism. However, on the surface, the ideal Mian is defined, as indeed is the *agurram*, as one descended from the Prophet, mediating between man and God, between man and man, dispensing blessing, a good and pious man, uncalculatingly generous and hospitable and one who does not fight or engage in feuds (ibid.: 74). This in the ideal is very much how the Mians would like to see themselves. If the Malik may be said to conform to a 'chiefly' model then the Mian conforms to a 'saintly' model in Pukhtun society; with the added and important clause that the latter are in no way pretenders to political authority unlike religious groups in complex societies such as Swat (Barth 1972). To the saintly model of the Mian knowledge (^{c}ilm) is the central feature just as the gun is to the Pukhtun model. The Mian contrasts himself and his ^{c}ilm with the diametrically opposed model of the Pukhtun and 'the gun he carries'. 'The work of the gun' (*the topak kar*) is the Pukhtun's, he will explain, and is seen as diacritical in determining social categories. This too is why he is an impotent judge or arbiter in disputes as he has no force to back his decisions, unlike the Pukhtun *jirga*.

In certain Islamic tribal societies like the Somalis there is a clear-cut distinction between men of God (*wadaad*) and men of the spear or warriors (*waranlah*) but 'in practice warriors and priests rub shoulders together in the same lineage' (Lewis 1969: 263) and both groups belong to the *diya*-paying group. Among the Mohmand the Mians, the men of God and the Pukhtuns, the men of the gun, do not rub shoulders in lineages, marriages or settlements. Both remain distinct groups with distinct functions. How then do the Mians, representing Islamic tradition and custom, and the Pukhtuns, tribal custom, accommodate to each other and at what point do they clash or come together? The Mian consciously inflates and exaggerates Islamic symbols within society to maintain his position and importance as interpreter of religion although painfully aware that in many ways he is outside the Pukhtun social world.

They see themselves as 'middle people' between the Pukhtuns, men of the world (*dunya*), and esoteric Sufi figures who have renounced it for religion (*din*). Their primary functions as viewed by them are: to arbitrate between warring factions; to provide religious blessing for medicinal purposes; and to remind Pukhtuns of Islam and their duties as Muslims. They may sometimes perform the more routine functions of the rites de passage normally reserved for the mullah. Unlike the mullahs they are neither paid in cash or kind by Pukhtun groups. Conceptually and ideally the functions of the Mian are to act as a neutral or buffer group or zone between two or more tribal segments. Their physical location and village is symbolic of this neutral position, being situated at the boundary where two or three sections or sub-clans meet. For example in the Gandab the Mians of Kassai are placed between the Yusuf Khel and Shati Khel, the Hamza Khel and the Kadai Khel. In practice

their role in effecting a ceasefire or even an agreement is
limited as they are not backed by any physical or coercive
force. They, however, play a useful role in keeping the lines
of communication open between two fighting factions to evacuate
the wounded, the sick, the women and children. Mian Halil described how the Mians would wear white clothes, and carrying a
white flag visit and talk to both parties whenever there was
shooting in Shati Khel between factions. In case of death they
would remove the corpse during the ceasefire. In the 1973
shooting when Yad Gul, the Ranra *mashar*, died, four Mians,
including Jalil, negotiated between Mazullah on the one side
and Major Sultan Jan and Shahzada on the other for a ceasefire.
Mian Jalil's car was used to convey and announce the news of
the agreement and request people to go home and later to take
the wounded to hospital. In normal times they attempt to live
lives that should ideally depict the saintly model. But as Mian
Jalil himself admitted the recent economic activities and involvements of the Mians especially in their market, Mian Mandi, have
not only decreased their prestige in the eyes of the Pukhtuns
but made the Mians themselves more worldly and correspondingly
less spiritual. Today they own flour mills, cars, buses and of
course, the most lucrative property in the Agency, the Mian
Mandi.

So we may come to the conclusion that although the Mians
may claim social equality with Pukhtuns they can in no way
attempt to appropriate or legitimate political power, for which
they have neither the guns, the men, nor the economic resources.
When I questioned the Shati Khel Maliks whether a Wali of Swat
could have emerged among the Mohmand they simply answered
with rather rude references to the 'manliness' of Swatis.
Shahzada explained the typical Mohmand social structure which
would never permit the emergence of local Pukhtun or non-
Pukhtun leadership among the Mohmand to the status of ruler.
His explanation is corroborated by the difficulties such famous
religious leaders as Chaknawar and the Hajji of Turangzai faced
in attempting to compose even a temporary united front among
the Mohmand clans against the British.

(ii) Mullahs
The role of the mullah is clearly defined and involves him fully
in the rites de passage. At birth he is to recite the *azan* in
the ear of the new born within twenty-four hours of birth.
He reads the prayer (*du^{c}a'*) after the circumcision of the boy.
He 'ties the marriage' (*nikah tari*) which formalizes and legalizes
the ceremony. He prepares the corpse and performs the death
rites (*janaza*) by wrapping the corpse in a white sheet about
ten yards long on which he writes the *kalima* and then outside
the village, in an open space, with the corpse lying in front,
leads the congregation in a special prayer. On such occasions
mullahs often gather from neighbouring villages and items such
as soap and a little money are distributed among them. The

mullah then accompanies the body to the cemetery with the male members of the community, the females visiting the grave later. He performs the final funeral rites by praying on a handful of mud and spreading it on the grave.

Apart from rites the mullah also tends to the mosque and calls the *azan* five times a day and leads the congregation in prayer. Depending on his powers of persuasion and medicinal knowledge he distributes talismans (*ta^{c}wiz*) for curing diseases, specially of children and cattle or keeping the evil eye away from them, for which he charges one or two rupees. Mohmand mashars believe that *ta^{c}wiz* given by a religous person, like Mian Kassai or the Imam of Bela, can cure diseases specially in women, children and cattle. Bela elders assured me that the Bela Imam had been giving them talismans, which worked in removing worms from cattle and increasing the output of their milk. Fever and headaches are commonly believed to be cured by him. The Imam says a prayer and usually gives a talisman with some Arabic writing on it. His payment is called 'payment in thanks' (*shukrana*).

Just as the Mian upgrades himself to Sayyid status so the mullah in a similar self-imposed upgradation, and usually after migration to a new locality, calls himself a Mian. The ignorance and indifference of the Pukhtuns ratify the upward mobility and in time the new status is accepted, genealogical fiction being converted to social legitimation. The mullah, or Imam, of Bela prefers to be called a Mian.

In *hujra* conversations Pukhtun mashars would question the role of the mullah: 'He is illiterate. What does he know of Islam? Why should he intercede between us and God?' Pukhtun Islam may be perhaps equated to the 'muscular Christianity' of the Victorian era: it is a laic, uncomplicated, surface reaction to an inherited tradition that is suspicious of dogmas, debates and formalized priesthood. Mohmand mashars would express their opinion of the religious groups just as Khushal Hkan Khattak did centuries ago, though perhaps with less eloquence:

> I have observed the disposition
> Of present-day divines;
> An hour spent in their company
> And I'm filled with disgust (Mackenzie 1965: 79).

They would reflect equal cynicism regarding traditional claims to payment by the religious groups:

> The plunder these *shaikhs* carry off
> While chanting God's great name (ibid.).

The duties of the mullah have been briefly enumerated. Primarily he attends to the demands in society regarding religious functions in the rites de passage. His behaviour and personality determine the respect he can command in the community.

The Mian is not prepared to accept Pukhtun social superiority. In his own ideal-type model he approximates to the 'saintly' model among Mohmands, a definition that precludes political activity. Conceptually the highest point of his 'saintliness' coincides with the lowest point of political activity. The presence of the Mian and the mullah among Pukhtun society are a visible and self-conscious reminder of Islamic values. Their presence acts as a social mechanism to sustain Islamic symmetry in Pukhtun society and correct cases of asymmetry. However in the ideal-type Pukhtun situation in Shati Khel both groups are clearly seen as client through the eyes of the Pukhtun and subordinate to his political authority. The Pukhtun casts himself in the role and status of patron. The Pukhtun world is still largely undisturbed in its traditional symmetry in 1975-6. However the role and importance of the religious groups vis-à-vis administration has undergone a significant change since the departure of the British. From a position of hostility to an infidel government the Mians and mullahs are now generally favourable to what they consider a Muslim government (Ahmed 1977. For the case of a mullah who led a movement recently against government in Waziristan see Ahmed 1982).

Clear deviances emerge, however, in the tribal village of Bela Mohmandan owing to its situation in the District. The social importance of non-Mohmand groups grows in direct proportion to the diminishing importance of the Pukhtun lineage and its code. This new emerging relationship is further complicated for the Pukhtun by their shift from traditional occupations to agricultural livelihood. They are now inextricably bound to the specialized and monopoly talents of non-Mohmand groups like the carpenters. The mullah is no longer client of the household head but a central and, because of his personal qualities, respected figure of the village community. In a sense he has risen above the status of client to the Pukhtun and become pivotal in the village rites de passage. The shifting relationships pose the dilemmas of encapsulation to Bela Pukhtuns within society. The Pukhtun is now confronted by the economic not political facts of his new situation and, because of the laws of settled districts, he is stripped of his own symbolic possession of Pukhtunness, his gun. As a small land-holding agriculturalist he is increasingly at the mercy of traditionally client groups. The traditional patron and client roles may not have been reversed in Bela but they are now in the process of being redefined, and, apart from the fading mystique of Pukhtun lineage, non-Mohmand groups are asserting themselves.

In conclusion: I have illustrated above the importance of symbols in society that are locally perceived as carrying religious significance and through their association or usage conferring status and merit. Such symbols are not necessarily ritual or religious nor seen as such but signify continuing social tradition, particularly in their association with the life and person of the Prophet and early Islam. I am thus arguing that however laic or religiously neutral a symbol, it acquires a religious significance by its repeated usage and invocation of its derivation from the times of the Prophet. These symbols maintain sanctity in the eyes of the social actor because of their association with the Prophet. Islamic symbolism is activated, interpreted and disseminated by religious groups living among Pukhtun tribes as I have described above. This ensures the potency and perpetuation within society of religious symbols. Such symbolism may often remain dormant in Islamic society, for long periods due to historical - cultural factors.(7) I have also attempted to show that it is not theoretically or methodologically possible to study an Islamic society in isolation as the symbols in society require a reference to the larger Islamic world outside the tribal or village universe.

NOTES

1 Data were collected from two areas, Bela Mohmandan, on the border of the Peshawar District and the Mohmand Agency but lying within the District, and Shati Khel deep in the Mohmand Agency. The regular civil and criminal laws of Pakistan do not extend to the Agencies in the Tribal Areas where problems are solved according to tribal law and custom.
2 The Mohmands in the Mohmand Agency in structure and organization are typical of segmentary, acephalous tribes believing in egalitarianism and basing their filiation on a tree-like genealogical charter with 'nesting attributes' (Fortes and Evans-Pritchard 1970; Middleton and Tait 1970). Rough population estimates of Mohmands who live in Afghanistan and Pakistan are about 400,000 to 500,000.
3 Approximately rupees 18-20 equal 1 pound sterling. Rs. is used as the abbreviation for rupees.
4 I will discuss the growth of saints among the Orakzai Shi[c]as in a separate paper, The Saints of Tirah: The Economic Base of Religious Leadership.
5 The Caliphs of the early dynasties of Islam, the [c]Umayyads (A.D. 661-750, 929-1031), the [c]Abbasids (A.D. 750-1258) and the Fatimids (A.D. 909-1171) were related to the Prophet on the genealogical charter and traced unilineal descent through agnatic ascendants to their common apical ancestor, Quraysh, and his descendant [c]Abd-Manaf (Hitti 1977).
6 Studies among Indian Muslims show the emergence of various castelike groups like the 'high' caste 'Ashraf', the Sayyids, Shaikhs, Mughals and Pukhtuns and the 'low' caste 'Ajlaf', mostly converts from low-caste Hindus (Ahmad 1973).
7 The social phenomenon of the late 1970s in the Islamic world commonly called the 'resurgence/revival of Islam', which may take highly political forms such as in Iran and Pakistan, is yet another aspect of this argument.

BIBLIOGRAPHY

Ahmad, A. (1964), 'Islamic Culture in the Indian Environment', Oxford University Press.

Ahmad, I. (ed.) (1973), 'Caste and Social Stratification among the Muslims', Manohar Book Services, Delhi.

Ahmed, A.S. (1976), 'Millennium and Charisma among Pathans: A Critical Essay in Social Anthropology', Routledge & Kegan Paul, London.

Ahmed, A.S. (1977), 'Social and Economic Change in the Tribal Areas', Oxford University Press, Karachi.

Ahmed, A.S. (1980), 'Pukhtun Economy and Society', Routledge & Kegan Paul, London.

Ahmed, A.S. (1983), 'Religion and Politics in Muslim Society: Order and Conflict in Pakistan', Cambridge University Press.

Bailey, F.G. (1972), Conceptual Systems in the Study of Politics, in R. Antoun and I. Harik (eds), 'Rural Politics and Social Change in the Middle East', Indiana University Press.

Barth, F. (1970), Pathan Identity and Its Maintenance, in F. Barth (ed.), 'Ethnic Groups and Boundaries: The Social Organization of Culture Difference', Allen & Unwin, London.

Barth, F. (1972), 'Political Leadership among Swat Pathans', The Athlone Press, London.

Béteille, A. (1977), 'Inequality among Men', Basil Blackwell, Oxford.

Coon, C.S. (1952), 'Caravan: The Story of the Middle East', Jonathan Cape, London.

Evans-Pritchard, E.E. (1973), 'The Sanusi of Cyrenaica', Oxford University Press.

Fortes, M. and Evans-Pritchard, E.E. (eds) (1970), 'African Political Systems', Oxford University Press.

Geertz, C. (1973), Religion as a Cultural System, in M. Banton (ed.), 'Anthropological Approaches to the Study of Religion', ASA Monographs 3, Tavistock Publications, London.

Gellner, E. (1969a), 'Saints of the Atlas', Weidenfeld & Nicolson, London.

Gellner, E. (1969b), A Pendulum Swing Theory of Islam, in R. Robertson (ed.), 'Sociology of Religion', Penguin Books, Harmondsworth.

Gilsenan, M. (1973), 'Saint and Sufi in Modern Egypt', Oxford University Press.

Hart, D.M. (1976), 'The Aith Waryaghar of the Moroccan Rif', Wenner-Gren Foundation, no. 55, University of Arizona Press, Arizona.

Hitti, P.K. (1977), 'History of the Arabs', Macmillan, London.

Home Department, Government of North-West Frontier Province, Tribal Research Cell (1932-5), 'Mohmand Situation', File 220.

Lawrence, T.E. (1962), 'Seven Pillars of Wisdom', Penguin Modern Classics.

Lewis, I.M. (1969), Conformity and Contrast in Somali Islam, in 'Islam in Tropical Africa', Oxford University Press.

Mackenzie, D.N. (1965), 'Poems from the devan of Khushal Khan Khattak', Allen & Unwin, London.

Merton, R.K. (1968), 'Social Theory and Social Structure', enlarged edn, Free Press, New York.

Middleton, J., and Tait, D. (eds) (1970), 'Tribes Without Rulers', Routledge & Kegan Paul, London.

Pettigrew, H.R.C. (1965), 'Frontier Scouts', published Clayton Road, Selsey, Sussex, England.

Spiro, M.E. (1973), Religion: Problems of Definition and Explanation, in M. Banton (ed.), 'Anthropological Approaches to the Study of Religion', ASA Monograph 3, Tavistock Publications, London.

Srinivas, M.N. (1966), 'Social Change in Modern India', University of California Press.

Tavakolian, B.M. (1976), 'The Role of Cultural Values and Religion in the Ecology of Middle Eastern Pastoralism', Anthropology UCLA, 8, USA.

Trimingham, J.S. (1973), 'The Sufi Orders in Islam', Oxford University Press.

Weber, M. (1962), 'The Protestant Ethic and the Spirit of Capitalism', Allen & Unwin, London.

NOTES ON THE CONTRIBUTORS

Akbar S. Ahmed was recently Visiting Scholar, Department of
Anthropology, Harvard University. He has written extensively
on the Pukhtuns, and his interests are Muslim society, tribal
groups and development anthropology. Dr Ahmed belongs to the
Civil Service of Pakistan. He is currently Director General,
National Centre for Rural Development, Islamabad, and Director,
Centre of Social Sciences and Humanities, University Grants Com-
mission, Pakistan.

V.N. Basilov is at the Institute of Ethnography, Academy of
Sciences, Moscow, and specializes in Central Asian peoples'
ethnography, Islam, and pre-Islamic beliefs, especially
shamanism. He has done most of his fieldwork in Soviet Central
Asia (predominantly Turkmenistan and Uzbekistan). Dr Basilov
is the author of 'The Cult of Saints in Islam' (Moscow, 1970)
and editor and co-author of 'Survivals of Pre-Islamic Beliefs
and Rites in Central Asia' (Moscow, 1975).

Donald P. Cole is Associate Professor of Anthropology at the
American University in Cairo. He is the author of 'Nomads of
the Nomads: The Al Murrah Bedouin of the Empty Quarter'
(1975) and of numerous articles about the bedouin and social
and economic change in the Arab world.

Fanny Colonna teaches sociology in Algiers. She has written
one book, 'Instituteurs algériens, 1883-1939' (1975) and has
contributed papers to various books and journals. Dr Colonna
is a member of the Centre National de la Recherche Scientifique.

Louis Dupree belongs to Universities Field Staff International
and is Adjunct Professor of Anthropology at Pennsylvania
State University. His thirty-four years of research, primarily
about Afghanistan and Pakistan, have resulted in over 300
publications, including 'Afghanistan' (first paperback edition
1980).

Ernest Gellner is Professor of Philosophy at the London School
of Economics. Intermittent fieldwork in central Morocco between
1953 and 1961 resulted in 'Saints of the Atlas' (1969). His other
publications include 'Muslim Society' (1981). Professor Gellner
is a Fellow of the British Academy.

David M. Hart has done fieldwork in Morocco and Pakistan
and has travelled extensively in the Arab world. His major
interest is the society and history of tribal Islam. His publi-
cations include 'Emilio Blanco Izaga: Colonel in the Rif' (1975),
'The Aith Waryaghar of the Moroccan Rif: An Ethnography and
History' (1976) and 'Dadda ^CAtta and His Forty Grandsons:
The Socio-Political Organisation of the Ait ^CAtta of Southern
Morocco' (1981).

I.M. Lewis is Professor of Anthropology at the London School
of Economics. His research has concentrated on the social and
political institutions of the peoples of the Horn of Africa and he
has visited the region regularly since 1955. His publications
include 'Peoples of the Horn of Africa' (1955: rev. ed 1969),
'Social Anthropology in Perspective' (1976) and 'A Modern
History of Somalia: Nation and State in the Horn of Africa'
(1965; rev. ed 1980).

Magali Morsy is a lecturer at the University of the Sorbonne
Nouvelle (Paris) who has specialized in the study of Morocco
and published several books on its history and civilization,
among them 'Les Ahansala' (1976), 'Une Lecture du Maroc au
18e siècle' (1982) and 'A History of North Africa, 1800-1900'
(forthcoming).

Stephen L. Pastner is Associate Professor of Anthropology and
Director, Asian Area Studies at the University of Vermont. He
has done fieldwork in Pakistan, Ethiopia and the Caribbean.

Emrys Peters is Professor of Social Anthropology at Manchester
University. He has done extensive fieldwork among the
Cyrenaican bedouin, on a Tripolitanian olive planatation, in a
Muslim Shi'ite village in South Lebanon and in a Maronite
Christian village in Central Lebanon. Professor Peters is a
former President of the British Society for Middle Eastern
Studies.

Richard Tapper is Lecturer in Anthropology with reference to
the Middle East at the School of Oriental and African Studies,
London University. He has done extensive field research in
Iran, Afghanistan and Turkey.

Bahram Tavakolian is Associate Professor and Chairperson of
the Department of Sociology/Anthropology at Denison University,
Granville, Ohio. He is also a Visiting Professor of Middle
Eastern Ethnology at Ohio State University.

INDEX